UNEQUAL AND UNREPRESENTED

Unequal and Unrepresented

Political Inequality and the People's Voice in the New Gilded Age

Kay Lehman Schlozman
Henry E. Brady
Sidney Verba

PRINCETON UNIVERSITY PRESS
PRINCETON AND OXFORD

Copyright © 2018 by Princeton University Press

Published by Princeton University Press,
41 William Street, Princeton, New Jersey 08540

In the United Kingdom: Princeton University Press,
6 Oxford Street, Woodstock, Oxfordshire OX20 1TR

press.princeton.edu

Jacket design by Faceout Studio

All Rights Reserved

ISBN 978-0-691-18055-7
Library of Congress Control Number: 2017958942

British Library Cataloging-in-Publication Data is available

This book has been composed in Adobe Text Pro and Gotham

Printed on acid-free paper. ∞

Printed in the United States of America

10 9 8 7 6 5 4 3 2 1

*To Stanley, Patty, and Cynthia,
our first and onlys,
with whom we have shared
nearly a century and a half of marriage*

Because half a dozen grasshoppers under a fern make the field ring . . . whilst thousands of great cattle, reposed beneath the shadow of the British oak, chew the cud and are silent, pray do not imagine that those who make the noise are the only inhabitants of the field.
—EDMUND BURKE
REFLECTIONS ON THE REVOLUTION IN FRANCE, 1790

People often say that, in a democracy, decisions are made by a majority of the people. Of course, that is not true. Decisions are made by a majority of those who make themselves heard and who vote—a very different thing.
—REP. WALTER H. JUDD (R-MINNESOTA)

Donald Trump's candidacy inspired millions of Americans to join his quest to give a voice to those who have long felt silenced.
—RNC STATEMENT "ON TONIGHT'S HISTORIC ELECTION VICTORIES"
HTTPS://WWW.GOP.COM/TOPIC/ELECTIONS-HILLARY-CLINTON/NOVEMBER 9, 2016

That's what our democracy demands. It needs you. Not just when there's an election, not just when your own narrow interest is at stake, but over the full span of a lifetime. If you're tired of arguing with strangers on the Internet, try talking with one of them in real life. If something needs fixing, then lace up your shoes and do some organizing. If you're disappointed by your elected officials, grab a clipboard, get some signatures, and run for office yourself. Show up. Dive in. Stay at it.
—PRESIDENT BARACK OBAMA
FAREWELL ADDRESS, JANUARY 10, 2017

CONTENTS

Preface ix
Acknowledgments xiii

1 Introduction 1

PART I

2 What Do We Mean by Political Voice?
   Does Equal Voice Matter? 23

3 The Roots of Citizen Participation:
   The Civic Voluntarism Model 50

PART II

4 Who Exercises Political Voice? 83

5 The Noisy and the Silent:
   Divergent Preferences and Needs 94

6 Do Digital Technologies Make a Difference? 112

7 Social Movements and Ordinary Recruitment 129

PART III

8 Who Sings in the Heavenly Chorus? The Shape of the
   Organized Interest System (with Philip E. Jones) 147

9 Representing Interests through Organizational Activity
   (with Philip E. Jones) 169

PART IV

10 Growing Economic Inequality and Its (Partially) Political Roots   187

11 Has It Always Been This Way?   206

12 Can We Do Anything about It?   227

13 Unequal Voice in an Unequal Age   255

Notes   279

Index   319

PREFACE

In the winter of 2015, one of us took a road trip on the California coast that included a visit to the immense, opulent Hearst Castle in San Simeon. When the obvious question arose, "Is this the biggest house in the United States?" curiosity led to a Wikipedia page titled "List of largest houses in the United States." Turns out that, according to Wikipedia, the Hearst Castle is not the largest house in the United States. At 175,000 square feet, that would be Biltmore House in Asheville, North Carolina, constructed during the 1890s in the "Châteauesque" style for George Washington Vanderbilt II. The Hearst Castle is not even in the top ten.

As social scientists, we could not help noticing a curious pattern in the listing in the Wikipedia article. Of the 110 houses on the list, more than three-quarters were finished during one of two relatively brief periods, 1891 through 1920 and 1991 through the present, eras that together account for less than one quarter of the years since 1776, when the first of the listed houses was completed. In contrast, only 6 percent of the mansions date from the six decades between the onset of the Great Depression and the end of the Reagan Administration.[1]

The recent construction of so many mega-dwellings lends concreteness to what economists have noted for some time. We live in a New Gilded Age, in which incomes for those at the top of the ladder have skyrocketed, while incomes for those in the middle class and below have languished. The result is greatly enhanced economic inequality. This increased concentration of income and wealth—at levels not seen since the late 1920s—has been accompanied by a heightened capacity of the affluent and well educated to pass along their advantages to their offspring and growing inequalities in many domains of life, for example, widening class-based gaps in health outcomes and life expectancy, not to mention house sizes.

For more than thirty years, the three of us have considered a different aspect of inequality: political inequality—in particular, inequalities of political voice. We have explored whose voices are heard in American politics through the activity of individuals and organizations that seek to influence political outcomes—either directly through expressions aimed at shaping policy or indirectly through efforts to affect the results of elections. Over and over, we have demonstrated that some people have a megaphone while others speak in a whisper. Disparities in political voice have been a feature of the American political landscape for at least as long as we have had instruments to measure them, and they are not simply random but reflect underlying patterns of advantage based on income and, especially, education.

This book seeks to present in a brief, user-friendly format what we have learned. Old friends will note that we have drawn directly on two earlier works. The first, *Voice and Equality*[2] (a.k.a. "the big blue doorstop"), provided an explanation of how the preferences and interests of all citizens come to be represented unequally. We used a series of statistical analyses to show how differences in participatory resources such as time, money, and skills; in psychological orientations to politics such as political interest, information, and efficacy; and in being recruited to political activity help explain why some people get involved in politics and others remain quiescent. A subsidiary theme was the consequences of this explanatory model for the shape of political voice: how representative are those who *do* speak?

The second, *The Unheavenly Chorus*[3] (a.k.a. "the big red doorstop") picked up the theme of whose voices are heard and extended the analysis of inequalities in political voice in several directions. We investigated inequalities of political voice that result not only from the participation of individuals but also from the multiple activities of the organizations involved in politics; the extent to which inequalities of political voice persist over decades; the possibility that political participation on the Internet might act as trip wire in breaking the patterns we had found; and the potential for reforms, ranging from procedural tinkering to broader social changes, to ameliorate the inequalities of political voice associated with inequalities in education and income.

In this volume, not only have we distilled two substantial books into a relatively short one, but we have also taken the opportunity to reflect and update. We have thrown into sharper relief the core themes of a larger body of work and considered the problem of unequal political voice in a changed environment shaped by increasing economic inequality and new rules of the political game. In the process, we cut away interesting but less essential material. Although there is no way to answer the questions we pose without engaging in systematic data analysis, we have tried to do the reader a favor by dispensing with complex statistical models and long explanations of our methods. As scholars, we have provided notes to aid the curious and the skeptical, but, in a departure from prior practice, we have relegated them to the back of the book.

Even though many of the fundamental concepts have been developed over a long history of scholarly inquiry and will thus be familiar to readers of *Voice and Equality* or *The Unheavenly Chorus*, much of the empirical material is new. We used more recent data wherever possible and even collected a new round of data about organized interests. The result is that more than three-quarters of the data in the tables and figures have been updated. Perhaps more importantly, we also take account of new scholarship and ongoing political developments. Since we published *The Unheavenly Chorus*, the consequences of the federal court decisions defining political contributions as a form of protected speech have become clearer. Furthermore, the Supreme Court subsequently decided *Shelby* v. *Holder* (2013), which declared unconstitutional the "preclearance" provisions of Section 5 of the Voting Rights Act, and the many state-level changes to voting procedures had either not yet been legislated or not yet implemented.

More recently, the insurgent candidacies of Bernie Sanders and Donald Trump in 2016 tapped into the deep well of anger and fear among middle- and working-class voters who, responding to the political and economic inequalities we analyze in these pages, feel that the system is rigged against them. Those who felt the Bern emphasize progressive economic policies, such as breaking up big banks, raising the minimum wage, and taxing the very rich. Trump followers have a less economic and more nationalist focus and emphasize limiting immigration and confronting the threat of terrorism. Still, they agree with one another about the dangers of increasing inequality and the pernicious impact of money in our politics. Yet these strong issue concerns have not translated into political action for these groups in the past, and perhaps not even in the future. As students of political participation, we were not surprised by the finding in a January 2016 American National Election Studies Pilot Survey that supporters of these two candidates were less likely to have voted in 2012 than the supporters of all other primary candidates. All these aspects of the environment for the exercise of political voice have given even greater urgency to our intellectual concerns. It certainly seems like the right time to revisit our work on political inequality in America.

We hope that we have provided new readers a congenial format for encountering our sometimes discouraging findings and old friends with an updated refresher course in unequal political voice in America.

ACKNOWLEDGMENTS

As always, we have incurred many debts in the course of completing this book. We continue to be very grateful to our home institutions—Boston College, the University of California–Berkeley, and Harvard University—for supplying us not only with critical research resources but also with congenial long-term homes in which to function as teachers and scholars. In particular, we thank Shirley Gee and Karina Ovalles of Boston College and Sarah Baughn and Bri Cuozzo of the University of California–Berkeley for having helped us in so many ways.

One of the rewards of academic life is working with the students, both undergraduate and graduate, who become part of the research family. Sonja Petek served as a fantastic analyst and manager of data. A superb team that included Brendan Buci, Erica Cross, Tanner Edwards, Laura Fedorko, Therese Murphy, and Greta Weissner coded and cleaned the 2011 data for the Washington Representatives Study. We also thank Alex Barton, Anne Bigler, Andrew Bowen, Daniel Geary, Sam Hayes, Marissa Marandola, and Jacob Wolfe for their creativity and perseverance in undertaking many and varied research tasks.

Over the many years that we have been studying inequality of political voice, it has been a joy to work with graduate students who become peers as co-authors and dear friends. We are deeply indebted to Traci Burch, Nancy Burns, Jennifer Erkulwater, Philip E. Jones, and Shauna Shames, who were co-authors of chapters of *The Unheavenly Chorus,* and to Hye Young You, who was a co-author of two of the later papers on which we drew for this book. We are also beholden to Casey Klofstad, who celebrated the twentieth anniversary of the publication of *Voice and Equality* by assembling a set of papers that use diverse methods and approaches to push the boundaries of what we know about political participation.

We express our appreciation to Lee Rainey of the Pew Internet and American Life Project for supporting a second round of data collection in 2012 so that we could continue to assess the ramifications of the rapidly changing digital environment for inequalities of political voice. We also thank Jeffrey Blossom of the Center for Geographic Analysis at Harvard for helping us learn to use the software that generated the maps in Chapter 12.

We are grateful to the two anonymous readers for Princeton University Press from whom we received helpful and thoughtful readings. Reader #2 (whom we surmise is Andrea Campbell) gave us a line-by-line reading of uncommon rigor and intelligence, to which we referred constantly as we revised. We also thank Larry Mischel and Joe Quinn for helpful readings of Chapter 10.

We are deeply grateful to Eric Crahan of Princeton University Press, who planted the original seed for this book and who stayed with us as it grew to maturity. We also thank the members of his team—Mark Bellis, Cyd Westmoreland, and Arthur Werneck—for their efforts in bringing the manuscript to print.

All three of us are extremely appreciative of the Rockefeller Foundation for supporting us as residents at the Bellagio Center—Kay and Henry together while this volume was being drafted and Sidney while we were working on *Voice and Equality*. It is hard to imagine a setting more conducive to uninterrupted work or more jaw-droppingly beautiful.

Once again, we thank Stanley, Patricia, and Cynthia, to whom we dedicate this work, for having the patience to hang in yet one more time.

Our friends, E. J. Dionne, Norman Orenstein, and Tom Mann, concluded the acknowledgments of their recent book by observing:

> Last, we thank each other. If this seems odd, consider that a three-way partnership could have been difficult. This one wasn't. We started as dear friends and ended as dearer friends. We're deeply grateful for that.

After a collaboration of more than thirty years that has meant a great deal to us professionally, intellectually, and personally, we can only say, "Amen."

KLS
HEB
SV
August 2017

We have drawn in various places on the following recently published works:

Kay Lehman Schlozman, Henry E. Brady, and Sidney Verba, "Growing Economic Inequality and Its (Partially) Political Roots," *Religions* 8 (2017): 97.

Kay Lehman Schlozman, Philip Edward Jones, Hye Young You, Traci Burch, Sidney Verba, and Henry E. Brady, "Organizations and the Democratic Representation of Interests: What Does It Mean When Those Organizations Have No Members?" *Perspectives on Politics* 13 (2015): 1017–1029.

Kay Lehman Schlozman, Philip Edward Jones, Hye Young You, Traci Burch, Sidney Verba, and Henry E. Brady, "Louder Chorus—Same Accent: The Representation of Interests in Pressure Politics," in *The Organization Ecology of Interest Communities: Assessments and Agendas*, ed. David Lowery, Darren R. Halpin, and Virginia Gray (London: Palgrave Macmillan, 2015), pp. 23–43.

Henry E. Brady, Kay Lehman Schlozman, and Sidney Verba, "Political Mobility and Political Reproduction from Generation to Generation," *Annals of the American Academy of Political and Social Science* 657 (2015): 149–173.

UNEQUAL AND UNREPRESENTED

1

Introduction

- On February 9, Shep Melnick and Joanne Linden went to the polls in Amherst, New Hampshire, to cast their ballots in the first presidential primary of 2016.
- During the same month, contributors were making donations in support of their favored candidates seeking the presidential nominations of the two parties. Travis Stanger, an Iowa high school student and part-time McDonald's cashier, made his monthly $3 donation to his candidate of choice. Meanwhile, hedge fund managers Paul Singer and Kenneth Griffin each gave $2.5 million to a candidate Super PAC.
- Blaring their horns, dozens of trucks paraded around the Rhode Island state capitol to protest pending legislation imposing tolls on tractor trailers to fund road and bridge repairs.
- In East Las Vegas, Laura Lozano was working a phone bank, urging Spanish-speaking voters to support her candidate's bid for the presidential nomination and explaining the complexities of how to take part in the upcoming caucuses.
- Hundreds of supporters gathered during the annual Kentucky Right to Life Rally to watch Governor Matt Bevin sign the first piece of legislation of his administration, an informed consent abortion bill.
- Outside the Twin Cities in Minnesota, a group of neighbors formed the Stockholm Township Concerned Citizens Group, hoping to

force Forsman Farms to scale back or drop plans to build a new facility that would house more than a million chickens.
- Resident leaders for Mitchell-Lama developments sent letters to New York City Mayor Bill de Blasio in support of affordable housing in the city.
- More than fifty people signed up to speak at a packed Seattle City Council briefing to give policymakers their views on how to best fight homelessness.
- Maple syrup producer groups from New England and the Upper Midwest as well as the International Maple Syrup Institute and the North American Maple Syrup Council lobbied the Food and Drug Administration to protest the mislabeling by major manufacturers of processed food containing imitation maple syrup.
- Stephen J. Ubl, president of the heavy-hitting trade group, the Pharmaceutical Research and Manufacturers of America or PhRMA, which spent $18.4 million on lobbying in 2015, worked to counter increasing criticism from doctors, consumer advocates, and politicians about the soaring prices of name-brand drugs.[1]

Democracies require mechanisms for the free expression of political voice so that members of the public can communicate information about their experiences, needs, and preferences and hold public officials accountable for their conduct in office. Working individually or collectively, they can communicate their concerns and opinions to policymakers in order to have a direct effect on public policy, or they can attempt to affect policy indirectly by influencing electoral outcomes. They can donate their time or their money. They can use conventional techniques or protest tactics. They can work locally or nationally. They can even have political input when, for reasons having nothing to do with politics, they affiliate with an organization that is politically active. As shown by the examples above, during the short days of mid-winter, 2016, Americans exercised political voice in all these ways.

In this volume, we explore how Americans use political voice to let public officials know what is on their minds and to generate pressure to respond to what is being said. But we are concerned not just with political voice but with equal political voice. Robert Dahl famously said: "A key characteristic of a democracy is the continued responsiveness of the government to the preferences of its citizens, considered as equals."[2] Later, in another context he argued that "all human beings are of equal intrinsic worth . . . and that the good or interests of each person must be given equal consideration."[3] If citizens are not equally able or likely to make efforts to let public officials know what they want or need, then some people will wield a megaphone, and others will speak in a whisper. Inequality of political voice has been a persistent and growing aspect of American democracy.

We examine inequalities of political voice—in the participation of Americans as individuals and in the activities of organizations that represent their interests—from a variety of perspectives. Among other topics, we consider:

- **Equal Political Voice in a Democracy:** What we mean by political voice and whether equal political voice matters in a democracy (Chapter 2);
- **The Civic Voluntarism Model:** How inequalities in individual political activity are rooted in differences in such resources as time, money, and civic skills; in such psychological orientations to politics as political interest, knowledge, and efficacy; and in the processes of recruitment by which friends, workmates, neighbors, and fellow organization and church members ask one another to take part politically (Chapter 3);
- **Unequal Voice among Individuals:** How active and inactive individuals differ with regard to their education and income, their race or ethnicity, and their gender (Chapter 4) as well as to their preferences, needs, and priorities for government action (Chapter 5);
- **The Role of the Internet:** How the possibilities for political participation on the Internet affect underrepresentation among the young or those of lower socioeconomic status (Chapter 6);
- **Social Movements and Recruitment to Participation:** How processes of political mobilization, whether rooted in protest movements or in ordinary interactions at work, in organizations, or religious institutions, affect inequalities of political voice (Chapter 7);
- **Unequal Voice among Organizations:** How inequalities of political voice among individuals are reinforced by the multiple forms of activity by organizations active in Washington politics (Chapters 8 and 9);
- **Growth of Economic Inequality:** How economic inequality has grown in the past thirty years, leaving some people with enormous resources and others with very few resources for the exercise political voice, and how public policies have contributed to those economic outcomes (Chapter 10);

- **Changing Political Inequality:** How inequalities of political voice have changed in an era of both increasing economic inequality and tinkering with procedural arrangements that govern politics (Chapter 11);
- **Possibilities for Reform:** Whether various procedural political reforms hold the potential to alleviate participatory inequalities (Chapter 12).

This book relies, in the main, on the analysis of participation by individuals and organized interests, but we place the subject in the broader context of the American political tradition and the contemporary increase in economic inequality.

Political Voice, Equal Political Voice, and Democratic Accountability

The exercise of political voice includes any activity undertaken by individuals and organizations "that has the intent or effect of influencing government action—either directly by affecting the making or implementation of public policy or indirectly by influencing the selection of people who make those policies."[4]

Political acts vary in their capacity to convey information about what citizens want and need. The vote is a notably blunt instrument of communication. Although winning candidates often claim a "mandate," in truth they usually have only an imprecise understanding of what was on the minds of the voters who placed them in office. In contrast, the many forms of direct expression of preferences—a sign at a demonstration, an e-mail to a senator's office, a prepared statement at a meeting of the local zoning board—can communicate clear and, in some circumstances, quite specific messages. Organized interests are especially likely to communicate detailed information when they contact public officials, and this information frequently helps in the process of policy formation, although it presents a particular point of view.

Political acts also vary in the pressure they can bring to bear on policymakers to listen and respond favorably to what they are hearing. When individual or organizational activists command valued resources—for example, campaign contributions, blocs of voters, political intelligence, or access to other powerful political figures—targeted public officials usually feel less free to ignore the accompanying messages. The senator engaged in a tight campaign for reelection, the state legislator drafting a tax bill, and the mayor confronting protests over an incident of alleged police brutality all have incentives to pay attention to activist publics.

THE LEVEL AND DISTRIBUTION OF POLITICAL VOICE

Public officials, journalists, and political scientists often worry about low levels of citizen participation in politics—especially if voter turnout is not high. We sympathize with these concerns. A vigorous civic life in which citizens are active as individuals and in organizations confers many benefits. For example, for individuals, political engagement can be educational—cultivating useful organizational and communications skills and broadening their understanding of their own and others' best interests. For the political system, citizens who have ample opportunities to express their political views are more likely to accept government actions as legitimate. Those concerned with well-functioning democracy have reason to monitor the level of individual and organized activity and to be uneasy if it decreases.

Still, we are primarily concerned with equality of political voice rather than with its quantity. Equal political voice does not require that everyone takes part. We know that scientific polls can provide a representative picture of public opinion by surveying only a small fraction of the population. Similarly, equal political voice follows if there is proportionate input from those with a variety of *politically relevant characteristics and circumstances:* for example, economic well-being; race or ethnicity; religious commitment; sexual orientation or identity; veteran status; immigrant status; or being a Medicare recipient, a student at a public university, or an employee of a defense contractor. Analogously, equal voice is achieved if varying *attitudes on issues* ranging from gay rights to the minimum wage to the regulation of coal mining to trade policy are expressed proportionately by political activists.

The individuals and organizations active in American politics are anything but representative in these ways. Those who are not affluent and well educated—that is, those of low socioeconomic status (SES)—are less likely to take part politically and are even less likely to be represented by organized interests. What is more, for as long as we have had the tools to measure political involvement, there has been continuity in the kinds of individuals and organized interests represented in politics. Inequalities of political voice are deeply embedded in American politics. Although public issues and citizen concerns may come and go, the affluent and well educated are consistently overrepresented.

EQUAL VOICE—EQUAL CONSIDERATION

One of the hallmarks of democracy is that the concerns and interests of each citizen are given equal consideration in the process of making decisions that are binding on a political community. As we shall demonstrate repeatedly in the pages that follow, the disparities in political voice across various segments of society are so substantial and so persistent as to preclude the minimal democratic requirement of equal consideration by decision makers. Public officials cannot consider voices they do not hear, and it is more difficult to pay attention to voices that speak softly. If some stakeholders express themselves faintly and others say nothing at all, there is little or nothing for policymakers to consider. As Lindblom and Woodhouse comment: "If poorer, less educated minorities participate less, their judgments about what problems deserve government's attention will attain less than proportionate weight in the process of partisan mutual adjustment."[5]

Because politics involves conflict among those with differing preferences and clashing interests, it is inevitable that politics will not leave all contenders equally satisfied with the outcomes. Yet it is not only feasible but desirable for all to be heard and for everyone's views to be considered on an equal basis.

Equal voice is not an absolute prerequisite for achieving equal consideration. Public officials have mechanisms besides participatory input from individuals and organizations for learning what is on the minds of citizens. They can, for example, consult polls or follow the media. And the influences on policy include many additional factors—ranging from an incumbent's values and ideology to partisan pressures to a desire to take a political career up a notch—other than policymakers' perceptions of what the public wants and needs. These other factors may substitute for equal voice. Still, if votes, campaign contributions, e-mails, lobbying contacts, comments on proposed agency regulations, or amicus briefs come from an unrepresentative set of individuals and organizations, equal consideration will be compromised and government policy will likely reflect the preferences and needs of the active part of the public.

MEASURING INEQUALITIES OF POLITICAL VOICE

Equal voice seems essential for democracy, but because voice can be expressed in so many ways, there is no fully satisfactory way to assess degrees of inequality across acts measured in different metrics.[6] We can compare the political input from a small protest with only ten demonstrators to one that is a hundred times bigger. But how do we compare the weight of a protest that attracts a crowd of 1,000 to the weight of 1,000 votes or 1,000 e-mails?

To complicate matters further, political acts vary in the extent to which activists can multiply their volume. At one extreme, within limits, votes have equal weight. We are each allowed only one per election contest. But the principle of one person, one vote does not obtain for other kinds of participation. Individuals are free to write as many letters to public officials, work as many hours in campaigns, or join as many political organizations as their time and commitment allow. When it comes to the extent to which the volume of activity can be multiplied, contributions to political campaigns and causes present a special case. Although there are no legal constraints on the number of phone calls a citizen can make to public officials or the number of marches a protester can attend, the fact that there are only twenty-four hours in a day imposes an implicit ceiling. In contrast, some lingering campaign finance laws to the contrary, there is no upper limit on the number of dollars that a person with a big bank account can contribute.

Individual and Collective Political Voice

Implicit in the concept of equal political voice is equality among individuals. In the vast political science literature concerned with public opinion and political participation, the individual is the main actor in the democratic system. However, the voice of a single individual is usually fairly weak. When individuals are coordinated within organizations, they can be a more potent force. Political voice in America is often the voice of organized interests speaking loudly and clearly.

Political participation by the public and by organized interests are often studied separately from one another with different frameworks and methods. When it comes to inequalities of political voice, however, they are two faces of the same thing. We consider politically active organizations of many kinds:

- Membership associations of individuals: for example, unions like the Teamsters, professional associations like the American Medical Association, and citizen groups like the Sierra Club;
- Trade associations like the National Restaurant Association that bring together firms in an industry;
- State and local governments that have residents but not members; and

- Memberless organizations like corporations, hospitals, and even universities, which do not have members in the ordinary sense but have important sets of stakeholders.

In considering political voice through organizational activity, we ask the same questions about political organizations that we ask about individual citizens: What interests do they represent through what kinds of activity, and how equal or unequal is that representation? The results for organized interests parallel the findings for individuals and show the extent and durability of political inequality in America.

WHO IS SPEAKING WHEN AN ORGANIZATION SPEAKS?

When individuals exercise political voice, they are representing themselves, and there is no ambiguity as to who is speaking. However, questions about representation immediately arise with organizations. Individual membership associations presumably communicate the interests of their members. But whose interests? Those of the executives who run the organization? The staff that support them? The board to whom they are accountable? The rank and file membership? If so, which ones among the rank and file? The old or the young? The most privileged or the least?

This problem is even knottier for the vast majority of politically active organizations that are not membership associations composed of individuals. Which of the various stakeholders are being represented when a corporation or a museum speaks in politics? In short, an organization may have a powerful voice in politics, but it may not be clear whose voice it really is.

MEASURING UNEQUAL VOICE WHEN ORGANIZATIONS ARE SPEAKING

When we move from the political voice of individuals to that emanating from political organizations, the problem of how to measure inequalities of political voice is exacerbated. Because organizations that are active in politics have very different numbers of members, we cannot count each organization as an equivalent unit as we would with individual citizens. The nation's largest membership association, AARP (formerly the American Association of Retired Persons) has nearly 38 million members. In contrast, the professional association of skin cancer surgeons, the American College of Moh's Surgery, has fewer than 1,300.[7] Indeed, the majority of politically active organizations—including some real heavy hitters like Boeing, which spent $21.9 million on lobbying in 2015—have no members at all.[8] On a level playing field, how much voice would each of these organizations have?

We shall consider ways to think about this question. For all the limitations on our ability to measure political voice with precision, the differences we find across individuals, aggregations of individuals, and organizations are sufficiently striking that there can be no doubt about the existence and persistence of real inequalities of political voice in America.

Who Exercises Political Voice? The Somewhat Level Playing Field of Democratic Citizenship

With some notable exceptions, the rights that inhere in citizenship place most members of the political community on an equal footing. The clearest and most basic requisite for equal political voice is the right to express that voice. For most forms of political activity, the right to take part is very widely dispersed and is not restricted to those who are formally citizens of the United States and eligible for a U.S. passport. As we proceed, when we discuss "citizen" activity, we generally include under that umbrella all adult members of the mass public residing in the United States, including resident aliens whether or not legal. Occasionally—for example, when we treat forms of activity such as voting that are restricted to those with formal citizenship status—we use the term "citizen" in its narrower legalistic sense.

As applied to the states through judicial interpretation of the Fourteenth Amendment, the basic participatory rights of the First Amendment—freedom of speech and press, the rights of assembly and petition—are generally available to all within the borders of the United States, regardless of citizenship status.[9] In fact, within limits, such rights may be available to non-citizens, even those who do not reside in the United States. The op-ed pages of major newspapers often feature opinion pieces by foreign commentators. Although their communications might not be heeded or even answered, non-Americans are free to get in touch with American public officials. Aware of the worldwide repercussions of American electoral outcomes, foreign visitors have been known to take part in presidential campaigns while visiting the United States.

The right to take part in particular ways is sometimes limited to subgroups of the relevant political community. For example, although making campaign contributions has been interpreted as a form of protected speech by the Supreme Court, foreigners are not permitted to donate to federal campaigns. Moreover, citizens residing in one town are not free to vote in the elections of an adjoining town. They may not even be free to attend town meetings in a neighboring community, even though an issue on the agenda—say, a pending decision to close the bridge that spans the river—might have an impact on them.

Important categories of citizens—including those without property, African Americans, and women—have been excluded from the franchise in the past. When Virginia Minor sued the Missouri voting registrar who denied her application to register under the Privileges and Immunities clause of the Fourteenth Amendment, the Supreme Court ruled unanimously in 1875 that, although Minor was a citizen, the franchise is not necessarily a right protected from state infringement.[10] Although racial, gender, and economic barriers to the vote have fallen after a long and bumpy journey, even today some categories of citizens are denied the vote. Children—whose First Amendment rights are also circumscribed—are the most obvious example of citizens who lack access to the ballot. Another category is convicted felons. All but two states have some restrictions on the voting rights of felons, restrictions that fall quite disproportionately on blacks, Hispanics, and the poor.[11] Nevertheless, despite the qualifications to the universal right to take part politically, political rights and liberties act as an equalizing force for political voice.

The political rights of organizations are not as broad as the rights of individuals. Organizations have free speech rights for communicating on public issues, but such rights may be constricted when it comes to partisan participation in elections. Nonprofits with 501(c)3 tax status must limit their lobbying or lose the tax deductibility of donations made to them. Starting with the Tillman Act of 1907, which prohibited corporations from giving money to federal candidates, restrictions have been placed on contributions from corporations. Recently, the right of corporations and other organizations to make electioneering expenditures has been contested in the courts, and the Supreme Court has ruled to permit greater freedom for such involvement.

Who Exercises Political Voice? The Tilted Playing Field of Unequal Participatory Factors

The equal right to act does not inevitably lead to equal political voice. It functions as a form of political equality of opportunity, a necessary but not a sufficient condition for political action. In Chapter 3, we focus on the participatory inequalities stemming from disparities in the factors that shape the activity levels of rights-bearing individuals. Among the factors that promote political activity are the motivation to take part; such resources as knowledge and skills, money, and time that provide the capacity to act; and location in the social networks that serve to stimulate activity and to mediate requests for participation.

THE PERVASIVE ROLE OF SOCIOECONOMIC STATUS

The factors that foster political participation are not independent of one another. Those who have the skills and information to take part are more likely to want to do so. Reciprocally, those with a concern about politics are predisposed to make efforts to learn the relevant skills. Similarly, those embedded in social networks are more often asked to take political action and to get involved politically. Moreover, those with the capacity to participate effectively—those who are able to contribute generously to a campaign or to make a coherent statement at a school board meeting—are more likely to be the targets of such requests. Thus, the processes that nurture political voice interact to create unequal political voice.

At the root of these self-reinforcing processes is SES. The well educated are likely to have a stockpile of a variety of other participatory factors: for example, to have the kinds of jobs that inculcate civic skills and generate high incomes; to be politically interested, knowledgeable, and efficacious; and to be connected to the networks that mediate requests for political activity. As we have continued our now decades-long investigation of unequal political voice, we have been surprised to uncover, under every intellectual rock we excavate, the deeply embedded and durable character of socioeconomic inequalities in political voice. Inequalities of political voice are found in every cross-sectional analysis, and they are linked to such politically relevant circumstances as living in dilapidated housing, needing Pell Grants, and suffering such problems of basic human need as having to cut back spending on groceries. They persist over time and flow across generations. The same biases apply to political voice expressed through organized interests—a fact that, over time, has consistently led to overrepresentation of the concerns and needs of business and other resource-endowed publics. However we look at the issue and however we analyze our wide-ranging data, SES always seems to return to the center of our explanation for differences in political voice.

OTHER BASES OF THE INEQUALITY OF POLITICAL VOICE

Our concern with inequalities of political voice extends to any politically relevant attribute—that is, to any characteristic that might become a source of conflict in politics. We emphasize how political voice varies with SES because it is not only significant for political conflict but also an important causal factor in the explanation of individual differences in political activity. Income and education are strongly associated with political participation. They also connect to many other attributes that, while not causal factors useful in explaining unequal political voice, are germane to political conflict in America.

Of particular concern is unequal voice on the basis of gender and race or ethnicity.[12] In a statistical analysis that controls for differences in people's characteristics that are rooted in SES (that is, in what is commonly referred to as "multivariate analysis"), disparities in participation among non-Hispanic whites, African Americans, and Latinos[13] or between men and women can be largely or fully understood in terms of these differences. That SES is behind racial or ethnic and gender differences in political participation does not justify the conclusion that these differences are all about SES and that race or ethnicity or gender is irrelevant. As long as there are politically relevant issues associated with policies that have a differential impact on men and women or on Latinos, African Americans, and non-Hispanic whites, it matters for politics that public officials hear disproportionately from members of some groups. If, for example, politicians hear less from African Americans because they are poorer and less well educated than whites, the fact remains that they have less voice, which is consequential for them as African Americans.

Furthermore, it is not exactly a coincidence that persons of color and women command fewer of the SES-based resources for political activity than do non-Hispanic whites or men. Indeed, these gaps in SES are intimately connected to the structures that sustain social and economic distinctions on the basis of race or ethnicity and gender in America. For these reasons, even though we give higher priority to SES in our analysis of inequalities of political voice, it is essential not to dismiss inequalities of political voice anchored in other bases of political cleavage.

TIME AND MONEY

A consistent theme throughout our investigation is the contrast between the roles of time and money in the exercise of political voice. Mark Hanna,

President McKinley's highly successful campaign manager, supposedly remarked more than a century ago: "There are two things that are important in politics. The first is money, and I can't remember the second." We might not go quite as far as did Hanna—many factors do matter in politics—but money certainly deserves a place of honor among the factors that facilitate political activity. While individuals use money to make contributions to electoral campaigns and to political organizations and causes, organizations use financial resources for many political purposes—to staff an office, hire lobbyists and other experts, make donations from their political action committees, or engage in independent spending in elections.

When political voice is based on inputs of dollars rather than hours, the possibilities for inequality of political voice expand. In contrast to time, there is no ceiling on income and wealth, and individuals are much more unequal when it comes to money than when it comes to time. Individual activity in making financial donations is, not unexpectedly, highly stratified, with a substantial gap between the affluent and the less well off. Moreover, compared to inequalities in income, inequalities in spare time are much less likely to adhere to the boundaries of politically relevant categories—not only SES but also race, ethnicity, and gender. Instead, the unavailability of extra time results from such life circumstances as paid work and having children at home.

For several reasons, including the strength of First Amendment protections, the United States allows more freedom in using market resources to influence political outcomes than do other countries. Because financial resources are so unevenly distributed and because differences in income hew to the fault lines of important political conflicts, political money raises the dilemma of how to reconcile inequalities of market resources with the desire to establish a level playing field for democracy.

Equal Voice and the Dilemmas of Democratic Governance

Could a circumstance of equal political voice endanger the democratic process? Philosophers of public life going back to the ancient Greeks have differed in the extent to which they trust the judgment of the public and in the role they assign to ordinary people and to those who are deemed wiser and more experienced in the ideal democracy.[14] At the Founding, James Madison expressed apprehension about those "particular moments in public affairs when the people, stimulated by some irregular passion . . . or misled by the artful misrepresentations of interested men, may call for measures which they themselves will afterwards be the most ready to lament and condemn."[15] Reflecting similar concerns about the lower classes, Alexander Hamilton argued: "The republican principle . . . does not require an unqualified complaisance to every sudden breeze of passion, or to every transient impulse which the people may receive from the arts of men."[16]

Distrust of the public is no longer as acute as it once was, but there is still reason for skepticism about the capacities of ordinary American citizens for enlightened self-government. Quantitative studies dating back at least to the 1950s demonstrate that many Americans have only limited commitment to civil liberties, tolerance for dissenting views, and command of political information—especially if they are not well educated.[17] Governing depends on expertise, on the capacity to understand and judge potential policies, and on the ability to make complex policy decisions that balance the concerns of many actors. The diverse members of the public, who have widely varied preferences and needs, devote limited attention to policy issues, making them ill equipped to judge among alternative policies. Equal voice for all—regardless of educational level, interest in and knowledge about politics, or relevant experience—might lead to government that is less effective, less efficient, and less prudent.

The institutional arrangement designed to resolve this tension is representative government. Representative democracy moves decisions away from the direct control of the citizens and into the hands of representatives who, relying on their own judgment and expertise, supposedly render politics more open and tolerant and policy more effective. Representative government thus ameliorates many democratic mischiefs: policy based on expertise would mitigate citizen incompetence; elected elites who are more committed to civil liberties would bolster support for the democratic process; the intermediation of representatives would reduce the danger of tyranny by a majority faction that squashes minority rights or by minority factions uninterested in the common good. Although there are plenty of episodes—the McCarthy era and Watergate come immediately to mind—suggesting that this characterization is idealized, more than two centuries later, American democracy remains based on representative government.

What is the role of political voice—and equal voice—in a democracy based on representative democracy? Within the American consensus on the wisdom of representative government as a compromise between rule from above and rule from below, there have been serious differences with regard to the extent to which public officials should defer to the expressed preferences of the public or exercise their own independent judgment in governing. The Progressives of the early twentieth century—who, in reaction to the corruption of party bosses, institutionalized such procedural arrangements as initiative, recall, and referendum—clearly believed in shifting the balance toward direct popular rule. In contrast, Joseph Schumpeter took a quite different view in his classic *Capitalism, Socialism, and Democracy*.[18] In his rather restricted interpretation of the role of the people in representative democracy, the task of the citizenry is to elect officeholders. Given the limited capacities of the public and the need for expertise in policymaking, citizen participation should begin and end with electoral participation. After they elect leaders from the choices offered, citizens should then leave the more expert elites free to rule.

From our perspective, all versions of representative government require continuous information from a representative group of citizens about their problems and experiences that might otherwise be overlooked. However, none addresses the fact that political activity by individuals and organizations derives disproportionately from the affluent and well educated. We take no position on the eternal question of the extent to which public officials in American democracy should be guided by the preferences of the public or by their own good judgment. Still, we believe firmly that broad exposure and information about everyone's wants and needs will permit whoever rules to do so more wisely.

EQUAL VOICE, MAJORITY TYRANNY, AND "MINORITIES RULE"

A related concern is reconciling support for equal voice with a concern about majority tyranny. For many issues in American politics, a relatively indifferent majority on one side is opposed by an intense but smaller public on the other. This pattern characterizes controversies as diverse as gun control, consumer product safety regulation, and community conflicts over the siting of facilities like sewage treatment plants or even new schools. That democratic procedures ordinarily provide for the majority to prevail raises no concerns about majority tyranny when the losers in the minority are not deeply invested in the outcome. However, if the losing minority has strong and intensely held views, majority rule may be more problematic—particularly if the triumphant majority compromises the basic rights of the minority or if the losing minority is defeated over and over on issue after issue.

How should a minority that cares deeply—especially a group that constitutes a more or less permanent minority—be treated in a democracy? Can equal voice be harmonized with deference to views that are intensely held? As Madison observed in "Federalist No. 10": "Measures are too often decided, not according to the rules of justice and the rights of the minor party, but by the superior force of an interested and overbearing majority."[19] In fact, Madison makes clear later in the essay that American government was designed to ensure that minority viewpoints have opportunities to block majority factions.

To ignore the fact that some people care deeply about a particular issue while the large and politically quiescent majority are more or less indifferent would seem unreasonable. Yet to allow an intense and active minority to prevail over and over again has other risks. The history of American political conflict demonstrates that majority tyranny is not the only danger and that an intense minority often carries the day in policy controversies, a circumstance sometimes dubbed "minorities rule." Indeed, later in life Madison expressed concern about the need for ordinary citizens to have a voice in politics and demonstrated greater congeniality to majority rule.[20]

As they seek to navigate between tyranny by majorities and rule by intense minorities, policymakers will be better informed if they hear all perspectives instead of having some systematically shouted while others are whispered. However they balance majority rule and deference to intense minorities, decision makers will benefit from equal voice.

Unequal Voice in the New Gilded Age

As we shall see in Chapter 10, systematic data substantiate that we do, indeed, live in a New Gilded Age. The concentration of income and wealth among the very rich has reached levels not witnessed since the 1920s. The minimum wage, which peaked in real terms in 1968, is now worth less than it was in the late 1970s, when wages for everyone below the top layer of earners began to stagnate. The proportion of those below the poverty line who are desperately poor has increased. These and related economic developments reflect such market forces as globalization and technological change. However, they are also influenced by, and reciprocally, have consequences for, politics. Not only is government policy part of the story of increasing economic inequality but the increase in economic inequality also has implications for unequal political voice in politics.

At the same time that economic inequality has increased, citizen politics in America has changed in ways that further enhance the long-standing participatory advantage of the well educated and well-off. Reflecting the relationship between education and income, the affluent have always spoken loudly and clearly in politics. While the rich have been getting richer, forms of activity based on money are occupying more space in the bundle of participatory acts through which Americans express political voice. The great political money chase enhances the relative importance of money in electoral politics, giving very, very affluent donors greater access to candidates and rendering successful candidates increasingly indebted to their funders. There has been simultaneous growth in organized interest activity, where the availability of economic resources has made it possible to hire more and more experts and lobbyists.

Procedural changes to the rules governing politics over the past decade, discussed in Chapter 12, have exacerbated patterns of participatory inequality deeply rooted in social structure. A series of federal court decisions, the best known of which is the 2010 Supreme Court decision in *Citizens United* v. *FEC*, have effectively lifted many of the limits on campaign money. We now have sufficient experience with this new campaign finance regime to know that at the same time that money has become more important in electoral politics, those with the wherewithal to make substantial contributions have become more important as well.

Procedural changes in voting at the state level also threaten to magnify participatory inequalities. Some states have legislated new requirements—some of them quite strict—for producing identification in order to cast a ballot. The impact of these new rules is not yet fully clear, but there is concern that voters of limited income and education—in particular, persons of color—will be disproportionately affected by the new requirements. At the same time that voter ID laws threaten to make it harder to vote in many states, a less-noticed contrary trend has eased ballot access in a majority of states. Unfortunately, even when such reforms as election day registration, online registration, early voting, and no-excuse absentee voting raise turnout (and they do not always do so), such procedural changes do not necessarily democratize the electorate. Even if voters show up at the polls in larger numbers, the additional voters mirror the characteristics of the core voters who show up without fail.

We were once asked whether what we were finding is an old disturbing pattern or a new disturbing trend to which we could only answer "Both."

Over and over in what follows, we demonstrate that pronounced inequalities of political voice are a longstanding feature of our politics and that such inequalities are anchored firmly in inequalities of education and income. However, both economic and political developments in the New Gilded Age are exacerbating the inequalities of political voice that have for so long characterized democracy in America.

A Note on Data

To pursue these multiple themes, we draw on evidence from various sources. However, for our systematic analyses, we rely principally on data from four sources:

- **The Citizen Participation Study**. Although the data from this 1990 survey are now more than a quarter century old, this survey contains the most comprehensive set of measures of individual participatory acts, the factors that facilitate participation, and the institutional contexts of adult life—work, nonpolitical organizations, and religious institutions.[21]
- **American National Election Studies (ANES)**. The ANES focus on forms of individual participation associated with elections and only occasionally include items about nonelectoral forms of activity. Still, they provide an invaluable ongoing portrait of the American electorate that dates back more than half a century. Electoral participation follows a zigzag pattern, spiking in years with presidential elections and falling off in the congressional elections two years later; therefore, unless otherwise noted, we use only the data from the surveys conducted in presidential election years.[22]
- **Pew Internet and American Life Project**. These surveys, which replicated some of the questions on the Citizen Participation Study, included items about Internet use as well as political engagement and activity both on the Internet and offline.[23]
- **Washington Representatives Study**. We have assembled the most extensive and comprehensive database to date of organizations active in Washington politics. The more than 33,000 organizations in the database include all the organizations listed in the 1981, 1991, 2001, 2006, and 2011 editions of the *Washington Representatives* directory[24]—along with additional organizations listed in archival sources as having been politically active by, for example, testifying in

Congress or filing an amicus brief. For each organization, we coded information about its history, the kinds of interests on behalf of which it advocates, and the activities it undertakes in the quest for policy influence.[25]

Our practice throughout is to use the most recent available data set that allows us to answer the intellectual questions we are posing and, whenever possible, to use other data sets to check our results. Because the Citizen Participation Study contained such rich measures, it often permits more complex—if cross-sectional and possibly dated—analysis. When we use that survey, we do so because we could not find a more recent data set containing appropriate measures.

PART I

2

What Do We Mean by Political Voice? Does Equal Voice Matter?

If political voice is essential to the democratic process through which policymakers learn about and respond to citizen preferences and needs, we need to understand what it is and why it matters. This chapter discusses the multiple ways that individuals and organizations express political voice and lays out some of the difficulties in assessing the extent to which political voice is unequal. We then tackle the complicated issue of whether there are actual policy consequences of the inequalities of political voice that we investigate in detail in the chapters to come.

The Many Forms of Political Voice

The American people do not speak in a single voice. If they did, we would not need to be concerned about equal political voice. In fact, if the people spoke as one, we would not need to be concerned with the central problem of democratic governance: solving public problems and meeting public challenges when citizens do not agree on the appropriate solutions—or even on the appropriate definition of the problems and challenges. Instead, the cacophony that constitutes political voice includes diverse messages on diverse subjects from diverse individuals and organizations undertaking diverse activities aimed at diverse targets in the three branches of government at the federal, state, and local levels.

TABLE 2.1. The Multiple Forms of Political Voice: Some Examples

	Individual Activity	Organizational Activity
INDIRECT INFLUENCE THROUGH ELECTIONS		
Principal input: Time	Vote	Organize a registration or get-out-the-vote drive
	Work in a campaign or for a party	Organize volunteers to work in a campaign or for a party
	Attend a campaign meeting or rally	Organize a meet-and-greet or fundraiser for a candidate
Principal input: Money	Donate to an electoral campaign or political organization or cause	Make a PAC donation
DIRECT INFLUENCE		
Principal input: Time	Contact a public official	Lobby a public official
	Take part in a protest	Present policy-related research
	Work with others in the community on a local issue	Organize a grassroots campaign
	Serve as a volunteer on a local board	Mobilize members to protest
		Testify in Congress or an agency
	Join an organization that takes stands in politics	File an amicus brief
Principal input: Money	Contribute to an organization that takes political stands	Hire professionals to undertake political advocacy

Political voice encompasses all activity undertaken by individuals and organizations with the intent or effect of influencing government action—either indirectly through participation in the electoral process or directly through expressions of preferences. Table 2.1, which lists a number of political activities undertaken by individuals and organizations, makes some critical distinctions among various ways to exercise political voice[1] and shows the extent to which parallels exist between individuals and organizations when it comes to political input.

We start by distinguishing two paths for the expression of political voice. The first one is indirect influence through elections and includes perhaps the most fundamental democratic act, casting a ballot. The vote is first among equals as a way to exercise political voice, and the right of citizens to hold their elected officials accountable through periodic elections is essential in democracies around the world. Among participatory acts, voting stands out. It is the most common participatory act. It is also the only political act for which there are strict limits on the volume of input: eligible voters get one and only one vote per election.[2] Individuals who wish to multiply their impact on electoral outcomes can, of course, get involved in elections by working for a candidate or making a campaign contribution. Although they cannot go to the polls to vote, organizations also take part in electoral politics by organizing get-out-the-vote drives, urging members or stakeholders to support particular candidates or parties, and making contributions through political action committees (PACs).

The second path for the exercise of political voice involves direct expressions of political preferences—for example, by protesting; contacting a public official; or, for an organization, testifying before a regulatory agency or filing an amicus brief.

The underlying logic of these two paths is that congenial policy outcomes can be achieved indirectly by affecting electoral outcomes so as to place likeminded people in office and directly by communicating what those public officials should do. Many of those who pursue the indirect path—by devoting considerable effort to campaigning or, especially, making major campaign contributions—do so with the objective of gaining access to convey detailed messages directly to public officials.

Participatory acts also differ with respect to whether the principal input is time or money. Both individuals and organizations undertake such time-based activities as, for individuals, working in a campaign or serving on a local board like the school board or, for organizations, preparing policy-related research or testifying before a government agency. Both individuals and organizations use financial resources to make contributions to electoral campaigns or other political causes. However, money plays a special role for most organizations that advocate in politics. When individuals use time to express political voice, they act on their own behalf and do not hire a Cyrano to compose an e-mail to a public official or a mercenary to march in a protest. In contrast, organizations—particularly those involved in national politics—ordinarily hire professionals to undertake their political representation. Thus, even when it comes to time-based activities, organizations are frequently using money to be active.

As resources for political activity, money and time have contrasting properties. Time is both more constrained and more evenly distributed than is money. Time cannot be banked for later use if not expended today. Furthermore, in contrast to money, there is a fixed upper bound on time: the best-endowed of us has only twenty-four hours in a day. Because time is inherently limited, disposable time is more evenly distributed across individuals than is disposable income. With all due respect to the difference in the metrics, the gap in dollars between the richest and poorest is far wider than the gap in hours between the busiest and most leisured. Indeed, of all the resources that facilitate political involvement, money is the most stratified. As we shall see in Chapter 10, in the New Gilded Age, income and wealth are especially highly stratified in the United States in comparison both with other developed democracies and with the decades between the end of World War II and the late 1970s. Compared to forms of political activity that rely on time as an input, those that involve money are likely to be highly stratified in the direction of the financially advantaged. A leitmotif of this book is that inequalities of political voice are especially pronounced when political input requires money rather than time.

Political activities vary in other ways not captured in Table 2.1. For example, while anyone with the time and inclination can attend a demonstration on a political issue, only citizens who are at least eighteen are permitted to vote. Political activities also vary in the extent to which their volume can be multiplied. At one extreme, the principle of one person, one vote enforces equality of input among voters. No other form of political input is characterized by such mandated equality. Individuals can send as many e-mails to public officials or spend as many hours canvassing for a candidate as they like. But time and money are different because the limitations on our spare time place an upper bound on the number of e-mails we can send or hours we can spend canvassing. Although some (rapidly diminishing) legal limits restrict campaign donations, the volume of money-based activity can be expanded well beyond the natural limits for time-based activity. When it comes to the professionalized domain of advocacy by organizations, variations in financial resources create tremendous differences across organizations in how much they do politically.

In addition, modes of political involvement vary in the extent to which, beyond requiring time or money, they demand such skills as the ability to make a speech, write a letter, or organize a meeting. Under most circumstances, it makes very little difference whether someone marching in a protest is an experienced and skilled demonstrator, but the volunteer member on the local zoning board who commands substantive expertise along with organizational and communications skills is likely to be much more effective than someone without such skills. Similarly, varied kinds of expertise—including, for example, public relations, law, lobbying, and economic research—are demanded of the professionals who work for organizations involved in Washington politics. Once again, financial resources matter. Organizations with deep pockets are in a position to hire many kinds of specialized professional expertise and can afford the best talent.

Moreover, political acts vary in their information-carrying capacity. All forms of political activity that entail direct expression of preferences communicate some amount of information about the issues and problems associated with the activity. However, especially if they are trenchant and compelling, some kinds of communications—for example, letters from individuals to government officials or statements made at community meetings—can transmit a lot of information. Similarly, communications from organizations—in such forms as advertisements, congressional testimony, research reports, or amicus briefs—can convey detailed messages. Organizations are particularly likely to be in a position to provide expert information that is useful in the formulation of policy. In contrast, the vote is a blunt instrument of communication, conveying a voter's decision to support a particular candidate, but, in the absence of an exit poll or other type of election follow-up, nothing about why the choice was made. Similarly, election-based forms of activity do not by themselves communicate detailed messages. However, under some circumstances, campaign workers and donors—especially those who work long hours or write big checks—have sufficient access to a candidate that they can make clear what is on their minds. Political acts also vary in the extent to which they give policymakers an incentive to heed the messages conveyed. When political input includes valued resources—whether votes, campaign contributions, campaign work, political intelligence, favors, or information germane to the making of policy—politicians may feel pressure to heed the accompanying messages. The member of Congress who is drafting a piece of legislation, the mayor who wants to pacify a restive group that has been staging regular protests, the state legislator who seeks votes and political support in anticipation of a run for governor, and the agency regulator who needs cooperation to ensure regulatory compliance all have incentives to pay attention to activist publics.

As we proceed, we shall often focus on particular participatory acts. However, we often find it useful to differentiate among voting, forms of political voice that depend on using time, and those that require inputs of money.

The Boundaries of Political Voice

Our understanding of political voice as activity having the intent or effect of influencing government action encompasses many forms of activity in multiple venues, but it excludes activities not aimed at influencing government. In recent years there has been considerable interest in extending our understanding of what constitutes political participation.[3] Although some argue that we must consider ways of engaging in civic life that bypass the usual institutions of politics and government and seek the public good without appeal to government intervention, we do not include them in our purview. Scholars have introduced such terms as "creative participation," "civic innovation," "postmodern participation," "lifestyle politics," "individualized collective action," and "DIY [do-it-yourself] engagement" to capture these forms of involvement. For convenience's sake, we shall refer to them as "creative participation."[4] Others have argued that we must include "discursive participation" where citizens talk and deliberate about public life.[5]

Creative participation includes a somewhat idiosyncratic set of actions that seek social change without involving public authorities. Some prominent examples are anti-sweatshop campaigns; protests against the World Trade Organization; and the most common form of creative participation, political consumerism—that is, buying, or refusing to buy, products with the objective of achieving a public good.

There is ample historical precedent—for example, the Boston Tea Party, nineteenth-century utopian communities, and the brief movement to get women out of their corsets and into bloomers—for efforts to seek public outcomes without appeal to government. Significant recent economic, technological, and social developments lead us to expect an upsurge of creative participation in our own era. For one thing, creative participation may be the only option when there is no governmental entity with the wherewithal or inclination to confront a particular problem. The proliferation of transnational economic and political institutions—in particular, multinational corporations and the World Trade Organization—imply that there may be no single governing authority with jurisdiction over a matter that activists seek to have addressed. In addition, technological developments make it feasible to communicate cheaply with large numbers of people over great distances. Social media can be used to assemble on short notice large groups of people who are connected by weak ties for some kind of goal-oriented action.

We also exclude discussion about politics and public issues from our definition of political voice.[6] With the proliferation of social media, such discussions, which once took place in person, can now be conducted through many channels. They can be informal and spontaneous or can occur in structured meetings; they can involve the exchange of views or self-conscious attempts to persuade. Obviously, this is an important set of activities. According to a recent survey, 68 percent of respondents reported taking part in political conversations in person or on the phone, a figure that is comparable to the share indicating having gone to the polls.[7] In addition, political discussions may foster political interest or clarify thinking about political matters and thus facilitate future participatory acts.

Limiting our understanding of political voice to actions directed at government that involve doing (not just talking) would matter if the excluded forms of participation were markedly different from the ones we study. However, the boundaries between our more conventional understanding of political participation and such forms of engagement as creative participation and discursive participation are quite porous. Moreover, as we show in Chapter 4, these alternative forms of civic involvement are characterized by the same kind of social class stratification typical of acts falling under our definition of political voice.[8]

How Much Political Voice? How Representative?

After nearly every election, there is a ritual handwringing about low levels of political participation. A decade or two ago political scientists asked whether all forms of political participation had been declining and, if so, why.[9] The level of participation certainly has consequences for democracy. Citizen voice emanating from a limited number of activists might lack the legitimacy of the activity of a larger group—as witnessed by the standard media practice of asking about the size of demonstrations. Similarly, the significant educative and community-building functions of political activity can be achieved only if participation is sufficiently widespread. In fact, political activity by individuals is not especially common in the United States. In a presidential election, a majority—59 percent in 2012—of voting-age adults go to the polls, a number that is substantial but not as high as in most developed democracies.[10] As shown in Figure 2.1, however, rates of activity are much lower for other forms of participation.

However, our concern is with the equality of political voice rather than the amount of political voice. While it matters for democracy that there be ample opportunities for the free expression of political voice and sufficiently high levels of participation across various political acts, the distribution of

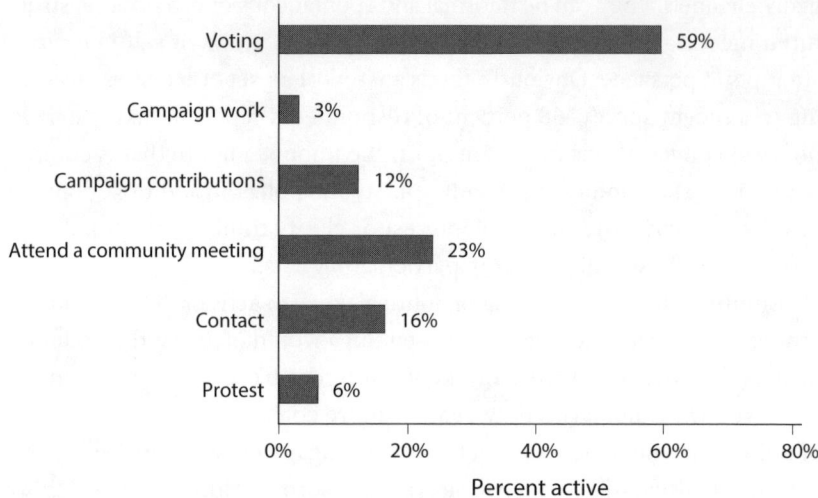

FIGURE 2.1. Participation in Political Activities
Sources: Voting: United States Election Project (2012), at http://www.electproject.org/2012g.
All other activities: American National Election Studies (2012).
Note: Figure for voting is based on all ballots counted for the Voting-Eligible Population (VEP).

that participation across individuals and groups is also significant. Equal political voice does not require universal or even a very high level of activity; it requires representative activity. Just as a few thousand responding to a carefully selected random-sample survey can yield a fairly accurate snapshot of public attitudes, a relatively small but representative set of activists might satisfy the requisites for equal voice. Thus, the conditions for political equality would be fulfilled if, across political issues, the total volume of activity were representative, containing proportionate input from those with characteristics that matter for politics. These politically relevant characteristics include such attributes as income, race or ethnicity, religion, gender, sexual orientation, age, veteran status, health, and immigrant status; attitudes on political matters ranging from immigration to student debt to climate change to U.S. policy toward China. These characteristics also include such policy-relevant circumstances as reliance on government benefits or employment in an industry that is regulated by or sells to the government. However, the individuals and organizations active in American politics are anything but representative. In particular, those who are not affluent and well educated are less likely to take part politically and are even less likely to be represented by the activity of organized interests.

Can We Measure Inequalities of Political Voice? The Problem of Multiple Metrics

Because so many avenues exist for the expression of political voice, there is no simple way to make a precise measurement of the extent to which political voice is unequal. How many hours of volunteering at the phone bank at campaign headquarters is the equivalent of a $5,000 check? How can we compare the information in a letter to an elected official with that in a vote for the official? How can we compare the pressure on a legislator from a monetary contribution with that from a confrontation in a town meeting? Because we cannot sum across differing acts to produce a number that can be compared across individuals, we consider both particular political acts and composite indexes of participation.

Among particular political acts, voting would seem to pose the fewest obstacles to measuring equal political voice. Even so, political arrangements like the selection of the president by the Electoral College and political disputes over the drawing of electoral districts—to gain partisan advantage or to ensure the election of candidates with particular racial characteristics—imply that even equal votes are problematic.

In contrast to votes, the quantity of other forms of political activity can be increased as the time and resources of the activist allow. Thus, the measurement of political voice requires that we consider not only how many people are active and whether they are a representative set but also how much they do. These considerations loom especially large when it comes to political money: even in the extremely unlikely circumstance that all eligible voters made some kind of political contribution, the tremendous range in amounts contributed would preclude equality of voice.

THE PUZZLE OF MEASURING POLITICAL VOICE WHEN THE ADVOCATES ARE ORGANIZATIONS

Defining political equality becomes even more complicated when representation is by organizations. For individuals, we can assess the volume and representativeness of participation among adults by comparing the number and characteristics of participants with information from the U.S. Census. When it comes to organizations, no such natural population exists to serve as a baseline. In fact, as we shall see in Chapter 8, because of barriers to the natural emergence of organizations among those who have common interests and concerns, if it were possible to enumerate all existing organizations, that census would yield a set of organizations that is already stratified by several criteria. The subset of politically active organizations drawn from the already partial group of all organizations is further skewed. Thus the two-stage process by which organizations may or may not come into being and then may or may not get involved in politics makes it very difficult to assess the representativeness of political voice through organizational activity.

Besides, moving from consideration of individuals to consideration of groups with their different political concerns and orientations and with radically different numbers of members—and sometimes no members at all in the ordinary sense—introduces additional complexities. With respect to political equality, how do we compare the relative political weight of AARP (formerly the American Association of Retired Persons), which has nearly 38 million members; the National Rifle Association with nearly 5 million; the United Food and Commercial Workers International Union with 1.3 million; the National Association of Home Builders with 140,000; the National Corn Growers Association with 40,000; and the American Beekeeping Federation, which has about 4,700 members? Just to complicate matters, many politically active membership associations do not have individual people as members. The American Petroleum Institute has roughly 650 member companies, and the Aerospace Industries Association has about 150.[11] How are we to construe the representation of companies in a democracy?

In a circumstance parallel to what we have already seen for individuals, organizations differ in their resources, especially money. Such disparities are not necessarily proportional to the number of their members, the number of politically relevant issues with which they are concerned, or the intensity of their political concerns. Budgetary resources are especially important, because they can be converted into a wide variety of inputs to the policymaking process: traditional lobbying activities, such as undertaking policy-related research, seeking to inform and persuade policymakers, drafting bills, testifying at hearings, and issuing policy statements and reports; making campaign contributions; conducting grassroots lobbying; and influencing public opinion through issue advertising, funding friendly authors and think tanks, and placing news and opinion pieces in mass media. Moreover, organizations with deep pockets can spend more generously on hiring the talent to undertake these activities.

An additional complexity is that politically involved organizations cover issues ranging from economic growth to racial equality to free speech to national security. It is complicated enough to characterize political equality considering just a single dimension, for example, the economic interests associated with making a living, which constitute the bulk of organized interest representation. It becomes even more so when the framework includes the many other dimensions around which interests are organized. When attempting to achieve equality of political voice, how much of the total organizational space should be allocated to organizations based on race? Sexual orientation? Attitudes toward capital punishment or the rights of homeowners? Hobbies?

Equal Voice and Representation by Organizations

When an individual speaks in politics, there is no ambiguity as to who is being represented by the message. The voice is that of the individual. When organizations serve as the conduits for giving voice to citizen interests, however, complex questions of who is being represented invariably arise. Even groups of people who have important attributes in common are rarely uniform in their interests, needs, and preferences. For example, consider a group that clearly has shared political interests: African Americans. But African Americans also vary in many ways—among them, income, gender, and sexual orientation—with consequences for their political needs and concerns. African American men and women have overlapping but not identical needs when it comes to government policy. Similarly, the political interests of black and non-Hispanic white women intersect but are not indistinguishable. Analogously, we would expect veterans who served during the Korean War to have different health-care needs from those who served in Iraq, Latinos to be divided along lines of national origin, and elderly people with private pensions to have different concerns than those who rely solely on Social Security.

Because the preferences and concerns of the members of an association are likely to vary, it can be difficult to determine for whom the organization is speaking. It is easy to imagine issues on which, say, younger workers and retirees in the Service Employees International Union or chemists in industry and chemists at universities in the American Chemical Society might part company with one another. Such divisions of opinion and interest are even more common when a voluntary association implicitly seeks to represent a constituency beyond its dues-paying members. The activists who join and run membership associations often have opinions that are, if not different in direction, more intensely held and more extreme than do others in the larger constituency. For example, while there is a substantial range of opinion on Middle Eastern policy among Jewish Americans, the most prominent and vocal organizations of American Jews tend to be supportive of hardline Israeli foreign policy. Finally, as Robert Michels famously pointed out a century ago, the leaders of a membership group develop their own interests, which may conflict with those of the rank and file.[12] In each of these cases, when an organization takes a stand in politics, there are ambiguities as to whose voice is being heard.

It is especially difficult to discern for whom an organization speaks for the vast majority of politically active organizations that are not membership associations composed of individual people.[13] Such "memberless organizations" as hospitals, universities, think tanks, and especially corporations do not have members in the ordinary sense. However, they are routinely involved in politics. There are also associations of such memberless organizations—for example, the Snack Food Association, which has firms as members, or the National Association of Children's Hospitals.

Although they do not have individual people as members, memberless organizations do have multiple sets of stakeholders, who can be defined as "any group or individual who is affected by or can affect the achievement of an organization's objectives."[14] The interests and preferences of various stakeholders—for example, the patients, physicians, nurses, other medical staff, nonmedical staff, administrators, board, third-party payers, suppliers, or neighbors of a hospital—are sometimes coincident and sometimes in conflict. Although government policies have an impact on stakeholders' lives and fortunes, it is not easy to ascertain who is being represented when memberless organizations seek political influence.

For example, who among multiple stakeholders—students, faculty, staff, administration, donors, alumni, and neighbors—is being represented when a university is active in politics? Consider for-profit colleges and universities, which account for 13 percent of college students, roughly a quarter of federal spending on Pell Grants, and 47 percent of student loan defaults.[15] According to a report from the U.S. Government Accountability Office, they frequently direct federal funding intended to benefit lower-income students toward marketing or administrative costs rather than financial aid.[16] When for-profit colleges and universities lobbied vigorously in opposition to the proposed "gainful employment rule," which targeted programs that leave students with high debt and limited earnings prospects, it is not clear that they were representing the best interests of their students.

Does Political Voice Make a Difference?

Inequalities of political voice would pose no challenge to democracy if either of two conditions holds: first, if the silent are no different from activists with respect to politically relevant characteristics, preferences, and concerns; or second, if the messages conveyed through the medium of political voice have no impact on public policy—a circumstance that might make us wonder about our understanding of democracy. We examine the first of these conditions—the representativeness of political expressions through individual and organized interest activity—in depth throughout the remainder of this volume. Before embarking on that investigation, we pause to consider the second question: Are policymakers responsive to what they hear from individuals and organizations? If, for whatever reason, political voice has no influence on policy, then no matter how unrepresentative political voice might be, it would be irrelevant for democratic equality.[17]

Policymakers say that they listen to and heed what they hear. In one study, 350 congressional staffers were asked how much influence visits from constituents, visits from lobbyists, individualized letters, and form faxes would have on their bosses' decision on an issue if they were undecided. It is striking that, although the staffers attributed more influence to individualized communications than to form letters, e-mails, and faxes, a majority deemed every single mode of advocacy as having at least some influence. When the communications are personalized, they are overwhelmingly seen as being influential. For example, 96 percent of the staffers considered individualized letters as having at least some influence, and 93 percent said that visits from lobbyists have at least some influence on undecided legislators.[18]

It is easy to cite examples where the exercise of political voice yields policy results. The securities industry swung into action in response to increased U.S. Securitites and Exchange Commission (SEC) regulation in the aftermath of the 2008 financial crisis—applying pressure deemed "relentless" by Sheila Bair, former chair of the Federal Deposit Insurance Corporation—and successfully watered down the proposed rules governing money market funds.[19] In a quite different example, activism by the middle-class, white parents of children affected by the recent heroin epidemic helped reshape the way that drug use is understood by politicians and police, who had emphasized zero tolerance and mandatory prison during the crack epidemic of the 1980s.[20] In fact, in July 2016, a Congress notable for partisan rancor and the inability to legislate passed a comprehensive drug bill with improved policies for dealing with heroin and opioid addiction.[21]

It is also easy to find examples where such political efforts come up short. Despite investing nearly $30 million in lobbying and advertising, the American Israel Public Affairs Committee was not able to block the six-nation nuclear pact with Iran negotiated by the Obama administration; and vigorous political efforts by Comcast—including spending $25 million on lobbying and making $5.9 million in campaign contributions during the 2014 electoral cycle—were not successful in eliciting approval for its proposed takeover by Time Warner Cable.[22] Thus, anecdotes suggest that voice often begets policy change but does not always. Systematic analysis is needed.

Unfortunately, determining whether political voice influences public policymakers—which requires linking the explicit and implicit messages sent by the public through their individual and organizational activities to the actions of governmental decision makers—presents difficulties at every step in the process. We have already discussed that different kinds of political participation vary in their capacity to carry specific information about public preferences. We have also pointed out the difficulties in aggregating expressions of opinion that lack a common metric of measurement and that vary in both their quantity and their intensity.

Governmental response is even more complex. Federalism and the separation of powers guarantee that policy in America is made in many venues, and it is unlikely that we can generalize across levels and branches of government. Moreover, consistent with the truism "If you want to know what a policy is all about, don't look at the title of the bill, look at the details," it is difficult to assess whether the policy output matches the citizen input. Even if the weight of political messages coming from individuals and organizations tilts strongly in one direction, it may be complicated to establish links between political voice and the detailed policies that ensue—between, for instance, overall public sentiment in favor of lower taxes and the precise provisions contained in a tax law that runs more than a thousand pages. In general, the less visible the issue—a procurement decision about a weapons guidance system as opposed to a decision to close an elementary school in a small town or to raise the federal income tax—the more freedom enjoyed by public officials to ignore participatory input from the general public (if, indeed, there is any input) and to act on their own or in response to expressions of political voice by narrow interests and organizations. Similarly, the less visible the action—a minor change of wording when a bill is marked up in committee as opposed to a recorded roll call vote on the floor—the greater autonomy public officials are able to exercise.

In addition, policymakers gain information about public attitudes and priorities from many sources other than participation by individuals and organizations—among them, the media, public opinion polls, party leaders, other public officials, and notables and experts outside politics. With multiple sources of information and multiple sources of pressure, public officials have incentives to interpret what they hear in ways that are congenial to their own political views, politically expedient, or consistent with budgetary constraints or legal requirements. Under the circumstances, it may be impossible to gauge which of many forces—among them the voice of the public—is having a decisive impact on a policymaker's actions.

In addition, congruence between expressed public preferences and the actions of public officials is not necessarily proof that the latter are responding to the former. In fact, the causality might run in the reverse direction, with expressed preferences shaped by those of the policymakers.[23] Or a similarity might reflect the impact of some other factor.

INDIVIDUAL PARTICIPATION AND GOVERNMENTAL RESPONSE

Despite the difficulty of making such connections, following the initial pioneering work of Warren Miller and Donald Stokes, studies have found congruence between the views of the public and government policy.[24] The mechanism connecting public opinion to governing officials is not always specified, but the links are clear.

Our major concern, however, is not with the overall connection between public attitudes and government actions but with the differential responsiveness of public officials that reflects the unequal political voice of citizens. Several studies using differing methods and data provide evidence that public officials do heed what they hear from citizen activists—who tend, as we shall see, to be more advantaged—and thus that policy responds to their particular preferences and needs.[25]

In an especially important investigation, Andrea Campbell analyzed a reciprocal relationship in which citizen activity influenced national policy on Social Security, which, in turn, created conditions that facilitated increased participation.[26] It is difficult to prove the impact on government policy of the spikes in participation among seniors that follow quickly on policy initiatives with implications for their interests. However, Campbell marshals persuasive evidence to show how members of Congress responded to pressure from the elderly with policy concessions in the case of the repeal of the Medicare Catastrophic Act. While many factors impinge on voting decisions in Congress, it seems likely that, in this case, communications from seniors were among those factors.

It is sometimes argued that policymakers compensate for the fact that they hear so much less from the disadvantaged by engaging in a kind of affirmative action in order to respond to the politically quiescent. However, growing evidence from both the national and state levels shows that policymakers do not seem to seek out and respond to information about the preferences and needs of lower-income constituents. On the basis of roll call votes in the Senate, Larry Bartels demonstrates that senators seem to ignore their lower-income constituents while voting in concert with the views of their upper-income constituents—a pattern that is especially pronounced when it comes to an economic matter like raising the minimum wage.[27] He concludes that "senators consistently appear to pay *no* attention to the views of millions of their constituents in the bottom third of the income distribution."[28]

On the basis of a large-scale study of nearly 2,000 survey questions on proposed policy changes between 1981 and 2002, Martin Gilens reaches a parallel conclusion—finding that policy change reflects the policy preferences of the most affluent and not at all the preferences of the poor.[29] Additional investigations have come to parallel conclusions with regard to differential representation on the basis of income at the state level as well as at the national level in other time periods.[30] Furthermore, evidence suggests analogous inequalities on the basis of race or ethnicity in governmental response.[31] In addition, with Benjamin Page, Gilens took the analysis one step further by incorporating information about the preferences of mass-based groups and organizations representing business interests.[32] They found that ordinary citizens and mass-based organizations have little independent influence on public policy; in contrast, policy outcomes reflected the preferences of business organizations and, especially, affluent citizens.

Although studies demonstrating differential policy responsiveness have been challenged, James A. Stimson queries: "Is representation pretty much equal? Or do some Americans—often richer Americans—command more than their fair share of attention in the policy process? No one asserts a third alternative, like the antiunion rhetoric of an earlier era, that the poor command more attention than they proportionally deserve."[33] In short, there is no evidence at all that policymakers are making special compensatory efforts to learn about and respond to the concerns of disadvantaged citizens. If anything, the opposite is the case.

DO ORGANIZED INTERESTS INFLUENCE POLICY?

Toward the end of *The Once and Future King*, T. H. White's rendering of the legend of King Arthur, the just order in Camelot is falling apart. Mordred, King Arthur's illegitimate son, whose claims caused the discord, proposes that, instead of resorting to combat to ascertain the truth of the allegations about an adulterous affair between the knight Lancelot and Queen Guenever, the matter be put to a jury. The dispirited King replies:

> You are still very young, Mordred. You have yet to learn that nearly all the ways of giving justice are unfair. If you can suggest another way of settling moot points, except by personal combat, I will be glad to try it. . . .
>
> You see, moot points have to be settled somehow, once they get thrust upon us. If an assertion cannot be proved, then it must be settled some other way, and nearly all these ways are unfair to somebody. It is not as if you would have to fight the Queen's champion in your own person, Mordred. You could plead infirmity and hire the strongest man you knew to fight for you, and the Queen would, of course, get the strongest man she knew to fight for her. It would be much the same thing if you each hired the best arguer you knew, to argue about it. In the last resort it is usually the richest person who wins, whether he hires the most expensive arguer or the most expensive fighter, so it is no good pretending that this is simply a matter of brute force.[34]

Do the organized interests in a position to hire the most expensive arguers—and many of the arguers are, indeed, very expensive—inevitably prevail in politics?

Inquiries by scholars and journalists yield mixed conclusions about the impact of organized interest activity on policy. They fall into two categories: case studies[35] that focus intensely on a single political organization or issue, and multicase systematic statistical studies of some aspect of interest-group activity. Case studies provide in-depth analyses that can encompass many aspects of the role of interest organizations in the making of public policy, but such studies face the twin problems of generalizability and potential selection bias. In contrast, studies involving multivariate analysis have weaknesses when it comes to the measurement of critical variables. Interestingly, when the studies are taken together, they come to similar mixed conclusions about the matter of whether organized interest activity has policy consequences.

That we do not always find policy consequences for organized interest involvement when we look closely occasionally leads political scientists to adopt a flippant counter-orthodoxy, to the effect that there is no evidence for organized interest influence on policy. Such a conclusion is a caricature of the mixed results. Sometimes there is evidence of significant influence; other times not. However, no evidence suggests that organizations are worse off in policy terms if they have been active.

PROBLEMS OF GENERALIZABILITY AND CASE SELECTION

Knotty problems bedevil investigations into the policy consequences of organizational action in politics. One is generalizability: the difficulty of specifying the larger class of instances to which a single case can be generalized. Another is related to selection effects: the distinct possibility that researchers will not bother with cases in which organized interests are unsuccessful or, indeed, with narrow issues in which few actors are involved and the stakes, while low for the general public are high for the participants.[36] Similarly, researchers may forgo cases in which presumed stakeholders do not take part.

Although these methodological concerns are of special relevance for case studies, statistical analyses do not necessarily escape them. With regard to generalizability, quantitative studies of organized interests in action often adduce systematic data about the activities of many organizations or the comportment of all members of the House and Senate, but they focus on just a single policy area or agency. It is widely recognized, however, that organized interest politics vary by policy area and do not fall into a single pattern. We would expect the politics to differ depending, for example, on whether government procurement or workplace safety regulation is at stake. Therefore, policy-specific statistical studies will not always yield the same results about the nature and extent of organized interest influence.

THE PROBLEM OF THE POLITICAL AGENDA

A number of investigations avoid the problem of selection bias by sampling political controversies. For example, Frank Baumgartner, Jeffrey Berry, Marie Hojnacki, David C. Kimball, and Beth Leech assembled a weighted random sample of organizations that lobby in Washington and then asked a government relations liaison in each organization to name the issue on which he or she had been working most recently, thus generating a random selection of issues of concern to lobbyists in national politics.[37] Still, Baumgartner and colleagues note that, by selecting issues on which Washington representatives are actually working, they fail to consider policy matters that do not make it into the policymaking process. Consequently, their analysis cannot take into account an important form of organized interest influence—influencing the agenda as opposed to determining the outcome once controversies become objects of political contention.

The political agenda is not simply a reflection of the issues that engage the attention of policymakers or the American public. Instead the construction of the political agenda is a political process in which organized interests take part. In his research on agenda setting in American policymaking, John Kingdon finds "many examples of items on the government agenda because of interest group activity" but notes that "a substantial portion of the interest group effort is devoted to negative, blocking activities," preemptive action designed to keep unwanted issues off the policy agenda.[38]

Using the term "agenda bias," Baumgartner et al. point out the extent to which the set of policy issues under consideration reflects the realities of political power. When they compare the list of policy matters in their sample with the issues that concern the public as revealed in public opinion surveys, they note the "relative paucity of issues relating to the poor and to the economic security of working-class Americans.... Although some marginalized constituencies—ethnic and racial minorities, gays, women—have organized with beneficial results, the same cannot be said of those who are simply poor.... There could be no more vivid evidence of the relationship between class and voice than the nature of the issues in our sample."[39]

Studies of organized interest influence also fail to consider the other end of the policy process—after policy controversies seem to have been settled. Even when it is over, it is not over. Policy matters are rarely concluded once and for all, and the issues that were the occasions for apparent victories or defeats may reappear with different results. Although the NRA may have lost in its 1994 confrontation with the administration of Bill Clinton over semi-automatic weapons, the assault weapons ban lapsed in 2004, and so far, the NRA has been successful in defeating numerous efforts to restore it.[40]

THE PROBLEM OF MEASUREMENT

Establishing causal links between inputs in the form of organized interest activity and policy outputs—that is, demonstrating that the policy outcome would not have occurred had the organized interest activity not taken place—turns out to be a very complicated business. It may be difficult to measure both the inputs of organizational activity and the outputs of organizational influence.

Some of the activities in which organized interests engage—for example, testifying at congressional hearings or filing amicus briefs—are officially documented and therefore measurable. But much of what organized interests do—not only the informal networking and socializing but also such vital activities as grassroots lobbying, conducting research, and providing information to policymakers—is not formally recorded and is therefore extremely difficult to measure across issues and organizations. That the relevant actors sometimes prefer their activities to be invisible renders measurement even more problematic.

Services provided to policymakers by organized interests frequently work better than direct attempts to persuade. By providing services, they seek simultaneously to enhance access, to frame policy positions in ways that are congenial, and to leave grateful policymakers in their wake.[41] This description of a lobbyist active on a medical privacy bill shows the multiple ways that Washington representatives can help policymakers, especially those in Congress:

> The corporate lobbyist, though not a witness, had been instrumental at every other step: she was heavily involved in drafting the bill, helping sign up congressional cosponsors, organizing the hearing and strategizing with staff about its timing and composition (she identified several witnesses and wrote testimony for two of them), and meeting with staffers during the hearing to clarify points and scribble questions for legislators to ask witnesses: all this even though the medical privacy issue was only a distant concern to the corporation she represents.[42]

Neither legislators nor lobbyists want to acknowledge fully their reliance on each other, even when such reliance is central to decision making in a complex democratic society.

Because they are readily observable, votes on the floor of the House or Senate are often used as the indicator of organized interest influence. However, organized interest influence is more likely to be manifest long before legislation reaches the stage of roll-call voting—in decisions by favorably disposed legislators to expend time and political capital on an issue, in the alteration of details when a bill is marked up, and so on.[43] Furthermore, the major policy action may be undertaken in other venues—for example, when regulations for meat inspections are written at the Department of Agriculture or the specs for a new transport plane are formulated at the

Department of Defense. In short, like organized interest inputs, policy outputs are complex and difficult to measure.

THE PROBLEM OF TALLYING THE VICTORIES AND DEFEATS

Similarly, it is a complicated business to assess the victories and defeats in any particular policy controversy. Knowing whether to tally an outcome as a win or a loss requires understanding an organization's goals, which are often ambiguous. Organizational goals may change along the way; there may be several objectives in play at the same time; and the leaders and staff of an organization may be pursuing one policy aim while holding another back, or they may be pursuing both at once. In addition, political organizations have their own institutional interests, and many organizations have leaders with different goals. For example, Catholic bishops share a profession, a religion, and a commitment to its principles, but they differ internally in terms of the priority they give to those principles as shown in debates over abortion, capital punishment, and other topics.[44]

Just as the objectives and advocacy methods are complex and varied, so are the outcomes. Whether an organization has prevailed may not always be clear. Policy influence is not the same as policy victory. A desired provision may be buried as a detail in an amendment. The objective might have been to block action, in which case success may not be obvious without close scrutiny of the process. Advocates, who often settle for half loaves, may give up some things to gain others. Suppose a new tax passes in spite of vigorous opposition by a reputedly powerful organization. However, in response to the lobbying, the rate is half what was originally proposed. Is that a victory or a loss? Even the loser in a policy controversy may be better off, or less badly off, for having been on the scene than it would have been had it not been involved at all.

THE PROBLEM OF ESTABLISHING INFLUENCE

Rarely does a clear-cut relationship exist between what an interest organization wants and what a policymaker does. Even under the magnifying glass of the case study, that kind of causality may be difficult to prove. Given the complexity of the policymaking process, it may not be possible to establish definitively that the outcome was the result of the actions of a particular corporation or professional association seeking to shape policy by inserting a clause in pending legislation or passing a favorable amendment. Was the clause inserted or did the amendment pass as the result of organized interest actions? As the result of the intervention of a powerful subcommittee chair with strong personal convictions or a particular constituency need? As the result of a threatened presidential veto? Or as the result of all these factors working together?

Taken together, the many case studies and the large number of well-executed quantitative studies yield mixed results—not so much from flawed research as from the fact that the studies focus on different aspects of a complex phenomenon. In her review of the unresolved debate on the effects of interest groups, Beth Leech finds striking continuity in the disagreements in current research: "Modern-day quantitative studies of the influence of lobbying and PACs are as contradictory as the classic cases were."[45] She elaborates:

> There are almost as many ideas about why studies of interest group influence disagree as there are studies that disagree. . . . [There are] a series of methodological problems, including a tendency to study one or a handful of issues, failure to include relevant variables, modeling influence as dichotomous, as well as a lack of attention to the political context of the issues in question . . . [and, in addition,] a tendency to select on the dependent variable, a tendency to focus on the end stage of the policy process, misconceptions about what it is that interest groups actually do, and misconceptions about how the policy process actually works.[46]

On balance, the evidence suggests that lobbying is more likely to have influence under two circumstances: for relatively narrow *issues* that do not receive a great deal of attention from the media; and for less visible *actions* rather than for roll-call votes on the floor of the legislature. More generally, intellectual skepticism about the impacts of organized interests should probably be tempered with a common-sense understanding that it would be hard to explain why so many lobbyists flock to Washington if they never made a difference.

DOLLARS AND POLICY INFLUENCE

Money plays an especially significant and complicated role in any consideration of equality of political voice. Observers in the public and the media often assume that we live in a "pay-to-play" environment, in which political spending has a direct and significant impact on policy.[47] Concern about explicit or implicit quid pro quos has led to regulations on the use of money to influence electoral and policy outcomes, but there are no equivalents for the mobilization of resources like time or skills to achieve favorable outcomes. The special status of money as a political resource has led political scientists to use sophisticated statistical approaches to investigate its political impact—with results that are rarely straightforward and sometimes surprising. The large multi-issue study of lobbying by Baumgartner and colleagues presents compelling evidence of a very weak relationship between policy success and a variety of measures of resources devoted to lobbying on a particular issue.[48] Still, in an explanation of "why resources matter but appear not to," the authors discuss the many factors that also need to be considered in addition to resources. They remark that their "findings do not suggest that it is better in politics to be poor than rich."[49]

One form of political spending—contributions to electoral campaigns by PACs, which function as the political giving arm of many organized interests—has been subject to systematic scrutiny for their consequences for floor votes in Congress. Quantitative studies seeking to link PAC contributions to the political actions of legislators show either no effect at all or, at most, small and inconsistent effects for PAC contributions; they point instead to the expected trio of factors—ideology, party, and constituency—as the important influences on roll-call voting.[50] In a summary assessment, Stephen Ansolabehere, John de Figueiredo, and James Snyder remark: "The evidence that campaign contributions lead to a substantial influence on votes is rather thin."[51]

Several arguments counter this assessment. For one thing, donations from a PAC associated with an organization may be dwarfed by individual contributions to the same legislator from executives of that organization. These individual contributions are frequently "bundled": rather than being sent in separately, they are combined and conveyed together to the legislator, often by a representative of the organization.[52] In an era when the legal environment for campaign giving has loosened the constraints on contributions from individuals, such practices are becoming increasingly widespread.

Perhaps most importantly, echoing our argument about where lobbying might have an impact, Michael Malbin argues that "the last place we should expect to find a change in a Member's behavior would be on a public roll-call vote."[53] According to Richard Smith, the "purpose of campaign contributions is to buy access rather than votes."[54] The impact of contributions is likely to be manifest in less visible ways—for example, in the particular issues to which legislators devote time and attention; in the lobbyists to whom legislators and their staff grant face time; in such low-key actions as planning legislative strategy or specifying details; or what legislators do in informal settings, committee hearings, and markup sessions. As John Wright puts it, "Representatives may 'hear you better,' for example, when a contribution precedes lobbying."[55]

What is more, both funders and elected officials frequently assert that contributions have implications for policy. Rarely is the tit-for-tat posed as starkly as it was by Charles Keating, the owner of the Lincoln Savings Bank, who said of his campaign donations to five senators in a position to intervene with the Federal Home Loan Bank Board on behalf of his failing bank: "Asked once whether his payments to politicians had worked, he told reporters, 'I want to say in the most forceful way I can: I certainly hope so.'"[56] Testimony from lobbyists and corporate leaders in the court case about the Bipartisan Campaign Reform Act gives anecdotal, if not systematic, support to the notion that contributions "buy access" as a first step to gaining influence, especially if unequal access means that only one side of a story is told.[57] According to Robert Rozen, a lobbyist for corporations, individuals, and trade associations: "The large contributions enable donors to establish relationships, which increases the chances they will be successful with their public policy agendas. Compared to the amounts that companies spend as a whole, large political contributions are worthwhile because of the potential benefit to the companies' bottom line."[58] Perhaps these political operatives rush to claim credit for political success with their bosses back at the headquarters of the organization, but they are less likely to make such claims when testifying in a federal court case.

Most of the nearly 3,000 legislators in state capitals across the country surveyed by Lynda Powell also believe that money has influence. They were asked: "To what extent is the content and passage of bills in your chamber influenced by the financial contributions of individuals and groups to candidates and parties?" Although state legislators might be expected to underplay the policy consequences of electoral money, only 13 percent responded that campaign contributions had no influence, and a majority, 54 percent, placed themselves in one of the three middle categories on a seven-point scale.[59]

Further evidence about how electoral money facilitates political access derives from a randomized field experiment, in which a political organization sent e-mails attempting to arrange meetings between organization members—all of whom were both constituents of the targeted legislators and campaign contributors (though not necessarily donors to the targeted legislators)—and legislators in Congress.[60] In communicating with congressional offices, the organization revealed on a random basis the information that its member for whom access was being sought was a donor. Senior policymakers—for example, members of Congress themselves or their chiefs of staff or legislative directors—were between three and four times more likely to make themselves available to organization members who had been identified as donors.

IF YOU'RE NOT AT THE TABLE, YOU'RE ON THE MENU: DOES NOT TAKING PART IN THE PROCESS HAVE CONSEQUENCES?

Silent voices are hard to study. As Heinz, Laumann, Nelson, and Salisbury put it in their study of the role of organized interests in policymaking: "We have no way to catalogue the segments of society that lack a voice in discussions of policies affecting them or who are unable even to initiate discussion of their concerns. Thus, despite the great range and diversity in the political orientations of the interest groups [we have studied] . . . we cannot conclude that national policy systems have overcome the problems of exclusiveness and limited participation noted by so many scholars."[61]

It is often said in Washington, "If you're not at the table, you're on the menu." It is undoubtedly too extreme to claim that interests not represented in the policymaking process will be roasted, sauced, and consumed. Nevertheless, close scrutiny of actual policy controversies demonstrates that, even if the organized interests that take part do not always win, they are better off for having gotten involved. By being in the process, they are in a position to achieve partial gains and to avoid the even larger losses that might have ensued had they not been on the scene. The interests that never get to the table are not in a position to engage in such defensive maneuvering or to realize even such limited objectives.

A BOTTOM LINE ON ORGANIZED INTEREST INFLUENCE?

What is the bottom line? A widespread view in the media and the public is that investments in political action by organized interests inevitably pay off. Political scientists sometimes claim that systematic assessments show organized interests to be paper tigers whose activity consists of a lot of motion to impress clients and constituents without having an effect on policy. Perhaps unexpectedly, case studies and statistical inquiries converge on similar conclusions. Clearly, lobbyists do not always get what they want. However, the various kinds of evidence do substantiate Anthony J. Nownes's maxim that "lobbyists sometimes get what they want."[62] In fact, lobbyists often get at least some of what they want. Organizations that go to court—usually because they have been sued but even because they have initiated legal action—can end up worse off than they were to begin with. Otherwise, they are rarely worse off, and are usually better off, for having gotten involved. Had they ceded the process to other actors, they would either have gained less or lost more. Therefore, it makes sense to inquire about the shape of political voice through organized interests, a question that we investigate in detail in Chapters 8 and 9.

Conclusion

Acting on their own, together with others, or through organizations, Americans can seek to have a direct effect on public outcomes by communicating their preferences and concerns to policymakers or to have an indirect impact by influencing election results. Working at the national, state, or local level, they can engage in activities that demand time or money. They can do a lot, a little, or nothing at all.

But are those voices representative of the citizenry as a whole? Put another way, if democracy is the level playing field on which we are equal as citizens, then we must be concerned about equality of political voice. However, any attempt to consider matters of equality of political voice immediately raises several caveats. For one thing, equal political voice does not require universal activity, only representative activity, but it is difficult to assess degrees of inequality of political voice. Different participatory acts involve different, and not easily compared, metrics of input—for example, hours versus dollars, a big check versus a small one, or a well-reasoned letter versus a cursory one; even the same act can vary in both volume and effectiveness. Furthermore, when advocacy is by organizations rather than by individuals, the measurement of inequalities of political voice becomes even more difficult.

A further complication in assessing departures from equality of political voice is that when organizations are advocates, it is difficult to know for whom the organization is speaking—especially if it is not a voluntary association composed of individuals. Nevertheless, the disparities across individuals, aggregations of individuals, and organizations are so striking that there can be no doubt about the existence and persistence of real inequalities of political voice in America.

Still, if public officials do not respond to what they hear, or if they take special pains to respond to the quiescent as well as to the noisy, inequalities of political voice would make no difference. Proving that expressions of political voice have consequences for policy outcomes is tricky, and the many studies (whether of individuals or organized interests) are not unanimous in their conclusions. Nevertheless, for all the difficulties in making definitive links between political voice and policy influence, critical examination of what we know about the consequences of political activity makes clear that concern about democratic equality forces us to contend with inequalities of political voice.

3

The Roots of Citizen Participation: The Civic Voluntarism Model

Why are people active in politics? We find it helpful to invert this question and to ask instead: Why don't people take part in politics?[1] Three answers immediately come to mind: because they can't, because they don't want to, or because nobody asked:

- "They can't" suggests a paucity of necessary resources—time to take part, money to contribute to campaigns and other political causes, and skills to use time and money effectively.
- "They don't want to" focuses attention on the absence of psychological engagement with politics—little interest in politics or little concern about public issues, a belief that activity can make little or no difference, little or no knowledge about the political process, or other priorities.
- "Nobody asked" implies isolation from the networks of recruitment through which citizens are mobilized to politics.

All three factors are helpful in predicting participation. Access to resources, the capacity to take part, and psychological engagement with politics (the motivation to take part) seem necessary for activity. Recruitment, being asked to take part, seems to act as a catalyst for participation among those with the wherewithal and desire to become active. We also demonstrate, not surprisingly, that issue commitments—for example, having a direct stake in some government policy or caring passionately about a controversial issue—can stimulate activity with regard to that issue. Different configurations of participatory factors matter for different forms of activity.

Our analysis of the participatory process takes us deep into the basic structures of American society—families, schools, jobs, nonpolitical organizations, and religious institutions—where resources are acquired, motivations are nurtured, and recruitment networks are established. The foundations for future political involvements are laid early in life—in the family and in school. Later on, experiences at work, in voluntary associations, and in religious institutions provide additional opportunities for acquiring politically relevant resources and enhancing psychological engagement with politics. These nonpolitical institutions also function as a location for recruitment to politics: not only do co-workers and fellow organization or congregation members ask one another to become politically active, but requests for activity originate from within the institutions themselves.

This model of the participatory process, which we call the Civic Voluntarism Model (CVM), considers the factors that foster political activity and demonstrates how they are stockpiled over the course of a lifetime, frequently conferring additional advantage on the initially privileged.[2] The elaboration of this model not only establishes that such basic institutions of American society as schools, voluntary associations, and churches affect participation but also delineates how they do so.[3]

Factors That Foster Participation: Resources

Of the three factors that foster participation, we place special emphasis on such resources as money, time, and civic skills. For most people, resource acquisition takes place outside the realm of political activity, which means that resources are more likely than either psychological engagement with politics or requests for political activity to be the cause, rather than the result, of activity. Focusing on resources provides a powerful and theoretically satisfying explanation of disparities across individuals and groups in the extent to which they take part in political life. And since resources are differentially available to groups with differing needs and preferences, paying attention to resources provides an important link to our concern with political equality.

The utility of particular resources varies across participatory acts. Contributions to candidates or political causes, a mode of activism that has skyrocketed in relative importance recently, obviously require money. Other forms of political activity—campaign work, informal efforts to solve community problems, even voting—require time. Finally, the citizen who possesses the requisite organizational and communications capacities—what we call civic skills—will find it less daunting to take part. Indeed, when inputs of time and money are coupled to civic skills, citizens become not only more likely to participate but also more likely to be effective when they do.

We trace the origin of these resources back to people's commitments and experiences in the family, at school, and in the workplace, voluntary associations, and religious institutions—all of which affect the portfolio of time, money, and civic skills available for politics. The result is disparities in resources not only among individuals but also among groups defined by their income, education, occupation, race or ethnicity, gender, and religion. The stratification of resources along lines of socioeconomic and other demographic cleavages is an important part of the story of differential political voice. Since the resources of time, money, and skills are differentially useful for various forms of activity, an explanation of political activity that is based on resources enables us to link basic life circumstances and choices to patterns of political activity and to explain both why some people are active and why they are active in particular ways.

MONEY AND TIME

Money and time are the resources expended most directly in political activity. It is impossible to contribute to a campaign or other political cause without some discretionary income. Similarly, it is impossible to write an e-mail to a senator, attend a school board meeting, or work in a campaign without the free time to do so.[4] Money plays a dual role in our analysis of political participation: it is simultaneously an important source of conflict in politics—associated with interests in public policy and with needs for government assistance—and an important resource for political action. In this crucial respect, money functions quite differently from time. Although citizens differ in their access to free time, American politics has not involved conflicts between the harried and the leisured in the way that it has sometimes involved conflicts between the affluent and the less-well heeled. Income groups are themselves politically relevant. Moreover, income inequalities, not unexpectedly, hew to other fault lines of political division. Those who are advantaged in other ways are likely also to report more income.

Whereas the affluent self-evidently have more money to spare for politics, it is less obvious whether they also have more free time to spare for politics. On one hand, we might guess that the rich would be better off when it comes to time, because they can hire others—gardeners, accountants, and the like—to do what most people have to do for themselves, and they do not have to moonlight to make ends meet. On the other, we might expect that the rich would have less free time, because they manage to accumulate wealth by dint of the long hours they log at work.

Time and money differ not only in the extent to which they are available to people but also in the way they are related to other characteristics. Not unexpectedly, those who are well educated and who have jobs that require high levels of education and on-the-job training command higher levels of family income. In contrast, no analogous pattern of stratification exists when it comes to free time. Those who never finished high school (a disproportionate share of whom are retired, keeping house, or permanently disabled) have more spare time; beyond this, however, educational level is not associated with differences in free time. Those at the top may feel harried—or they may complain especially loudly—but they are not disadvantaged when it comes to time.

Interesting patterns emerge with respect to the availability of money and time to Latinos, African Americans, and non-Hispanic whites and to men and women. As we would expect, non-Hispanic whites and men have higher family incomes. However, they enjoy no analogous advantage with respect to free time. Men and women are equally busy. Non-Hispanic whites have slightly more time than African Americans do, and Latinos report somewhat less time than the other two groups. But the differences are minimal compared with the gaps in income.

If free time does not vary with socioeconomic advantage, race and ethnicity, and gender, what does influence the amount of leisure an individual enjoys? The answer is strikingly simple: life circumstances. Having a job reduces free time. So does having young children at home, especially preschoolers, although having grown children seems to have no effect. Having a spouse with a job also diminishes free time. In addition, among those not in the work force, the retired have the most time not committed to other activities. The extent to which life circumstances determine the availability of leisure time helps us understand that, on average, women and men are equally busy, a finding that is sometimes greeted by skepticism from readers.[5] The explanation is that, on average, men and women devote their busy hours to different pursuits. Even among those with full-time jobs, men spend more time than women at work. In contrast, men—even the husbands of women with full-time jobs—devote less time to housework and child care. On average, women with full-time jobs and young children at home are especially time-strapped, even when compared to men in that situation, and women at home full time without paid work have much more spare time. The overall result is that women and men have, on average, the same amount of free time—time that can be devoted, if desired, to taking part in politics.

EDUCATION

Civic skills are acquired throughout the life cycle beginning at home and, especially, in school. Investigations of citizen political participation in democracies around the world repeatedly find that more education leads to more activity.[6] Various explanations are adduced for this close relationship. Education enhances participation more or less directly by developing skills that are relevant to politics—the ability to speak and write, the knowledge of how to cope in an organizational setting.[7] Education also imparts information about government and politics and encourages attitudes, such as a sense of civic responsibility or political efficacy, that predispose an individual to political involvement. The participatory consequences of schooling are not limited to the classroom: taking part in extracurricular activities in high school—in particular, student government but also various clubs and activities—has a positive impact on later political activity. In addition, education affects activity indirectly: those who have high levels of education are much more likely to command lucrative jobs and to have opportunities to exercise leadership and develop politically relevant skills at work, in church, and in voluntary associations.

Differences in political participation among groups distinguished by gender and race or ethnicity reflect educational disparities among these groups.[8] Even though minorities, especially blacks, have made strides in education in the past half century, as shown in Table 3.1, marked gaps remain. Considering the population as a whole, African Americans are only slightly less likely than non-Hispanic whites to have graduated from high school. Latinos, however, lag behind both groups. The disparities are wider with respect to higher education, with non-Hispanic whites much more likely than African Americans, and especially Latinos, to have graduated from college, a pattern that is even more pronounced for achieving advanced degrees.

In contrast, the gender differences in education are quite small. Historically, men were better educated than women: although less likely to graduate from high school, men were more likely to attain an undergraduate or,

TABLE 3.1. Educational Attainment by Race or Ethnicity and Gender, 2014

	Non-Hispanic White	African American	Hispanic	Men	Women
Not a high school graduate	8%	15%	32%	13%	12%
High school graduate	29	34	30	31	29
Some college or associate's degree	30	32	25	27	30
Bachelor's degree	21	13	9	18	19
Graduate degree	12	6	4	10	10
Total	100%	100%	100%	99%	100%

Source: U.S. Census Bureau, Current Population Survey, 2014 Annual Social and Economic Supplement, http://www.census.gov/hhes/socdemo/education/data/cps/2014/tables.html.
Note: Persons 18 years and older (civilian noninstitutionalized population including armed forces living off post or with their families on post).

especially, a graduate degree. In the last generation, these patterns have changed. Sometime around 1990—coincidentally, at just the time that the "Title IX babies" born in 1972 were entering college—women began to surpass men in the share of those between 25 and 29 who had earned a B.A., a trend that has accelerated since then and that is especially pronounced for blacks and Hispanics. Due to the gains of the younger cohorts of women, the education gap between all adult men and women has now narrowed to the point that women have essentially achieved parity with men.

ADULT CIVIC SKILLS

With the end of schooling, the nonpolitical institutions of adult life—the workplace, voluntary associations, and churches—operate in several ways to enhance activity in politics. Perhaps most importantly, in the context of activities having nothing to do with politics, these nonpolitical settings foster the organizational and communications capacities that facilitate the effective use of time and money in politics. Managing the introduction of a firm's new IT system, coordinating the volunteers for the PTA Teacher Appreciation Day, or arranging the details for the church Thanksgiving food drive—all these undertakings represent opportunities in nonpolitical settings to learn, maintain, or refine civic skills. In short, those who develop skills in an environment removed from politics are likely to become politically competent. Indeed, those who enter the higher levels of politics—who, for example, run for office—have almost always developed civic skills at work, in nonpolitical organizations, or in church, regardless of their previous political experience.

We asked respondents who are employed, who give time or money to a nonpolitical organization, or who give time to educational, charitable, or social activities in their churches beyond simple attendance at services whether, in the relevant context, they had within the past six months:

Written a letter
Gone to a meeting where they took part in making decisions
Planned or chaired a meeting
Given a presentation or speech

Whether someone gains civic skills in a nonpolitical context depends on several factors. A necessary condition is connection to the institution—having a job or being affiliated with a secular voluntary association or a religious institution. Beyond mere affiliation, institutions vary in the extent to which they nurture civic skills: a job at a hedge fund rather than a big box retailer or membership in a professional association rather than a softball league is more likely to yield opportunities to acquire resources relevant to political participation. Moreover, within institutions, individuals vary. Some people are more inclined than others to assume responsibility voluntarily and are more capable than others of undertaking acts that demand—and, thus, hone—skills. To the extent that the initiative in apportioning tasks rests with leaders and staff rather than with the individual, we would expect them to be more likely to recruit workers or members with existing skills or previous experience and with demonstrated willingness to undertake activities that involve practicing civic skills. Among workers or members with similar credentials and experience, however, leaders and staff might also be more likely to call on those with particular characteristics—say, gender or race—to take on these responsibilities.

As shown in Figure 3.1, the exercise of civic skills varies systematically with education, income, race, and gender. Not unexpectedly, on average, skill acquisition rises sharply with both education and family income. Of the three venues under consideration, the workplace is especially skill endowing. Well-educated people are more likely to be in the work force and, if in the work force, to have the kinds of jobs that pay well and are rich in opportunities for skill development. They are also more likely to be affiliated with nonpolitical organizations although not necessarily with religious institutions. Within organizations and churches, those with high levels of education are disproportionately likely to volunteer, or be called on, to undertake

3.1.A. Education

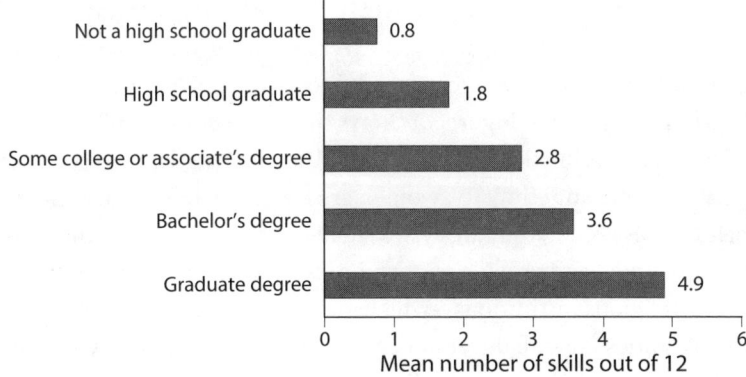

3.1.B. Family income

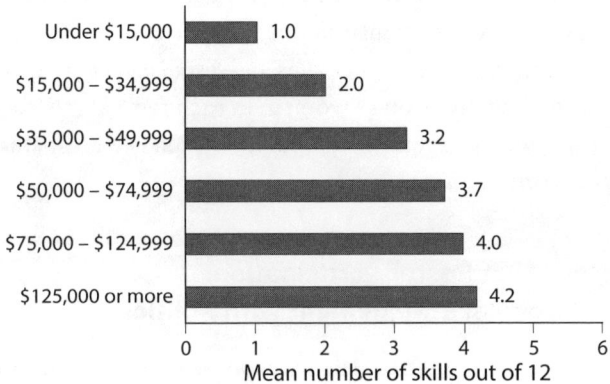

3.1.C. Race/ethnicity and gender

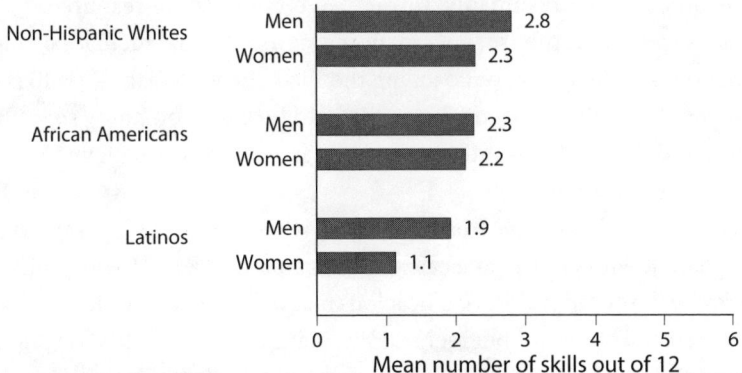

FIGURE 3.1. Mean Total Skills by Selected Characteristics
Source: Citizen Participation Study (1990).
Note: Mean for the sum of skills exercised on the job, in a nonpolitical organization, and in a religious institution.

the kinds of activities that develop civic skills. Hence, it is not surprising that the well-educated and affluent are, on average, more likely to develop civic skills in the institutional venues of adult life.

The bottom panel of Figure 3.1 shows that skill acquisition is also structured by race or ethnicity and by gender. The patterns are quite complex.[9] Regardless of race or ethnicity, women are less likely than men to be in the work force. Moreover, they are systematically less likely to have the kinds of jobs that pay well and provide opportunities for skill development. When it comes to religious institutions—which are much less rich than work places in opportunities for skill development—women are more likely than men, and African Americans are more likely than non-Hispanic whites or, especially, Latinos to be affiliated with a church or other religious institution. The bottom line is that, with respect to the average number of skills developed across the three sets of institutions, non-Hispanic whites are advantaged in comparison to African Americans and, especially, Latinos, and men are advantaged in comparison to women. In each racial or ethnic group there is a gender gap with regard to civil skills—which is widest among Latinos and quite narrow among blacks.

Factors That Foster Participation: Psychological Engagement with Politics

A lack of resources can explain why someone does not participate in politics. However, having resources does not automatically translate into participation, because the resources that facilitate political activity can be put to many other uses. Presumably, those who commit these resources to political purposes—rather than to spending time on social media, putting in extra hours at the office, or coaching the Little League team—are likely to be psychologically engaged with politics: to be aware of, know something about, and care about politics and public issues; and to believe that they can, in fact, have a voice.

For several reasons, we tread cautiously when considering psychological engagement with politics as a cause of participation. First, being politically interested, knowledgeable, or efficacious may enhance the likelihood that an individual will be active; but reciprocally, being active may increase interest, information, and efficacy.[10] Causality can go from activism to engagement as well as from engagement to activism. Second, because political engagement is so close to what we seek to explain—that is, political participation—an explanation based on political engagement is less interesting. That people who are politically interested are politically active seems to tell us less than an explanation based on resources, which have their origins in commitments and involvements further removed from politics. Third, we have more confidence in our ability to measure resources, which are concrete and based on units having standard metrics, than in our ability to measure political engagement. With the possible exception of political information, the various aspects of political engagement are more ambiguous in meaning. Finally, resource-based explanations of participation are relevant for real issues of American politics: conflicts between the rich and the poor—or between those with rewarding, skill-producing work and those with lesser employment or no work at all—have recurred in American politics; competition between the interested and the indifferent or the confident and the inefficacious has not been a theme in American political life.

Even so, we need to pay attention to these subjective factors. People with equivalent bundles of participatory resources differ in their actual activity. Those who choose to devote scarce resources to political activity rather than to other pursuits would, presumably, be distinctive in their orientation to politics.

Students of participation use numerous measures of political engagement. We concentrate on four that seem conceptually distinct: political interest, political efficacy, political information, and strength of party identification.

> *Political Interest.* Citizens who are interested in politics—who follow politics, care about what happens, and are concerned with who wins or loses—are more politically active. Our measure of political interest combines expressed interest in national and local politics and affairs.
>
> *Political Efficacy.* The belief that it could make a difference if one got involved has been shown to be strongly associated with political activity. Political efficacy has been measured in many different ways. The measure that we use puts together four items: one each about how much attention a local or national government official would pay if the respondent had a complaint; and one each about how much influence the respondent has over local or national government decisions.
>
> *Political Information.* Citizens vary substantially in their political information or knowledge. This information can be of many

sorts—from the "who" of the individuals active in politics and government to the "what" of current political controversies, from the actual workings of the political system to the constitutional principles underlying government. Political information differs from the other components of political engagement in being objective rather than subjective. Our political information scale tests knowledge of government and politics as well as the names of public officials.

Strength of Party Identification. Party identification holds a special place in the study of the political behavior of the American public. Although it is usually used to predict the direction of the vote, it has also been shown to play a role in electoral turnout. We measure the strength, not the direction, of partisan leanings, categorizing respondents as strong partisans, weak partisans, partisan leaners, or nonpartisans—regardless of whether they are Republicans or Democrats.

Not surprisingly, political interest, efficacy, and information are all positively related to one another. Strength of party identification is somewhat separate, significantly related to political interest but not to efficacy or information.

Analogous to what we show for participatory resources, psychological orientations to politics map onto other social cleavages. Figure 3.2 displays the means of the engagement measures for educational groups and shows that the well educated are, on average, more politically interested, efficacious, and informed than those who are lower on the educational ladder. In contrast, highly educated respondents are not particularly likely to be strongly identified with a political party. Data not presented show that the pattern for income closely tracks that for education.[11]

With regard to race or ethnicity and gender, although the size of the disparities varies across the different measures of psychological orientations to politics, on average, non-Hispanic whites tend to score highest, followed by African Americans and then Latinos. The one exception is that African Americans are somewhat more likely to be strong partisans. In addition, men are more likely to be psychologically engaged with politics than women are.[12] However, the gender differences are considerably smaller than those based on race or ethnicity and range from almost imperceptible for strength of party identification to appreciably larger for political information.

So far, we have seen a cumulative process in which the resources and psychological orientations to politics that facilitate participation accrue to

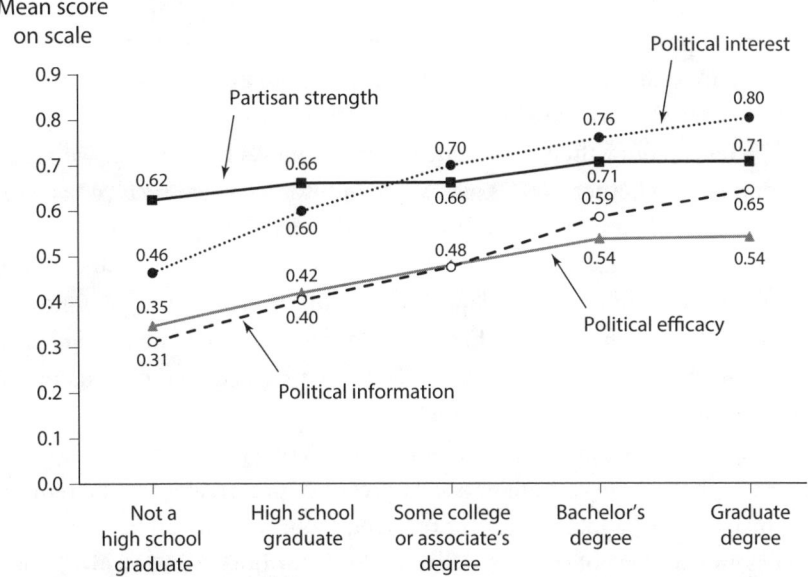

FIGURE 3.2. Mean Psychological Engagement with Politics by Education
Source: Citizen Participation Study.

those who command a disproportionate share of other factors. The differential accumulation of participatory factors is further reinforced by processes of recruitment to participation.

The Factors That Foster Participation: Recruitment to Politics

Often individuals become politically active more or less spontaneously when they are excited about issues, connect politics to their basic commitments and concerns, or get involved out of a sense of civic duty. Frequently, however, they become active because someone asked. Such requests arise from a variety of sources—for example, from a campaign that e-mails a solicitation to support a candidate, from the pastor during a sermon in church or the officers of an organization of which one is a member, or directly from a neighbor or co-worker.

Showing that appeals for activity cause participation is, however, not a straightforward task. Requests might beget activity, but activity might just as easily beget requests. Who is a better prospect for an appeal for money than a past donor? Those who ask others to take part in politics have no incentive to waste their efforts on unlikely prospects who have been inactive in the past. As we shall see, requests for participation are not made in a scattershot fashion but are highly structured by socioeconomic status (SES) and by related characteristics.

To learn about their experiences with requests for activity, we asked respondents whether in the past twelve months they had received any requests to work in a campaign; to give money to a campaign; to contact a government official; to take part in a protest, march, or demonstration; or to take some active role in a local, public, or political issue.[13] If so, we followed up by inquiring whether they had received more than one such request and whether they had said yes to it. In addition, we asked about the nature of their connections to the people making requests.

Although common, requests for political activity are far from universal. Just over half of the respondents, 52 percent, reported at least one request in the past year; a mere 1 percent received requests to do all five activities. These appeals for political involvement do not ordinarily bear fruit. Taking all requests together, only 44 percent of those asked said yes. The proportion of the sample successfully recruited—a function of the likelihood of being asked and saying yes, if asked—varies across political acts and ranges from a high of 17 percent for contacting public officials to a low of 3 percent for protesting, an activity for which the relatively small number of requests are less likely to bear fruit.

The likelihood of being asked to get involved politically is not randomly distributed. Those who are socially connected to family, neighbors, coworkers, or fellow organization or church members are positioned to receive more requests for political activity. Furthermore, whether they are individuals soliciting friends, fellow club members, or firms developing lists for the purpose of mass solicitations, those who seek to mobilize others to take part politically make efforts to focus their efforts on likely prospects. The result is that requests are aimed disproportionately at those who command factors that foster participation.

Figure 3.3 shows the mean number of requests for activity for members of groups defined by levels of education and family income, race or ethnicity, and gender. The results repeat familiar patterns. Whether because they are more likely to be in networks through which requests for activity are mediated or because those who seek to get others involved target them as likely activists, or both, the probability of being recruited to political activity rises with educational attainment and family income. In contrast, the differences based on gender and race or ethnicity are relatively muted.

3.3.A. Education

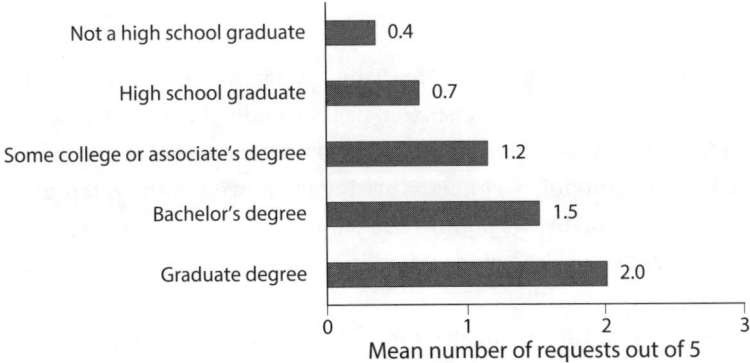

3.3.B. Family income

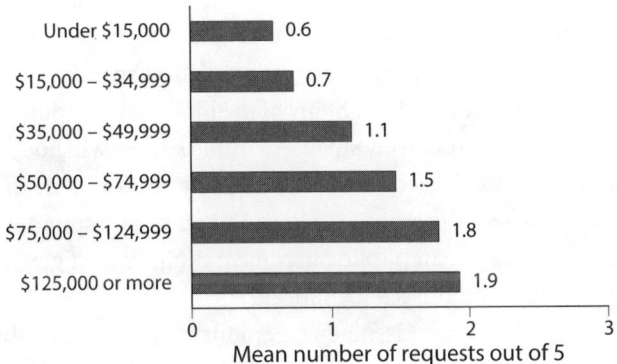

3.3.C. Race/ethnicity and gender

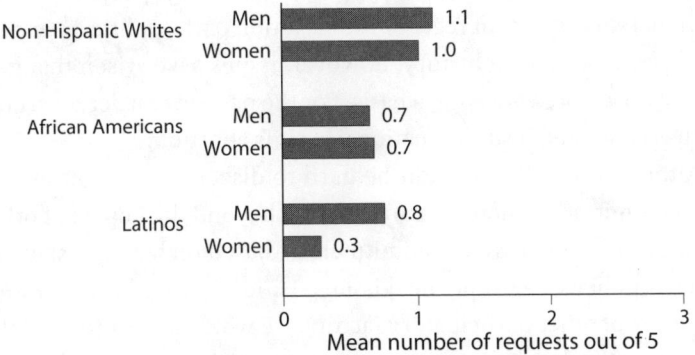

FIGURE 3.3. Mean Requests for Political Activity by Selected Characteristics
Source: Citizen Participation Study (1990).
Note: Average number of five political acts (work in a campaign; give money to a campaign; contact a government official; take part in a protest, march or demonstration; or take some active role in a local public or political issue) for which at least one request for activity was received.

The Role of Issue Commitments

The three participatory factors described so far are devoid of substantive issue content. However, activists told us repeatedly that their participation was founded, at least in part, on a desire to influence what the government does. Focusing on policy concerns arising from needs and preferences for government action brings politics back into an analysis that started by self-consciously locating the roots of political action in experiences outside politics.

The policy commitments that might stimulate participation can have diverse origins, but two come immediately to mind: first, having a personal stake in government policy; and second, caring deeply about a particular political issue. Government policies that affect citizens in different ways create potential constituencies of activists. All of us—ranging from farmers to veterans to the wheelchair-bound to auto executives—have interests in what the government does. Many of the identifiable groups having a stake in public policy are relatively small. A sample survey will not contain sufficient cases for analysis of those who have a joint interest in most policies. In our survey, however, we are able to locate two sets of respondents for whom we might infer a stake in public outcomes: recipients of government benefits and parents of school-aged children.

Another source of issue engagement is citizens' deeply held views on controversial matters. Many issue controversies—conflicts over, for example, the siting of a public housing facility or an allegation of bribery against the mayor—are sufficiently localized that, even though people are exercised, a national survey cannot register the elevation of the political temperature. Throughout American history, however, issues have arisen that generate passion on a more widespread basis. For the past several decades, one issue that has generated heat on a national basis is abortion.

Although the effects might be hard to discern, we might expect that issue commitments increase participation beyond the impact of other participatory factors. If issue commitments—based on having a stake in government policy or a deeply held issue position—foster participation independently of other participatory factors, we would expect to see enhanced activity directed toward the specific policy at stake. For example, we would anticipate—and, later in the chapter, we show—that intense views on abortion influence the likelihood of contacting a public official about abortion but not the likelihood of contacting an official about Middle East policy or the city's failure to collect the garbage.

From Generation to Generation: The Legacy of Family for Political Participation

The promise of the American Dream to the contrary, when it comes to occupational and economic success, we do not start off on an equal footing. Families provide very different launching pads that affect future wealth and status—as well as political voice. Experiences in the family and at school ramify throughout the life course, generating participatory factors and, ultimately, political activity. It is widely acknowledged that economic and social stratification reproduces itself from generation to generation, so that those from affluent families are more likely to end up affluent themselves and those from poor families more likely to end up poor. Less well known is the reproduction of political stratification across generations.[14] On average, those whose parents did not take part politically turn out to be relatively inactive as adults, and the offspring of politically active parents tend to be highly participatory as adults.

We consider two pathways by which the family might operate to influence future political participation. The first emphasizes political learning: in the family, children absorb cues and lessons about politics and the rights and responsibilities of citizens. The second, which has rarely been mentioned by students of political socialization, focuses on the way that the SES of one's family of origin shapes opportunities for educational attainment and experiences in school, which, in turn, affect the likelihood of acquiring many other attributes that foster political participation.

Although the family does not figure especially prominently in contemporary political science, students of political socialization once deemed it significant among the institutions that shape the political orientations, attitudes, and behaviors of the young.[15] For example, children and adolescents who come from higher social class backgrounds or whose parents had high levels of formal education were found to have higher levels of political information and understanding and also to be more politically interested and efficacious, more tolerant, and more politically active.

Political scientists assumed that family mattered for politics through learning and culture. Children were presumed to look to their parents as role models when it comes to politics; to absorb implicit lessons about authority, autonomy, and decision making from their parents' household management practices and child-rearing styles; and to pick up political orientations and attitudes from explicit political instruction by their parents. The connection between parents' social class and their offspring's future political activity derived from the fact that high-SES parents are more likely to create a politically rich home environment—in which frequent political discussions take place and politically active parents serve as role models—and children who grow up in such an environment would be distinctive in their political orientations. The lessons that are absorbed in a politically stimulating home would carry into adulthood, creating motivated citizens who are politically interested, informed, and efficacious, and therefore more likely to take part.

However, being raised by parents who are well educated and affluent is potentially politically enabling in another way, one that is less explicitly political.[16] Parents' social class influences the ultimate socioeconomic position of the next generation—including the experiences their children have in school, the level of education they attain, the jobs they get as adults, and the incomes they earn. Position in the socioeconomic hierarchy, in turn, affects the acquisition of such participatory factors as civic skills developed in adult institutional settings, psychological orientations to politics, and the location in networks through which recruitment to political activity takes place.

Perhaps surprisingly, growing up in a rich political environment has much less powerful consequences for adult political activity than does achieving a high level of education. Those who have been exposed to a rich political environment at home while growing up do turn out to be more politically active as adults. However, even more substantial than the effect of the political environment at home is the impact of socioeconomic processes. The single most important is the strong relationship between parents' education and that of their offspring and, in turn, the multiple direct and indirect consequences of education for political participation.

EXPERIENCES IN SCHOOL

An additional dimension is germane to the class-based transmission of political activity across generations. Parental education is associated with the kinds of experiences that students have in high school, experiences that have downstream effects on adult political life. To investigate how high school experiences shape future political participation, the Citizen Participation Study asked about both respondents' own tastes and commitments when they were in secondary school and about the environment of the school and the opportunities offered for involvement.[17]

Perhaps unexpectedly, the strongest predictors of future participation are not the attributes of the school—the political involvement of fellow students, or the extent to which the school encouraged students to debate current events or permitted them to complain. Instead, a better predictor of subsequent participation is the respondent's activity as a high school student—in particular, involvement in high school government but also involvement in other clubs and activities (though not activity in high school sports, which has a small, but statistically significant, negative relationship to future activity).[18] In the chain of effects, activity in high school is strongly predicted by parents' education and, in turn, is a strong predictor of various factors associated with adult activity: civic skills, political interest and information, and requests for political activity.

A NOTE ON THE CREATION OF GROUP DIFFERENCES

As we shall see in Chapter 4, men are somewhat more politically active than women, and non-Hispanic whites more politically active than African Americans and, especially, Latinos. It turns out that the intergenerational processes that perpetuate class-based inequalities of political voice have no impact on the participation gap between men and women, but they do exacerbate political inequality on the basis of ethnicity or race.[19] Because boys and girls are born randomly into families, there is, as we would expect, no significant difference in the educational attainment of the parents of men and women and, therefore, no gender difference in experiences with respect to politics at home. In contrast, non-Hispanic white respondents are more likely than African Americans or, especially, Latinos to report that their parents were very well educated. These differences in background translate into aggregate disparities in youthful political exposure. Non-Hispanic whites are more likely than blacks or Latinos to report having had a stimulating political environment at home.

The contrast between the two sets of groups is noteworthy. Parental characteristics are not an important factor when it comes to explaining gender differences in participation. Men and women differ in neither the kind of families into which they are born nor the way that they convert the legacy of their parents' characteristics into political activity. Of course, women and men do not have the same experiences in childhood, adolescence, or adulthood, but gender disparities in participation are created during the life course, not as the result of parents' level of education. In contrast, the parental legacy has much more substantial consequences for participatory inequalities among Latinos, African Americans, and non-Hispanic whites.

For both blacks and Latinos, group differences in parental education and the political environment at home play an important role in creating a participation gap with non-Hispanic whites.

The Institutional Nexus: Accumulating Participatory Factors in Adulthood

Youthful experiences continue to ramify outward in adulthood, channeling individuals differentially into nonpolitical institutions, where affiliated adults accumulate bundles of participatory factors. These stockpiles are affected by the *level* of participatory factors available in the institutions into which they have been sorted and the *distribution* of participatory factors across different kinds of people within the institution.

SELECTION INTO INSTITUTIONS

To exercise civic skills or be the target of requests in a nonpolitical institution, one must be in the workforce, join an organization, or be a member of a religious congregation. Interestingly, nearly identical proportions of respondents are connected to each domain: 66 percent have jobs; 68 percent are affiliated with a nonpolitical organization; and 67 percent are members of religious institutions.

As shown by the schematic summary in Table 3.2, however, selection into these institutions varies substantially across demographic groups defined by SES, race or ethnicity, or gender. Starting with the workforce, the relationship between SES and having a job is of medium strength. It is hardly surprising that a larger proportion of people have jobs as we move up the income ladder. Leaving income aside, even when we exclude younger people who may not have completed their education and older people who may have retired, with each step up the educational ladder, the proportion who are in the workforce rises. With regard to race or ethnicity, the differences among non-Hispanic whites, blacks, and Latinos are quite small. In contrast, as expected, men are much more likely than women to be in the work force.[20] Affiliation with nonpolitical organizations also rises with education and income, and non-Hispanic whites are considerably more likely to be affiliated than are African Americans or, especially, Latinos. There is, in contrast to jobs, no disparity on the basis of gender. The pattern is significantly different for membership in a local religious congregation. In this case, the SES gradient is small, but differences occur on the basis of race or ethnicity

TABLE 3.2. Who Is Affiliated with Adult Institutions? Selection into the Work Force, Nonpolitical Organizations, and Religious Institutions

	Workforce	Nonpolitical Organization	Religious Institution
Extent to which selection process is structured by:			
SES (Unless otherwise noted the advantage is to high-SES)	Medium	High	Low
Race or ethnicity (Unless otherwise noted the advantage is to non-Hispanic whites)	Low	High	Medium African Americans advantaged
Gender (Unless otherwise noted the advantage is to men)	High	None	Medium to High Women advantaged

and gender: blacks are somewhat more likely to be members than are non-Hispanic whites or, especially, Latinos, and women are notably more likely to be affiliated with religious congregations than are men.

WHAT HAPPENS ON THE JOB, IN ORGANIZATIONS, OR IN CHURCH: CIVIC SKILLS

For those who are affiliated, all three of these nonpolitical settings provide many opportunities to practice skills relevant to politics. Chances to develop civic skills are especially plentiful in the workplace. For example, more than two-thirds of those with jobs reported attending a meeting where decisions were made and more than one-third had planned such a meeting. Nonpolitical organizations provide fewer—and religious congregations somewhat fewer still—opportunities to practice civic skills: in these two domains, about a third of those affiliated attended a meeting where decisions were made, and close to a fifth planned such a meeting.

Opportunities to exercise skills are not distributed evenly along lines of class, race, or gender. In some cases, the allocation of opportunities to exercise civic skills reinforces other processes that create advantage; in others, it counterbalances these processes. The workplace is particularly rich in opportunities to practice civic skills. However, as shown in the schematic

TABLE 3.3. Distribution of Participatory Factors in Institutions of Adult Life (among Institutionally Affiliated)

A. Civic Skills

	Workforce	Nonpolitical Organization	Religious Institution
Extent to which distribution among institutionally affiliated structured by:			
SES (Advantage to high-SES)	High	High	Low to Medium
Race or ethnicity (Advantage to non-Hispanic whites[a])	Medium	Medium	Medium Latinos disadvantaged[b]
Gender (Advantage to men)	Low to Medium	Low	Low

B. Requests for activity

	Workforce	Nonpolitical Organization	Religious Institution
Extent to which distribution among institutionally affiliated structured by:			
SES (Advantage to high-SES)	High	Medium	High
Race or ethnicity (Advantage to non-Hispanic whites[a])	Medium	Medium Latinos disadvantaged[b]	Medium Latinos disadvantaged[b]
Gender (Advantage to men)	Low	Low	Low

[a]Non-Hispanic whites advantaged over African Americans; African Americans advantaged over Latinos.
[b]Non-Hispanic whites and African Americans equivalent or close; Latinos disadvantaged.

presentation in Table 3.3.A, work-based civic skills are not only highly stratified but they also reinforce the biases introduced by processes of selection into the workforce. Occupations requiring high levels of education and professional training are much more likely to permit the development of civic skills than are occupations demanding less education and training. Teachers or lawyers are more likely to have opportunities to enhance civic skills—to organize meetings, make presentations, and the like—than are fast-food workers or nursing home attendants. Jobs that demand education and training are unevenly allocated across social groups with the result that, among those with jobs, non-Hispanic whites are considerably more likely to develop skills on the job than are African Americans or, especially, Latinos. In addition, men are somewhat more likely than women to develop civic skills at work.

The patterns for nonpolitical organizations are similar though less pronounced. Just as particular occupations vary substantially in their skill-endowing possibilities so, too, do different kinds of nonpolitical organizations. Members of service clubs and fraternal organizations (such as the Lions or Kiwanis) and members of literary, art, discussion, or study groups are, not unexpectedly, more likely to exercise civic skills in the course of their organizational activities than are donors to public radio or social service organizations like the Salvation Army. On average, nonpolitical organizations provide fewer opportunities to develop civic skills than do workplaces, and selection into nonpolitical organizations is highly structured by both SES and race or ethnicity. Reinforcing the results of class-stratified selection processes, opportunities for the development of civic skills accrue disproportionately to the better-educated and more affluent members of nonpolitical organizations and, to a somewhat lesser extent, to non-Hispanic white members. The gender gap in favor of men is extremely small.

When it comes to the development of civic skills in religious institutions, the results are quite different and provide some counterweight to processes in which those who have already accumulated participatory factors are positioned to stockpile even more. Although the very poorest members of religious congregations are less likely to exercise civic skills in their houses of worship, there is otherwise no income advantage in the development of civic skills in religious institutions. In contrast, those at the top of the educational ladder enjoy a marked advantage when it comes to religiously based civic skills. With regard to gender, among church members, men have only a very small advantage over women in the chance to exercise civic skills in religious institutions. The unexpected pattern is that African American church members are, on average, more likely to develop civic skills than are non-Hispanic whites or, especially, Latinos.

What is the origin of this perhaps puzzling gap? Just as the possibilities for skill development vary across different kinds of occupations and organizations, they also vary across different religious denominations. Compared to the Catholic Church, most Protestant denominations allow for greater lay participation in the liturgy; and most Protestant denominations are organized on a congregational basis with authority vested in the congregation rather than in the hierarchy.[21] Systematic data show that, although Catholic and Protestant respondents are equally likely to attend religious services, there is a dramatic difference in terms of both the amount of time devoted to church-related educational, social, or charitable activity and opportunities to exercise politically relevant skills in church. Protestants are three times more likely than Catholics to have reported a skill opportunity.[22]

Although the share of Latinos who are evangelical Protestants has been rising, African Americans are much more likely than Latinos to be Protestants, a pattern that partially explains why African Americans are more likely to develop civic skills in church. Among Protestants, Latinos reported exercising, on average, fewer civic skills than did African-American and non-Hispanic whites. However, Latino Protestants reported considerably more skill-building opportunities than did Latino Catholics.

The contrast between Protestants and Catholics makes clear that institutions matter. These patterns emerge from the characteristics of the two denominations and the way their congregations are governed rather than from distinctive characteristics of the congregants or any lesser commitment to political issues on the part of Catholics. In fact, parishioners at Catholic churches are no less likely than Protestants to be exposed to political cues and messages in church.

WHAT HAPPENS IN ADULT INSTITUTIONS: REQUESTS FOR ACTIVITY

The institutions of adult life also facilitate political participation by serving as the locus of requests for political activity. In all three adult nonpolitical settings, not only are requests for political activity less frequent than opportunities to exercise civic skills, but also the pattern of requests is different. Requests for activity are most frequent in religious institutions, followed by workplaces, and then nonpolitical organizations.

What kinds of people are targets of requests for political activity in each of these settings? Table 3.3.B demonstrates that institutionally based recruitment to politics rises with SES. Contrary to what we saw for civic skills, religious institutions show no pattern of counter-stratification: just as they are at work, the well educated and affluent are disproportionately likely to be asked in church to take part politically. The pattern is similar, though less pronounced, for nonpolitical organizations. Across all three sets of institutions, the disparities on the basis of race or ethnicity are less pronounced than the SES gaps. In each case, Latinos are least likely to have reported being asked to take part. The disparity is particularly noticeable for congregation-based requests: among members of religious institutions, 38 percent of African Americans, 35 percent of non-Hispanic whites, and only 16 percent of Latinos received requests at church to take part politically. With respect to gender, across all three institutional settings, the differences between men and women in the proportion receiving requests for political activity are minimal.

Putting It All Together: The Civic Voluntarism Model

Three components comprise the CVM. The first is *resources*, in particular, the time, money, and skills that make it possible to take part. The second is a set of *psychological orientations to politics*, for example, political interest, information, and efficacy as well as identification with a political party, that predispose a citizen to want to take part. The third is *recruitment*, requests for activity that serve as a catalyst for participation. We have shown how people accumulate different portfolios of participatory factors as they move through their lives. The process begins in the family and continues as people move through school into adult institutional involvements on the job, in nonpolitical organizations, and in religious institutions.

We now assemble the various pieces to show how these factors work together to foster both overall participation as well as particular forms of activity.[23] We lay out our findings schematically in Table 3.4, which lists the factors shown in multivariate analysis to be predictors of overall participation, voting, undertaking time-based acts (such as getting in touch with a public official or working with neighbors to solve a community problem), and making political contributions. Two things are immediately obvious. First, political participation is an outcome that involves the complex interaction of many factors. Second, different types of participation involve quite different configurations of these factors.

OVERALL PARTICIPATION

What matters in predicting overall participation—measured by an index that includes voting, forms of activity that take time, and making contributions?[24] The brief answer is more or less everything. Resources—education; civic skills; family income; and to a lesser extent, free time—have a strong relationship to overall participation, even when the impact of political interest and information, both powerful predictors, is taken into account.

The continuing direct effect of involvement in high school activities and, again to a lesser extent, exposure to politics in the family is striking confirmation of the multiple roles that the family and school experiences play

TABLE 3.4. Factors That Foster Participation

	Substantial Effect	Some Effect
Overall participation	Education High school activity Income Civic skills Political interest Political information Citizenship	Politics at home Free time Recruitment
Voting	Political interest Political information Partisan strength Citizenship	Politics at home High school activity Religious attendance Political efficacy Recruitment
Time-based acts	Education Civic skills Political interest Recruitment	High school activity Free time Political information Political efficacy
Political contributions	Income	Political interest

in bringing individuals into politics, indirectly by shaping opportunities to acquire education, jobs, and income and more directly by providing political stimulation. Over and above their effects on political activity through political interest, these factors have direct consequences for participation. The fact that actual participatory experiences appear to be the most important school effect is a significant finding for understanding civic education. To writers like Tocqueville, local governments and voluntary organizations are "schools of democracy," not because they give formal instruction in democratic governance but because they give opportunities to practice democratic governance. At least as far as our data suggest, American high schools have a similar effect, not by teaching about democracy but by providing hands-on training for future participation.

RATIONAL PROSPECTING: THE IMPACT OF RECRUITMENT

We often hear people say, "I never would have gone to that demonstration/worked in that campaign/joined that community effort if my neighbor hadn't asked me." Besides, we know from scholarly work about get-out-the-vote techniques that, under specified conditions, contacting voters can successfully mobilize them to turn out. Why, then, is recruitment not an even more powerful predictor of activity in Table 3.4? Our answer has to do with the process—discussed at greater length in Chapter 7—that we call "rational prospecting." Those who seek to get others involved in politics act as rational prospectors, targeting their requests to individuals who would be most likely to assent and to participate effectively. They look for people who have attributes—ranging from organizational and communications skills to a big bank account to a demonstrated interest in politics—that are associated with participation. In the course of locating likely targets, rational prospectors direct their requests to at least some people who would have taken part anyway, even in the absence of a request—which has the effect of weakening the relationship between recruitment and participation. By focusing on those who have "participatory characteristics," rational prospecting also mobilizes those who are even higher in SES than are those who become active on their own initiative, an effect that is most notable for campaign contributions.

DOES ANYTHING NOT MATTER?

Does anything not affect participation? Institutional affiliations do not, on their own, enhance political participation. What matters is what happens in institutions. Only when having a job, being a member of a nonpolitical organization, or going to church develops civic skills or yields requests for political activity does it have an impact on activity. Being there is a necessary first step but is no guarantee of a participatory boost.

Interestingly, once their effects on subsequent factors are taken into account, certain initial characteristics have almost no *direct* influence on participation. The blessing that comes from having well-educated parents has a very weak direct impact on political participation, because it works through its strong impact on eventual educational attainment. In addition, with other factors controlled, neither being African-American nor being Latino has a direct impact on activity.[25] Note what this finding means. Our analysis does not imply that groups defined by their race or ethnicity are identical in their levels of participation. Quite the contrary. As we shall see in Chapter 4, there are disparities in participation among non-Hispanic whites, African Americans, and, especially, Latinos—disparities that are anchored in social class differences among these groups. Understanding that group differences in political activity reflect disparities among them in SES does not, however, reduce their significance for politics. That the government hears more from certain kinds of people than from others has political implications.

VOTING

The pattern of participatory factors for voting, the most common political act, differs strikingly from that for other political activities. A prerequisite for voting—citizenship—of course plays a significant role, as it does for overall activity. What is distinctive about voting is that, with other factors taken into account, resources and even educational attainment play no role. Instead, indicators of psychological engagement with politics come to the fore, with political interest especially powerful and partisan strength also important. Three other factors are also relevant: the legacies of youth (growing up in a politically rich environment and engaging in extracurricular activity while in high school); recruitment; and a measure of institutional affiliation (attending religious services). In short, the path to voting is distinctive.

It seems surprising that education, generally considered the dominant single factor boosting participation, is not a significant predictor of voting. We do not conclude, however, that education is unimportant for voting. Rather, it plays an indirect role by fostering political interest and information.

TIME-BASED ACTS

Time-based acts include all forms of participation in the scale of overall activity except for voting and giving money. Since time-based activities figure so importantly in the scale of overall political activity, it is not surprising that the configuration of factors is quite similar to what we saw for overall activity. The resources of education and civic skills retain primary importance, as do being interested in politics and having been targeted by requests for activity. Having taken part in activities in high school as well as free time and other measures of psychological engagement with politics are of secondary importance.

POLITICAL CONTRIBUTIONS

The configuration of factors for political contributions contrasts with what we have discussed so far. We consider not just whether people have donated but how much they gave, and the amount of the contribution is predicted chiefly by family income. Education and civic skills play no role. Even the impact of psychological orientations to politics is muted: only political interest, which plays a secondary role, seems to matter. Thus, with other factors taken into account, contributors are, when compared to other activists, affluent but not especially politically engaged. This result has important implications for political stratification and for politics: the great bulk of the public—a group that has distinctive politically relevant needs—is greatly disadvantaged when it comes to this activity, which has increased substantially in significance in recent years.

THE ROLE OF ISSUE COMMITMENTS

Earlier we identified several issue constituencies large enough to show up on a survey: two groups having a stake in government programs, namely, beneficiaries of means-tested government programs and parents of school-aged children, as well as two groups having extreme attitudes (pro-life and pro-choice) on the issue of abortion. In our survey we asked those who indicated having taken part in politics whether there were any issues and problems associated with their political activity and recorded their replies. We placed into categories these verbatim discussions of the issues and problems that led to activity. In this way, we were able to locate political activity directed toward problems of basic human needs, educational concerns, and abortion. We then added having a direct stake to the analysis of participation directed at each of these issues. Even with the many other factors associated with participation taken into account, we found that having a stake in a particular policy (in this case, either receiving means-tested government benefits or having school-aged children, or having passionate views on a controversial issue, in this case, abortion) has a strong additional impact on the likelihood of being active on issues related to that policy. Thus, issue engagements can play an independent role in generating activity related to that issue.

These issue constituencies differ in important ways. Compared with both the public at large and with parents of school-aged children, recipients of means-tested benefits are, not unexpectedly, less well educated and less well off financially. Although they attend church regularly, they exercise very few civic skills in nonpolitical institutions and are relatively uninterested in and uninformed about politics. It is not surprising that they are not very active in politics. More than half of their participation is directed at issues of basic human needs. Still, because their overall activity is so low, the volume of their participation on issues of basic human needs is quite limited. The lift given to their participation by their interest in issues of basic human needs is insufficient to overcome their other resource deficits.

The contrast between the participatory profiles of those who are passionately pro-choice and passionately pro-life is particularly striking. Those in the most extreme pro-choice category in their attitudes on abortion enjoy many advantages with regard to participatory factors and are quite active in politics. However, they do not focus their activity on the issue of abortion. Of the four groups with a stake in an issue discussed here, members of the pro-choice group are the least likely to engage in a participatory act inspired by the issue that defines them as a group. Only a small proportion of the issue-based activity of the pro-choice group is dedicated to abortion. The much smaller group with strongly held attitudes at the opposite end of the abortion scale is very different. Those with pro-life attitudes are neither especially advantaged in socioeconomic terms nor particularly interested in or knowledgeable about politics. Moreover, they are relatively inactive in politics. Where they are distinctive is in their remarkably high level of church attendance and in the extent to which they concentrate on the issue of abortion when they do take part politically. The fact that a majority of their issue-based activity is directed at the issue of abortion makes those with extreme pro-life attitudes the closest to a single-issue constituency of the four issue-oriented groups.[26]

In sum, issue commitments can function as a significant factor in motivating participation—even for those who are disadvantaged when it comes to the factors that foster political activity. Still, issue engagements are only one piece of the puzzle. For a group that is resource deprived, issue engagements go only so far in elevating a depressed level of participation. For a group that is well endowed with participatory resources, issue engagements can give an additional participatory push. What happens in politics does have implications for who is active in politics. Nonetheless, the way in which political issues and conflicts affect participation also depends fundamentally on the structure of participatory factors having their origins outside politics.

Beyond SES: Understanding the Roots of Participation

One of the strongest empirical patterns noted by social scientists is the association between higher levels of education and income and greater political participation. Since income and education are basic components of the stratification system in any society, what is often referred to as the "SES model" of participation is also a model of political inequality. It predicts participatory disparities across groups having differing preferences and needs for governmental action that are in potential political conflict with one another. However, the SES model has weak theoretical underpinnings, failing to provide a coherent rationale for the connection between the explanatory socioeconomic variables and participation. By specifying the factors that facilitate participation and showing how those factors are anchored in basic institutions of a society, the CVM fortifies the SES model theoretically, providing an explanation as to why those with high SES are more politically active.

The CVM begins with the paths by which one generation passes on its socioeconomic position to the next. Highly educated parents confer advantage on their offspring, because their children tend to take part in activities in high school and, more importantly, to end up becoming well educated and, thus, to have high-level jobs, to be affluent, and to get involved with organizations. These outcomes, in turn, enhance a number of factors that foster political participation: civic skills developed at work and in nonpolitical organizations; political interest, information, and efficacy; and requests for political activity. In addition, parents who are well educated are more likely to expose their children to politics—by taking part in politics themselves, and thus serving as role models and by creating a politically rich environment at home—which has consequences for later political activity through enhanced political interest.

The factors that foster participation—resources, psychological engagement with politics, and recruitment—are thus shaped by the basic institutions of society: families, schools, jobs, voluntary associations, and religious institutions. Depending on the level of their educational attainment; the extent of their commitment to the labor force and the kinds of jobs they hold; the number and kinds of organizations with which they get involved; the kinds of congregations they attend and the level of activity in ancillary educational, charitable, and social activities in those congregations, individuals amass different amounts and mixes of participatory resources. The process is cumulative. Those with greater resources at the outset collect more as their resource endowments allow them to move into institutional positions conducive to further resource acquisition. These processes also create psychological engagement with politics and place individuals in recruitment networks.

The sole exception to the way that participatory factors accrue disproportionately to those who are already advantaged is the way that, depending on the denomination and the nature of the congregation, religious institutions provide opportunities to cultivate civic skills for people who would not always have such chances at work or in nonpolitical organizations. Religious institutions distribute opportunities for skill development in a way that is less structured by education and income than do workplaces or nonpolitical organizations.

In elaborating the CVM, we detailed the mechanisms by which SES is translated into participation—not simply for overall activity but for particular modes of involvement. We demonstrated that what is true for voting cannot be generalized to other forms of activity. Similarly, a unique configuration of factors—dominated by a single factor, family income—predicts financial contributions to politics. By specifying how the components of SES operate to enhance various forms of participation, we made clear that education and income are not simply interchangeable: the narrow and powerful effect of income on political contributions contrasts sharply with the broader role of education.

Education plays a role in generating participation at every stage of this process and enhances nearly every participatory factor: the well educated have higher incomes and exercise more civic skills; they are more politically interested and informed; they are more likely to be in institutional settings from which they can be recruited to politics. In short, educational attainment affects not only the kinds of resources individuals accumulate but also the kinds of citizens they become.

Analysts of the American educational system characterize its contributions to American society in several ways. Some stress its role in producing a skilled and competent work force. Others focus on its contribution to the creation of a citizenry committed to the ideals of democracy. For still others, of a more critical posture, the educational system is a means of reproducing social stratification from one generation to the next. Our analysis makes clear that education functions in each of these ways: training workers, preparing citizens, and transmitting social class across generations. And in all three capacities—not only in transmitting social class—educational differences beget participatory inequalities.

PART II

4

Who Exercises Political Voice?

After thirteen white male Republican senators were named to a panel to revise a health-care law passed by the House in early May 2017, CNN host Erin Burnett asked "Why couldn't they find one woman to represent the concerns of 126 million female adults in the United States of America? What can they realistically bring to the table when the conversation turns to, let's just say, childbirth, maternity leave, ovarian cancer or breast cancer?"[1] A GOP aide responded by saying:

> We have no interest in playing the games of identity politics, that's not what this is about; it's about getting a job done. We'll work with any member of any background who wants to pass a health reform bill that will reduce premiums and take away the burdens that Obamacare inflicted. To reduce this to gender, race or geography misses the more important point of the diverse segments of the conference the group represents on policy—from members who support Medicaid expansion, to those opposed to it, to those who have called for long term full repeal.[2]

Representative with Respect to What? Politically Relevant Characteristics

People differ in many ways, among them, their attitudes on public policy issues ranging from taxes to immigration to abortion. It is sometimes argued that, so long as activist publics are representative with respect to their policy attitudes, we do not need to be concerned if they are not representative in terms of their other characteristics. CNN host Erin Burnett is not the only one who disagrees. *Politically relevant characteristics*—that is, those attributes whose visibility to a public official might make a difference in the response to citizen participation—include not only attitudes toward policy matters but also a wide range of social and economic characteristics that make government policies relevant to an individual.

The range of politically relevant characteristics is quite broad and the content ever-changing. Indeed, new groups with shared politically relevant characteristics are being created all the time. A natural disaster like a hurricane, a technological innovation, a new government program supporting medical research for a particular disease, and an emerging social movement are but a few examples of the kinds of developments that leave in their wake groups of individuals who have common interests in or preferences for government policies.

We cannot dismiss demographic characteristics from the list of characteristics that are potentially politically relevant. Demographic distinctions are pertinent to political conflicts ranging from racial profiling in police behavior, the age at which Social Security benefits become available, the availability of Section 8 housing vouchers, and the way that sexual harassment is treated under civil rights law to the coverage of contraception under the Affordable Care Act. Under such circumstances, disparities in participation among demographic groups may be significant. Apart from the explicit demands made by activist publics, their social characteristics convey implicit information. When a group is active—especially one with identifiable, politically relevant characteristics—it becomes visible to an elected representative and is incorporated into his or her salient constituency. Politicians attend to their constituencies and know who is watching what they do. (As a former representative is said to have remarked about the town in which one of us lives, "One-tenth the votes. Half the mail.") Even in the absence of explicit directives—and constituents often do not send detailed messages—elected officials anticipate the needs and make inferences about the preferences of potentially active constituents. Thus, it matters not only how participants differ from the nonparticipants in their opinions—whether they want lower taxes, greater funding for medical research, or protection from foreign trade competition—but also who they are.

BUNDLES OF POLITICALLY RELEVANT CHARACTERISTICS

Politically relevant characteristics rarely travel on their own. Instead, they ordinarily come bundled together. Often, to know that a set of people with a particular attribute is active is to know something about the other characteristics that are being well represented through participation. For example, if the elderly in a community take part, it also means that there is activity coming from people who benefit from Social Security or Medicare and who are very likely to support these programs politically.

That politically relevant characteristics are often packaged together complicates the problem of participatory representation. Accurate representation of a group sharing one politically relevant characteristic does not guarantee accurate representation with respect to other group attributes, because it also matters which group members are active. Senior citizens might be proportionally represented among activists. However, if elderly activists are drawn disproportionately from those who are between sixty-five and seventy-five years old, then participatory input from the aged would underrepresent the preferences and needs of what are sometimes called the "old-old," a group that is less healthy and less well-off financially than those whose Medicare cards were issued more recently. Similarly, even if minority group members are proportionally represented among activist publics, we would want to inquire whether African-American or Latino activists are representative in their opinions on political issues or in their actual circumstances, such as their homelessness or reliance on government benefits. Analogous dilemmas can present themselves with respect to any combination of politically relevant characteristics.

We have made the point that political acts vary in their capacity to convey information. Votes tell little about the preferences of voters, but a sign carried at a demonstration or an e-mail to a public official can communicate more. Analogously, some characteristics are more immediately apparent to those at whom activity is targeted. For example, among demonstrators, a group of handicapped citizens in wheelchairs concerned about access to buildings has a more visible set of characteristics and needs than a group of dyslexic citizens concerned about special education programs. Thus, in evaluating the messages that activity sends to policymakers, we need to consider both the nature of the participatory act and the nature of the politically relevant characteristic.

Socioeconomic Status and Political Participation

Those who take part in politics are distinctive in many ways that have implications for political debates. One of the most important is that, as Chapter 3 made clear, those who are higher in the socioeconomic status (SES) hierarchy are more likely to be active—more likely both to vote and to undertake other political acts.[3] In Figure 4.1 we have used data from the 2012 American National Election Study (ANES) to show the relationship between political participation and a measure of SES constructed by ranking respondents in terms of the sum of their educational attainment and family income and dividing them into five equal groups, or quintiles.[4] The top line shows the percentage of respondents in each SES group who reported having engaged in one or more of the five acts in the participation scale. The other lines show the data for the five individual acts: contacting a government official, engaging in informal community activity, making a political contribution, working for a political party or candidate, and attending a protest.[5] Figure 4.1 makes clear that political activity rises with SES.

Because, as we shall see in Chapter 10, those at the very top of the SES ladder have made such disproportionate economic gains in the New Gilded Age, we were interested in looking more closely at the participation of those in the highest quintile. To obtain enough data to consider smaller slices of the SES hierarchy, we combined the more than 26,000 respondents from all

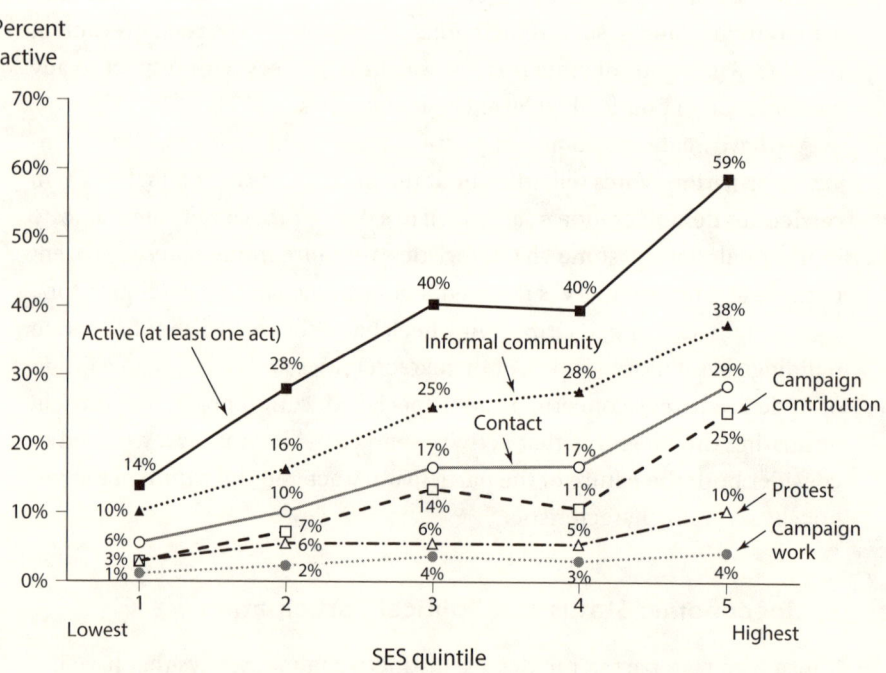

FIGURE 4.1. Participation in Political Activities by SES Quintile
Source: American National Election Study (2012).

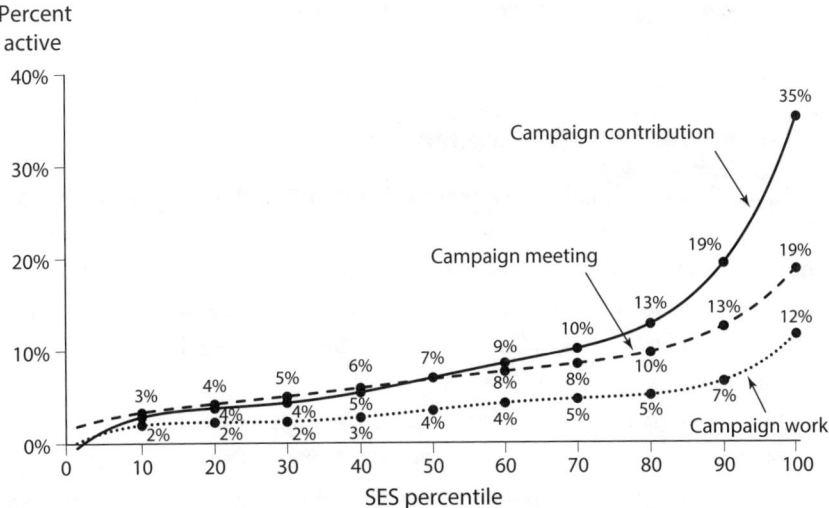

FIGURE 4.2. Participation in Campaign Activities by Percentile, 1952–2012
Source: American National Election Study (1952–2012).
Note: Data smoothed by using fitted percentages from quintic polynomial regressions of people giving money (solid line), attending campaign meetings (dashed line), and working in campaigns (dotted line).

quadrennial American National Election Studies between 1952 and 2012 and divided them into SES percentiles. Figure 4.2 presents data about the proportion of individuals in each of these socioeconomic groups who engaged in three campaign acts: donating money to a party or campaign, working for a party or candidate, and attending campaign meetings or rallies.[6]

As expected, the share engaging in each of the three activities climbs with SES, especially among those in the upper third of the SES hierarchy. What is striking, however, is the pattern for contributing money. In the lowest percentiles, contributing money is rarer than attending a campaign meeting or rally, or even working for a candidate or campaign. The line for giving money crosses the other two lines and then skyrockets upward into the upper-SES ranges. By the 90th percentile, only 7 percent reported working for a campaign, about 13 percent reported going to campaign rallies or meetings, and 19 percent reported donating money. In the highest percentile, about 12 percent indicated working in a campaign and 19 percent attending a campaign rally or meeting. In contrast, 35 percent reported having made a contribution. Because the members of this upper-SES group are in a position not only to make campaign donations but also to give more generously when they do, these data reinforce our understanding of the extent to which making campaign contributions places the affluent in a position to amplify their political voices.

Is Local Politics More Hospitable?

Although decisions made in Washington have profound consequences for our lives, local politics is in many ways closer to ordinary citizens. Many of the most important public services, ranging from schools to garbage collection, are under the control of local authorities. Depending on the size of the community and the nature of its politics, we may know local officials personally and encounter them in our daily lives. We wondered whether local politics might be more hospitable to those who do not enjoy high levels of income or education, thus ameliorating the social class structuring of citizen participation.

The data in Figure 4.3 tell a more complicated story.[7] The top two lines in Figure 4.3 show a well-known pattern: across all five SES quintiles, the

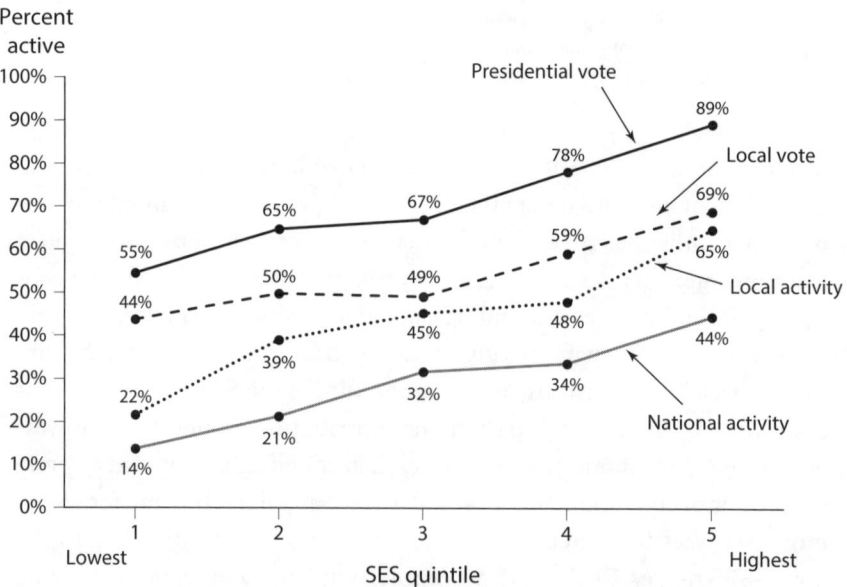

FIGURE 4.3. Voting and Activity beyond the Vote in Local and National Politics by SES Quintile

Source: Citizen Participation Study (1990).

Note: Shown are the percentages of those who voted in all or most local or presidential elections and the percentage who engaged in one or more of six political activities (working in a campaign, making a campaign contribution, being affiliated with an organization that takes stands in politics, attending a protest, contacting an elected official, or contacting a nonelected official) at the local or national level.

proportion claiming that they had voted in all or most presidential elections is higher than the proportion claiming that they had voted in all or most local elections. Even though local politics may be closer to ordinary citizens, local elections do not receive the sustained attention given to presidential elections, with the result that local turnout is lower. However, the gap between the upper and lower SES groups is smaller for local elections than for presidential elections. The bottom two lines in the figure, which reflect the data about six acts other than voting for which activists indicated whether they took part at the national or local level, show a pattern that is in certain ways the reverse of that for voting. In this case, a higher proportion engaged in at least one of the political acts at the local level. However, the social class gradient for local activity is more pronounced than for national activity.

In sum, the evidence that political voice is less unequal in local politics is mixed. Voting turnout is more structured by SES in national elections than in local elections. For participatory acts other than voting, however, the association with SES is stronger at the local level than at the national level.

What If We Construe Civic Involvement More Broadly?

We do not include two other important categories of civic involvement—the various ways that citizens seek the public good without appeal to government intervention and the various ways that they talk and deliberate about public life—in our conceptualization of political participation. However, it is interesting to note that they are characterized by the same social class structuring as the explicitly political forms of participation at the center of our inquiry. Figure 4.4 shows for five SES groups the proportion who engage in two acts of civic engagement (making a campaign donation and contacting a public official) that fall under the rubric of our definition of political voice;[8] and two more (boycotting a product to express one's position on an issue or cause and engaging in political discussion) that do not. For all four forms of activity, the propensity to take part rises with SES.[9] Thus, a more expansive definition of what constitutes political participation does not change the generalization that activity is strongly associated with SES.[10]

Social Class and Participatory Inequalities on the Basis of Race or Gender

Historically, American politics has involved contestation along a number of fault lines—on the basis of not only economic concerns but also such

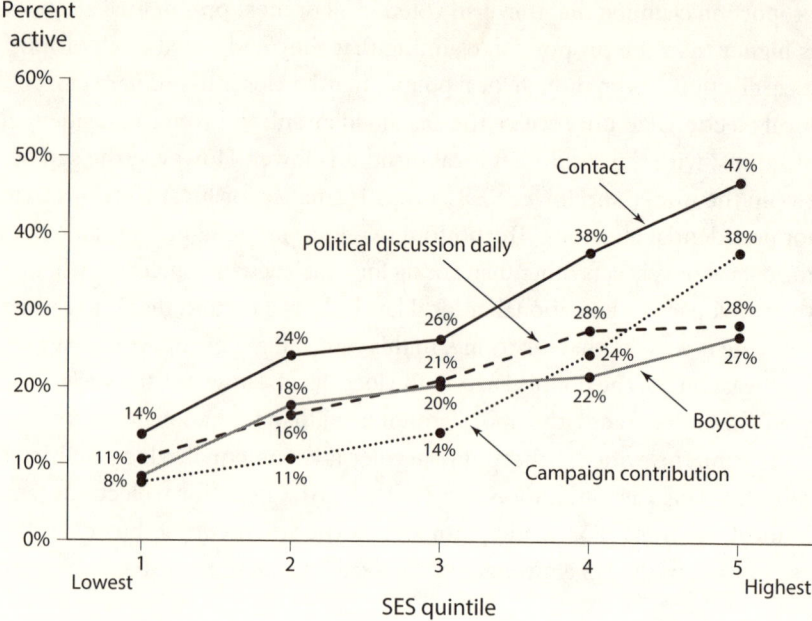

FIGURE 4.4. Political Voice and Political Engagement by SES Quintile
Source: Pew Internet and American Life Project (2008) (campaign contribution, discussion, contact); Citizenship, Involvement, Democracy (CID) Survey (2006) (boycott).
Note: Shown are the percentages contributing money, contacting government officials, discussing politics, or participating in boycotts.

divisions as region, religion, and moral commitments. Participant publics are also unrepresentative with respect to a variety of characteristics that are relevant to such political conflicts—perhaps most importantly, gender and race or ethnicity. Traditionally, men have been on average somewhat more politically active than women, and non-Hispanic whites somewhat more active than African Americans and, especially, Latinos. At least when it comes to participatory differences among such groups, social class is an important part of the story.[11]

With regard to gender, although the education gap has now closed, until very recently, women lagged behind men with respect to both education and income. Men continue to have, on average, higher incomes than women have. Consistent with the continuing income deficit, data from the 2012 ANES show a small gap in participation: on a scale measuring participation in the five acts shown in Figure 4.1, men scored an average of .80 and women .73.[12] Figure 4.5 presents data, for women and men, on the average score on the scale of political participation for each of the SES quintiles.

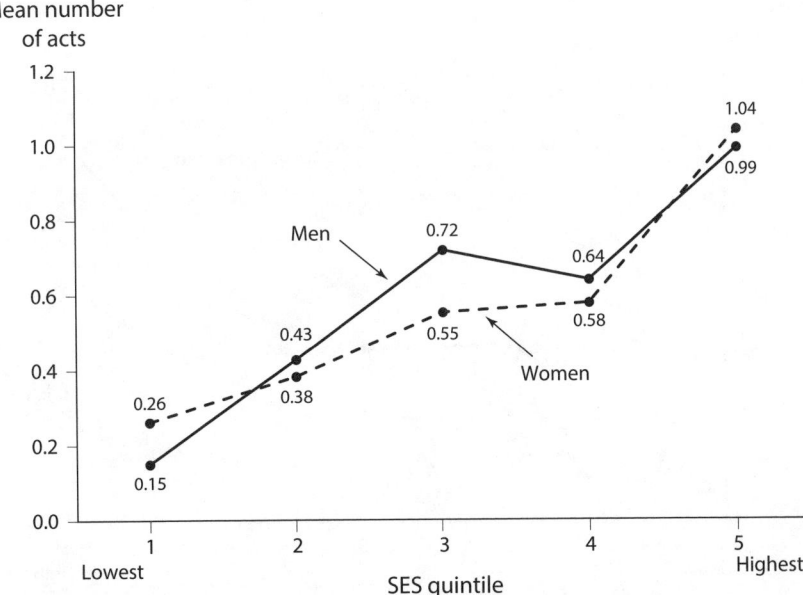

FIGURE 4.5. Political Activity by Gender and SES Quintile
Source: American National Election Studies (2012).
Note: Shown is the mean number of acts on a five-act scale. The five-act scale includes working in a campaign, making a campaign contribution, attending a community meeting, contacting a public official, and attending a protest.

The gender differences within SES quintiles are small in magnitude and inconsistent in direction. What stands out is the extent to which, as we have emphasized, political activity rises with SES. What these data, which present gender differences with regard to averages on an additive scale of political acts, do not show, however, is the extent to which men dominate among top campaign donors. According to the Sunlight Foundation, in the 2014 election cycle only 22 percent of the small group of mega-donors—what they call "the 1 percent of the 1 percent"—were women. Forty-one of the top fifty funders, and all the top fifteen, were men.[13]

The pattern with regard to race or ethnicity is somewhat more complicated. Compared to non-Hispanic whites, African Americans and Latinos are disadvantaged in both educational attainment and income. Consistent with those differences, average political activity for non-Hispanic whites is slightly higher than for African Americans or, especially, Latinos. As shown in Figure 4.6, for each of the three groups, average political activity rises with each rung on the socioeconomic ladder. Once education and income are

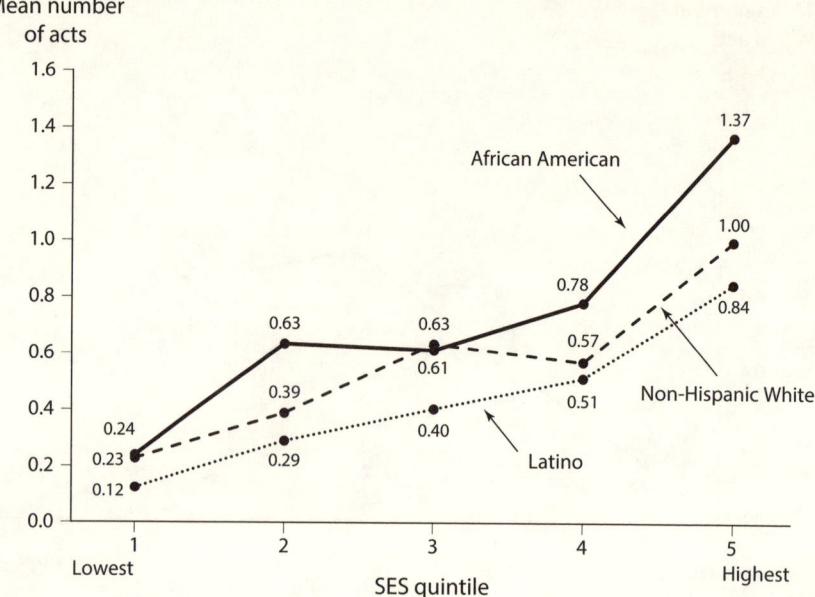

FIGURE 4.6. Political Activity for African American, Latinos, and Non-Latino Whites by SES Quintile
Source: American National Election Studies (2012).
Note: Shown is the mean number of acts on a five-act scale. The five-act scale includes working in a campaign, making a campaign contribution, attending a community meeting, contacting a public official, and attending a protest.

taken into account, racial or ethnic differences in political activity diminish substantially—often to the point of statistical insignificance. We should note, however, that within SES quintiles, Latinos are somewhat lower in average participation, and African Americans are slightly higher in average participation, than non-Hispanic whites. Since the pattern of SES-adjusted advantage for African Americans also appears in 2008, we speculate that it reflects the mobilizing impact of the Obama presidential campaigns.

The fact that inequalities of political participation on the basis of gender or race or ethnicity reflect in large part group differences in education and income—disparities that are hardly mere coincidence but are instead rooted in group differences in socially structured experiences—does not vitiate their implications for political voice. Whatever their origins, there are inequalities of political voice between women and men and among Latinos, African Americans, and non-Hispanic whites. Thus participant publics are unrepresentative in yet another way that is germane to politics—not only on the basis of class but also on the basis of race or ethnicity and, to a lesser extent, gender.

Conclusion

This chapter begins our inquiry into the extent to which political activists are representative of the public with regard to a variety of politically relevant characteristics, focusing on the association between participation and SES. Whether we consider working in a campaign or donating to one, getting involved in an effort to solve a community problem, contacting a public official, being active locally or nationally, seeking the public good without appealing to government intervention, or engaging in political discussion, those who are well educated and affluent are more likely to take part. To a considerable degree, group differences in political activity on the basis of gender and race or ethnicity are a reflection of the way that political activity is structured by SES. Whatever the origin of disparities in political activity on the basis of gender and race or ethnicity, the result is that public officials are hearing disproportionately from non-Hispanic whites and from men.

5

The Noisy and the Silent: Divergent Preferences and Needs

> These unhappy times [the Great Depression] call for the building of plans that . . . put their faith once more in the forgotten man at the bottom of the economic pyramid.
> —FRANKLIN DELANO ROOSEVELT, RADIO ADDRESS, APRIL 7, 1932[1]

Franklin Delano Roosevelt grew up in privilege. Yet as governor of New York and as president of the United States, he spoke for the "forgotten man at the bottom of the economic pyramid." Despite the inequality of political participation graphically depicted in Chapter 4, might rich people speak for those at the bottom? Is it possible that at the very least, on average those who participate in politics have the same preferences, needs, and concerns as those who do not?

Is Citizen Political Voice Representative?
Voters and Nonvoters

Consider voters first. Are there politically significant policy differences between voters and nonvoters? In an important book on citizen activity, *Who Votes?*, Raymond Wolfinger and Steven Rosenstone reported little or no difference in policy preferences between voters and all citizens as revealed by answers to a series of forced-choice policy questions in the 1972 American

National Election Study.[2] Work following that of Wolfinger and Rosenstone has found similar patterns of quite marginal differences between voters and nonvoters in their responses to survey questions on policy matters.[3]

But a more recent study suggests that the matter is far from settled. Using American National Election Studies data from 1972 until 2008, Jan Leighley and Jonathan Nagler find that Republicans and self-identified conservatives are overrepresented among voters.[4] A closer look at the 2004 data shows that for a variety of economic issues such as trade agreements and overseas tax breaks "voters . . . are *not* representative of the electorate on issues that go to the core of the role of government in modern democracies."[5] In contrast, on social issues like gun control, stem cell research, and abortion, Leighley and Nagler find no systematic bias and consider voters representative of the electorate as a whole.

Beyond Voting—Beyond Attitudes Expressed in Surveys

Voting and attitudes expressed in surveys are among the ways that people's concerns get communicated to decision makers.[6] People also express their perspectives through acts such as contacting officials or protesting that can convey more precise messages to policymakers. Moreover, activities like giving money to political candidates, parties or movements or protesting can be multiplied beyond the enforced equality of ballots. And citizens not only have policy views but, even more fundamentally, they have policy-relevant concerns and needs. People differ in their personal circumstances and dependence on government benefits, in their priorities for government action, and in what they say when they get involved.

BEYOND VOTING: CAMPAIGN WORK AND CONTRIBUTIONS

Using data from the 1990 Citizen Participation Study and the 2005 Citizenship, Involvement, Democracy (CID) Survey project,[7] we were able to locate the average opinion with respect to economic and social issues of several groups defined by their political participation: all citizens, voters, campaign workers, and campaign contributors. We present the results for 2005 in Figure 5.1. The further a group is to the right on the x-axis, the more conservative it is, on average, with regard to economic issues as measured by a question about whether the government should take measures to reduce differences in income levels. The higher on the y-axis, the more conservative it is, on average, in terms of such social issues as abortion and gay rights.[8]

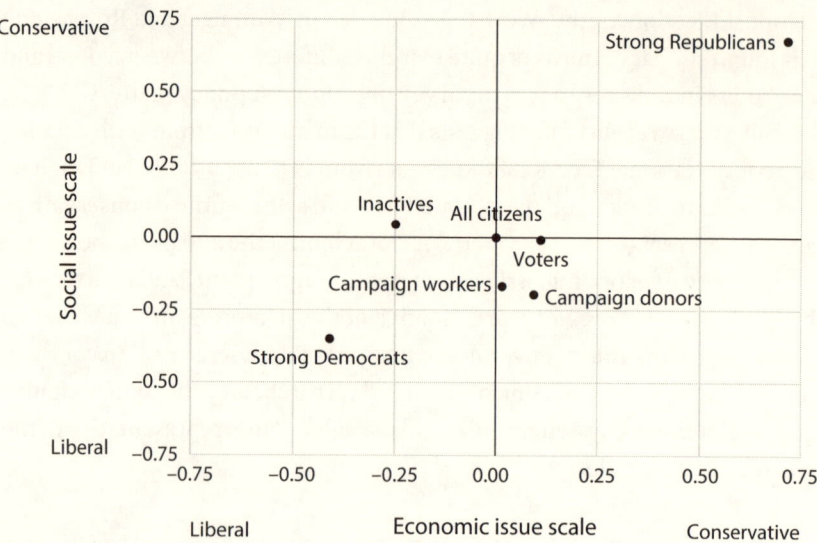

FIGURE 5.1. Mean Social and Economic Issue Positions of All Citizens, Inactives, Strong Partisans, and Election Activists
Source: Citizenship, Involvement, Democracy Survey (2006).
Note: The one-item economic issue scale and the three-item social issue scale are described in the text. The scales were constructed so that the position for "all citizens" was at zero and they ran from more liberal (negative values) to more conservative (positive values).

Figure 5.1 also locates the average opinions of those who consider themselves Strong Democrats and Strong Republicans. As expected, the strong partisans are more extreme—with Democrats more liberal and Republicans more conservative—on both the economic and social dimensions.

There are several striking aspects of Figure 5.1. First, these data echo Leighley and Nagler's finding that the average voter is to the right of the average citizen on economic issues (the horizontal dimension) but is at the same location (on the vertical dimension) as the average citizen with respect to opinions on social issues. Second, opinion on social issues among campaign activists—whether they give time or money—is, on average, more liberal than among voters or all citizens. That is, compared to all citizens and voters, campaign activists have attitudes that push American politics in a less conservative direction on social issues like abortion and gay rights. Third, those who give money to politics push in a conservative direction on economic policy. In contrast, those who are not active are more liberal on economic issues but somewhat more conservative on social issues.

Data from 1990 show a remarkably similar pattern, but amplify these results in an important way. The 1990 questionnaire asked about the *size* of campaign contributions. Compared to all citizens, all voters and, even, all contributors, those who made large campaign contributions were considerably more conservative on economic issues.[9]

Representing Moderate and Extreme Opinions in an Era of Polarization

We have just seen that political activists differ from the average citizen in the direction of their opinions. There is another way to think about the representativeness of political voice—in terms of the *extremity* of opinion. Do political activists tend to take more extreme positions, so that the moderate middle is underrepresented?

The debate on whether the party polarization so evident in Congress has reached down to the level of ordinary citizens provides us with clues. Alan Abramowitz shows that engaged citizens—who are well educated, politically interested, and politically active—are also less centrist in their political views, a relationship that has become more pronounced since the early part of this century.[10] Inverting this logic leads us to expect that political voice underrepresents moderate opinions. Figure 5.2.A considers seven categories of people in the 2012 American National Election Study (ANES) ranging from those on the left (extremely liberal) to those on the right (extremely conservative), according to their response to a standard survey item measuring liberalism or conservatism with regard to the percentage undertaking at least one of seven high-information activities.[11] The V-shaped line indicates that those who are either extremely conservative or extremely liberal are much more politically active than those in the middle who define themselves as "moderate" or "middle of the road." In other words, public officials are hearing disproportionately from those at the extremes at the expense of moderates.

We find the same pattern when we examine two political issues using 2012 ANES data. The first, shown in Figure 5.2.B, substitutes a scale of attitudes on economic issues for the measure of overall liberalism or conservatism.[12] As before, the line showing participation scores for people defined by their economic liberalism or conservatism is V-shaped, indicating that that those at the extremes of economic liberalism or conservatism are much more active than those whose attitudes on economic issues are moderate or

5.2.A. Percentage active by overall ideology scale

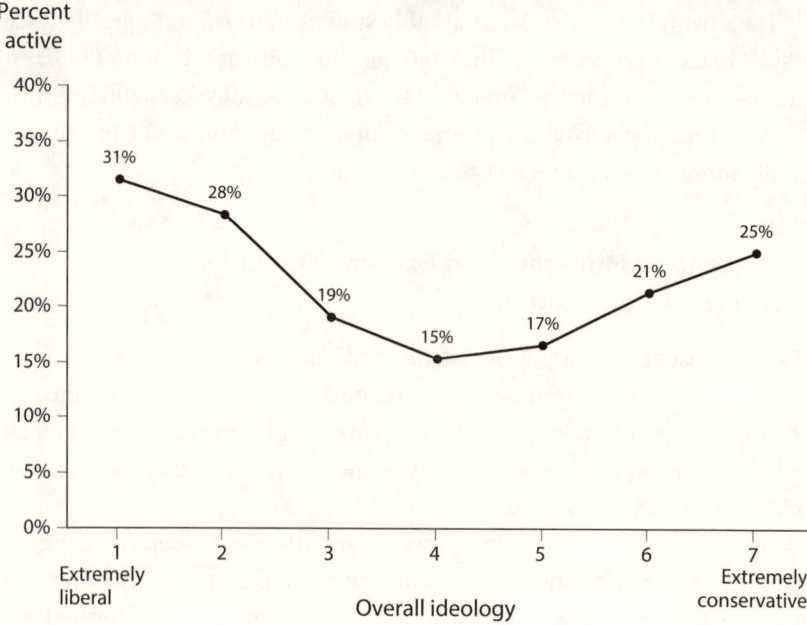

5.2.B. Percentage active by political activity and economic issue scale

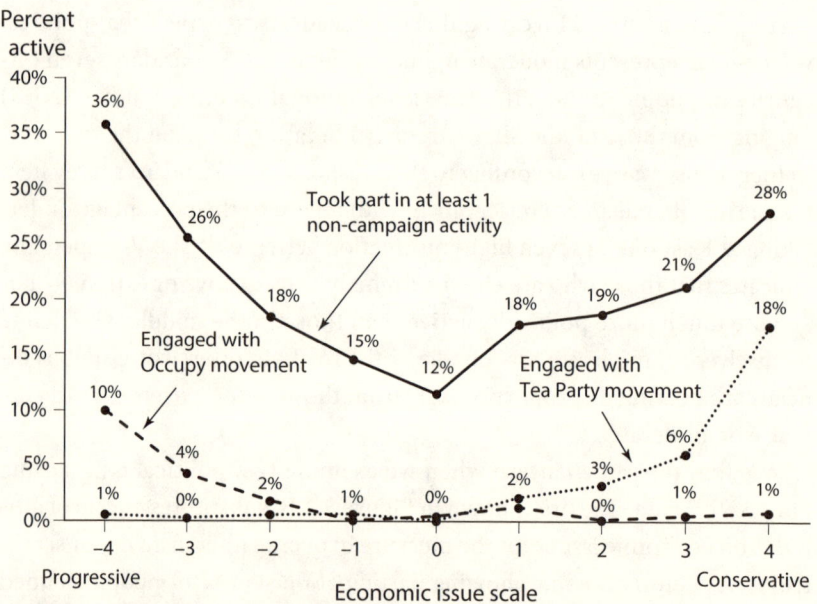

FIGURE 5.2. Political Activity by Extremity of Political Attitudes
Source: American National Election Study (2012).
Note: Measure of overall activity is having participated in at least one of seven information-rich acts described in the notes. Respondents are defined as having engaged with a movement if they reported that either they "actively participated" or had, "in the past 12 months . . . attended a meeting, protest, rally or any other event associated" with it.

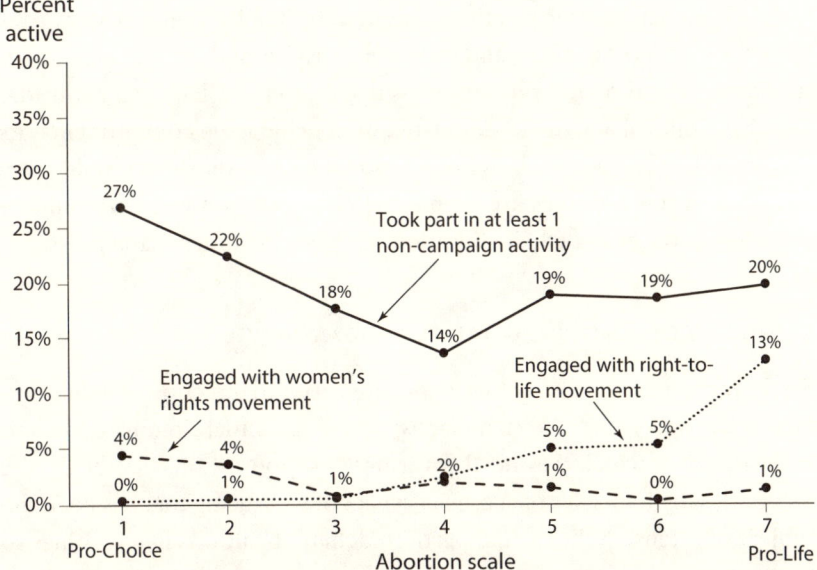

FIGURE 5.2. Political Activity by Extremity of Political Attitudes (*continued*)

mixed. Thus, once again, the moderates are whispering, while those far to their left and far to their right have megaphones. Figure 5.2.B contains two other lines indicating activity associated with the Occupy movement on the left and the Tea Party (Taxed Enough Already) movement on the right.[13] As might be expected, activity associated with the Occupy movement rises sharply among those who are at the left end of the scale measuring economic attitudes, and activity in a group associated with the Tea Party rises even more sharply among those who are at the right end of the scale.

The other issue, shown in Figure 5.2.C, is abortion, measured by a seven-point scale in which the most pro-choice position is on the far left and the most pro-life position is on the far right. Consistent with what we have seen for overall ideology and for economic issues, the V-shaped pattern indicates that public officials are hearing a lot more from those with extreme opinions on abortion than from those who are middle of the road. Figure 5.2.C also gives information about issue-relevant movement activity. The bottom two lines in the figure show the proportion in each group defined by attitudes on abortion who are active in the women's rights and the pro-life movements. Respondents who express the most unambiguous pro-choice views have some tendency to be affiliated with the women's rights movement, and there

100 CHAPTER 5

is a distinct uptick in the probability of pro-life movement activity among those with the strongest pro-life attitudes.[14]

The noncentrist issue positions espoused by Tea Party and Occupy supporters on economic issues and by women's rights and pro-life movement supporters on abortion reinforce our discussion in Chapter 3 about the way that political activity is stimulated by specific issue commitments. As predicted by the Civic Voluntarism Model (CVM), those who hold issue positions at the extremes are even more politically active than would be expected on the basis of their education, income, and other characteristics.[15]

BASIC NEEDS AND UNEQUAL POLITICAL VOICE

Not only are activists distinctive in the intensity and direction of their opinions, but they also differ from nonactivists in their actual circumstances and in the extent to which they need government support. Consider the data in Table 5.1, which focuses on a crucial aspect of well-being that has been the subject of intense political and partisan debate: health. When it comes to health needs, the electoral activists and campaign contributors from whom

TABLE 5.1. Are Activists Typical? Health

	Nonvoters	Political Inactives[a]	All Respondents	Top 12 percent in Activity[b]	Campaign Contributors
Health "excellent" or "very good"[c]	36%	44%	49%	53%	59%
Has health-care insurance	76%	77%	85%	92%	92%
Able to pay for health care[d]	37%	48%	56%	72%	74%
Put off health care[e]	34%	25%	23%	17%	11%
N	470	438	2,054	252	236

Source: American National Election Study (2012).
[a]Respondent may or may not have voted but did not engage in any of ten election-related activities (other than voting).
[b]Top 12 percent on a scale of ten election-related activities (other than voting).
[c]Respondent rates current health as "excellent" or "very good."
[d]Respondent considers it "extremely" or "very likely" that he or she will be able to pay for all health-care costs in next twelve months.
[e]Respondent or someone in the household has put off getting regular health care ("getting regular checkups and vaccinations as well as treatment for illness and injury") during the past twelve months because of the cost.

TABLE 5.2. Are Activists Typical? Cutting Back to Make Ends Meet and Receipt of Means-Tested Benefits

	Cut Back to Make Ends Meet[a]	Received Means-Tested Benefits[b]
Inactives	59%	17%
All respondents	46%	9%
Voters	40%	6%
Campaign workers	40%	5%
Campaign contributors	35%	2%

Source: Citizen Participation Study (1990).
[a]Did any of the following to make ends meet: put off medical or dental treatment, delayed paying the rent or making house payments, cut back on the amount or quality of food, or worked extra hours or took an extra job.
[b]Indicated that they or any family member in the household received food stamps, Aid to Families with Dependent Children, housing subsidies, or Medicaid.

public officials hear are not typical of the public. In 2012, they were considerably more likely to assess their health as "very good" or "excellent" and, because the Affordable Care Act had not yet kicked in at the time that this survey was conducted, more likely to report having health insurance. Contributors were twice as likely as nonvoters to say prospectively that were "extremely" or "very" likely to be able to pay for all their health care in the next twelve months and only one-third as likely to report retrospectively, that, within the last twelve months, they had put off regular health care such as checkups and vaccinations or treatment for an illness or injury because of the cost.

The voters to whom politicians are ultimately responsible and the campaign activists and contributors to whom candidates are exposed and, presumably, beholden differ substantially from the inactives, whose experiences are less visible. The distinctiveness of campaign contributors with respect to such experiences is noteworthy. Observers of elections have commented that the need for candidates to raise vast sums of money to make a credible run for office implies that they spend more and more time rubbing elbows with wealthy donors rather than interacting with constituents. The consequence is that they are more likely to encounter the rarified concerns and experiences of the affluent and less likely to come into contact with those who face such basic problems as needing health care or shelter.[16]

The same pattern emerges in Table 5.2, which presents similar data for government benefit programs from the 1990 Citizen Participation Study.

TABLE 5.3. Political Activity Related to Government Benefit Programs by Benefits Recipients[a]

	Among Those Who Receive Income Benefits		Among Those Who Receive Medical Benefits	
	AFDC[b]	Social Security[c]	Medicaid[b]	Medicare[c]
Vote	10%	25%	10%	26%
Campaign contribution	0%	6%	0%	5%
Contact public official	6%	7%	3%	6%
Organization member	2%	24%	4%	22%
N	109	546	123	423

Source: Citizen Participation Study (1990).
[a]Respondents who indicated that they or any family member in the household received a particular government benefit were asked whether they had, in the past five years, taken into account the position of a candidate in relation to the program in question in deciding how to vote, made a campaign contribution with the program in mind, contacted an official to complain about the program, or belonged to an organization concerned about the program.
[b]Means tested.
[c]Not means tested.

Respondents were asked whether they had been forced to do any of the following to make ends meet: put off medical or dental treatment, delay paying the rent or making house payments, cut back on the amount or quality of food, or work extra hours or take an extra job. They were also asked whether they or any member of their immediate family living with them received any of the following: housing subsidies, Medicaid, or the means-tested government benefits then known as food stamps and Aid to Families with Dependent Children (AFDC).[17] The campaign contributors are, once again, distinctive in having been much less likely than voters, or especially those who undertook no activity at all, to have reported cutting back on essential expenses or receiving means-tested government benefits. Those whose political quiescence renders them less visible have very different life experiences than the people whom candidates encounter at campaign fund-raisers.

Beneficiaries of such programs clearly have incentives to be politically active in defense of these programs. The 1990 Citizen Participation survey asked those who received some form of government benefit whether they engaged in political activity in relation to that program. Table 5.3 presents data about political activity by beneficiaries of four federal programs: two programs providing income support (AFDC and Social Security) and two providing medical care (Medicaid and Medicare).[18] Each category includes one means-tested program assisting the indigent and a second benefiting elderly people regardless of income that is not means tested.

It is striking whose interests are represented when program beneficiaries exercise political voice. In each case, the beneficiaries of programs that are not means tested were more active than their counterparts in means-tested programs. For some forms of activity, the differences are quite small; for others, the disparities are substantial. While relatively few program beneficiaries made campaign contributions in relation to the program, it is striking, if hardly surprising, that not a single beneficiary of a means-tested benefit did so. Presumably reflecting the role of AARP, the massive membership association that acts as the political advocate for those who are fifty and older, the disparities with respect to joining an organization concerned about the government program from which they benefit are especially noteworthy. In summary, among recipients of non-means-tested benefits, 44 percent undertook at least one political activity in relation to that benefit; among recipients of means-tested benefits, only 18 percent did so.

What Do They Say?

A constant refrain of leaders of movements that range from the Tea Party to Black Lives Matter is that their supporters must mobilize politically because no one is listening to their particular concerns. This formulation suggests that what matters is not just what activists think about the issues on the preselected menu presented in a survey but what issues they care enough about to make the subject of their activity. In the context of a survey, affluent liberals might register their views about police behavior or homelessness, but are these the issues about which they organize community efforts or send e-mails to public officials? Or is their political involvement animated instead by a concern with the environment, foreign policy toward Cuba, or a narrow issue connected with work? To assess whether citizen voice through individual activity is representative, we need to consider the actual messages that accompany that activity.

In the 1990 Citizen Participation Study, we inquired about the issues that animate citizen activity. Respondents who reported having taken part in some form of political activity were asked whether there were "any issues or problems ranging from public policy issues to community, family, or personal concerns" that led to the activity. For those who replied that there was such an issue, we followed up with an open-ended question about the

> **BOX 5.1** Issues Mentioned by Political Activists
>
> *Basic human needs*: various government benefits (welfare, AFDC, food stamps, housing subsidies, Social Security, Medicare, and Medicaid); unemployment (either as an economic issue or in terms of the respondent's own circumstances); housing or homelessness; health or health care; poverty or hunger; aid to the handicapped or handicapped rights.
> *Taxes*: all references to taxes at any governmental level.
> *Economic issues*: local or national economic performance; inflation; budget issues or the budget deficit; government spending; other economic issues.
> *Abortion*: all references to abortion, whether pro-choice, pro-life, or ambiguous.
> *Social issues*: traditional morality; pornography; family planning, teenage pregnancy, sex education, or contraception; school prayer; gay rights or homosexuality.
> *Education*: educational issues (school reform, school voucher plans, etc.); problems or issues related to schooling of family members; guaranteed student loans.
> *Environment*: specific environmental issues (such as clean air, toxic wastes) or environmental concerns in general; wildlife preservation; animal rights.
> *Crime or drugs*: crime; gangs; safety in the streets; drugs.
> *International*: relations with particular nations or to foreign policy in general; defense policy or defense spending; peace, arms control, or international human rights issues.

content of those concerns. The bulk of the replies, 86 percent, contained recognizable public policy issues.[19]

We coded the verbatim responses into the nine categories, presented in Box 5.1, that reflect the dominant policy concerns of citizen activists. The categories reflect in part the era in which the survey was conducted. Had the data been collected twenty-five years earlier, different issues—for example, the war in Vietnam or civil rights—would have figured prominently. Had we been able to replicate the study a quarter century later, some issues—for example, pornography, which has been rendered politically moot by virtue of its easy availability on the Internet—would undoubtedly have fallen out. Others, such as gun control or economic inequality, for which there were so few mentions in 1990 that they were not included under our rubrics, might have gained greater prominence. But overall, we were struck that categories constructed in 1990 do a surprisingly good job of accommodating the issues on the political agenda today.

ECONOMIC CIRCUMSTANCES

Although those who are advantaged and disadvantaged[20] in terms of education and income are similar in having wide-ranging policy concerns, as shown on Table 5.4, they differ in the distribution of their concerns.[21] Compared with the issue-based activity[22] of the advantaged, the activity of the disadvantaged is more than twice as likely—and the activity of respondents

TABLE 5.4. What Respondents Say: Issue-Based Political Activity (Information-rich acts only)[a]

	All	Advantaged[b]	Disadvantaged[c]	Receives Means-Tested Benefits
Proportion of issue-based activity animated by concern about:				
Basic human needs	10%	8%	21%	32%
Taxes	6%	6%	4%	8%
Economic issues (except taxes)	5%	7%	1%	1%
Abortion	8%	11%	0%	4%
Social issues (except abortion)	2%	1%	5%	6%
Education	12%	15%	10%	18%
Environment	9%	8%	2%	2%
Crime or drugs	9%	6%	10%	8%
Foreign policy	3%	3%	0%	0%
Number of respondents[d]	2,517	425	480	288
Number of issue-based acts[d]	1,556	432	123	73

Source: Citizen Participation Study (1990).
[a]Information-rich acts are those in which an explicit message can be sent to policymakers: contacting, protesting, campaign work or contribution accompanied by a communication, informal community activity, or voluntary service on a local board. The numbers in the cells represent the proportion of such acts having identifiable issue content for which there was a reference to the particular issue.
[b]Advantaged: At least some college and family income of $50,000 or more.
[c]Disadvantaged: No education beyond high school and family income below $20,000.
[d]Numbers shown are the weighted numbers of cases and issue-based acts.

in families receiving means-tested benefits four times as likely—to have been animated by concerns about basic human needs: poverty, jobs, housing, health, and the like. Moreover, the activity of the disadvantaged is more likely to have been motivated by concern about drugs or crime. In contrast, the activity of the advantaged is more likely to have been inspired by abortion, the environment, or economic issues (such as taxes, government spending, or the budget).

When we consider the actual number of communications, however, a very different story emerges. Because the disadvantaged are so much less active than the advantaged, public officials actually hear less about issues of basic human needs from the disadvantaged than from the slightly smaller group of advantaged respondents—even though references to basic human needs occupy relatively greater space in the bundle of communications emanating from the disadvantaged.

Not only are the disadvantaged more concerned about basic human needs, their messages differ in two fundamental ways from those sent by others. First, when the disadvantaged communicate with public officials about such matters of basic human need as hunger or homelessness, they are much more likely (in 56 percent of the cases) than the advantaged (in only 8 percent of the cases) to be concerned about problems that affect them personally, such as a question about eligibility for Social Security, a complaint about the conditions in a housing project, or a request by a disabled respondent for special transportation, to cite some actual examples from the survey. Even when respondents framed human-needs issues as a matter of policy rather than as a solely personal concern, the disadvantaged were much more likely to report that the problem is one that affects themselves or their families as well as others in the community. All in all, of those who communicated to public officials about issues of basic human needs, 71 percent of the disadvantaged but only 29 percent of the advantaged were discussing something with an immediate impact on themselves or their families.

Second, the responses of the advantaged and the disadvantaged can be distinguished in terms of their actual policy content.[23] To the extent that disadvantaged respondents make policy statements about such issues in association with political activity—as opposed to making statements or requests regarding their own personal circumstances—they never suggest reducing public attention to issues of basic human needs. In contrast, the policy messages about matters of basic human needs originating with advantaged respondents are quite mixed with respect to whether they urge increased or decreased support for government programs aimed at alleviating problems like poverty, hunger, and homelessness. Some advantaged respondents make such statements as "welfare should be done away with" or that they have a "dislike of big government, welfare state, and big brothers."

RACE OR ETHNICITY

We can ask analogous questions about the messages that accompany the participation of non-Hispanic whites, African Americans, and Latinos. Table 5.5 shows that African Americans and Latinos were much more likely to mention basic human needs, education, children or youth, civil rights or minorities, and crime or drugs. Non-Hispanic white respondents are more

TABLE 5.5. What Latinos, African Americans, and Non-Hispanic Whites Say: Issue-Based Political Activity (Information-rich acts only)[a]

	Non-Hispanic Whites	African-Americans	Latinos
Proportion of issue-based activity animated by concern about:			
Basic human needs	9%	13%	13%
Taxes	7%	3%	3%
Economic issues (except taxes)	6%	2%	1%
Abortion	9%	3%	3%
Social issues (except abortion)	2%	2%	2%
Education	11%	17%	19%
Children or youth (except education)	5%	12%	10%
Environment	10%	1%	9%
Crime or drugs	7%	25%	16%
International	3%	1%	4%
Civil rights or minorities	1%	6%	6%
Number of respondents[b]	2,074	233	141
Number of issue-based acts[b]	1,341	129	50

Source: Citizen Participation Study (1990).

[a]Information-rich acts are those in which an explicit message can be sent to policymakers: contacting, protesting, campaign work or contribution accompanied by a communication, informal community activity, or voluntary service on a local board. The numbers in the cells represent the proportion of such acts having identifiable issue content for which there was a reference to the particular issue.

[b]Numbers shown are the weighted numbers of cases and issue-based acts.

likely to have focused on taxes and other economic issues. They are also more likely to mention abortion.

The particular emphasis in these 1990 data on issues of crime, violence, and drugs by African Americans and Latinos deserves mention. Among candidates and public officials, these issues have been the traditional bailiwick of non-Hispanic white conservatives. In contrast, the minority and non-Hispanic white liberal politicians who represent African American and Latino constituencies have often kept issues like drug use and crime at arm's length. It is noteworthy how importantly these issues figured on the agenda of the citizen activists whose communities are most affected by them. More systematic content analysis reveals that blacks and Latinos were somewhat more likely than non-Hispanic whites to mention drugs and to refer to their own neighborhoods or communities in discussing these issues, while non-Hispanic whites were somewhat more likely to discuss a neighborhood effort to set up a crime watch. With the more recent emergence of the opioid crisis and the Black Lives Matter movement, we would expect a different pattern if we conducted the survey again today.

We were also interested in the extent to which the concerns associated with political activity involved civil rights issues. We include under this rubric both general references to "civil rights," "racial issues," or "discrimination" and specific concerns—for example, getting translators for Spanish-speaking prison inmates, hiring more minority teachers in the school system, or opening up the all-Anglo cheerleading squad to Hispanics in a majority-Mexican-American high school. Table 5.5 indicates that 6 percent of the information-rich, issue-based activity of both African Americans and Latinos involved reference to such issues. These issues figured in a very small portion, less than 1 percent, of the participation of non-Hispanic whites. Because African Americans and Latinos constituted only a fraction of the population, and because in 1990, African Americans were somewhat—and Latinos were substantially—less likely to participate than were non-Hispanic whites, only an extremely small proportion of the messages communicated through the medium of information-rich participation concerned policy matters germane to civil rights or racial or ethnic minorities. Moreover, public officials heard as much about these matters from non-Hispanic whites as from African Americans and Latinos combined. In terms of co ntent, since some of the references to civil rights issues by non-Hispanic whites consisted of negative views of affirmative action, what public officials heard from non-Hispanic whites was more mixed than what they heard from either of the other groups.

GENDER

Given women's traditional role in the family as well as the particularistic orientation to politics that has been ascribed to them since the ancient Greeks, women might be expected to bring to politics narrower, more personal or family concerns. To investigate, we examined the contacts with government officials, which are often focused on narrow personal concerns. We discovered that men and women who got in touch with public officials did not differ in whether they were motivated by personal or public concerns. Discussing their most recent contact, 22 percent of the men and 21 percent of the women indicated that the subject was a matter of particularized concern. Thirty-five percent of the women who contacted public officials indicated that the issue of concern affects the whole community, and 25 percent stated that it affects the entire nation (or the whole world); the analogous figures for men who contacted officials were 38 percent and 22 percent, respectively.

TABLE 5.6. What Men and Women Say: Issue-Based Political Activity (Information-rich acts only)[a]

	Men	Women
Proportion of issue-based activity animated by concern about:		
Basic human needs	9%	10%
Taxes	7%	5%
Economic issues (except taxes)	6%	4%
Abortion	5%	12%
Social issues (except abortion)	2%	2%
Education	9%	15%
Children or youth (except education)	5%	6%
Environment	9%	9%
Crime or drugs	8%	9%
International	4%	2%
Civil rights or minorities	<1%	1%
Number of respondents[b]	1,191	1,327
Number of issue-based acts[b]	821	736

Source: Citizen Participation Study (1990).
[a]Information-rich acts are those in which an explicit message can be sent to policymakers: contacting, protesting, campaign work or contribution accompanied by a communication, informal community activity, or voluntary service on a local board. The numbers in the cells represent the proportion of such acts having identifiable issue content for which there was a reference to the particular issue.
[b]Numbers shown are the weighted numbers of cases and issue-based acts.

When it comes to the actual issues that animate activity, there was also more similarity than difference between women and men in the 1990 data. Table 5.6 shows the proportion of information-rich, issue-based activity arising from concern about various subjects. Both men and women participate about many things with a similar, though not identical profile of concerns. For example, education figures more importantly in the activity of women, who have traditionally been the family members more likely to deal with teachers and schools. Also, women were twice as likely as men to refer to abortion.

Apart from the issue of abortion, women's issues—for example, sexual harassment or discrimination against women—were mentioned extremely rarely as the subject matter of activity. Women discussed these issues in connection with just under 1 percent of their information-rich, issue-based activity, and men did so even less frequently. All those who did act on this concern thought that the government should be making greater efforts to help women. But overall, public officials were hearing very little on the subject in 1990.

Conclusion

What decision makers hear from political activists is not representative of the opinions, concerns, and needs of the general population. Activists are more conservative on economic issues and sometimes more liberal on social issues. They are more extreme on both economic and social issues, so that the moderate middle is underrepresented. Activists have less need for health care, they are less likely to have to cut back on spending to make ends meet, and they are less likely to use government benefit programs. In addition, those who benefit from such non-means-tested programs as Social Security or Medicare are much more likely to undertake political action—for example, to make a voting decision or to contact a public official—in association with that program than are beneficiaries of such means-tested programs as food stamps (now SNAP) or Medicaid, who are by definition economically needy.

As for the messages sent through political participation, activists with low levels of education and income were much more likely than their more advantaged counterparts to report that their activity was animated by a matter of basic human need, such as hunger, housing, or health care. Similarly, African Americans and Latinos were more likely than non-Hispanic whites to indicate that their political participation was anchored in a concern about basic human needs. In addition, when these groups characterized their issue-based political activity, they were much more likely to identify a problem in their own lives. It is a truism about lobbying that public officials listen more carefully to those who are directly affected by the policies they advocate and who speak on their own behalf. Presumably, the analogous principle applies to communications from individuals: stories about basic human needs sound different to policymakers when told by those who are in need. Stories about the need to control crime in the community sound different to policymakers when told by residents.

Looking more closely, we discovered that, because of differences in rates of participation—and, in the case of Latinos and African Americans, because they are numerically relatively small groups in the adult population—public officials are hearing less from the disadvantaged or from racial or ethnic minorities, even about the issues that weigh relatively heavily in their bundles of participatory concerns. Compared to those who are well educated and affluent, the disadvantaged send fewer participatory messages concerning matters of basic human needs. What is more, in terms of the actual content of such messages, the advantaged communicate a mixed set of policy preferences with respect to whether government should be doing more to address issues of basic human needs. In contrast, to the extent that they speak at all, disadvantaged participants are uniformly favorable to greater government assistance.

In short, we have good reason to believe that public officials are receiving a skewed set of messages about what citizens care about, want, and need in policy terms.

6

Do Digital Technologies Make a Difference?

- More than 116,000 Texans signed an online petition—posted at Change.org by a victim of sexual assault—proposing to alter Texas prison rules to prohibit those serving terms for violent crimes from going online to seek pen pals.
- Business leaders sent letters and e-mails urging Tennessee legislators and Governor Bill Haslam to reject proposed legislation requiring all students in public schools and universities to use bathrooms and locker rooms that matched their gender at birth.
- In a state with no mandate for maximum class size and larger-than-average public school classrooms, a Portland, Oregon, parent whose first grader was assigned to a class with thirty-two students posted a video on YouTube advocating smaller classes.
- Seeking to persuade the state to require their insurers to cover their losses, members of the Connecticut Coalition against Crumbling Basements used Facebook and Twitter to locate other Connecticut homeowners whose basements were collapsing as the result of defective concrete.[1]

Digital technologies have changed the way we shop, navigate unfamiliar streets, listen to music, make airline reservations, keep up with friends, and look for romance. The ongoing technological revolution has also opened up new possibilities for citizen politics: for gaining political information more quickly and easily than ever before; for broadcasting opinions about political subjects to friends, to the media, and to public officials; and for disseminating messages to large numbers of like-minded people and coordinating them for joint action; and for undertaking such political actions as registering to vote, making a campaign contribution, or signing a petition from the comfort of an easy chair.[2] Digital participation certainly broadens the options for taking part, and it may bring new people into politics, but is it bringing *new kinds of people* into political activity? Even if these rapidly evolving technologies are effective in generating additional political activity, is the new activity simply replicating the same participatory inequalities? The development of the Internet immediately generated optimistic predictions about its democratic effects:

> Extensive claims have been made about how the Internet changes everything, including politics. Enthusiasts have speculated that this medium will at long last eliminate the dominance of the established mass media, create an engaged and active citizenry, and redistribute power in more egalitarian ways. They assert that we should free democratic theorizing from the constraints of advanced industrial or post-industrial society and replace liberal democratic pluralism with direct democracy, strong democracy or more radical democratic theories.[3]

We, too, were initially hopeful that digital technologies, if more and more widely accessible, might act as the trip wire disrupting participatory inequality.

To investigate whether Internet-based citizen participation alters the powerful association between social class and participation, in the summers of 2008 and 2012, we collaborated with Lee Rainie and Scott Keeter of the Pew Internet and American Life Project to design surveys about the use of digital technologies and about political activity both off and on the Internet.[4] All studies of the impact of digital technologies on democratic politics—including, of course, this one—are hampered by the fact that they report on a moving target. Technological changes clearly proceed much more quickly than the time line for publication in political science.[5]

In addition, these two surveys reflect the particularities of the two presidential campaigns in which Barack Obama, a candidate who made self-conscious efforts to incorporate digital technologies into his campaigns, was running. Obama held special appeal for persons of color as well as younger voters—who tend not to be politically active and, because they have not reached their peak earning years and may not even have completed their educations, have relatively low levels of SES. Therefore, these surveys would be more likely to understate than to overstate the extent of class- and age-based participatory inequalities.

Nevertheless, just as it has become abundantly clear that the anonymity afforded by the Internet (where "nobody knows you're a dog") has hardly led to a flowering of civil discourse, patterns of unequal political voice are replicated in digital participation. Although Internet access has grown, it remains stratified by class and race, a phenomenon widely known as the "digital divide." Moreover, access to the Internet has not led to an upsurge of participation among those who are less likely to take part in traditional ways.

Does the Internet Increase Citizen Participation?

Because the Internet lowers barriers to citizen political activity, observers have been optimistic that the Internet would raise political participation.[6] Certain forms of political participation—in particular, making campaign donations and contacting public officials—are simply easier on the Internet. The networking capacities of the Internet are also suited to facilitate forming political groups, recruiting adherents and sympathizers, and mobilizing them to take political action—either on- or offline. Moreover, the Internet provides a wealth of political information and opportunities for political interaction, discussion, and position taking.

However, the Internet may have the effect of repackaging political activity instead of increasing it.[7] Rather than citizens undertaking additional actions, they might simply be transferring online what they would have undertaken offline. In fact, investigations of whether Internet use enhances political activity show mixed results.[8]

The Digital Divide and Participatory Inequality

Even if it were unambiguous that Internet use increases political participation, more political activity does not necessarily imply a less unequal distribution of activity. While we often associate the Internet with emergent groups and underdog candidates operating on a shoestring and seeking support from the previously inactive, the Internet has also been used effectively by established interests. As Pippa Norris notes, if an increase in political participation derives from the same people, or the same kinds of people, who are already active, a likely result is the replication, or even the exacerbation, of existing political inequalities.[9]

For some time, social observers have been concerned that the digital divide is leaving behind a substantial portion of the public—with implications for equal opportunity in economic life and equal voice in political life. During the 1990s, concern about unequal access to the Internet led to a mandate in the Telecommunications Act of 1996 specifying that "elementary and secondary schools and classrooms, health-care providers, and libraries should have access to advanced telecommunication services."[10] The Act created a program of federal grants under the E-Rate program. According to a September 2000 report by the Department of Education, fully 75 percent of all public schools and districts and 50 percent of libraries had applied for funds under the E-Rate program.[11] By the turn of the twenty-first century, 95 percent of public libraries offered Internet access to patrons.[12]

Although the metaphor of the digital divide originally referred to lack of hardware access and suggests a chasm separating techno haves from the techno have-nots, it is now more appropriate to think of a continuum ranging from those who have no digital access or experience to those who use the Internet with great frequency in a variety of ways on a variety of devices. But what is critical for our concern with participatory inequalities is not simply that some Americans have been left behind in the technological advances of recent decades but that the digital divide mirrors the socioeconomic stratification of political activity in the United States.

Early adopters of new technologies tend to be disproportionately affluent and well educated. If the technology takes off and the price comes down, use becomes more widespread and includes the less affluent, thus reducing stratification. Pew data for 2008 and 2012 about Internet use and, for comparison, cell phone ownership, illustrate that pattern. Overall, in the four years separating the surveys, the share of respondents who could be categorized as Internet users—that is, who either use the Internet or send or receive e-mail, at least occasionally—increased from 75 to 90 percent.[13] At the same time, ownership of cell phones (or other hand-held devices) rose from 75 to 91 percent. Figure 6.1 shows, for five quintiles of socioeconomic status (SES), that both Internet use and cell phone ownership are structured by SES. However, the digital divide has closed much more substantially for cell phone ownership than for Internet use.[14] At the high end of the SES ladder, both Internet use and cell phone ownership were nearly universal in 2008 and 2012. At the low end, while cell phone ownership rose from 45 to 83 percent over the period, Internet use increased less sharply (from 44 to 66 percent).

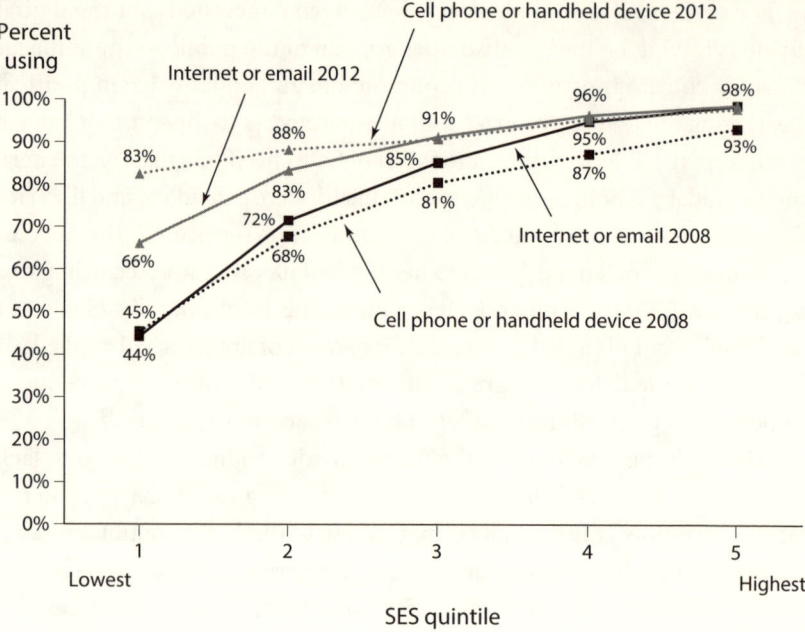

FIGURE 6.1. Internet and Cell Phone Use by SES Quintile, 2008 and 2012
Source: Pew Internet and American Life Surveys (2008 and 2012).

However, an important exception shows up in the pattern of the association between Internet use or cell phone ownership and the characteristics that predict political participation. The young, who are relatively inactive politically, are more likely than their elders to be both Internet users and cell phone owners.[15] Every study of Internet access and use, no matter what the measure, shows a steady decline with age.

Figure 6.2 shows that, in 2012, 96 percent of those between eighteen and twenty-four years of age, compared with only 48 percent of those seventy-one and older, use the Internet or e-mail at least occasionally. The generation gap for cell phone ownership is slightly less pronounced: the corresponding figures are 94 percent and 65 percent. Since the young are less active than their elders in most forms of political participation, digital technologies may have a potentially significant counterstratificational effect. However, this age-related digital divide may diminish as members of the younger generation come of age and replace their tech-phobic elders.[16]

Using the Internet does not necessarily mean using it for political purposes. The overwhelming share of Internet use is for nonpolitical activities that range from purchasing shoes to viewing pornography to keeping up

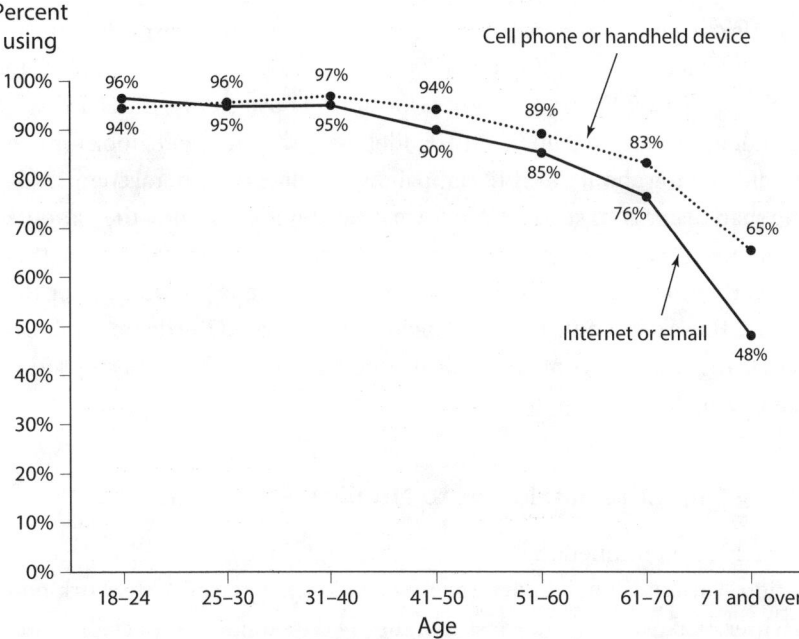

FIGURE 6.2. Internet and Cell Phone Use by Age
Source: Pew Internet and American Life Survey (2012).

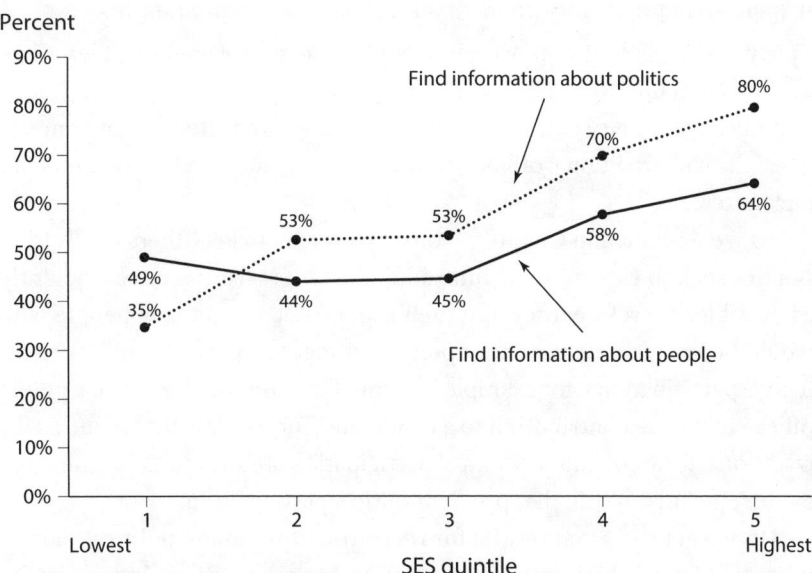

FIGURE 6.3. Finding Information on the Internet about Politics or about Someone You Might Know or Meet, 2012
Source: Pew Internet and American Life Survey (2012).

with friends on a social networking site. How does the use of the Internet for political purposes compare to its use for these economic, personal, and social purposes? Figure 6.3 shows, for Internet users only, the share of respondents at each step up the SES ladder using the Internet to look for news or information about the 2012 campaigns or politics in general compared to the share using it to search for information about somebody they know or might meet. When it comes to using the Internet to find information, there is clearly more class structuring if that information is political rather than social. These data confirm our suspicions that, beyond the demographic biases in digital access, online political opportunities might simply reproduce familiar patterns.

Using Digital Technologies to Mobilize Participation

Earlier we mentioned that digital technologies facilitate political mobilization. Various digital media, ranging from e-mail to social networking to Twitter, make it nearly costless to multiply the number of specially crafted messages targeted at selected publics to recruit political activists.[17] Figure 6.4, which presents 2012 data about the proportion of respondents who were asked to take political action through various media, demonstrates that digital political recruitment figures significantly in mobilization efforts. Thirty-seven percent of those surveyed had been recruited by at least one of the digital methods: an e-mail, a request on a social networking site, a text message, or a tweet. In contrast, 59 percent reported at least one request through traditional offline means: a letter, a phone call, or an in-person encounter.

As we discussed in Chapter 3, those who seek to get others involved in politics seek to expend their time and effort on recruitment as efficiently as possible. Therefore, they aim their requests at the kinds of people who would be likely to say yes and, upon assenting, to follow through with effective participation—for example, a compelling communication to a public official or a large contribution to a candidate. The result is that requests for traditional forms of offline political participation are structured by the same factors, including SES, that predict political participation.

Do we get the same results for recruitment to online political participation? Figure 6.5 shows the association between SES and requests for political activity through on- and offline channels. As expected, offline requests by letter, by phone, or in person rise sharply across the rungs of the SES ladder. Contrary to rosy predictions that the Internet would have an

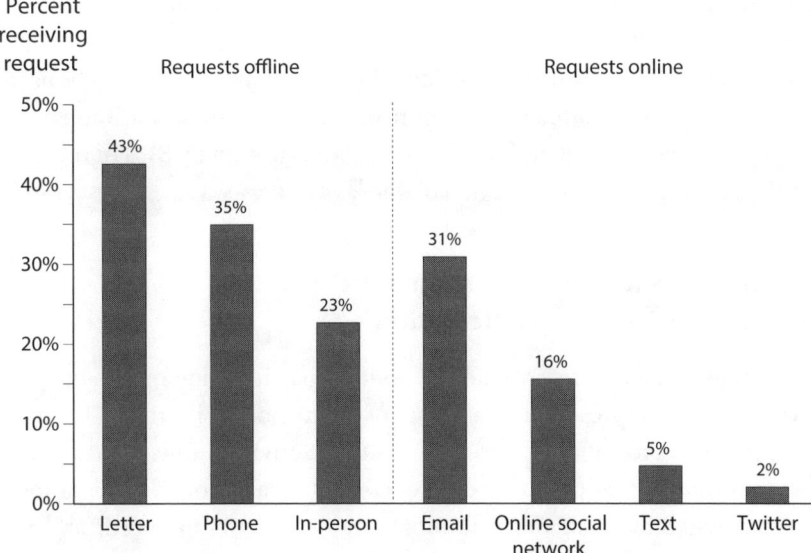

FIGURE 6.4. Requests for Political Activity Offline and Online
Source: Pew Internet and American Life Survey (2012).

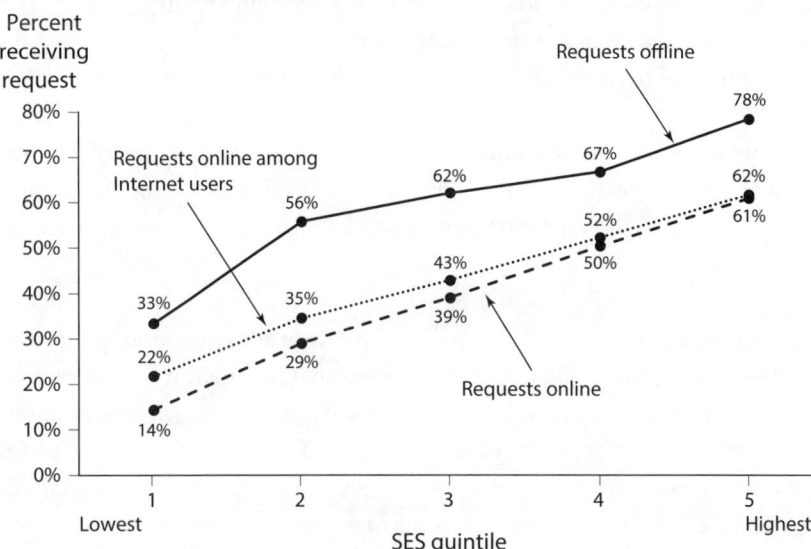

FIGURE 6.5. Requests for Political Activity Online or Offline by SES Quintile
Source: Pew Internet and American Life Survey (2012).
Note: The measure of requests offline is having been asked at least once by letter, by phone, or in person. The measure of requests online is having been asked at least once by e-mail, by text, by tweet, or through a social networking site.

equalizing impact on politics, the likelihood of digital recruitment by e-mail, text, tweet, or through a social networking site increases no less steeply with levels of SES. When we consider digital recruitment of Internet users only, shown by the dotted line in Figure 6.5, the association is still apparent, though somewhat weaker, indicating that stratification by SES of requests is shaped by more than the digital divide.[18]

The Representativeness of Online and Offline Political Participation

We can investigate directly whether political participation on the Internet overcomes the representational biases of offline political activity. The 2012 Pew survey asked about a series of political activities, four of which can be performed either online or offline: contacting a national, state, or local government official; signing a petition; sending a "letter to the editor"; and making a political contribution. Using these items, we constructed separate activity scales for online activity and for offline activity for those acts with online counterparts.[19] Overall, online political participation is somewhat less common than engagement in their traditional offline variants. Twenty-eight percent of respondents took part online in at least one of the four acts, and 41 percent engaged in at least one in its offline version.

Figure 6.6 presents data for quintiles based on SES and shows that, whether on- or offline, political activity rises sharply with SES.[20] The solid top line shows the proportion who undertake offline at least one of the four activities that have online and offline versions; the dashed bottom line shows the proportion who take part in at least one of the online counterparts of these four activities.

The dotted middle line in Figure 6.6 shows the proportion who engage in at least one of the four Internet-based political activities among Internet users—that is, among those who use the Internet or e-mail at least occasionally. On one hand, because Internet use itself has a social class component, when we consider the online political activity of Internet users only, the SES gradient is, not surprisingly, slightly less sharp than when we consider all respondents. On the other hand, the data make clear that lack of access is only a small part of the story of the class structuring of online political activity. At the upper end of the SES scale, where Internet use is nearly universal, the level of online activity is not affected by lack of access to hardware. In contrast, some—but only a small part—of the participatory deficit of those at the bottom end reflects lack of Internet access. Thus, far from acting as a

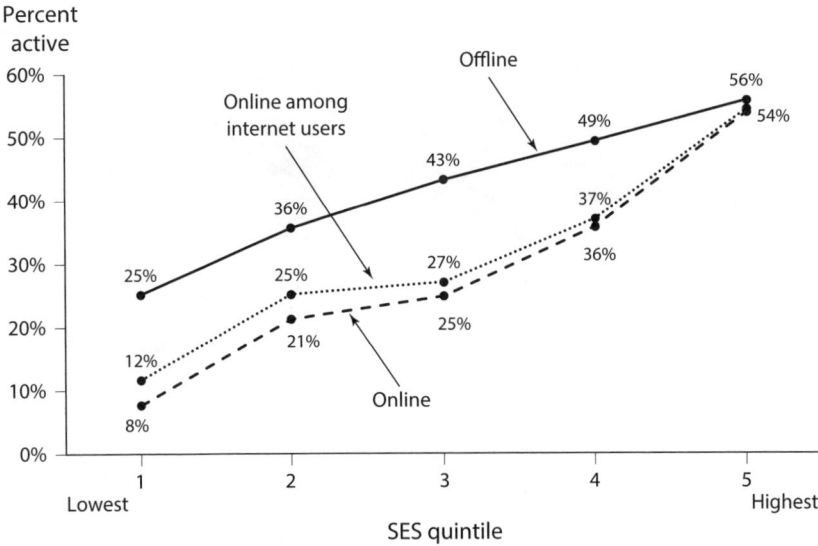

FIGURE 6.6. Political Activity Online or Offline by SES Quintile
Source: Pew Internet and American Life Survey (2012).
Note: The measure of offline political activity is having undertaken at least one of the following offline: contacting a national, state, or local government official; signing a petition; sending a "letter to the editor"; or making a political contribution. The measure of online political activity is having undertaken at least one of these activities online.

great equalizer, political activity on the Internet seems to replicate familiar patterns of socioeconomic stratification. It does so not only because the digital divide has a social class component but, more importantly, because lower-SES Internet users are not using the Internet to take part politically.[21]

The patterns for age groups, shown in Figure 6.7, are quite different. Age is much less powerful in structuring political activity than is SES: the distance between the most and least active of the seven age groups is much smaller than the distance between the lowest and highest of the SES quintiles. Most forms of political participation have been shown to rise with age until they peak in middle age before falling off among the elderly. We see the roughly curvilinear pattern in the scale of four offline acts for which there are online counterparts, shown by the solid top line in the figure. However, when it comes to online activity, shown in the dashed bottom line, we see a contrasting pattern. The likelihood of undertaking online political activity is lower among those older than seventy. For those under seventy, however, there is no relationship between age and online political participation. In contrast to what we observed for offline political activity, the absence of online

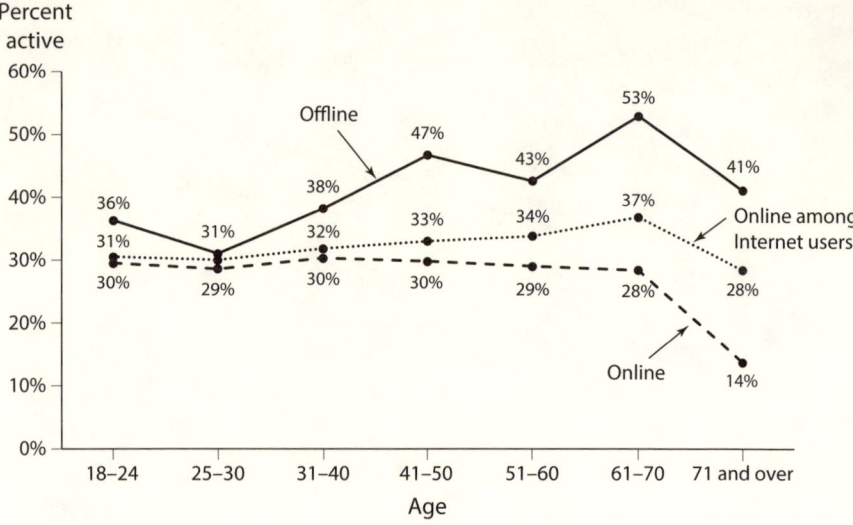

FIGURE 6.7. Political Activity Online or Offline by Age
Source: Pew Internet and American Life Survey (2012).
Note: The measure of offline political activity is having undertaken at least one of the following offline: contacting a national, state, or local government official; signing a petition; sending a "letter to the editor"; or making a political contribution. The measure of online political activity is having undertaken at least one of these activities online.

activity among the elderly represents, we assume, not a fall-off from previous Internet-based participation but instead a case of never having used the Internet. This suspicion gains credence when we consider the online activity of those who use the Internet or e-mail at least occasionally, shown by the dotted middle line in Figure 6.7. Among Internet users, online political participation rises gradually across age groups until it drops off among those over seventy. Still, it is notable that the traditional underrepresentation the young among political activists is not evident for political acts undertaken online.

Citizen Politics and Social Media

The activities just considered are political acts that existed before the advent of the Internet, allowing us to compare them in their off- and online manifestations. Clearly, such a definition of participation is extremely restricted, omitting multiple forms of traditional participation that have no digital analogue: for example, attending a protest, volunteering for a candidate for office, or working with community members to solve a local problem. Reciprocally, there are Internet-based forms of political engagement without an offline counterpart—in particular, political involvement anchored in social media. In the spirit of "the Internet changes everything," we wondered whether the evolving possibilities for political engagement on social media disrupt the recurrent patterns of SES stratification. The past decade has witnessed striking growth in the availability and use of various social media. In the 2008 Pew survey, 25 percent of respondents reported that they used a social networking site like Facebook or LinkedIn or used Twitter. By 2012, that figure had risen sharply to 59 percent. The increase is not simply a matter of the narrowing of the digital divide. Considering Internet users only, the figures are 33 percent and 69 percent, respectively.[22]

Social media provide opportunities for political engagement. A member can, for example, use a social network site to join a group that is involved in political or social issues, to follow political figures, or to post links to political stories or articles. Such possibilities for political engagement through social media do not simply reproduce participation as we have defined it so far. They instead reflect some of the distinctive civic tastes of post-Boomer cohorts: their preference for participatory forms that are anchored in nonhierarchical and informal networks and that eschew such traditional political intermediaries as campaigns, parties, and interest groups.[23]

These possibilities for political engagement through social media sites may lead to conventional forms of online and offline political participation. In a well-known pattern, new technologies initially resemble the older technologies they eventually replace before their unique capacities have developed. For example, before the power of visual images was refined, early campaign ads on television used talking heads with wordy messages suitable for radio. In certain ways, as increasing numbers of politicians move from maintaining Web sites to establishing a presence on Facebook, what is happening is almost the opposite. More conventional forms of political discourse and advocacy have also established a beachhead in the world of social media.

Of course, most social media use has nothing to do with politics. Still, among Internet users, a growing minority—7 percent in 2008 and 29 percent in 2012—used social media for political purposes.[24] Even though these forms of political involvement are, on average, less demanding than the activities that we usually group under the umbrella of political participation, they might indicate future trends.

The data in Figure 6.8 make clear that among Internet users, social media use (of all sorts) has grown substantially in recent years and, not surprisingly, that the young are much more likely than their elders to exploit these rapidly developing Internet capabilities. In both years, social media use declines

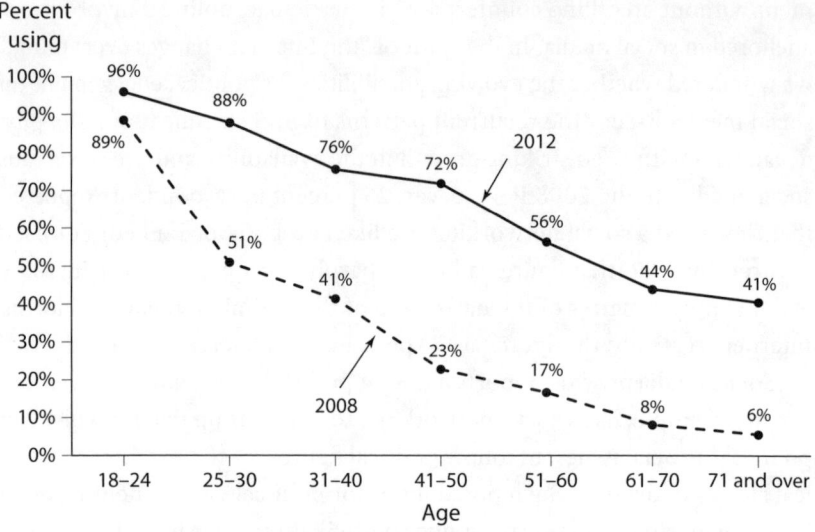

FIGURE 6.8. Social Media Use among Internet Users by Age, 2008 and 2012
Source: Pew Internet and American Life Surveys (2008 and 2012).
Note: To reflect the changing digital environment, the measures of being a social media user were somewhat different in the two surveys. In 2008, a social media user reported using at least one of the following: Twitter; a "micro-blogging service"; or a social networking site such as MySpace, Facebook, or LinkedIn. In 2012, a social media user reported using at least one of the following; Twitter; or a social networking site like Facebook, LinkedIn, or Google Plus.

precipitously as age increases, and in all age groups social media use rose over the four-year period. The increase is much less substantial for those younger than twenty-five, simply because the overwhelming majority of the youngest adults used social media in 2008.

The pattern is similar but not identical for the minority of Internet users who become politically involved on social media. As with general social media use, political involvement on social media falls off sharply across age groups. Once again, there was a marked increase even across a brief period of four years. However, when it comes to political engagement on social media, the growth was less pronounced among older respondents and sharpest among those in their late twenties.

DOES POLITICAL ENGAGEMENT ON SOCIAL MEDIA SEVER THE SES LINK?

When we investigated then-emergent social media in 2008, we were hopeful that the possibilities for political engagement on social media might overcome the familiar structuring of political participation by social class. Figure 6.9 shows social media use among SES groups for all respondents and for Internet users. Consistent with what we have seen, at each step along the SES ladder, social media use is higher in 2012 than in 2008. When we consider all respondents, the digital divide introduces an SES bias in social media use. However, among Internet users, there is no consistent association between SES and social media use. In 2008, Internet users on the lowest rung of the SES ladder were the most likely to be social media users. For the other four SES quintiles, there is no obvious pattern.[25] By 2012, the line for Internet users is essentially flat and shows no association between social media use and SES.

With regard to political involvement on social media, Figure 6.10 shows a somewhat bumpy pattern for 2008, with the digital divide a factor only for the lowest SES group. By 2012, political engagement on social media is not only more common at all levels of SES, but a familiar pattern also can be discerned. Although the slope is not especially steep, political engagement

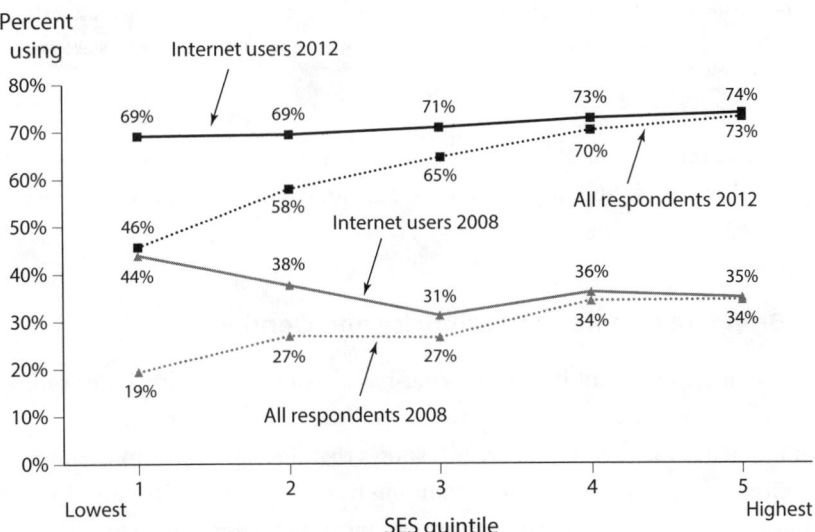

FIGURE 6.9. Social Media Use by SES Quintile, 2008 and 2012
Source: Pew Internet and American Life Surveys (2008 and 2012).
Note: To reflect the changing digital environment, the measures of being a social media user were somewhat different in the two surveys. In 2008, a social media user reported using at least one of the following: Twitter; a 'micro-blogging service'; or a social networking site such as MySpace, Facebook, or LinkedIn. In 2012, a social media user reported using at least one of the following; Twitter; or a social networking site like Facebook, LinkedIn, or Google Plus.

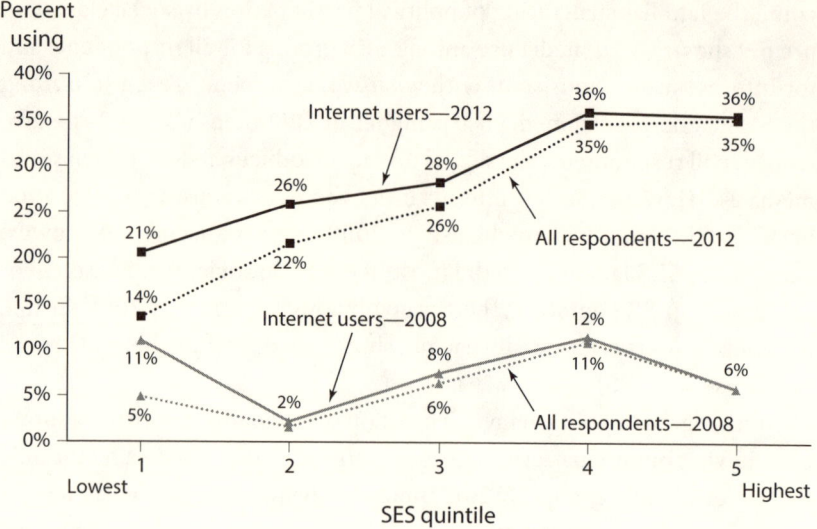

FIGURE 6.10. Political Use of Social Media by SES Quintile, 2008 and 2012
Source: Pew Internet and American Life Surveys (2008 and 2012).
Note: The measures are slightly different in 2008 and 2012. However, the definition of political use of social media is essentially having done at least one of the following: belonging to a social network site involved in political or social issues; following an elected official or candidate for office on a social networking site; or posting political news or one's own thoughts on political or social issues.

on social media rises steadily with SES, a pattern that is only partially explained by the digital divide. Once again, social class intrudes into the expression of political voice.

A Brief Note on Race or Ethnicity and Gender

Before leaving the subject of Internet-based political activity, let us return to our concern with two other sets of politically relevant categories: race or ethnicity, and gender. Figure 6.11 shows that, just as we saw in Chapter 4, political participation is highest among non-Hispanic whites and lowest among Hispanics, with African Americans in between. However, the disparities in political activity among the three groups are wider for online than for offline participation. One striking aspect of the data in Figure 6.11 is that, in contrast to what we saw for SES-based differences in political activity, the gaps do not narrow when we consider the online participation of Internet users only. Further analysis shows that socioeconomic disparities among non-Hispanic whites, African Americans, and Latinos do not fully

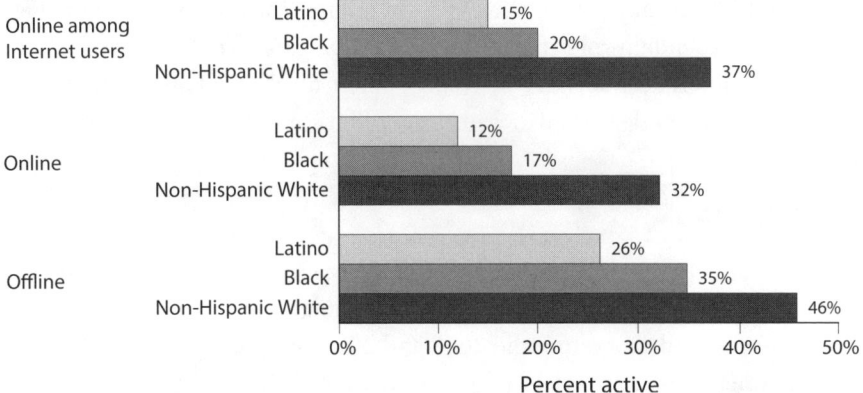

FIGURE 6.11. Political Activity Offline and Online by Race and Ethnicity
Source: Pew Internet and American Life Survey (2012).
Note: The measure of offline political activity is having undertaken at least one of the following offline: contacting a national, state, or local government official; signing a petition; sending a "letter to the editor"; or making a political contribution. The measure of online political activity is having undertaken at least one of these activities online.

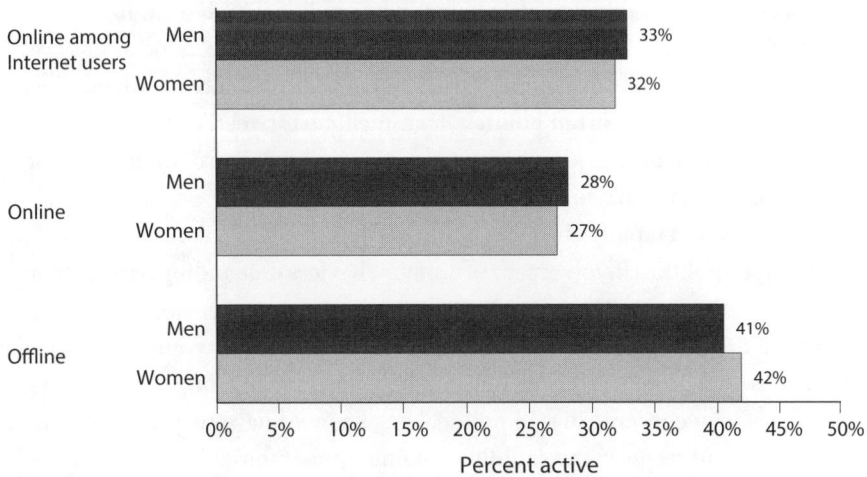

FIGURE 6.12. Political Activity Offline and Online by Gender
Source: Pew Internet and American Life (2012).
Note: The measure of offline political activity is having undertaken at least one of the following offline: contacting a national, state, or local government official; signing a petition; sending a "letter to the editor"; or making a political contribution. The measure of online political activity is having undertaken at least one of these activities online.

explain the gaps in political participation online. Thus, race and ethnicity play an independent role apart from SES with regard to online activity.[26]

As for differences between men and women, the data in Figure 6.12 show no significant gender disparities in either offline or online participation.[27]

Conclusion

Not unexpectedly, in recent decades the possibilities for political voice through the Internet grew markedly and changed in form—even in the four-year period separating the 2008 and 2012 Pew surveys. Not only are more Americans connected to the Internet, but the Internet also provides increasing opportunities for political engagement both through traditional activities that can be undertaken on the Internet and through social media.

Although these revolutionary technological changes provide citizens with new means of expressing political voice, they have not severed the deep roots that anchor political participation in social class. Although the digital divide—that is, the gap between those who have access to and use of the Internet and those who do not—has become somewhat narrower in recent years, it hews closely to SES level. The class structuring of the digital divide is partly, but only partly, responsible for the fact that online political mobilization and activity are strongly associated with SES. Even though these associations are weaker when we consider Internet users only, the probability of either being asked online to take part in politics (by e-mail, text, tweet, or through a request on a social networking site) or engaging in the online counterpart of a traditional offline participatory act rises with SES.

The new and rapidly changing world of social media also presents opportunities for political involvement of a somewhat less demanding nature than offline involvement. The early days of social media showed some promise that the SES stratification of participation might be overcome. As social media use has grown, diffusing beyond the youngest age group, durable patterns of socioeconomic bias in political engagement have reappeared.

But in one respect, the rapidly evolving opportunities for political engagement online do not simply mirror traditional patterns. While the digital divide reinforces the class bias in political participation, it does the opposite when it comes to age. It is well known that younger citizens, who are underrepresented when it comes to expressing political voice, are especially likely to be Internet users. As a result, disparities among age groups in the various forms of online political participation tend, at present, to be quite muted.

7

Social Movements and Ordinary Recruitment

- In December, 1773, a group of angry, hatchet-wielding men boarded three ships anchored in Boston Harbor, descended into the cargo holds, hacked open chests of tea, and dumped the contents overboard to protest an import tax, imposed by the English Parliament, on tea sold to Americans. The Boston Tea Party is sometimes considered the event that made the American Revolution inevitable.
- Organized by Lucretia Mott and Elizabeth Cady Stanton, a group met in Seneca Falls, New York, in July 1848, to discuss the "condition and rights of women." The declaration that emerged from that convention contained the revolutionary assertion, "We hold these truths to be self-evident: that all men and women are created equal" and the equally revolutionary demand for women's right to vote.
- To win recognition of the United Auto Workers as their bargaining agent, autoworkers locked themselves in General Motors Fisher Body Plant Number One in Flint, Michigan, on December 30, 1936. After a sit-down strike lasting several weeks, the workers gained, among other concessions, permission to speak to one another in the lunchroom.
- Four African-American students at North Carolina Agricultural and Technical College sat down at the lunch counter at a Greensboro, North Carolina, Woolworth's in February, 1960. Although they

waited all day, they were never served. Nevertheless, they were soon joined by many others, and the sit-in campaign they started spread throughout the South.
- Beginning in January 1974 and every year since then, pro-life forces have staged a "March for Life" on the anniversary of the 1973 Supreme Court decision legalizing abortion. Organized by the March for Life Education and Defense Fund, the march attracts thousands who advocate overturning *Roe* v. *Wade*.
- During the August 2009 congressional recess, supporters of the nascent Tea Party movement mobilized to "pack the hall" and disrupt town hall meetings held by congressional legislators to deliver a conservative message about personal and economic freedom and concern about the growing national debt.

From the colonial era to the present day, political outsiders have undertaken joint actions, often disruptive, to challenge the status quo and those in power. Social movements inevitably involve grassroots mobilization and bring new issues and new perspectives into politics. Might social movements interrupt the patterns of educational and income advantage deeply embedded in the processes that shape political voice? Whether composed of animal rights activists, environmentalists, advocates of school prayer, backers of same-sex marriage, or opponents of immigration, do such movements function as vehicles for the political activation of those who would otherwise be quiescent?[1]

To determine whether political movements bring in a more representative set of activists and thus moderate the accent of the political chorus, we look systematically at the ordinary processes by which friends, coworkers, fellow organization or church members, and strangers who call during dinner recruit others to become politically active. What we find is somewhat surprising—a process of "rational prospecting": those who wish to get others involved in politics follow a strategy of seeking out prospects who are likely to assent to a request for political activity and to participate effectively when they do. The result is that ordinary processes of recruitment actually amplify the class bias in political voice instead of reducing it.

Social Movements and the Mobilization of Outsiders

Social movements take on many forms in the amorphous space between categories of people with common characteristics, beliefs, or needs and structured organizations with membership rules, official leadership, and administrative apparatus. By speaking for and mobilizing outsiders, social movements serve to bring attention to challenging viewpoints.[2] They unite people who operate outside established institutions and contest the political, economic, or social status quo. The outsider status of social movements is directly related to another aspect of these movements—their contentiousness: "The irreducible act that lies at the base of all social movements, protests, and revolutions is *contentious collective action* . . . because it is the main and often the only recourse that ordinary people possess against better-equipped opponents or powerful states."[3]

Bottom-up endeavors succeed by using existing networks to activate "an unmobilized constituency."[4] Networks can be located in informal social ties, in existing institutions—workplaces, voluntary associations, churches, student groups, and the like—that can be repurposed for movement activism, and in organizations that are created to serve as a movement base.[5] Black churches in the South generated civil rights insurgency in perhaps the most widely cited example of the appropriation of an existing institution for movement purposes.[6] Recent technological innovations—in particular, the ever-changing capacities of social media—lower the cost and raise the speed of mobilization.[7] The Black Lives Matter movement, which emerged in 2013 in opposition to violence, especially police violence, against African Americans, took advantage of social media.[8]

Throughout American history, bottom–up movements of outsider constituencies have catalyzed social and political change. Discussions of American social movements generally focus on movements of the left—of which the labor and civil rights movements, the American Indian Movement, the Townsendites (who advocated for a universal pension system during the 1930s), and the striking California grape pickers are but a few examples. However, several important recent social movements—including the pro-life movement; the Christian right; the militia movement; and most recently, the Tea Party movement—are on the right, not the left. Like many of their progressive counterparts, they mobilize alienated non-elites to activity in contentious politics and confront entrenched adversaries.

SOCIAL MOVEMENTS AND THE ACCENT OF THE HEAVENLY CHORUS

Because they bring large numbers of ordinary people into politics, social movements presumably democratize participation and render the accent of the heavenly chorus less upper class. For example, describing civil rights organization in the early 1960s in Greenwood, Mississippi, Charles M. Payne suggests that "yardmen and maids, cab drivers, beauticians and barbers, custodians and field hands"[9]—who were not even permitted to vote, much less to be political regulars—were mobilized to become active. Still, the question of the extent to which social movements entail the political activation of new people, and new kinds of people—and thus ameliorate the SES bias of participation we have documented so extensively—is complicated.

For one thing, while they face well-organized and resource-endowed opponents both inside and outside the government, the challenging groups that coalesce around social movements are not necessarily socially and economically disadvantaged. The nineteenth-century abolition and temperance movements; the peace movement of the 1960s; and more recently, the environmental and animal rights movements, ACT-UP (which mobilized AIDS activists), MADD (Mothers Against Drunk Driving), and the Tea Party are examples of movements that have involved oppositional activism on behalf of initially overlooked or unpopular ideas by foot soldiers drawn from the middle class. While their causes rendered them political outsiders, the individual supporters of each of these movements were not socioeconomically disadvantaged.

Furthermore, even when a movement appeals to a disadvantaged group, it rarely mobilizes those who are worst off in absolute terms.[10] Resource mobilization theorists have argued convincingly that certain basic resources—for example, organizational networks, leadership capacity, and access to some financial backing—are required to launch and sustain a movement.[11] Lacking a stake in the system, a sense that they can make a difference, and the skills and resources that facilitate political participation, the worst off in disadvantaged groups usually do not join social movements. Thus, even though social movements serve as vehicles for those who lack conventional political resources, their supporters may not be typical of the larger constituency from which they are drawn. Instead they may be characterized to some degree by the same kind of tilt that we have seen with regard to conventional political activity.

In addition, the internal dynamics of social movements are often characterized by hierarchy and privilege. Even social movements that challenge the status quo on behalf of disadvantaged groups frequently favor some voices in these groups over others.[12] For example, in the student movements of the left during the 1960s, women resented the dominance of men, who occupied the leadership positions. At roughly the same time, Filipino Americans complained that the Asian American movement was being run by the numerically dominant Chinese and Japanese Americans, who presumed to speak for all Asian Americans. Within the civil rights movement, black members of the Student Nonviolent Coordinating Committee chafed under the leadership of white counterparts, while black women fought against sexual stereotyping from both black and white men. In fact, sensitivity to such patterns has led several egalitarian movements—one branch of the second wave women's movement, the Occupy movement, and the Black Lives Matter movement—to eschew traditional leadership and structures of hierarchy.[13]

To determine whether social movements provide a counterweight to the SES bias in political voice clearly requires more systematic inquiry. However, social movement tactics are not easily differentiated from conventional modes of the expression of political voice. For example, many rights-based movements—ranging from the civil rights movement to the movement for marriage equality to the pro-life movement—have used the courts to promote their objectives. The Tea Party movement has supplemented disruptive tactics, such as holding demonstrations and badgering politicians at local town halls, with conventional methods like supporting conservative candidates in Republican primaries.[14]

The intersection of social movement and conventional politics goes even further. Because social movements have difficulty maintaining a high level of fervor over the long run, they risk fading away without having much impact. More commonly, they are absorbed into a political party or—especially in the United States, where the pressure system is quite permeable—they leave political organizations in their wake.[15] The lack of a clear boundary between movement and conventional politics implies that it would be extremely difficult to enumerate activity by movement activists and use it as a basis for assessing the extent to which movement activity ameliorates inequalities of political voice.

Ordinary Recruitment

Even if we are unable to isolate and enumerate political activity rooted in specific social movements, we can use evidence from surveys to investigate processes of political mobilization more generally and systematically—including not only processes of social movement mobilization but also the less colorful, and less often studied, ordinary processes by which friends, friends of friends, and even strangers recruit others to become active politically. These everyday processes might entail a request to attend a meeting to support a local school bond referendum or to oppose a zoning change that will bring more commercial development to the neighborhood; a request to give a campaign donation to a business associate who is running for state treasurer; a request to volunteer in the campaign of his opponent; a request to write a legislator about a proposal to abolish the National Endowment of the Arts; or a request to attend a pro-Trump rally. These solicitations may be associated with a social movement, but ordinarily they are not.

Respondents in the Citizen Participation Study were asked about these everyday processes—whether, over the past twelve months, they had received any requests to take part in a campaign (to work in the campaign, to contribute money, or both); to contact a government official; to take part in a protest, march, or demonstration; or to take some active role in a public or political issue at the local level.[16] If so, they were asked whether they said yes to the request as well as about the characteristics of people making requests and the nature of their connections to respondents.[17] Just over half of the respondents in our survey, 52 percent, reported having received a request over the past year to take part in at least one of the five kinds of activity about which we asked; of those asked, 53 percent said yes to at least one request.

Of those who engaged in any of these five activities, 70 percent undertook at least one spontaneously, because they either received no requests to become active in that particular way or were asked once and did not say yes. Forty-two percent of those who engaged in any of the activities undertook at least one in response to a request by assenting to the most recent solicitation. In sum, recruitment is an important factor in generating political activity, and therefore in influencing the accent of political voice, in the United States.

Recruitment and Equality: Who Is Recruited?

We are concerned, of course, with the impact of political recruitment on participatory stratification. For respondents in each of five groups defined by socioeconomic status (SES), Figure 7.1.A shows the percentage who were asked to take part in any of the five acts just listed and the percentage who undertook at least one of these five acts—either through recruitment or spontaneously. As expected, the share who reported activity rises steeply across SES groups—as does the share who reported receiving at least one request for activity, which tracks actual activity quite closely. Figure 7.1.B is more striking. It shows the proportion in each socioeconomic quintile that engaged in at least one such act as the result of a request and the proportion who engaged spontaneously in at least one act.[18] Predictably, those at the

7.1.A. Percentage asked to be active and percentage active by socioeconomic quintile

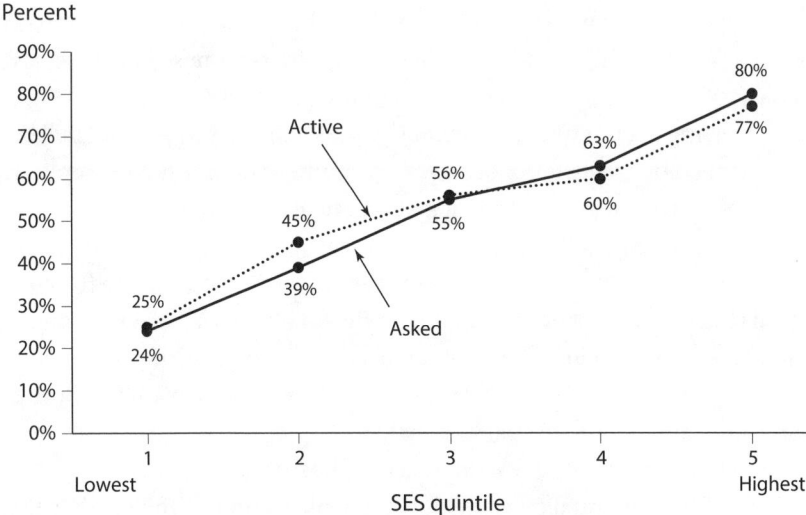

7.1.B. Percentage who engaged in recruited and spontaneous acts by socioeconomic quintile

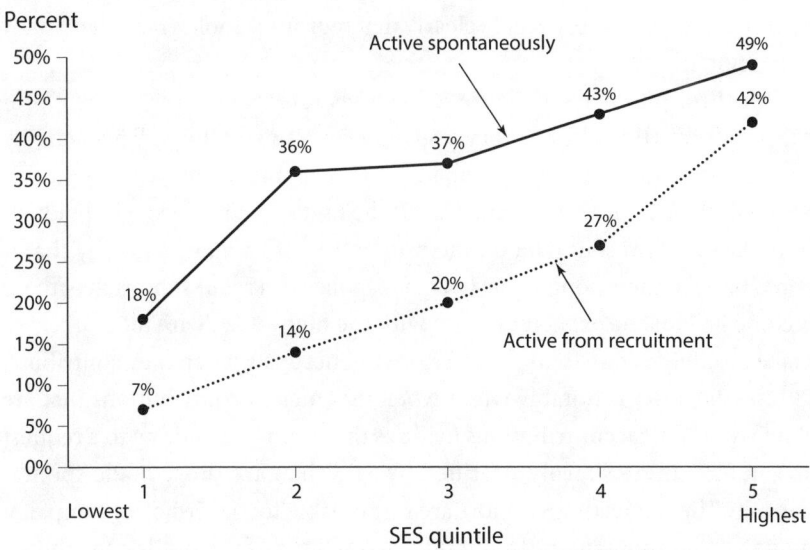

FIGURE 7.1. Who Is Recruited and Who Acts Spontaneously?
Source: Citizen Participation Study (1990).
Note: Figure 7.1.A shows the percentage asked to engage in at least one of five acts (work on a campaign, make a campaign contribution, contact an official, protest, or take part in a community activity) and the percentage who engaged in at least one of these acts—either spontaneously or after recruitment.
Note: Figure 7.1.B shows the percentage who were active spontaneously without having been asked and those who were active from recruitment after being asked. Some people were active both spontaneously and after being recruited. Therefore, the sum of the numbers in this figure equals or exceeds the percentage active in Figure 7.1.A.

low end of the SES scale are less likely to be active, whether they were asked or acted on their own. What is noteworthy is that, compared to those in the bottom SES quintile, those in the top quintile are six times as likely to have been active in response to a request but less than three times as likely to report having been active spontaneously. Thus, contrary to what might have been expected, processes of ordinary recruitment do not merely replicate the stratification of political participation but actually amplify it.

In an era of big political money and nearly ubiquitous fundraising, what about the recruitment of political contributions? Not unexpectedly, compared to activities that depend more heavily on time rather than on money, family income plays an especially important role with respect to financial contributions. As we saw in Chapter 3, the affluent are more likely both to contribute and to donate sizable sums.

When it comes to political fundraising, those who ask others for contributions target potential givers with large bank accounts. The result is that those who donate in response to a request are even more affluent than those who contribute spontaneously, and both groups have higher incomes than those who do not contribute at all. Taking into account the size of the donation demonstrates especially clearly that recruiters look where the money is and find it.[19]

The three pie charts in Figure 7.2 demonstrate that the recruitment process reinforces the participatory overrepresentation of the well heeled. Figure 7.2.A shows the share of campaign donors coming from each of the five SES quintiles. Figures 7.2.B and C shift the unit of analysis from individuals to dollars and present data on the proportion of campaign money that is contributed either spontaneously or in response to a request by each of these income groups. As expected, those with the highest SES are more likely to make campaign contributions and to give generously when they contribute.

The disparity is notably wider when it comes to contributions that are solicited. Political contributions made as the result of assenting to a request are, in fact, more sharply stratified by SES than are those made spontaneously. The highest SES donors are responsible for a third of all campaign money given spontaneously and fully three-fifths of the funds contributed in response to requests. These figures, which are based on data from 1990, would surely be much more pronounced if we had analogous data from the current period in which the limits on giving have been lifted and "bundlers" pursue large donations and receive political credit for the aggregate amounts that they raise.

7.2.A. Distribution of campaign contributors by SES quintiles

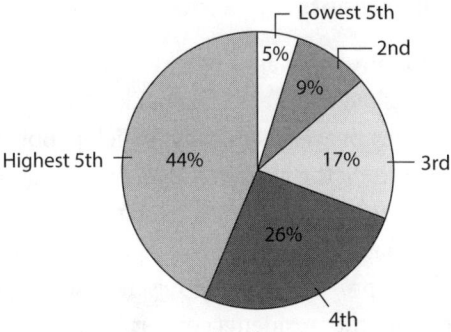

7.2.B. Distribution of campaign contributions (dollars) given spontaneously by SES quintiles

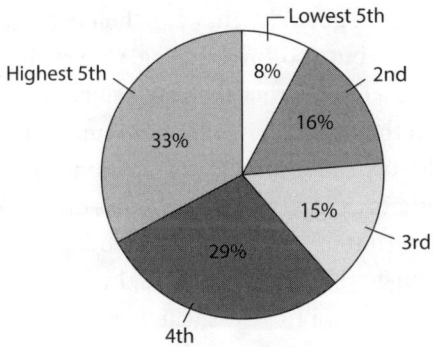

7.2.C. Distribution of campaign contributions (dollars) given as a result of recruitment by SES quintiles

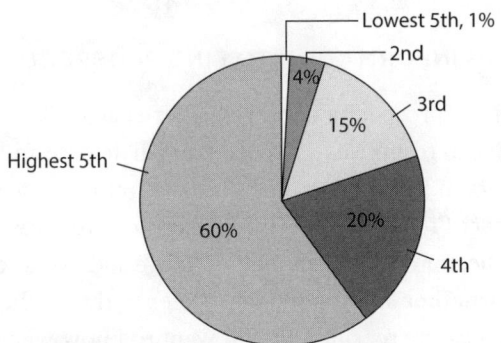

FIGURE 7.2. Where Do the Political Contributors and Dollars Come From?
Source: Citizen Participation Study (1990).

Rational Prospecting: The Everyday Process of Recruiting Participants

In an oft-quoted—and probably apocryphal—remark, Willie Sutton is said to have replied when asked why he robbed banks, "Because that's where the money is." The ordinary processes through which people are asked to take part do not help overcome the class bias in individual political voice. They do not even involve random selection of targets, thus reproducing the socioeconomic structuring of participation. Instead, those who wish to recruit others to politics—from professional fund-raisers in search of large campaign contributions to community residents concerned about the schools—heed Sutton's advice and target the advantaged.

In Chapter 3, we introduced the concept of rational prospecting and made the point that those who wish to get others involved expend their time and effort as efficiently as possible. They aim their requests at those who are likely not only to say yes but also, on assenting, to participate effectively—by, for example, making a large rather than a small contribution or writing a compelling letter rather than an incoherent one. Thus the upshot of the process of rational prospecting is that participation undertaken in response to requests from others exaggerates the SES bias of political activity.

The process of recruitment takes place in two stages: finding likely prospects to ask and then getting them to say yes. In the first stage, the rational prospector uses information to assess whether potential targets are likely to have the capacity and inclination to be active. In the second stage, the rational prospector seeks to get these recruits to say yes by apprising them of participatory opportunities and of the gratifications attendant to activity.

STAGE 1: USING INFORMATION TO FIND PROSPECTS

How does a rational prospector decide whether a particular prospect is likely to become active in response to a request to participate and, beyond that, whether the person has the capacity and motivation to participate in an effective manner? First, and most obviously, because previous activity is such a good indicator of the likelihood of future activity, a recruiter would want to know whether an individual has been active in the past. Beyond that, however, a canny recruiter would want to know whether prospects have other characteristics that might predispose them to take part in politics: the resources of time, money, or skills needed to take effective political action, as well as psychological engagement with politics—that is, political interest, knowledge, and efficacy. Indeed, multivariate analysis shows that the characteristics that predict being active in politics—education, family income, psychological engagement with politics, and civic skills—also predict being asked to take part.

STAGE 2: GETTING TO YES

Having chosen a target, recruiters, like real estate agents and fund-raisers, need to close the deal. Of course, selecting promising prospects maximizes the probability of assent. But having made the selection, the rational recruiter can use two further tactics to obtain a positive response. First, the recruiter can inform or remind the prospect of participatory opportunities: a town meeting the prospect might want to attend, a phone bank that needs volunteers, or a forthcoming election. Second, and perhaps more important, the recruiter can use various inducements to get the prospect to say yes. These can be of many sorts, ranging from the social rewards of working with people one enjoys or making friends to the gratification that accompany fulfilling a civic obligation or furthering a worthwhile policy goal. Of special interest to us are inducements that involve some form of *leverage*: instances in which the relationship to a particular recruiter gives the prospect a special incentive to say yes. When the person making the request controls rewards or punishments, the appeal is more likely to be successful. An employer or supervisor is an example of someone commanding this kind of leverage.

The likelihood of having good information and wielding some kind of leverage would seem to vary with the closeness of the recruiter to the prospect. In contrast to the recruiter who approaches a stranger, or even a friend of a friend, the recruiter who is personally acquainted with the prospect is certainly more likely to know about characteristics of the prospect that are relevant to participation—not just relatively visible ones like income but less apparent ones like political interest or concern about policy issues. In addition, close relationships enhance leverage. We tend to trust and to want to please those we know best. For rational prospectors, devoting attention to targets to whom they are close has another virtue as well: efficiency. Not only does closeness imply the likelihood of greater information and an enhanced ability to elicit affirmative responses, but rational prospectors will presumably find it easier to locate, connect with, and get the message across to those with whom they have close relationships. Connection through networks thus plays a role in finding prospects and getting them to say yes.

Closeness and Recruitment

A close relationship between prospector and quarry has implications for both steps of the two-stage process of recruitment—facilitating the location of attractive prospects and enhancing the likelihood that they will say yes. It turns out that the factors that predict political recruitment vary, depending on whether the target is someone known personally, someone in a secondary network (that is, a friend of a friend or someone whose name was recognized), or a complete stranger. Even if they do not know their targets personally, recruiters can make some rough guesses about educational level and family income from zip code. Even more helpfully, they can make inferences about past political activity from lists of contributors or volunteers. Multivariate analyses show that, in locating promising targets, strangers rely for their cues on more visible characteristics, including past participation, family income, and especially, educational attainment.

In contrast, recruiters who have close relationships with those they approach are in a better position to assess characteristics related to participation that are less readily apparent, among them the potential recruit's civic skills and political interest. Unlike strangers, friends and acquaintances rely heavily on these less visible characteristics when making requests for activity. Recruiters who have personal relationships with their targets also aim their requests at people who have taken part in the past.

Rational prospectors seeking to recruit others to political activity must not only locate the prospect, they must also gain acquiescence. When we turn our attention from who gets asked to who says yes, it turns out, not unexpectedly, that recruiters who target people with whom they have close relationships are much more likely to get a positive response. Compared to those who make requests of strangers, recruiters who have a secondary connection also do better—although, not surprisingly, not as well as those who ask someone they know. In short, friends and relatives are more effective as recruiters for two reasons. First, because they have much better information, they are able to select especially promising targets. Second, because we ordinarily seek not to offend those to whom we are attached, we are more likely to say yes when asked by a friend or relative than when asked by a stranger.

In addition, when recruiters have some kind of relationship that would enhance the likelihood that the prospects would say yes *to them*—that is, when they select people over whom they have some leverage—they are more likely to be successful. Of the various kinds of relationships in which the recruit has a particular incentive to comply with a request, bosses at work seem to be in an especially privileged position. Indeed, supervisors at work have the highest success rate when making requests: fully 70 percent of those asked by a supervisor acceded to the request for political activity.

In fact, it seems that, recently, employers have been taking advantage of their leverage over employees to urge—or even require—them to take part politically.[20] In a recent survey, one in four employees recalled having been contacted by management about some political matter. Employer mobilization is not confined to nonpartisan efforts to encourage employees to go to the polls. Instead, it may involve mandatory, but unpaid, attendance at meetings called by management to educate workers about political issues with a potential impact on the company, or even participation in partisan electoral politics. Workers have very little legal protection from political coercion.

We now can understand the fallacy of our original conjecture that processes of recruitment might operate to overcome the ordinary biases in political participation in favor of the advantaged. Those who ask others to become active politically seek individuals with characteristics—among them, high levels of income and education—that would predispose them to participate in politics. Since the same factors are associated with both being asked to be politically active and actually being politically active, those who take part as the result of requests are no less advantaged than the spontaneous activists who take part on their own initiative. That many participatory acts result from requests by people who know their targets personally reinforces these processes. If they use any information they have based on personal connections to find promising recruits and exploit their personal ties to induce their targets to say yes, rational prospectors who approach people to whom they are close are especially likely to generate political activity from the ranks of the SES-advantaged. Ordinary processes of recruitment seem to exaggerate the patterns already evident in political participation.

Political Parties and Recruitment of Activity

In a democracy, a central function of political parties, especially parties of the left, is the mobilization of ordinary citizens—in particular, those who might not otherwise be active. During the nineteenth century, strong political parties played a critical role in organizing and mobilizing voters in America—or at least the white males among them—regardless of class or immigrant status. Recent scholarship about the role of American parties

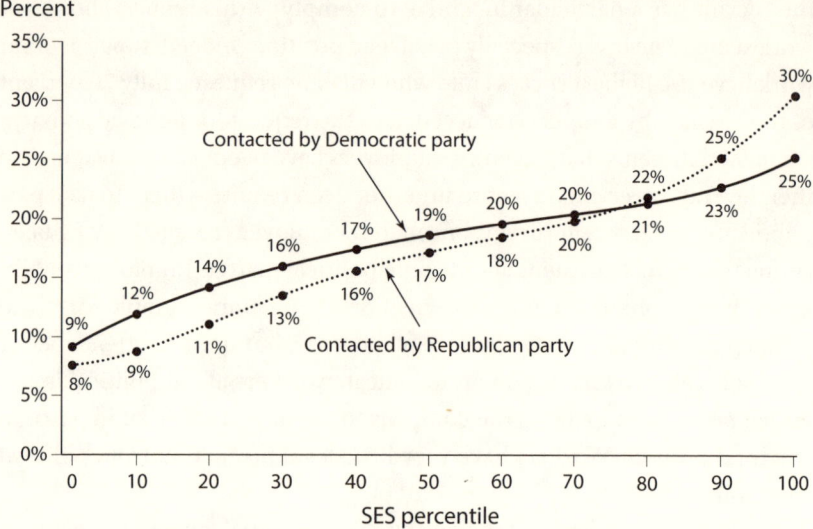

FIGURE 7.3. To Whom Do the Parties Talk during a Campaign? Percentage of Respondents Contacted by Democratic Party or Republican Party by Socioeconomic Percentile
Source: American National Election Studies (1956–2012).
Note: Data smoothed by using fitted percentages from quintic polynomial regressions of people contacted by the Democratic Party and contacted by the Republican Party on SES Percentiles for 1956–2012.

in mobilizing publics for political action has focused, in particular, on immigrants. The incorporation of the foreign born into politics depends on a variety of factors, including their nation of origin, the length of their stay in the United States, their command of English, and many aspects of the communities in which they settle.[21] Nonetheless, no one argues that contemporary American political parties mobilize lower-SES or immigrant voters as effectively as they once did. Besides, American parties are well known for being organizationally fragmented, and there are no working-class or peasant parties.

American National Election Study (ANES) surveys routinely ask: "Did anyone from one of the political parties call you up or come around and talk to you about the campaign this year?" In Figure 7.3, we combine the respondents from the ANES from 1956 to 2012 and array them in terms of SES percentiles. The data make clear that a majority of respondents never hear from someone connected with either party, but that the probability that a voter has been contacted rises sharply with SES. Both parties are more likely to attempt to mobilize upper-SES voters than those in the middle or, especially, in the lowest SES ranks. The curve is steeper for the Republican Party, but the Democrats are also acting as rational prospectors, targeting those higher on the SES ladder. Further analysis not shown makes clear that this pattern of partisan rational prospecting goes back at least to the 1950s, which is when political scientists first had systematic survey evidence. Because political parties increasingly recognize the importance of getting out the vote and because contacting costs have declined dramatically in the era of robocalls, e-mail, Twitter, and Facebook, contacting rates increased significantly starting in 2000. Still, the SES bias has persisted.

In short, parties have unambiguously played an important historical role in mobilizing voters who might otherwise not go to the polls and in representing the concerns of broad groups whose views might otherwise not be voiced. But in terms of whom they bring in as activists, the result is more mixed. Especially when seeking contributions, the parties hunt where the ducks are and target the well educated and affluent among their supporters.

Conclusion

Social movements hold the promise of overcoming the long-standing biases in the voices heard in public life by drawing attention to neglected issues and, sometimes, bringing into politics new and unrepresented publics. Our politics today would be quite different if Tea Party supporters had not shown up in 2009 at legislators' town halls. But not all social movements are as successful as the Tea Party in reconfiguring politics or policy, and different movements mobilize different strata of the population.

Respondents to the 2012 ANES were asked whether, in the past twelve months, they had actively participated in or attended a meeting, protest, rally, or any other event for eight prominent American social movements: the Tea Party, Occupy, Right to Life, women's rights, environmental rights, racial equality, peace/anti-war, and LGBT (lesbian, gay, bisexual, and transgender) rights. Most of these movements mobilized people from all SES groups with a slight tilt toward the top; the Right to Life Movement appealed much more strongly to those of lower SES and the Tea Party to those in the middle SES quintile. Each of these movements showed a positive correlation between movement activity and self-reported voting in 2008, which suggests these movements were not bringing new people into politics. The sole exception was LGBT rights, presumably because of its strong support among young people who were either ineligible or unlikely to vote in 2008.

By focusing on prominent social movements, however, we stack the deck in favor of finding widespread mobilization.

We take a somewhat different approach from social movements theorists in conceptualizing processes of political mobilization and citizen recruitment. Rather than looking at particular social movements, we started with a random sample of the population to see how the recruitment process, seen comprehensively, brings citizens to politics. Our results demonstrate that studies of social movements yield only a partial picture.

Whether they use as cues the socioeconomic characteristics associated with participation in politics—or use what is perhaps the best indicator of future potential to participate, previous activity in politics—rational prospectors target citizens who are politically engaged and who have the resources to be active. In addition to selecting people who might participate on their own, they seek prospects over whom they have some leverage—some connection that would make the targets feel a special obligation to say yes. Critical to the process is information. Because close relationships increase information and leverage, rational recruiters look close to home, contacting people they know. When they do so, they are more likely to locate targets with the relevant characteristics, to elicit a positive reply, and to produce effective participation.

Because rational prospectors target recruits who possess attributes associated with participation, those brought into politics by recruiters actually exaggerate the traits characteristic of activists. Although this pattern holds for all forms of participation, it pertains especially to campaign contributions. Money is the most unequally distributed of inputs into American politics, and political recruiters exacerbate participatory inequalities by locating affluent potential donors, who proceed to give especially generously. The result is that policymakers in America hear even more disproportionately from those who command the resources that make participation possible. In the aggregate, processes of recruitment whereby citizens are asked by others to become involved are less likely to transform than to replicate the representational outcomes of a participatory system in which the privileged speak more loudly than the disadvantaged.

PART III

8

Who Sings in the Heavenly Chorus? The Shape of the Organized Interest System

Even before Tocqueville famously noted the American propensity to form associations in pursuit of joint ends, political and otherwise, organizational activity served as an important channel for the expression of political voice. In parallel with political acts by individual citizens, organized interests send out a flood of messages to policymakers. Collective political efforts raise the same kinds of questions about inequalities of political voice that we have been considering with respect to individual activity. We want to know what kinds of organizations are involved, for whom they speak, and how much they say. We explore these problems in this chapter. In the next, we consider the various activities undertaken by organizations in politics.[1]

Political Organizations, Equal Voice, and the Problem of Money

Individual citizen voice and organized interest voice are linked by the fact that many individual participatory acts—for example, joining a demonstration organized by a gun rights or gun control group or writing a letter to

Philip E. Jones is coauthor of this chapter.

a government official at the behest of a professional association of which one is a member—are catalyzed by organizations. Yet most organizations active in political life have no members in the usual sense of the word, so that individual political activity in membership associations constitutes only a small part of the sum total of organized interest involvement in politics.

Like individual participants, organizations pursue political influence through multiple avenues, ranging from lobbying to the production of specialized research to making electoral contributions through a political action committee. And like individual activists, organizations must use some combination of the resources of time, money, and skill. However, individuals act for themselves. They do not hire a designated protester to fill in for them at a march or a ghost writer to compose an especially moving communication to a public official. In contrast, organizations often undertake political activity by employing well-compensated professionals who may command extensive experience and expertise. Thus, organizations can use money to buy time and skills—with consequences for inequality of political voice.

Because they often have deep pockets, organizations can use money not only to buy the time and skills of professional advocates but also to provide inducements to public officials—whether a favor, a campaign contribution, or even a bribe. Every so often, a substantial impropriety results in media attention and public outcry, and scandal ensues. Well-known examples include:

- The Teapot Dome scandal, which broke in 1921 and involved the decision by the Secretary of the Interior to lease drilling rights to private oil companies in the naval petroleum reserves;
- The Abscam scandal during the late 1970s and early 1980s, in which a sting operation set up by the FBI resulted in videotapes of public officials accepting bribes from operatives posing as representatives of a fraudulent Arab company in exchange for policy favors;
- And, during the late 1980s, the Keating Five scandal, in which five senators, all of whom had received campaign donations from the chairman of the Lincoln Savings and Loan or his associates, intervened with the Federal Home Loan Bank Board, which was then investigating Lincoln.

Although political scandals involving money always generate at least temporary explosions of appropriate public indignation, we rarely inquire why such corruption offends so deeply. As James C. Scott explicates succinctly, in a modern democratic polity, corruption seems especially damaging since it undermines both the egalitarian assumptions of majority rule and the principles of even distribution of civil and social rights of which we normally approve. Under liberal democratic regimes, corruption represents an additional and *illegal* advantage of wealthy interests over and above the *legal* advantages they ordinarily enjoy by virtue of large campaign contributions, muscle in the courts, and so forth.[2]

A concern with bribery reflects the same set of concerns that underlie the democratic principle of one person, one vote. Of the resources for political persuasion and influence—skills, time, and money—money is not only the most unevenly distributed but also the one whose distribution hews most closely to fault lines of political conflict. Given how unequal our bank accounts are, allowing cash gifts or emoluments to public officials from the stakeholders in a policy controversy places citizens on a very unequal footing when it comes to potential political influence.

We cannot know how common the shenanigans characteristic of the periodic lobbying scandals are in American politics. Presumably, cover-ups are sometimes successful. Nevertheless, we believe that illegal influence peddling is not the norm—an assessment substantiated by the consistent ranking of the United States among the twenty least corrupt countries in the world on the Transparency International Corruption Perceptions Index.[3]

Furthermore, we depart from popular stereotypes of pressure politics by recognizing that organized interest representation is essential both for democratic governance and for the formation and legitimation of sound public policy. Any polity legitimately considered a democracy must permit citizens to organize in order to communicate their preferences to office holders, to have an impact on the peaceful and lawful selection of public officials, and to influence policy outcomes. But organized interests are not merely to be tolerated in a democracy; they also have a central part to play in its functioning. Representatives of organized interests perform a crucial role by providing information in the policymaking process: they call attention to issues, furnish evidence about how problems are being experienced on the ground, and provide expertise about the anticipated consequences—both substantive and political—of proposed solutions. Furthermore, by making possible a two-way process of communication, organized interests facilitate the acceptance and legitimation of policies by interested stakeholders.

The problem with organized interest representation in American politics is not that the unsavory practices exposed during lobbying scandals are the norm. As revealed by systematic assessment, the problem is instead that inequalities of political voice are characteristic of the day-to-day, completely legal functioning of organized interest politics.

The Puzzle of Political Equality When Representation Is by Organizations

As hard as it is to define political equality for individual political acts, the difficulties increase for organizational activity.[4] When we assessed inequalities of political voice through individual activity, we began with the adult population of the United States—as enumerated, perhaps imperfectly, by the Census—and then we evaluated the extent to which individual political participation is representative of that population. There is no such census enumerating all existing organizations to provide a baseline from which departures in political activity could be measured in a manner analogous to the procedure for individual participation. Even if we had such an enumeration, however, it is not clear how to match organizations to individual citizens and thus to the one-person, one-vote principle underlying political equality. Many people's interests are not represented by organizations. Besides, it is often hard to discern exactly who is being represented by organizations.

BARRIERS TO ENTRY INTO PRESSURE POLITICS

If it were easy to bring a new organization into being and to take it into politics, then the population of organizations would be more likely to represent the population of individuals. In fact, political scientists once argued that interest groups emerge more or less automatically in response to disturbances in the political environment and regularly enter and leave the pressure system as dictated by their concerns about the particular political issues at any given time.

Scholars subsequently challenged the once-dominant analysis of American politics that emphasized the low barriers to entry to the organized interest system and its fluid nature.[5] Two influential though quite different analyses, one by E. E. Schattschneider and the other by Mancur Olson, pointed to barriers confronting new interest groups.[6] Schattschneider famously observed that "the flaw in the [organized interest] heaven is that the heavenly chorus sings with a strong upper-class accent."[7] Speaking directly to our concern with equality of political voice, Schattschneider argued that what he called the "pressure system" is biased in favor of groups representing the well off, especially business, and against groups representing two other kinds of interests: broad public interests and the economically disadvantaged.

According to Schattschneider, broad public interests or public goods constitute the first kind of interest that is unlikely to achieve organized representation. These are objectives like safer streets or safer consumer products, cleaner water or cleaner government, enhanced domestic security or reduced domestic violence that are broadly beneficial to all in society. Schattschneider argued that, while everyone has a stake in such broad public interests, relatively few people care intensely about them or give them the highest political priority.

In an influential formal analysis, Mancur Olson reached through logical deduction the same conclusion about advocacy on behalf of public interests that Schattschneider reached by empirical observation. Olson pointed out that large, diffuse groups lacking the capacity to coerce cooperation or to provide selective benefits available only to organization members—for example, discounts on travel or insurance—often face severe collective action problems that prevent them from organizing on behalf of their joint political concerns. According to Olson, the rational individual has an incentive to free ride on the efforts of others rather than to spend scarce resources of money and time in support of favored causes. An organization will emerge and prosper only when it has the capacity to force a potential free rider to support group efforts or when it supplies benefits exclusively available to those who assist in the collective effort. Moreover, contrary to the common understanding that the larger the interested constituency, the more likely it is to be represented by an organization, the free rider problem is exacerbated when the potential group is large.

Thus Olson's logic gives a formal foundation to Schattschneider's empirical statement that the proportion of people who take part in an organization seeking public goods is far smaller than the proportion that would benefit from those conditions.

Consistent with our findings about inequalities of individual political voice, Schattschneider pointed to a second kind of interest that would be less well represented in politics: the disadvantaged. While Olson's argument rests on the notion that there are costs to starting an organization or keeping one going, he neglected the disparities among groups in the capacity to assume those costs. In contrast, Schattschneider understood that not all potential constituencies are in a position to bear the costs of political organization and advocacy.

Olson's collective action model has elicited many efforts that seek to square its compelling logic with empirical reality. Clearly, the political arena contains many large organizations that are not in a position to force members to join and that do not provide selective benefits of significant economic value. Moreover, ongoing groups that do offer selective benefits to induce membership had to overcome the free rider problem at the outset to get off the ground. They may have done so by offering non-material selective benefits—for example, the rewards of working with others and enjoying their fellowship and esteem, and the satisfaction associated with supporting a cherished cause—before the fledgling organization is in a position to offer material ones.[8] In addition, it is easier to found and nurture new organizations when there are entrepreneurs willing to bear the costs,[9] patrons such as foundations or even governments to provide support,[10] or large donors among members.[11] Sometimes, "unexpected" organizations representing broad public interests or disadvantaged groups—that is, organizations like the National Organization for Women, the Human Rights Campaign, the National Council of La Raza, and the Friends of the Earth, to name a few—emerge when social movements leave conventional political organizations in their wake.[12]

In short, although the barriers are not insurmountable, both the free rider problem and the resource problem function as impediments to the natural emergence of organizations among those who have common interests and concerns. Thus, even if it were possible to enumerate all existing organizations, that census would yield a set of organizations that systematically underrepresents certain kinds of potential interests. In addition, just as the set of politically active individuals is not a representative sample of all adults, the set of politically active organizations drawn from the already partial group of all organizations is further stratified.

EQUAL VOICE AND ORGANIZATIONAL REPRESENTATION: FURTHER DILEMMAS

Moving from the consideration of individuals to consideration of organizations introduces additional complexities, as discussed in Chapter 2. The principle of one person, one vote that establishes equal political voice among individual voters is impossible to apply to organizations, because organizations have radically different numbers of members. Moreover, even organization

TABLE 8.1. Organizational Membership Status

Associations of individuals	11.3%
Memberless organizations	56.5
Associations of memberless organizations	13.9
Governments/associations of governments	14.3
Mixed or other	4.0
Total	100.0%
N	14,305

Source: Washington Representatives Study (2011).
Note: We omit from this table the small number of organizations ($N = 62$) whose membership status could not be ascertained.

members who are united in their commitment to an organization's goals are unlikely to be uniform in their interests, needs, and preferences.

Studies of interest group politics give disproportionate attention to organizations of individuals—for example, labor unions like the Amalgamated Transit Union, professional associations like the American Dental Association, and rights groups like the National Organization for Women—but such groups are only a small minority of organizations active in Washington. The predominant organizational advocate in Washington is an organization without members in any traditional sense—for example, a corporation, university, think tank, or hospital.[13] Besides, many membership associations—most notably the trade associations that bring together companies in a single industry—are composed of memberless organizations, not individual people.

Table 8.1 draws on the Washington Representatives Study, an extensive data archive containing information about the organizations listed in the *Washington Representatives* directory, because they have a presence in national politics—either by maintaining an office in the capital or by hiring Washington-based consultants or counsel to manage their government relations activities.[14] For each of these organizations, we coded what we call "organizational membership status": that is, whether it is an association composed of individual members, an organization without members, an association of organizations without members, a mixture of types, or something else.[15] As shown in Table 8.1, just 11.3 percent of the more than 14,000 organizations active in 2011 were membership associations of individuals—less than memberless organizations (56.5 percent), associations of memberless organizations (13.9 percent), or subnational governments or consortia of governments (14.3 percent). Because fewer than one in eight of the organizations listed is a classic voluntary association composed of individual members, it is inappropriate to use "interest groups" and "pressure groups" as umbrella terms to denote the organizations that seek to influence political outcomes.

That the preponderance of organizations in the pressure system have no members in the ordinary sense raises knotty questions for equality of political voice. When representation is by institutions like corporations or universities, whose concerns and preferences are being represented? As Justice John Paul Stevens put it in his dissent in the campaign finance case *Citizens United* v. *FEC* (2010):

> It is an interesting question "who" is even speaking when a business corporation places an advertisement that endorses or attacks a particular candidate. Presumably it is not the customers or employees, who typically have no say in such matters. It cannot realistically be said to be the shareholders, who tend to be far removed from the day-to-day decisions of the firm and whose political preferences may be opaque to management. Perhaps the officers or directors of the corporation have the best claim to be the ones speaking, except their fiduciary duties generally prohibit them from using corporate funds for personal ends.

Similar questions can be raised about any politically active memberless organization. For example, when a university takes stands in politics, whose interests are being represented—those of the administration, professors, staff, graduates, or students? Surely, on many occasions the interests of these various stakeholders coincide. At the very least, all these university constituencies have an interest in seeing the institution prosper financially. Nevertheless, there is ample evidence that what is good for one part of an institutional constituency is not necessarily good for all. Consider, for example, the policy of some retailers making managers' bonuses dependent on keeping labor costs below a specified ceiling.[16] When managers stand to gain financially by keeping workers' wages down, it is hard to argue that their interests coincide with workers' interests.

Still, as difficult as it might be to specify the requirements for equality of political voice when interest representation is by organizations, it is possible to identify when we have substantial departures from political equality and to make comparative assessments of relative inequality. The systematic data analysis in the remainder of this chapter and in Chapter 9 show a configuration of organized interests and distributions of organized interest activity that is very far from approximating equality of political voice.

The Contours of Organized Interest Representation

The array of organizations active in Washington politics is nothing short of dazzling. Reporting on national politics in *CQ Weekly* for one four-month period in 2015 included references to dozens of organizations. Table 8.2 presents examples of some of the common kinds—along with the issues on which they were working—and makes clear the broad range of organizations and policy concerns.

The organizations listed in the Washington Representatives Study capture the astonishing range of organizations active in Washington. It includes such memberless organizations as JetBlue Airways, Southern Methodist University, and the Denver Art Museum;[17] the governments of places as diverse and far-flung as Dayton, Ohio, the state of New Mexico, and Angola; organizations of garlic growers, movie actors, motorcycle riders, Turkish businessmen, pawnbrokers, candle manufacturers, fish and wildlife agencies, exporters of Brazilian textiles; advocates for causes that range from the protection of ducks, historic buildings, and young children to the reform of marijuana laws to the rights of the disabled; organizations based on how people earn a living, how they spend their leisure, and how they define themselves in religious or ethnic terms; organizations, especially corporations,

TABLE 8.2. Examples of Organized Interests and Their Policy Concerns

Organization	Policy Issue
Pandora	Compensation to song writers and music publishers
American Football League	Antitrust exemption for football
U.S. Chamber of Commerce	Trade embargo of Cuba
National Association of Criminal Defense Lawyers	Sentencing guidelines
AFL-CIO	Trans-Pacific Partnership (Free trade)
National Rifle Association	Trade in elephant ivory
National Gay and Lesbian Task Force	Same-sex marriage
Parkinson's Action Network	Funding for the National Institutes of Health

Sources: All organizations were mentioned in articles in *CQ Weekly*: Eliza Newlin Carney, "Left Meets Right In Prison Politics," April 13, 2015; Finlay Lewis, "Trading Places on Free Trade Pacts," April 13, 2015; Kate Ackley and Tamar Hallerman, "As Door to Cuba Opens, Castro Foes Push Back," April 20, 2015; Kate Ackley, "K Street Joins Fight Over Elephant Ivory," June 15, 2015; Melissa Attias, "Dueling Diseases: The Race for Cure Dollars," June 15, 2015; Shawn Zeller, Sounds and Fury: Songwriters Battle over Royalties from Streaming," July 6, 2015; Alan Ota, "NFL Launches Charm Offensive on the Hill," July 20, 2015; Kate Ackley, "Long Road Still Ahead on Gay Rights" July 27, 2015.

TABLE 8.3. Organized Interests in Washington Politics[a]

Corporations	36.6%
Trade and other business associations	10.2
Occupational associations	5.4
Unions	0.7
Education	5.7
Health	5.2
Social welfare or poor	1.1
Identity groups[b]	3.6
Public interest	4.4
State and local governments	12.3
Foreign	6.2
Other	7.9
Don't know	0.7
Total	100.0%
N	14,365

Source: Washington Representatives Study (2011).
[a]Distribution of organizations listed in the 2011 *Washington Representatives* directory.
[b]Includes organizations representing racial, ethnic, or religious groups, the elderly, women, or LGBT.

that have billions in assets and others that live from hand to mouth; organizations with liberal views; and organizations with conservative views.

Given our concern with the extent to which political voice through organizations is representative, a crucial part of the construction of the Washington Representatives database was to place each organization listed in the directory into one or more of ninety-six organizational categories.[18] These categories were designed to capture the nature of the interest being represented—business, an occupation, a foreign government, a group of universities, a religious or ethnic group, a conservative think tank, and so on—as well as something about its organizational structure. In contrast to most studies of organized interests that rely on highly aggregated categories, we deliberately proliferated the number of categories to capture fine distinctions.

For all the number and diversity of organizations, it turns out that both the free rider problem and the resource constraint problem have profound effects on whose voices are heard through the medium of collective representation. Table 8.3 summarizes, in all its multidimensional complexity, the distribution of the organizations listed in the *Washington Representatives* directory in 2011. The data make clear that the essential outlines of Schattschneider's analysis of the pressure system pertain in the New Gilded Age and that the set of organized political interests continues to be organized principally around economic matters. This domain includes economic enterprises in the for-profit and nonprofit sectors, along with associations of such enterprises and large numbers of membership associations such as unions and professional associations that join people on the basis of their shared occupations. In this domain, the representation of business is dominant.[19]

Consistent with Schattschneider's analysis, just as in individual political participation, the economically disadvantaged are underrepresented in pressure politics. Even those with ordinary jobs and middle-class incomes are vastly underrepresented. Organizations of the poor themselves are extremely rare, if not nonexistent, and organizations that advocate on behalf of the poor are relatively scarce. In addition, as both Olson and Schattschnider predicted, the number of public interest groups is relatively small, accounting for less than 5 percent of the organizations active in Washington. Both size and resources matter. A large group of jointly interested citizens that is reasonably well endowed with a variety of kinds of resources—for example, veterans—is more likely to achieve organizational representation than is a resource-poor group of similar size and similar intensity of concern, say, public housing tenants or nursing home residents.

Table 8.3 also indicates the substantial presence of other kinds of organizations that are often neglected in discussions of Washington pressure politics—in particular, state and local governments in the United States and a variety of foreign interests.[20]

Although this brief synopsis identifies ongoing inequalities in political voice, the highly aggregated categories in Table 8.3 obscure a great deal. It seems useful to take a closer look at some of the more important categories of interest organizations.

Economic Organizations in Washington Politics

More than two-thirds of the organized interests in Washington are directly related to political concerns arising from economic roles and interests.[21] Among the thousands of organizations in this remarkably diverse sector, those representing business—domestic and foreign corporations, multiple kinds of business associations, occupational associations of business executives, and business-oriented think tanks and research organizations—constitute the overwhelming share. Of all the organizations active in Washington, 51 percent represent business in one way or another.[22] And of these business groups, corporations are by far the most numerous. American corporations accounted for nearly two-thirds of business organizations and more than a third of all the organizations with Washington representation in 2011.[23] Although they are, by a factor of more than three, the most numerous of the organizations active in Washington, it is interesting to note that only a small proportion of American corporations are represented.

Trade and other business associations, which have for-profit American corporations as members, make up most of the remainder of business organizations and constitute 10 percent of all organizations in the Washington pressure system. Trade associations include well-known heavyweights like the American Bankers Association and the Petroleum Institute along with such smaller fry as the Baby Carrier Industry Alliance, the National Armored Car Association, the National Association of Theatre Owners, and the Pet Food Institute. They bring together companies in a single industry, companies that are ordinarily marketplace competitors, to work together on common problems. Part of their mission is nonpolitical: trade associations often provide technical services on such nonpolitical matters as accounting practices or employee benefits. However, their shared concerns usually also include political matters, in particular the kinds of regulatory issues on which government action affects an entire industry. In addition to trade associations, a smaller but more diverse group of associations also bring together American firms ranging from peak associations like the U.S. Chamber of Commerce and the National Federation of Independent Businesses (which bring together businesses across industries) to diverse ad hoc coalitions.

Our emphasis on the sheer number of organizations that represent business interests in national politics should not be interpreted as implying that business speaks with one voice.[24] The many issues in which business interests are active involve varying patterns of organized interest interaction, not a single structure of power. Very few issues involve the mobilization of the entire business community. While there are issues—for example, competition among military suppliers for a defense contract—that involve conflict among business interests, much more common are issues on which a portion of the business community is opposed by interests drawn from outside business or by no organized interests at all.[25] Therefore, the absence of business unity is not necessarily evidence of business weakness.[26]

The education and health sectors contribute a much smaller but still notable set of organizations. In both cases, roughly four-fifths of the organizations are memberless organizations. In the education sector, these are overwhelmingly universities—with public and nonprofit private universities more or less equally represented, along with a handful of for-profits. Health institutions include hospitals, clinics, nursing homes, and other institutions that care for the infirm or disabled. The health sector has a much more substantial, and often difficult-to-discern, component of for-profit institutions.

Constituting little more than 1 percent of all organizations in the Washington pressure system is the highly influential set of organizations representing the agricultural sector.[27] Most are crop-specific organizations, like the American Peanut Council, the American Sugar Alliance, and the U.S. Apple Association, which often include processors and equipment manufacturers along with individual farmers and corporate agricultural producers.

LABOR UNIONS AND OCCUPATIONAL ASSOCIATIONS

Individuals gain significant representation through their memberships in occupational associations that have individuals as members. Because occupational hierarchies are so deeply rooted in disparities in education and income, the many membership associations that organize people on the basis of what they do for a living matter for inequalities of political voice. Those who do work requiring high levels of education—and, to a lesser extent, conferring high levels of income—are highly likely to be represented by an organization in Washington. In contrast, with the exception of unions, those who do unskilled work have no occupationally based membership groups at all to represent them.[28]

Labor unions traditionally receive attention in discussions of Washington representation. We distinguish labor unions from other membership associations that bring together people who share a common occupation by whether the organization bargains collectively on behalf of its members. These members may be well educated. Many white-collar unions—for example, unions of teachers or nurses—are made up of professionals, especially professionals employed in the public sector. Unions are not especially numerous, comprising only 12 percent of the occupational membership associations, or 1 percent of all organizations, in the Washington pressure community. Because there are so few of them, and because so few other organizations represent the economic interests of nonprofessional and nonmanagerial employees, their political efforts are spread thinly across a wide range of issues.[29]

Rates of union membership, which are more than five times higher for public sector than for private-sector workers, also vary quite substantially across occupations and industries. Interestingly, because public-sector professional workers such as teachers are relatively likely to be unionized, professionals have, overall, higher rates of union membership than do service, sales, or production workers. In the private sector, workers in transportation, construction, and telecommunications have much higher rates of union membership than those in agriculture or financial services.[30]

Most membership associations that represent individuals on the basis of their occupations do not bargain collectively. By far the most numerous such organizations—accounting for nearly half—are professional associations. These organizations unite people—for example, criminal defense lawyers, plant physiologists, landscape architects, historians, transportation engineers, and thoracic surgeons—on the basis of a shared occupation that usually requires a prescribed course of educational training and at least a college degree.[31]

Of particular relevance to our concern with the relationship between disadvantage and political voice is the 9 percent of occupational associations, or less than 1 percent of all organizations in the Washington pressure community, that bring together those in nonprofessional and nonmanagerial occupations. Examples of such groups include associations of realtors, master printers, meeting planners, travel agents, medical sonographers, and pilots. Comparing the list of these organizations with the U.S. Census list of all occupations makes it evident that even the associations that enroll nonprofessional and nonmanagerial workers tend to represent those in occupations that demand relatively high levels of skill, pay, and status.[32] Unless they are unionized, no associations represent those in many occupations: bellhops, telemarketers, hotel desk clerks, laundry workers, bus drivers, bartenders, custodians, bank tellers, or tool and die makers. A conservative estimate is that for only one-tenth of the nearly 90 million American workers in nonprofessional and nonmanagerial occupations is there an occupational association, other than a union, that brings together people in their occupation. Indeed, other than unions, there are *no occupational associations at all* to organize those who labor at low-skill jobs.

Figure 8.1 provides a perspective on the uneven organizational representation of economic roles. The left column shows the distribution of adults in the 2010 U.S. Census: 58 percent were in the labor force in various kinds of jobs; 6 percent were out of work; and 35 percent were out of the workforce by virtue of being in school, at home, disabled, or retired. The right column shows the distribution for the subset of organizations in the 2011 *Washington Representatives* directory organized around economic roles. The correspondence between the people in the column on the left and the organizations on the right is at best approximate, because it is extremely difficult to match all the relevant organizations in the right column to the economic roles in

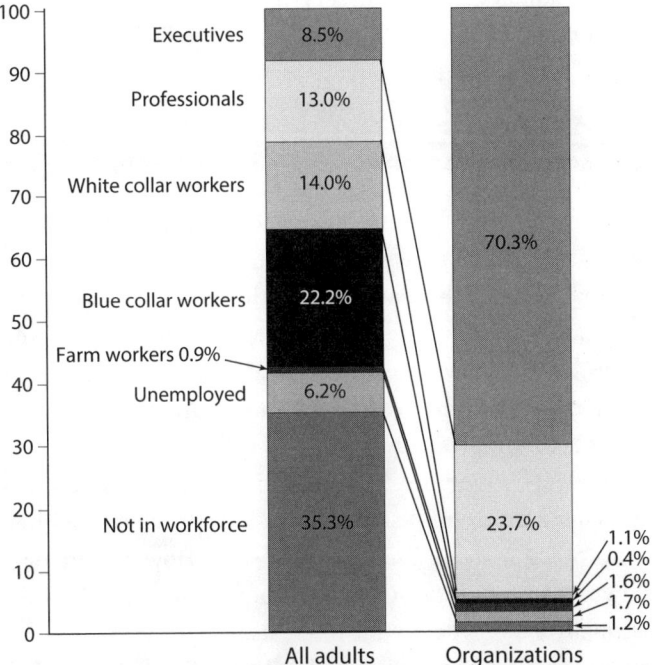

FIGURE 8.1. Distribution of Adult Workforce Statuses and Parallel Economic Organizations

Sources: All adults: Calculated for the 2010 civilian population age sixteen and older from the 2012 Statistical Abstract, 131st ed. (tables 586 and 616) as reported on the Web site of the U.S. Bureau of the Census: https://www.census.gov/library/publications/2011/compendia/statab/131ed.html (accessed on January 11, 2016). Organizations taken from the Washington Representatives Study (2011).

the left column.[33] Insofar as possible, we made assumptions that would have the effect of coding against the expected patterns in the data.

Whatever the imperfections in the data, the overall pattern is striking. The 8 percent of adults who work in an executive, managerial, or administrative capacity are represented by 70 percent of the economic associations and institutions. Professionals, who constitute 13 percent of adults, are represented by 24 percent of economic organizations. The remaining 79 percent of adults—a group that includes lower-level white-collar, blue-collar, and service workers as well as those who are unemployed, in school, at home, disabled, or retired—are represented by a mere 6 percent of the economic organizations.[34] In short, when it comes to economic organizations, those representing business are vastly disproportionate in their numbers, and nearly all adults who work in service, blue-collar, or lower-level white-collar jobs or who are out of the workforce entirely have a very small share of organized representation.

ORGANIZATIONS THAT REPRESENT THE LESS PRIVILEGED

By focusing on how adults are represented in terms of their occupations or workforce status, we may have overlooked other forms of representation of the economic needs of those who are on the middle and lower rungs of the economic ladder. As discussed in Chapter 10, workers today, even highly skilled ones, are squeezed by many trends designed to cut labor costs. These include the export of jobs overseas, the outsourcing of service functions, job-cutting technological advances, and the increased use of part-timers and independent contractors. Such developments create potential economic constituencies—for example, workers in jobs providing neither paid sick leave nor protection from disability or job loss. However, no organizations in Washington seek to represent groups organized around these joint non-occupationally defined economic interests.

Furthermore, like those who work in low-skill jobs, those at the bottom of the economic ladder are also underrepresented in pressure politics. Table 8.3 shows that only about 1 percent of the organizations active in Washington in 2011 were in the category we label as "social welfare or poor." Nearly two-thirds of these are providers of direct services, like the Capital Area Food Bank, Goodwill Industries, Twin Cities RISE, Meals on Wheels America, or the American Red Cross. The remainder are organizations that advocate on behalf of the poor in the United States or in favor of more comprehensive guarantees with respect to basic human needs. Such organizations, which may or may not also attempt to organize the poor, include the Coalition on Human Needs, the Food Research and Action Center, and the Center on Budget and Policy Priorities.[35]

We might expect that certain needy constituencies with an obvious stake in policy outcomes—for example, unemployed workers, public housing tenants, or those eligible for the Earned Income Tax Credit—would advocate on their own behalf based on their concern with a social program or tax provision from which they benefit. A very few such organizations—for example, the Full Employment Action Council and the Section 8 Housing Group—had appeared in earlier directories. However, of the more than 14,000 organizations enumerated in the 2011 directory, not one was an association of beneficiaries of means-tested government benefits representing themselves. Furthermore, as Jeffrey Berry points out, the health and human service nonprofits that have as clients "constituencies that are too poor, unskilled, ignorant, incapacitated, or overwhelmed with their problems to organize on their own" are constrained by the 501(c)3 provisions in the tax code from undertaking significant lobbying.[36]

Political representation of resource-poor constituencies is more likely when the need for government assistance is assumed to be permanent. The wag who once observed, "You are only old once" made a powerful observation about the possibilities for organized advocacy. Various explanations are possible for the potent organization of the elderly and their ability to protect their government benefits: benefits for the elderly are not means-tested, and therefore many of the beneficiaries are not poor; the elderly have high rates of electoral turnout; and AARP has found a formula for generating a large membership based on the provision of selective benefits. Still another explanation is that, in contrast to the other age-related statuses through which we pass, we do not graduate from being elderly. The elderly know that they will always be dependent on Medicare and Social Security and act accordingly in politics. In contrast, economic need often results from conditions that are unforeseen or expected to be temporary—for example, unemployment, mortgage foreclosure, or medical emergency not covered by insurance. Under the circumstances, organized advocacy by the economically disadvantaged acting on their own is especially unlikely.

Organizations That Represent Identity Groups

The evidence on the representation of economic interests in pressure politics is compelling: the overwhelming share of organizations represent the well off. But when it comes to identity groups constellated around noneconomic axes of cleavage—for example, race, ethnicity, nationality, religion, age, gender, sexual orientation, or gender identity—the less advantaged have greater representation.[37] Numerous groups represent the interests of, for example, women, the elderly, Muslims, Asian Americans, or African Americans. Some of these identity organizations are positioned at the intersection of more than one identity: the National Council of Negro Women and the National Hispanic Council on Aging are examples.

Few, if any, of these organizations are explicitly organized around the interests of, for example, men or WASPs. Nevertheless, the interests of middle-aged, straight white men, especially those who have high levels of education and income, are surely well represented in the mainstream economic organizations that form the bulk of the organized interest community.

To what extent can identity groups substitute for class-based groups in advocating for economically needy members of constituencies defined by other affinities? For all their diversity, organizations representing racial, ethnic, or nationality groups; religious groups; women; the elderly; and gays and lesbians comprise only a tiny proportion of the organizations in the pressure system. They constitute 2.3 percent, 0.7 percent, 0.4 percent, 0.2 percent, and less than 0.1 percent, respectively, of the organizations listed in the 2011 *Washington Representatives* directory.

Interestingly, nearly half of the organizations in this category represent Native Americans. By a factor of six, organizations representing Native Americans outnumber those representing African Americans, a group traditionally viewed as the vanguard with respect to minority politics—and having, according to the 2010 U.S. Census, nearly fourteen times the Native American population. We discovered that 74 percent of the Native American organizations are federally recognized tribes, which makes them in some ways more analogous to the state and local governments in the intergovernmental lobby than to the kinds of civil rights organizations that traditionally represent racial and ethnic groups. The number of Native American tribes that have Washington representation reflects not only the legacy of historical engagement with the federal government but also more recent events. The 1988 Indian Gaming Regulatory Act stimulated the political involvement of Indian nations both because it enhanced their stake in public policy and because the resources that accrued to them through gaming have given them the wherewithal to undertake political action. In fact, 83 percent of the federally recognized tribes with Washington representation are involved in casino gambling.[38]

Public Interest Groups

The free rider problem implies that public goods will receive less vigorous organized advocacy. Indeed, the number of public interest groups is relatively small, accounting for less than 5 percent of the organizations active in Washington. While they are not especially numerous, the causes they advocate are remarkably diverse. Table 8.4 gives examples of various kinds of public interest groups.

Although we commonly refer to such public goods as public interests, we should make clear that those who advocate on behalf of public interests have

TABLE 8.4. Examples of Public Interest Groups in Washington Politics

Environmental and wildlife
    Environmental Defense Fund
    Greenpeace, USA
    Wildlife Advocacy Project
Consumer
    Consumer Federation of America
    National Association of Railroad Passengers
    Public Citizen
Government reform and citizen empowerment
    Common Cause
    Project on Government Oversight
    Rock the Vote
Other liberal groups
    American Civil Liberties Union
    Death Penalty Information Center
    Planned Parenthood Federation of America
Other conservative groups
    Americans for Tax Reform
    Committee on the Present Danger
    National Rifle Association
Other public interest
    Campaign for Tobacco-Free Kids
    National Crime Prevention Council
    National Safety Council

no monopoly on virtue. Just like supporters of policies that benefit particular constituencies, advocates of broad public interests can be sanctimonious or even not fully forthcoming. Besides, in any real political controversy, there is competition between opposing conceptions of the public interest: for example, wilderness preservation versus economic growth, consumer product safety versus low prices, and national security versus low taxes. When a public interest is on one side of an issue, there is usually a competing public interest on the other side.[39]

Many political conflicts have supporters of public and private goods on the same side. Consider the dispute over whether wilderness areas in national parks should be opened for snowmobile use in winter. Environmentalists might find it useful to ally with manufacturers of cross-country skis against snowmobile dealers. When a controversy brings together advocates for both public and private interests, the latter often attempt to cloak their policy positions in the mantle of the public good. However, even though all of them may be sincere in their support for the public good in question, it is possible to distinguish analytically between the cross-country ski manufacturer and the environmentalist when it comes to wilderness preservation or between the defense contractor and the advocate for national security when it comes to military preparedness. In each case the former stands to benefit selectively from the policy in question in a way that the latter does not.

It is extremely difficult to summarize the overall ideological position of the diverse organizations that seek to represent the public interest. The set of organizations representing public goods probably leans somewhat to the left. Still, Table 8.4 makes clear that there is also considerable representation of public goods valued by conservatives. In fact, explicitly ideological public interest groups—for example, anti- or pro-gun control groups on the domestic front or pro–national security or pro-peace groups in the international domain—are balanced between conservative and liberal organizations. Moreover, many public interest groups in various presumptively liberal categories are, in fact, either ideologically neutral or conservative. Examples include consumer groups like the American Automobile Association and the American Motorcyclist Association, wildlife organizations like Pheasants Forever, and government reform organizations like the Citizens against Government Waste. Furthermore, compared to advocates of liberal public interests, conservative public interest organizations are more likely to find themselves on the same side of a policy controversy as an intense private interest—for example, a corporation or trade association representing real estate developers or the manufacturers of infant car seats.

Conclusion

It is sometimes argued that "almost everybody" is in government relations, a circumstance that, if true, would surely contrast with our results about citizen voice expressed through individual activity. Our exploration of the contours of the organized interests in Washington politics has unearthed an astonishing number of organizations representing an astonishing number of interests—all with a stake in the outcome of some policy controversy and a legitimate story to tell to the public officials whose decisions affect their lives and livelihoods. Very few of these organizations sometimes gathered under the rubric of "interest groups" are membership groups, and only a tiny minority, less than one in eight, are associations composed of individual members.

Nevertheless, for all the variety of interests represented by organizations in Washington, the pressure system is far from universal. Many constituencies with a seeming interest in federal policies—parents of children in Head Start programs, women at home, office receptionists, Wal-Mart associates, criminal defendants awaiting trial, recipients of Temporary Assistance for Needy Families benefits, parking lot attendants—have no organization dedicated specifically to their interests. Powerful evidence of the extent to which the pressure system is not representative emerges from data of a very different kind: a study of political controversies sufficiently important that questions were asked of the American public on surveys. It turns out that almost no relationship exists between the positions taken by the average citizen and the positions taken by interest groups.[40]

What is more, both the free rider problem and the resource-constraint problem imply that organized interest representation in Washington is riddled with inequalities. The free rider problem implies that public goods like automobile safety, crime reduction, an end to capital punishment, or lower taxes are less likely to receive organizational support. When we considered the set of organizations that act on behalf of such public goods, we saw, on the one hand, that a wide variety of such causes receive organized advocacy. On the other hand, public goods-seeking organizations are less common than might be expected on the basis of the number of people who would potentially benefit from the conditions being sought.

In other respects, the public interest groups active in Washington defy some popular conceptions. The prominence of certain public interest groups—for example, environmental groups—leads some to the conclusion that the public interest sector is uniformly liberal. In fact, in most controversies involving a public good, an alternative public good is also at stake, usually on the opposite side of the ideological spectrum: there are, for example, trade-offs between consumer product safety and low consumer prices. Taken together, the public interest groups in the pressure system lean in a much less decisively liberal direction than is sometimes imagined.

This observation leads to a second point, one that fits with the themes that emerged in our consideration of participatory inequalities among individuals. While they take seriously the costs of founding and maintaining an organization, formal presentations of the free rider problem often miss the differences among constituencies in their ability to bear those costs. Resource constraints have a powerful impact on which voices are heard through the medium of collective advocacy.

Compared to those well endowed with resources (especially business interests), economically disadvantaged constituencies—including economically disadvantaged groups defined by another characteristic, such as race or gender—have limited representation in pressure politics if they are represented at all.[41] Two especially notable findings in this regard bear repeating: first, unless they are members of a union, unskilled workers have no occupational associations at all to represent their interests in Washington; and second, although a small number of organizations advocate for the poor, no single organization brings together recipients of means-tested government benefits (such as Medicaid) acting on their own behalf.

Understanding the barriers to the formation of organizations helps us understand why the voices in the heavenly chorus continue to sing with an upper-class accent and why there are some notable political silences. Some argue that the absence of organized representation for what would seem to be a politically relevant interest is prima facie evidence for an absence of political concern on the part of those who might be presumed to have shared political interests. However, the lack of an organized political voice for convenience store clerks, beneficiaries of the Earned Income Tax Credit, office receptionists, parents at home full-time with children, and people who have been denied coverage for costly medical treatments does not necessarily imply satisfaction with current public policies or a preference for spending time and energy going fishing, attending the opera, or putting in more hours on the job. In sum, the barriers to group mobilization are especially high when the group in question is relatively large and not well endowed with political resources. Under the circumstances, we cannot assume that the amount of organization activity is a surrogate for the intensity of group political preferences or that the paucity of organized political groups representing the disadvantaged resource indicates indifference to political outcomes.

9

Representing Interests through Organizational Activity

> Every other rich country uses the same medical technology, gets the same or better health outcomes, and pays vastly lower sums. Why the disparity? Health care in America is big business, and in America big business means big lobbying and big campaign contributions, the public interest be damned.
>
> —JEFFREY SACHS[1]

As shown in Chapter 8, the free rider problem and the resource problem tilt the set of organizations active in national politics toward the advantaged. In this chapter we use this already skewed baseline to assess the representativeness of political voice through organizations. The Washington Representatives Study uses data from a variety of sources to measure whether organizations are involved in politics—and, if so, how much they do.[2] These extensive systematic empirical data allow us to describe the political voice emerging from organized involvement in national politics.

The Founders deliberately designed the governing structure in Washington to establish multiple, often overlapping, institutions with numerous points of access for those who seek a hearing by policymakers. Sometimes, organizations seeking policy influence have no choice of venue: they must testify before the particular Senate subcommittee or executive agency that

Philip E. Jones is coauthor of this chapter.

is currently holding hearings or respond in the appropriate court if sued. Ordinarily, however, there are options.

Organized interests must start by asking whether—and, if so, how intensely—to become involved. Such an assessment requires consideration of the availability of appropriate resources and skills, the importance of an issue to the organization or its members, the likelihood of support or opposition from other organizations, and the probability of achieving the desired policy objectives. When the necessary resources are lacking, the possibilities for policy influence remote, the political configuration unfavorable, or the issue of secondary importance, the decision may be to do nothing—a decision that may send signals to the organization's members, if any; to other organized interests; and to policymakers.[3]

Organizational leaders need to make choices not only about whether to act but also about where to locate their political actions. These decisions reflect the mission of the governmental arena, its rules for handling political matters, its receptivity to particular points of view, and the resource requirements for becoming active. Organizations frequently engage in forum shopping, seeking to locate a controversy in the institutional setting that, by dint of institutional mission or the particular incumbents in place, promises the greatest likelihood of a favorable outcome.

The choice of venue affects the tactics used. Tactics that are appropriate when lobbying Congress—for example, meeting personally with those responsible for making policy or doing favors for them—are proscribed when dealing with the federal judiciary.[4] Furthermore, in any venue there may be choices about which particular policymakers to target. No single strategy works for all organizations, for all issues, or for approaches to all policymakers.[5] Although it seems logical to focus on persuading a legislator who is on the fence, it may be worth attempting to persuade a legislator who seems to be opposed, especially if the lobbyist can point to a link to interests in the district. It may be productive to work with allies, for example, urging them to give higher priority to the matter at stake or helping them shape legislative strategy. Just to make matters more complicated, these are not mutually exclusive options. Organizations may create synergies by combining tactics, for example, grassroots lobbying or spending by political action committees (PACs) with direct attempts at influence.[6] Or they may play simultaneously in more than one institutional arena. For example, corporations use political expenditures aimed at Congress to signal to a bureaucratic agency that overly rigorous regulatory treatment will result in an appeal for relief from Congress.[7]

Organizational Resources for Political Action

Many resources are relevant for political advocacy—ranging from having an appealing message to having skilled personnel on staff. Such resources vary in the extent to which they can be substituted for one another in the policy fray, but money is ordinarily the most fungible. In a world in which most activity and advocacy is undertaken by hired professionals rather than by volunteers, a large budget can purchase personnel—especially talented personnel with specialized expertise.

Some organizations have large staffs and big budgets, and others are much leaner operations. Besides, some organizations have millions of members, others have thousands, and the majority have none at all. Fortunately, the *Washington Representatives* directories contain a valuable surrogate measure of an organization's political capacity: the number of in-house lobbyists it has on staff and the number of outside law, public relations, or consulting firms it hires.

Washington lobbyists are often characterized as fat cats with bottomless war chests to fund their political operations. In the 2011 directory, General Electric listed 44 in-house lobbyists and 21 outside firms; the Pharmaceutical Research and Manufacturers of America (PhRMA) listed 32 and 39; the U.S. Chamber of Commerce weighed in at 109 and 19, respectively. Nevertheless, most organizations fielded much smaller staffs. In fact, just over four-fifths (81 percent) of the organizations in the directory either hire a single outside firm or have only one or two people on staff in Washington and hire no outside firms.[8]

Informing and Activating Potential Supporters

One time-honored tactic of political influence is grassroots lobbying: communicating either with the public at large or with organization members and supporters to highlight issues, shape opinions, or generate communications to public officials in support of favored political positions.[9] In contrast to direct lobbying efforts, which usually involve paid professional advocates and specialized or technical information, grassroots lobbying can be used to call attention to policy matters deemed important to a political organization and to provide legislators with a sense of public—or, especially, constituency—opinion. Organized interests often combine outsider strategies with traditional insider tactics.[10] Arguments made by organized interests when they lobby become more compelling in the context of evidence of constituent concern about an issue.

Given the natural predilection of elected officials, especially legislators, to feel compelled to listen and respond to constituents, grassroots lobbying is an obvious tactic for associations that have individuals as members, but it can also work effectively for memberless institutions like corporations or universities. They can mobilize employees seeking to protect their jobs, customers seeking to protect a valued product (for example, vitamin supplements) threatened with federal regulation or taxation, or stockholders or executives seeking to protect a company's profits. Corporations and other resource-endowed organizations perceive constituent lobbying as so effective that they sometimes weigh in on public debates surreptitiously by undertaking "astroturf lobbying"—hiring public relations firms to manufacture artificial grassroots campaigns.[11] These grassroots mobilization strategies not only facilitate the pursuit of policy objectives but also serve to raise the visibility of an organization and to attract new members or supporters.[12] Furthermore, they can be used to reassure existing members or supporters, demonstrating that the organization's leadership and staff are busy fighting the good fight on behalf of shared goals.[13]

In spite of the obvious political benefits of grassroots lobbying, it can be costly in terms of time and resources.[14] Furthermore, going public entails the risk of activating opponents as well as supporters. Besides, once a grassroots campaign has been initiated, it may be difficult to control.[15] In fact, if the policy views of an organization's members and staff conflict, mobilizing the membership to lobby can be downright counterproductive.[16] Most attempts at political influence take other forms.

Organizational Activity in Washington

We used archival sources to code information about the extent of organizational involvement in other forms of Washington political activity.[17] Table 9.1 presents the distribution of organized interest activity of different kinds. One striking aspect of the data in Table 9.1 is the sheer volume of what organizations do. The figures in the bottom row of the table show that organizational political action is a massive enterprise involving more than 14,000 listed organizations, nearly 13,000 in-house lobbyists and more than 16,000 contracts with outside firms, more than $6 billion in spending on lobbying, more than 12,000 congressional testimonies, and nearly 7,000 signings of amicus briefs.

TABLE 9.1. Distribution of Political Activity by Organized Interests

	All Organizations[a]	In-House Lobbyists[a]	Outside Firms[a]	Lobbying Expenditures[a]	Congressional Testimony[b]	Amicus Briefs[b]
Corporations[a]	36.6%	27%	44%	54%	16%	6%
Trade and other business associations	10.2	21	11	20	13	8
Occupational associations	5.4	11	3	5	9	11
Unions	0.7	3	<1	1	3	1
Education	5.7	3	5	3	3	4
Health	5.2	3	5	4	3	1
Social welfare or poor	1.1	1	1	<1	2	2
Identity groups[c]	3.6	5	3	2	6	10
Public interest	4.5	10	3	2	11	13
State and local governments	12.3	4	12	4	18	36
Foreign	6.2	3	6	3	2	1
Other	7.9	10	6	3	15	8
Don't know	0.7	<1	1	<1	1	<1
Total	100.1%	101%	100%	101%	102%	101%
N	14,365	12,830	16,531	$6,566,988,000	12,619	6,894

Source: Washington Representatives Study.

[a] Distributions for all organizations listed in the 2011 *Washington Representatives* directory.

[b] Data from 2001 includes all organizations that undertook this activity regardless of whether they were listed in the 2001 *Washington Representatives* directory.

[c] Includes organizations representing racial, ethnic, religious, or LGBT groups, the elderly, or women.

When interpreting the figures in Table 9.1, it is important to keep in mind that, only in the first column of numbers, which shows the distribution of organizations in the 2011 *Washington Representatives* directory, is the organization the unit of analysis. Other columns show the distribution of the number of in-house lobbyists on staff in organizations' Washington offices, outside lobbying firms hired, dollars spent on lobbying, testimonies before congressional committees and subcommittees, and signings of amicus briefs filed before the Supreme Court. Although it will be useful to compare the share of activity in any realm for a particular category of organization with its share for all organizations, it is critical to recognize that the distribution of organizations in the first column of numbers is a skewed population. Most obviously, it underrepresents the economic interests of all but the most affluent Americans—not only needy ones like recipients of means-tested government benefits but also nonunionized workers in nonprofessional, non-managerial occupations. In addition, the interests of a variety of noneconomic groups—ranging from students to women at home to non–English speakers to supporters of various public goods—receive scant representation through organizations.

IN-HOUSE AND OUTSIDE LOBBYISTS

The columns in Table 9.1 labeled "In House" and "Outside" bring together information about the share of lobbying capacity—whether in-house lobbyists or outside firms—for each category of organization. The relative size of the shares reflect, first and foremost, the number of such organizations and thus their weight in the overall distribution of organizations. Corporations and trade and other business associations hire a large share of lobbyists: 48 percent of in-house lobbyists and 55 percent of the outside firms. Compared to their share of all organizations, corporations and state and local governments—which have good reasons for being located in places other than Washington and for which dealings with the federal government can facilitate, but do not define, their overall mission—field a smaller share of in-house lobbyists and hire a larger share of outside firms. For occupational associations, labor unions, organizations representing public interests, and groups based on identity, the opposite is true.

SPENDING ON LOBBYING

The best single surrogate measure of how much an organization does in Washington is its lobbying spending. For each organization in the 2011 directory, we recorded the amount spent on lobbying in 2010 and 2011 as reported in the lobbying registrations filed under the Lobbying Disclosure Act (LDA), which was passed in 1995 and has been amended since.[18] Of the activities we consider, spending on lobbying is the only one that allows an organization to use its financial resources on its own initiative—constrained only by the registration requirements under the LDA and the restrictions on lobbying by nonprofits.[19]

The LDA superseded the relatively toothless 1946 Federal Regulation of Lobbying Act and covers both oral and written communications about legislative or administrative issues not just with members of Congress but also with their staff members as well as high-level policymakers in the White House and executive branch agencies. Although the LDA is stronger than the act it replaced, registered lobbyists are not required either to name specific government contacts or to divulge expenditures on such political activities as monitoring political developments, grassroots lobbying, conducting and publicizing research, holding fundraisers, or filing amicus briefs—activities that can absorb substantial amounts of organizational resources, time, and skills. Therefore, the reports cover only part, and often a very small part, of the funds spent by an organization in pursuit of political influence and only a fraction of the number of individuals who are associated with the business of influencing policy outcomes.[20]

Data from lobbying registrations show that, even when we omit organizations that registered no lobbying expenses, the vast bulk of spending on lobbying is concentrated among a very small share of political organizations. Of the more than $6 billion spent on lobbying during 2010 and 2011 by the registered organizations listed in the 2011 *Washington Representatives* directory, 39 percent was spent by the top 1 percent of lobbying spenders. Fully 80 percent was spent by the top 10 percent of lobbying spenders, and a mere 1 percent by the bottom 50 percent of lobbying spenders. Had we been able to include in the denominator the organizations that did not register because their lobbying expenses fell below the threshold in the LDA, these figures would have shown an even greater concentration of lobbying spending.

When it comes to the distribution of money spent on lobbying in Table 9.1, spending by corporations and trade or other business associations is substantially higher than their already notable share of organizations and dwarfs the share of spending by any other kind of organization.[21] Of the $6.57 billion spent on lobbying in 2010–2011 by the organizations listed in the 2011 *Washington Representatives* directory, 54 percent was spent by corporations and 20 percent by trade and other business associations.

TABLE 9.2. Lobbying Expenditures, 2010–2011

	Average Lobbying Spending	Total Lobbying Spending
Corporations	$675,000	$3,538,965,000
Trade and other business associations	$885,000	1,290,552,000
Occupational associations	$406,000	311,676,000
Unions	$658,000	70,646,000
Education	$204,000	165,489,000
Health	$333,000	246,959,000
Social welfare or poor	$108,000	17,823,000
Identity groups[a]	$231,000	118,900,000
Public interest	$175,000	111,182,000
State and local governments	$151,000	265,360,000
Foreign	$224,000	198,776,000
Other	$197,000	222,610,000
Don't know	$81,000	8,050,000
Total	$459,000	$6,566,988,000

Source: Washington Representatives Study (2011).
[a]Includes organizations representing racial, ethnic, religious, or LGBT groups, the elderly, or women.

Table 9.2 shows the average amount and the total spent on lobbying for the organizations in various categories. Trade and other business associations and corporations spend the highest average amounts, $885,000 and $675,000, respectively. Unions are not far behind at $658,000, and occupational associations at $406,000. On average, state and local governments, public interest organizations (which also face legal constraints on lobbying), and organizations advocating on behalf of social welfare and the poor spend much less on lobbying. In this last category, if we omit the organizations that deliver services directly, we find that the small number of organizations that advocate for the poor average only $73,000 on lobbying.

The figures for total lobbying spending in the right-hand column of the table reflect not only average lobbying spending for the organizations in any category but also the number of organizations in that category. Total spending by trade and other business associations and, especially, corporations dwarfs lobbying spending by the organizations in any other category. Corporations and trade and other business associations alone accounted for $4.83 billion of the total of $6.57 billion spent on lobbying—almost three-quarters of the total spending. Although unions are competitive when it comes to average spending per organization, there are so few unions that their lobbying spending of $70 million is only 1 percent of the total. In contrast, reflecting their more limited resources and, in some cases, restraints on lobbying by tax-exempt organizations, organizations advocating on behalf of public goods spent $111 million, those advocating on behalf of African Americans and Latinos $3.2 million, and those advocating on behalf of social welfare benefits or the poor $18 million—of which most derived from service providers and not a single penny came from a group of recipients of means-tested benefits acting on their own behalf.

Buried in these aggregate categories are additional disparities in lobbying expenditures:

- Among occupational associations, the higher-status professional associations represent a majority, 63 percent, of the lobbying spending.
- Organizations representing African Americans spent a mere 2 percent, and organizations of women only 3 percent, of the quite limited lobbying spending by identity groups. Instead, organizations, mostly tribes, representing Native Americans and organizations representing the elderly—responsible for 35 percent and 40 percent, respectively—dominated lobbying spending by identity groups.
- Among organizations seeking public goods, environmental and wildlife groups account for almost a third, 30 percent, of lobbying spending for this diverse group of organizations.
- Many organizations—some of which are identifiably liberal or conservative—do not fit easily into one of these aggregate categories. The imbalance in lobbying spending between such liberal and conservative organizations is noteworthy: total lobbying spending by the "other conservative groups" was just about double the total spending by "other liberal groups."

TESTIFYING BEFORE CONGRESS

At the discretion of their chairs, congressional committees and subcommittees hold hearings that give organized interests an opportunity to state a public case either by sending written comments or by testifying in person.[22] Organizations retain control over whether and how much they lobby, but the initiative rests with legislators and their staffs when it comes to congressional testimony. Depending on the underlying purposes of the hearing—whether, for example, to explore policy alternatives and their consequences or to create a public record in favor of one approach—the list of witnesses may be balanced among various perspectives or stacked in one direction.[23]

As shown in Table 9.1, testifying in Congress represents a broader set of interests and a quite different skew than the distribution of lobbyists and lobbying expenditures.[24] The modal testifier represents a subnational government or consortium of governments. Corporations and trade and other business associations, which together accounted for nearly three-quarters of the dollars expended on lobbying, account for a much smaller share of the testimonies: 16 and 13 percent, respectively. Labor unions have high rates of testifying. Because they are few in number, however, they constitute only 3 percent of the testimonies. At 11 percent, advocates of broad public interests constitute a much larger share of the testimonies than of lobbying dollars. A similar point can be made about organizations representing identity groups (6 percent of the testimonies) and organizations representing social service providers and the economically needy (2 percent of the testimonies). Indeed, for the first time we see the barest trace of activity by an organization composed of means-tested public benefits recipients: 8 of the nearly 13,000 testifiers (0.06 percent) represented such an organization.

FILING AMICUS BRIEFS

Unlike legislatures, which function so importantly as arenas for organized interest efforts to influence policy, courts cannot initiate political action. Litigants do. Going to court requires a real dispute, not a hypothetical concern, in which the contending parties have a stake. The adversarial nature of the judicial process implies that the sides are sharply defined in a way that they are not always in legislative matters, and the outcomes are more likely to be zero sum.

Although they cannot engage in conventional lobbying of judges and their clerks, organized interests that seek to influence federal judicial outcomes have several options. They can focus on nominees to the bench and attempt to have an impact on Senate confirmation processes. They can file suit. Or they can file an amicus curiae ("friend of the court") brief.[25] Although any party wishing to file an amicus brief must secure the permission of the court, scholars agree that the Supreme Court is unlikely to deny permission and that amicus briefs are becoming more and more common, especially at the merits stage of Supreme Court cases.[26]

Filing amicus briefs is explicitly about the expression of political voice and can be thought of as the judicial counterpart of legislative lobbying.[27] However, in contrast to legislative lobbyists, who can increase their leverage by linking a forceful presentation to inducements, including campaign donations and other favors, those filing amicus briefs can deliver nothing more than a compelling argument.

Under ordinary circumstances, the objective of filing an amicus brief is to influence the outcome of the decision—whether a decision to grant *certiorari* (that is, to hear a case) or a decision on the merits. However, even when organized interests have no expectation of changing which side prevails in the present case, they may seek to have an impact on how the argument in the decision is framed, to influence details of the decision if not its overall direction, to shape the direction of dissenting opinions, or to alter the terms of future debate not only in judicial proceedings but in the media or in other political arenas. While amicus briefs often repeat and reinforce the arguments made by one of the parties to the case, they ordinarily provide additional information to justices who are aware that the decision in the particular case in front of them may have implications beyond its impact on the immediate litigants. An amicus brief can make arguments that litigants cannot make, inform the court of the broader implications of the case, provide additional background information, indicate the lineup of political and social forces concerned about the case, and clarify who besides the immediate litigants might be affected by the outcome.[28]

Because filing an amicus brief is expensive in terms of costly lawyers' time, organizations often make strategic calculations.[29] Beyond seeking to influence what cases the Supreme Court hears and how they are decided, organized interests may be animated by the need to reassure members or donors of the association's vigorous efforts in promoting its objectives.[30] In addition, litigants often encourage the filing of amicus briefs, and those who plan to file amicus briefs often encourage others to sign along with them—as a way of forging alliances with organizations having similar political predispositions, demonstrating wider support before the Court, and sharing the costs.[31] Regardless of the pressures that might impel organized interests to file amicus briefs, however, amici do not seem to select only cases that are sure winners.[32]

Our data show that only a small share of organizations listed in the 2001 *Washington Representatives* directory filed an amicus brief in a case in which a petition of certiorari was filed during either the 2000–2001 or the 2001–2002 term and that the share varies substantially across various kinds of organizations.[33]

The pattern for amicus briefs parallels that for Congressional testimonies.[34] State and local governments, which account for more than a third of the signings, are by far the biggest hitters. Because Supreme Court decisions so often involve issues of federalism or consequences for the states, this finding is hardly remarkable. At 6 and 8 percent, respectively, corporations and trade and other business associations account for a much smaller share of the signings in 2001 than they do for any other form of political activity listed in Table 9.1. Even so, unions filed only 1 percent of the briefs during the period. Besides, business organizations, especially the U.S. Chamber of Commerce, may have subsequently discovered the utility of filing briefs with the business-friendly Roberts Court.[35]

Given the significance of the courts in matters surrounding public goods, civil rights, and nondiscrimination, it is not surprising that organizations based on public goods, (13 percent of the signings) and identity groups (10 percent of the signings) figure even more importantly in signing briefs than in testifying in Congress. Organizations that provide services to or advocacy on behalf of the economically needy constitute, as they did for testimonies, 2 percent of the signings. Still, there is a trace of activity attributable to organizations of recipients of means-tested benefits: 29 of the 6,922 signings (0.4 percent) came from such groups, usually representing public housing tenants.

A NOTE ON MAKING PAC DONATIONS

To supplement their attempts at policy influence through direct communications to public officials, organizations become involved in elections by, for example, recruiting and assisting candidates; communicating with and mobilizing their own members; and especially if, like labor unions, they have large memberships, providing campaign volunteers to work on behalf of favored candidates.[36] A common organizational strategy for electoral action that may be declining in relative importance is making contributions to candidates and parties through political action committees (PACs).

Concern about campaign finance in America has a long and twisting history. The 1907 Tillman Act, part of the Progressive-era reaction to the free-for-all campaign contribution practices of the late nineteenth century, outlawed direct campaign contributions in federal elections by corporations. In 1943, the Smith-Connally Act (or War Labor Disputes Act) proscribed unions from making direct contributions. The 1947 Taft-Harley act made this ban permanent. At the urging of labor unions seeking to ensure that the separate PACs they had established as their campaign finance arms would not be put out of business, the 1974 amendments to the Federal Election Campaign Act gave them legal standing. In the aftermath, corporations sought clarification as to whether they also had the right to establish PACs. In its 1975 *Sun Oil* decision, the Federal Election Commission gave corporations a green light to use resources from the corporate treasury to establish and administer PACs and solicit managers and shareholders to make contributions.

After the *Sun Oil* decision, PAC giving—by corporations and a variety of other kinds of institutions and associations—took off quickly. In constant dollars, total PAC expenditures shot up from $77.4 million to $2.20 billion between 1977 and 2012. Corporate PAC expenditures multiplied more than fourteen-fold, from $15.2 million to $343.0 million, and labor PAC expenditures grew from $18.6 million to $279.4 million.[37]

PAC giving generates concern about the possibility of undue influence on electoral results or policy outcomes by interests with deep pockets and identifiable policy agendas. We have pointed out consistently that forms of political expression that rely fundamentally on inputs of money rather than on such resources as time or skill raise concerns about equal political voice, arguing that citizens are much more unequal with respect to the size of their bank accounts than with respect to the amount of their leisure or the acuity of their skills. That said, through the giving by union PACs, ordinary people gain greater representation than they do through other forms of organization-based political activity. Three unions of skilled, blue-collar workers—the International Brotherhood of Electrical Workers, International Union of Operating Engineers, and International Association of Machinists and Aerospace Workers—were among the top twenty PAC donors to candidates in the 2016 electoral cycle.[38] In contrast, the list of fifty most generous individual donors in the 2016 electoral cycle, composed mostly of entrepreneurs, investment and hedge fund managers, heirs to substantial fortunes, and those with private foundations, includes not a single practicing physician or lawyer in a firm—much less an electrician, crane operator, or airplane mechanic.[39] PAC donations from unions accounted for 26 percent of the total PAC giving in the two electoral cycles between 1999 and 2002, a figure that is roughly half the size of PAC giving associated with business over the same period.

In spite of the substantial sums involved, PAC contributions have never been the most significant source of money for campaigns. What is more, in recent years the campaign giving environment has changed substantially. Corporations are increasingly giving "dark money," that is, directing contributions to organizations that do not have to disclose their donors and have broadened their focus to encompass low-profile races at the state and local levels.[40] Furthermore, donations from affluent individuals—sometimes bundled by a corporation or other organization lest there be any ambiguity about the collective source—have skyrocketed. Thus, at the same time that the total amounts spent on campaigns have shot up, the relative importance of—and concern about—PAC giving has faded.

Distribution of Organized Interest Activity: Summing Up

The pie charts in Figure 9.1 reconfigure some of the findings in Table 9.1 to emphasize the categories of organizations to which we have paid special attention: organizations representing business, the economically less privileged, identity groups, and broad public interests. Among business organizations we include U.S. and foreign corporations, U.S. subsidiaries of foreign corporations, for-profit firms of professionals (such as law and consulting firms), U.S. and foreign trade and other business associations, and business-affiliated research organizations. We define organizations representing the economic interests of the less privileged extremely broadly and include

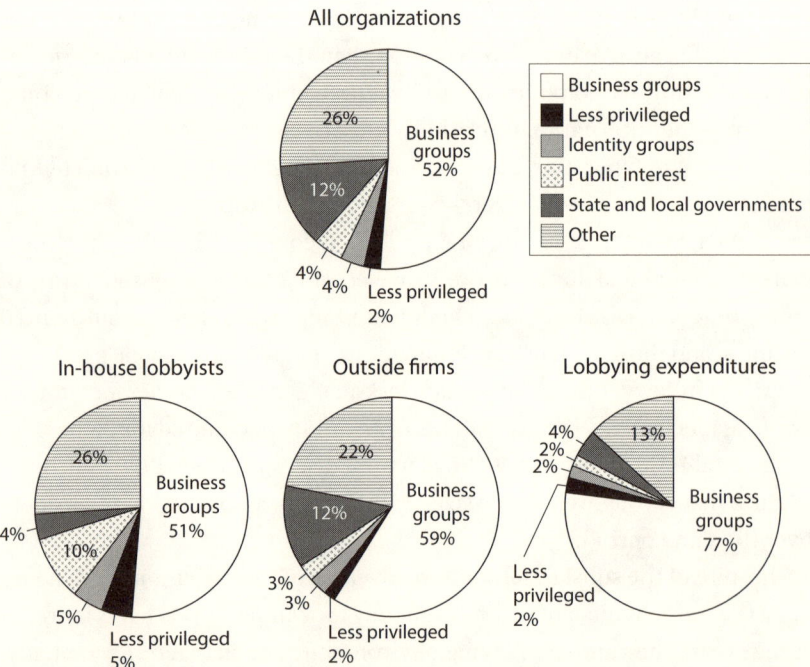

FIGURE 9.1. Distribution of Political Resources by Type of Organized Interest
Source: Washington Representatives Study (2011).
Note: For-profit firms of professionals that hired more than one in-house lobbyist are excluded from this distribution.

blue-collar and white-collar unions, social service providers, organizations advocating on behalf of the poor, and other occupational associations.

Figure 9.1 underlines that, in the New Gilded Age, business interests weigh heavily—and the interests of broad publics and the less privileged, whether defined in terms of economic well-being or identity, much less heavily—in organized interest politics. This formulation holds whether we are considering the number of organizations or their capacity to get involved as measured by the number of lobbyists on staff or the number of outside firms they hire. This pattern is especially pronounced when it comes to spending on lobbying, a domain in which economic resources are paramount. More than three-quarters of the dollars spent on lobbying in the two-year period originated with business.

Political Voice through Organized Interest Activity: The Bottom Line

In Chapter 8 we saw that the representation of politically relevant interests is anything but inevitable. The shape of the pressure system reflects both the free rider problem and the resource constraint problem, with the result that broad public interests—whether liberal, conservative, or neither—and the economically disadvantaged have limited organizational representation.

In this chapter we have explored political voice through the medium of organized interest activity and learned the following:

- Like income or wealth, the vast bulk of spending on lobbying is concentrated among a very small share of political organizations. Of lobbying spending during 2010 and 2011 by the registered organizations listed in the 2011 *Washington Representatives* directory, over a third, 39 percent, was spent by the top 1 percent of lobbying spenders. Fully 80 percent was spent by the top 10 percent of lobbying spenders and a mere 1 percent by the bottom 50 percent of lobbying spenders.
- Although the weight of advocacy by organizations representing business interests varies across domains of organized interest activity, in no case is it outweighed by the activity of either organizations representing the less privileged or public interest groups. The weight of business advocacy is particularly notable when it comes to forms of input in which the metric is dollars. It is striking that 77 percent of expenditures on lobbying originate with organizations representing business.

- Testifying in Congress and filing amicus briefs are the only forms of organizational advocacy for which identity, public interest, and especially state and local governments achieve political voice at a volume close to that of occupational associations and business.
- In no domain of organized interest activity does activity by organizations that provide services to or political representation of the poor register more than a trace. Activity on their own behalf by recipients of means-tested benefits barely exists at all. Unless nonprofessional, nonmanagerial workers are union members, their economic interests receive very little representation in any arena of organized interest activity. The interests of unskilled workers receive none at all.
- As individual organizations, unions are quite politically active. However, because there are so few of them, they rarely register collectively as a significant share of organized interest activity.
- Identity groups are, across the board, also a small share of organized interest activity.
- In the multidimensional issue space of American politics, it is impossible to specify what share of activity should represent public goods. However, in no domain does activity by public interest organizations outweigh activity by organizations representing business, and activity by conservative public interest organizations is a more substantial share of activity on behalf of public interests than is generally acknowledged.

As a medium for the expression of political voice, pressure politics contrasts with political participation by individuals in the extent to which financial resources can be used to purchase professional advocacy not only to enlarge the number of voices but also to substitute skilled professionals for citizen amateurs. As with any form of political voice in which the principal resource is money, the advantaged are able to speak more loudly. The heavenly chorus does sing with an upper-class accent, and the voices of advocates of broad publics and the less privileged are much more muted.

PART IV

10

Growing Economic Inequality and Its (Partially) Political Roots

- In 2013, America's twenty-five highest-paid hedge fund managers made more than twice as much as all the kindergarten teachers in the country taken together.[1]
- In 2013, the combined family wealth of just six members of the Walton family added up to more than the wealth of 52.5 million, or 42.9 percent, of American families.[2]
- The minimum wage was $2.65 per hour in 1978. Had it kept up with the cost of living, it would have been $9.62—not $7.25—in 2014. If it had kept up with the increase in compensation of CEOs of large corporations, it would have been $95.97 in 2014.[3]
- As measured by the poverty gap—that is, the percentage by which the mean income of the poor falls below the poverty line—the poor in the United States are quite poor indeed. In a group of thirty-four rich countries, only in Korea, Mexico, and Spain is the poverty gap higher.[4]
- In state university systems, merit aid flows disproportionately to those who are less needy: about one in five students from households with annual incomes over $250,000 receive merit aid—in contrast to one in ten from families making less than $30,000.[5]

When it comes to money, Americans are very unequal. Economic inequality has grown over the last generation, and as we have shown repeatedly, participatory inequalities are grounded in disparities in income. Those who are economically well-off speak more loudly in politics by giving more money and by engaging more frequently in almost all forms of political participation—even ones that cost nothing. The affluent are also better represented and more active when it comes to political voice through the organizations that hire professionals as lobbyists.

Political and economic inequalities intersect in several ways. Not only is money a critical resource for both individual and organizational input into politics, but also economic disparities shape the content of political conflict. Although the list of contentious political issues in contemporary America is long and varied, matters associated with differences in income and material well-being—ranging from tax policy to health-care policy to Social Security—generate a great deal of political conflict.[6] Economic differences produce political conflict. Besides, growing economic inequalities result from public policy as well as from economic and technological change.

Increasing Economic Inequality

By a variety of metrics, economic inequality has grown over the past generation.[7] Detailed information on household income—earnings, dividends, rents, and such government transfers as Social Security—goes back to the passage of the constitutional amendment authorizing the federal income tax in 1913. The share of pretax national income commanded by the top 10 percent and the top 1 percent of American households rose after World War I and peaked in the late 1920s. Then, during World War II, it decreased markedly, remaining relatively stable until the 1970s. During this period, increased income resulting from growth in both productivity and national income benefited the vast majority of middle-class and poor households below the top tenth while the most affluent lagged behind. Then, in the late 1970s, income inequality began to climb.

Figure 10.1 presents striking evidence about what happened between 1979 and 2011. As measured in constant dollars, average after-tax household income for those at the bottom of the economic ladder—and for the middle-class households in the middle three-fifths—grew quite modestly over the period. In contrast, household incomes for those in the top fifth increased substantially: the growth in dollars in household income of those in the highest fifth was larger than the average 2011 income of those in the fourth quintile on the economic ladder. Even more notable is the extent to which this growth was concentrated in the top 1 percent of households. This

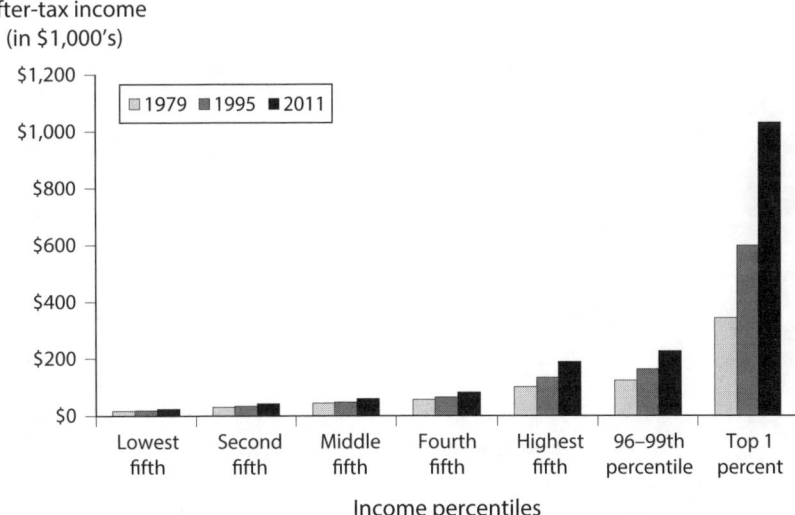

FIGURE 10.1. Growing Economic Inequality: After-Tax Household Income by Income Group, 1979–2011 (2011 Dollars)
Source: Congressional Budget Office, "The Distribution of Household Income and Federal Taxes, 2011," November 12, 2014, Supplemental Data, at https://www.cbo.gob/publication/49440 (accessed on December 26, 2015).

upward redistribution benefited an extremely narrow slice of households: only the top 10 percent saw their share of after-tax income grow, and the gains went disproportionately to the top 1—and even the top 0.1—percent.

Discussions of increasing economic inequality tend to focus on the extent to which the rich have become richer compared to the middle class. A trend less often noticed is the fact that, by some metrics, the poor have gotten poorer. After decreasing for a number of years during the 1960s, the poverty rate leveled off and has varied within a relatively narrow range since then.[8] The relative stability of the poverty rate, which separates families into groups of poor and non-poor, obscures the trend toward deeper poverty among poor households. Between 1996 and 2011, the number of people who live in extreme poverty—that is, who live for at least one month a year on no more than $2 a day per person—doubled.[9]

EARNINGS

The story about earnings and wealth parallels that for household income. For most households, the principal source of income is earnings, that is, wages

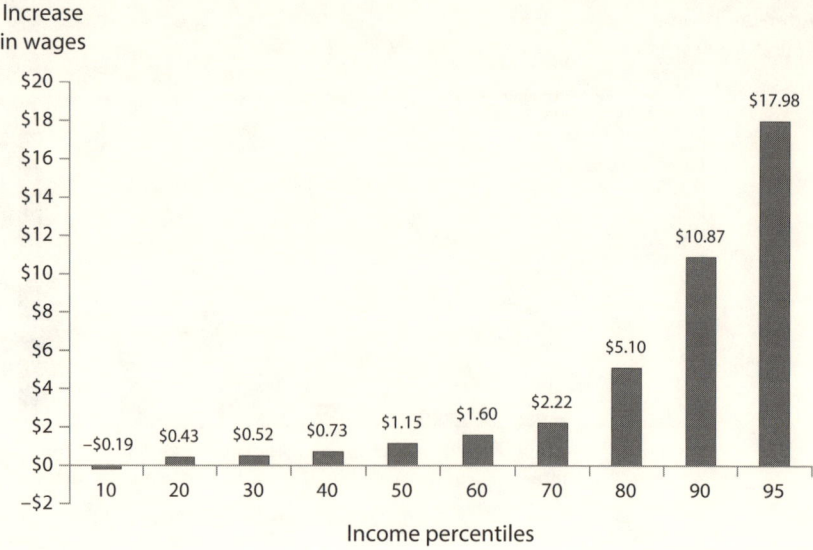

FIGURE 10.2. Growing Economic Inequality: Change in Hourly Wages by Wage Percentile, 1979–2015 (2015 Dollars)
Source: Economic Policy Institute analysis of Current Population Survey Outgoing Rotation Group microdata, State of Working America Data Library, "Wages by Percentile," 2016.

and salaries derived from paid work. Wage and price controls during World War II resulted in substantial wage compression, especially among high-wage earners. Surprisingly, when the controls were lifted, the share of wages commanded by top earners did not immediately bounce back to prewar levels. However, in the 1970s it began to increase steadily before skyrocketing in the late 1980s and late 1990s. As shown in Figure 10.2, between 1979 and 2015—a period during which productivity gains were substantial—workers in the lowest decile actually lost ground in terms of real wages, and improvements in real wages for all but those in the top two deciles were modest.

Although much has been made of the increasing returns to education, what is striking is the extent to which the fruits of economic and productivity growth in recent decades accrued so disproportionately to those at the very, very top and not to low- and middle-wage workers or even to workers who have college diplomas or advanced degrees. Between 1979 and 2010, the wage and salary income of the vast majority of Americans in the bottom 90 percent grew in real terms by 15 percent. Those at the top of the pyramid (in the 90th to 99th percentile) saw their paychecks grow by 46 percent. The analogous figures for those in the stratosphere, the top 1 percent

> **BOX 10.1** Compensation for CEOs and Ordinary Workers
>
> In the nation's largest firms, CEO compensation rose 941 percent between 1978 and 2015, a rate far higher than the increase in the stock market (543 percent) or the pay of the top .1 percent of earners (320 percent).
>
> Between 1973 and 2015, productivity increased 73 percent in the United States—at the same time that the average hourly earnings of nonsupervisory workers went up a mere 11 percent.
>
> *Sources*: Lawrence Mishel and Jessica Schieder, Economic Policy Institute, "CEO Compensation Grew Faster Than the Wages of the Top 0.1 Percent and the Stock Market," July 13, 2016, http://www.epi.org/publication/ceo-compensation-grew-faster-than-the-wages-of-the-top-0-1-percent-and-the-stock-market/; and Economic Policy Institute, "The Productivity–Pay Gap," August 2016, http://www.epi.org/productivity-pay-gap/ (accessed January 14, 2017).

and tippy-top .1 percent, are 131 percent and 278 percent, respectively (see Box 10.1).[10]

Meanwhile, total compensation of CEOs at the nation's largest corporations shot up by almost 1,000 percent between 1978 and 2014,[11] a trend fueled, at least in part, by the restructuring of executive pay, in particular the inclusion of stock options in compensation packages. In 1965, CEO compensation was, on average, 20 times that of the median worker in the firm. By 2013, that ratio had jumped to 295.9. In that year, Disney's CEO earned 2,238 times the median worker's salary in his company.[12] What is noteworthy is that colossal CEO pay packages seem unrelated to performance.[13] One study showed the compensation of CEOs of large companies that had been through bankruptcy to be only 4 percent below the median for all CEOs of large companies.[14] Executives seem not to be held to account, even when the profits being rewarded turn out to be based on fraud.[15]

At the same time, the safety net provided by fringe benefits from private employers frayed in terms of both availability and generosity.[16] Although the Affordable Care Act increased the share of Americans with health insurance, copays and deductibles also increased. In addition, the share of workers who qualify for unemployment compensation if they lose their jobs declined, and defined-contribution retirement plans replaced defined-benefit pensions, so that workers cannot rely on a steady, predictable pension when they retire. In 1980, 84 percent of full-time workers in private establishments with at least 100 employees had defined-benefit pension plans. By 2015, that figure had fallen to 25 percent.[17]

WEALTH

The pattern of substantial, and increasing, inequality is even more dramatic for wealth: that is, the assets held by a household—for example, housing, consumer durables such as cars, businesses, savings, or investments—minus any outstanding mortgage, college loans, or consumer debt. Wealth—especially financial wealth like equities, bank deposits, or bonds—has always been more unevenly divided than either earnings or household income. In 2012, the top 1 percent commanded fully 42 percent of national wealth.

Over time, changes in the concentration of wealth parallel the U-shaped pattern for earnings and household income. The share of wealth owned by the top 1 percent reached a peak in the late 1920s and bottomed out in the 1970s before turning upward again in the late 1970s. Between 1978 and 2012, the share of the nation's wealth held by the top .1 percent rose sharply from 7 percent to 22 percent. In fact, the share of wealth commanded by those at the very top was nearly as much as for all those in the bottom 90 percent, 23 percent, down from 35 percent in the mid-1980s.[18]

An important aspect of the unequal division of wealth is the divide by race or ethnicity. Black and Latino households command, on average, much less wealth than non-Hispanic white households, and these inequalities in wealth are much more pronounced than analogous inequalities in income or wages. Blacks and Latinos are less likely to be homeowners and more likely to owe more than they own.[19]

The United States in Comparative Perspective

Most rich countries have witnessed increasing income inequality in recent decades,[20] but the United States and the United Kingdom have led the way. The United States was actually less economically unequal than the powers of Europe in the early twentieth century. By the twenty-first, the United States was the most economically unequal of a group of fourteen rich countries.[21]

A key driver of increasing inequality in the United States is the explosion in compensation to those at the top. In what Thomas Piketty calls a "hyper-meritocratic society," the "peak of the income hierarchy is dominated by very high incomes from labor rather than by inherited wealth."[22] Whether quarterbacks or Oscar-winning actors or, more commonly, financiers and corporate chieftains, America's winners are very well paid indeed. In contrast, at the bottom of the hierarchy, compensation for low-skilled work is quite stingy compared to other countries. Furthermore, government benefits are not particularly generous, and taxes are not especially redistributive in the United States. Taken together, these multiple factors interact to produce a higher level of inequality in disposable income in the United States than in other developed democracies.[23]

DOES AMERICAN AFFLUENCE COMPENSATE?

Two arguments are made to blunt concerns about the level of income inequality in the United States. The first is that the high level of affluence in America implies a higher, even though unequal, standard of living for all. Not unexpectedly, Americans in top deciles continue to be better off than their counterparts in other affluent countries. In the middle, the United States has long outranked other affluent countries with respect to median income, but other countries are catching up fast. In 2014, median income in Canada surpassed that in the United States.[24] Toward the bottom of the income ladder, however, the United States lags behind other rich nations. According to one comparative study, "Low paid workers in the United States—the most productive economy in the world—have markedly lower living standards than low paid workers in other advanced economies."[25] The combination of the relatively low wages of low-paid American workers and the lack of income supports for the non-working poor implies that the incomes of households in the lowest decile in the United States are quite low compared to their counterparts elsewhere.[26] In sum, American affluence compensates somewhat for those in the middle and not at all for those at the bottom of the ladder.

WHAT ABOUT THE AMERICAN DREAM?

The second argument focuses on the opportunities for achieving the "American Dream." Discussions of realizing the American Dream come in two versions. One emphasizes that life gets better with absolute improvements in standard of living over the life cycle or across generations, regardless of whether the improvement also involves a relative as well as an absolute rise. The sluggish wage growth over much of the period since the mid-1970s implies that achieving this version of the American Dream has become harder for middle- and lower-income Americans. Over the life cycle, earnings tend to increase with age as workers gain experience and seniority, but they increase less sharply than they once did.[27] American standards of living have improved even though wages have stagnated, but only because families are smaller in the post–Baby Boom era; work force participation, especially by married women, has risen; and consumer indebtedness has increased.

Another definition of achieving the American Dream posits that opportunities for success, while differential, are available to the talented and industrious, irrespective of initial circumstances of disadvantage. American ideology to the contrary, rags-to-riches—and riches-to-rags—stories, however newsworthy, are exceptional. We are not all equal at the starting point, and recent research shows considerable correspondence in the economic rewards that accrue to successive generations.[28] Children who have the good fortune to be born to affluent, well-educated parents are better off in myriad ways. Among others, they are more likely to

- Grow up with two biological parents;
- Live in a home environment that cultivates attitudes, interests, habits, and personality traits that are helpful in school and the marketplace;
- Benefit from parental investments in their development, ranging from stimulating conversations to music lessons to summer camp;
- Attend schools with experienced teachers, educationally engaged fellow students, Advanced Placement courses, and organized sports;
- Achieve academically in school;
- Be able to afford rising college tuitions and to have advisors at home and school able to guide them through the process of applying to college and finding financial aid, if needed;
- Matriculate in college and, ultimately, graduate;
- Be located in social networks that provide mentors and contacts along the way.[29]

The investments made by parents in their children's development and well-being are not necessarily financial: although private school tuition costs money, story time before bed does not. On average, it is probably more advantageous to have well-educated parents than rich ones. Still, it is hardly surprising that those who are savvy enough to have chosen affluent, well-educated parents are much more likely to end up affluent and well educated themselves.

These class-based gaps in the experiences and well-being of children have, unfortunately, grown markedly in recent decades, with potential con-

> **BOX 10.2** The Income Gap in Parental Expenditures on Children
>
> The class-based gap in parental expenditures on their children's development—in such things as books, high-quality child care, summer camp, and private school—has grown. During 1972–1973, families in the highest income group spent $2,701 more per year on child enrichment than did families in the lowest income group. By 2005–2006, the disparity had grown to $7,557.
>
> *Source*: Greg J. Duncan and Richard J. Murnane, "Introduction: The American Dream, Then and Now," in *Whither Opportunity? Rising Inequality, Schools, and Children's Life Chances*, eds. Greg J. Duncan and Richard J. Murnane (New York: Russell Sage, 2011), p. 11. Data for lowest and highest income quintiles in 2008 dollars.

sequences for the current circumstances and future mobility prospects of children whose parents are less affluent and well educated.[30]

The United States is anything but the leader when it comes to providing opportunities for success regardless of previous condition of disadvantage. In a group of thirteen affluent democracies, the Nordic countries exhibit the most social mobility from generation to generation as measured by a relatively weak relationship between fathers' and son's earnings. Along with the United Kingdom and Italy, the United States has the least social mobility. What is more, among rich countries, those with higher levels of income inequality tend also to be those where advantage passes from one generation to the next.[31] In sum, there is no evidence at all that the opportunities for success for the talented and industrious promised by the American Dream compensate for inequality in America.

How Do We Explain Increasing Economic Inequality?

There is widespread agreement both that multiple factors contribute to increasing income inequality and that those factors are difficult to disentangle. There is also consensus that structural and economic trends exacerbate economic inequality. Among them are skill-based technological change, with machine tools, computers, and robots operated by high-skilled workers replacing low-skilled workers; international trade and domestic outsourcing, with lower-paid workers substituting for better-paid ones; and winner-take-all markets, with the most successful not only in athletics and entertainment but also in the corporate and financial sectors able to command stratospheric compensation.[32]

At this point, the agreement breaks down. Some maintain that the growth of economic inequality can be explained primarily by the operations of increasingly efficient markets. Others point out that markets reflect more than simply an equilibrium achieved by impersonal forces of supply and demand and that market outcomes are "the result of the bargaining power of different participants."[33] This insight provides the conceptual framework for the Progressive-era observation that "an empty stomach can make no contracts."[34]

A special point of contention is the role of politics. Economists differ with regard to the weight they place on government policy in explaining increasing economic inequality. Clearly, technological and economic developments are significant causes of growing economic inequality. Still, the economic argument about increasing return to education does not explain the explosion of compensation at the very top. Furthermore, these economic and technological changes, which are present across developed economies, cannot explain why the growth of inequality has differed so substantially across nations and why it has been especially pronounced in the United States. Christopher Jencks has a blunt rejoinder, "The answer turns out to be pretty simple: 'It's politics, stupid.'"[35] If it is politics, then to what extent have policies exacerbated inequality or failed to deter its growth?

BENEFITS AND TAXES

Discussions of how policy affects income inequality usually begin with the government benefits and taxes that modify market outcomes. In all rich democracies, the sum total of what governments distribute, often on a means-tested basis, in benefits and extract in taxes ameliorates income inequality. The reduction in inequality from these tools is not especially pronounced in the United States. Since the late 1970s, the redistributive effects of benefits and taxes have clearly not kept pace with growing inequality in market outcomes before benefits and taxes.

In 1988, Ronald Reagan famously observed, "We fought a war against poverty, and poverty won." While Reagan may have the better quotation, in fact, government benefits do reduce poverty,[36] and decreases in benefits increase poverty. The 1996 welfare reform replaced the major income support program, Aid to Families with Dependent Children (AFDC), with Temporary

Assistance to Needy Families (TANF), which is time-limited and on average provides a less generous level of support. While the welfare rolls were already declining at the time that welfare reform was passed, the drop in coverage has been marked: in 2014, the TANF caseload was only 27 percent of what it was at the height of the old welfare program in 1994.[37] That a much smaller share of poor families receive TANF benefits and that inflation-adjusted TANF benefits are, on average, lower than at the time of welfare reform is at least part of the story of the increase of the proportion of families with children that are deeply poor. The decline of TANF has reduced government benefits that redistribute income, but that is not the end of the story.

The main income support for the poor is now the Earned Income Tax Credit (EITC), a tax benefit that is tied to work. The EITC ameliorates income inequality, but the link to employment means that it only helps those who are able to find jobs. As a result, it has limited countercyclical impact in economic downturns.[38] Two other programs partly fill the gap. During the Great Recession, SNAP—the Supplemental Nutrition Assistance Program, the heir to what was known as "food stamps"—and Unemployment Insurance provided compensatory assistance with the result that, according to a Congressional Budget Office Report, the reduction in income inequality from government benefits was somewhat higher in 2011 than it had been in 1979.[39] With economic recovery and the expiration of the temporary boost to SNAP benefits, SNAP spending has declined and with it the temporary boost in the redistributive impact of government benefits.[40]

The American tax system is complicated. While it is broadly progressive, in certain respects, it is friendlier to those with higher incomes. Most people's federal taxes are fairly straightforward and are withheld from their paychecks.[41] In contrast, for those with complex investments and financial dealings, the federal tax code is riddled with tax-reducing deductions and loopholes inserted by lobbyists and exploited by lawyers and accountants. Because such provisions are so byzantine, they are open to legitimate differences of interpretation as well as flagrant dishonesty. Significantly, in the late 1990s, Congress passed legislation crippling the tax enforcement capacity of the IRS and has subsequently eroded its funding. Nevertheless, after federal taxes, income inequality is somewhat less pronounced than before the federal government takes its bite.

Unlike federal taxes, state and local taxes, which vary substantially from state to state, are not progressive. With each rung up the economic ladder, the proportion of income paid in state and local taxes diminishes. In 2015, the share of income paid in state and local taxes by the lowest 20 percent of households, those with incomes below $19,000, was 10.9 percent; by the middle 20 percent, those with incomes between $35,000 and $56,000, 9.4 percent; and by the top 1 percent, who had incomes over $471,000, only 5.4 percent.[42]

After decades of tinkering with the federal tax code, federal taxes now do less to ameliorate income inequality than they did in 1979.[43] Some of the alterations to federal taxes have had a regressive impact.[44] Compared to those further down, the affluent realize a higher share of their incomes from unearned income—that is, income like rents and dividends not derived from wages and salary. Therefore, the successive reductions of the capital gains tax to 15 percent have, on average, reduced the tax bills of those at the top of the income ladder. Similarly, changes to the federal estate tax have reduced estate taxes for the very wealthy.[45]

Perhaps most notably, income taxes on high salaries have been reduced substantially. Beginning in the 1980s, most affluent countries lowered marginal income tax rates, but the United States and the United Kingdom, which had relatively higher rates during the 1960s, went further than most.[46] During the Reagan administration, the marginal federal income tax rate fell from 70 percent to 28 percent. Since then it has fluctuated within a narrower range. The tax bill passed in December 2017 reduced it from 39.6 to 37 percent. In fact, the most important effect of reductions in the marginal rate on earned incomes may be less on who pays what in taxes than on what the best-paid workers earn. The era of lower marginal income tax rates has also been the era of soaring compensation. When federal taxes gobbled so much of high pay, there was less incentive to try to extract the last dollar. With lower marginal rates, the payoff for demanding a big raise has skyrocketed.[47]

GOVERNMENT POLICY AND THE SHAPING OF MARKET OUTCOMES

Less widely discussed than the way that government benefits and tax policies modify market incomes is how profoundly government policies shape the operations of markets. Beginning with the capacity of governments to enforce the contracts on which market exchanges rely, capitalist systems are embedded in myriad policies that shape their functioning. Two issues at stake in the 2016 presidential election—immigration and trade agreements, both of which have implications for economic distribution—are shaped fundamentally by policy decisions. These are but two of the many matters germane to economic inequality for which both market operations and government policies have consequences. That is why, according to Joseph Stiglitz, we must understand "the array of laws and policies that lie beneath the surface—the rules that determine the balance of power between public and private, employers and workers, innovation and shared growth and all the other interests that make up the modern economy."[48]

As with immigration and trade, policies with the potential to enhance workers' paychecks often have politically powerful opponents and inevitably involve trade-offs among valued outcomes. Furthermore, agreement on a desired result may not be matched by consensus among economists on how to achieve it.

One policy, not always cited in discussions of growing economic inequality, is the use of fiscal and monetary tools to maintain full employment and thus promote higher wages. Slack labor markets tend to place workers, especially low-wage workers, at a disadvantage. Since the Reagan years, economic policy has not always made full employment a priority.[49] Another rarely cited partial explanation for growing economic inequality is reduced competition among firms in various economic sectors. When fewer employers are competing for workers, employers gain leverage in setting wages. Concerns about the impact of mergers on competition for employees, and therefore on wages, are notably absent from merger complaints.[50] Besides, antitrust enforcement has not been especially vigorous in recent decades.

A policy that is mentioned more frequently is the minimum wage, which by placing a floor under wages, has a mildly equalizing effect on earnings. Unlike many policies ranging from Social Security benefits to the cap on payroll taxes, the minimum wage, established in the Fair Labor Standards Act of 1938, is not indexed to inflation or to the median wage. The value of the minimum wage peaked in real terms in 1968 and has declined 24 percent since then, even though the half-century since then has witnessed substantial economic growth.[51] It is also not especially generous in comparison with other affluent democracies. In a group of thirteen affluent countries, only in Spain and Japan is the minimum wage a smaller percentage of median earnings than in the United States.[52] Therefore, what the government has not done—or, at least, what it has not done very often since the Reagan Administration—namely, raise the minimum wage, has contributed to income inequality.

Overtime pay presents a parallel case. Like the minimum wage, guaranteed overtime pay, mandated in the Fair Labor Standards Act, is not indexed. Because the threshold for overtime eligibility is not automatically adjusted with inflation, the share of salaried workers who qualify for overtime pay had sunk to 11 percent in 2014—from 65 percent in 1975.[53] As we are finishing this book, the Trump administration is seeking to roll back an Obama administration rule extending overtime pay to more than 4 million workers.[54]

In an era when workers have on average reduced leverage in bargaining with employers, employers have adopted practices to keep labor costs down. Among them are hiring outside contractors to do work once undertaken by regular employees who qualified for such fringe benefits as health insurance; requiring employees with complaints about pay or employment practices to submit to binding arbitration rather than to sue in court; enjoining employees not to discuss matters of pay with one another; failing to pay mandated minimum wage or overtime; and requiring new employees—not just engineers in Silicon Valley who might have access to trade secrets but also such low-wage employees as fast-food workers or camp counselors—to sign non-compete agreements limiting their freedom to seek better-paid jobs.[55] In a related practice that limits worker mobility and, therefore, keeps wages down, fast-food companies like Burger King and Pizza Hut require franchise holders to agree not to hire workers from one another.[56]

All these practices could be modified by government policy. In some cases, policymakers have chosen to eschew any policy remedy or have been met by successful opposition from affected business interests. In others, the policy tools are in place but are inadequately enforced. For example, when it comes to paying below minimum wage or depriving employees of overtime, the number of federal inspectors was cut by nearly a third between 1980 and 2007. Even with the reduced capacity to enforce wage and overtime guarantees, more than $1 billion of stolen wages were recovered in 2012, a figure that is thought to be a small fraction of the national total.[57]

The growth of the financial sector, the explosion of its profitability, and the compensation of its higher-ups along with consumer losses during the Great Recession constitute market forces that clearly exacerbated income inequality. It is difficult to assess how much that outcome also reflects government action and inaction with respect to investments, borrowing, and other financial transactions.[58] Political conflict about government regulation of finance tends to involve lobbying by organized interests—for example, credit card companies, banks, and other financial institutions. As is so often the case, policy impact is buried in the details—details that have been scrutinized and shaped by interests with insider status, policy expertise, and deep pockets.

Several government actions in the post-2000 era seem to have been particularly friendly to business. For example, the 2005 bankruptcy reform that made it harder for consumers—and nearly impossible for indebted students[59]—to discharge debts by declaring bankruptcy is surely more advantageous to credit card companies, mortgage lenders, car lenders, and for-profit universities than to indebted consumers. Similar arguments are made about policy developments with regard to the increased protection of intellectual property and the relaxation of antitrust enforcement.[60]

Much of the story of the financial sector in recent decades, however, involves the absence of regulation. The 1999 repeal of the 1933 Glass-Steagall Act, which had separated investment banking from commercial banking, involved explicit deregulation. However, absence of regulation can also reflect successful industry opposition, as in the case of the complex financial instruments known as derivatives, as well as the failure of enforcing agencies to regulate vigorously—whether out of ideological conviction, coziness with the industry, or insufficient budgets.

Combined with technological developments that transformed how financial transactions take place, this unregulated environment incubated new ways of doing financial business. Speculation in arcane and complex financial instruments and other forms of financial risk-taking, predatory lending, and sometimes actual fraud ended up jeopardizing the solvency of financial institutions and leaving many consumers indebted or foreclosed during the 2008 Great Recession. When the collapse of major financial institutions threatened, the government came through with a bailout that, while eventually repaid in full, cost more than the government spent on the unemployed who lost jobs during the ensuing recession and helped bankers retain their bonuses while leaving behind those who had lost homes to foreclosure. In the aftermath, Congress legislated new financial regulations in the 2010 Dodd-Frank Wall Street Reform and Consumer Protection Act. Although passed with a party-line vote, the bill involved substantial compromise. Both the bill itself and its implementation, which has not been especially forceful, have been controversial.

DECLINING UNIONS AND GROWING ECONOMIC INEQUALITY

Any account of the growth of economic inequality must include a discussion of the decline of labor union membership and power, a development with consequences for both economic and political inequality. Unions operate in several ways to boost workers' power and enhance their earnings. For one thing, union members are more likely to be politically active—even beyond what we would expect on the basis of their education and incomes. For another, as discussed in Chapter 8, labor unions represent their members' economic interests—and the economic interests of ordinary citizens more generally—in politics. Unions also provide workers with a collective voice in the workplace.

The share of the workforce that is unionized actually peaked in the 1950s, but the past three decades have witnessed striking attrition in the proportion of workers who are union members and the slightly higher proportion who are covered by union contracts. It is notable that, even as the size of the workforce expanded substantially, the absolute number of union members declined by nearly 5 million over the period. In 1977, 26.5 percent of all wage and salary workers were members of unions; by 2014, the figure had dropped to 11.1 percent.[61] America's circumstances are not unique. Over the last generation, erosion in the proportion of the workforce that is unionized has been common across industrial democracies. In a group of twenty advanced democracies, the proportion of unionized workers diminished between 1979 and the late 1990s in fourteen of them.[62] Still, even if the United States is hardly alone in the drop in union density, the United States has, in comparative terms, very low levels of union membership.

The decrease in union ranks has occurred entirely in the private sector. The proportion of union members among private-sector workers decreased steadily, from 21.7 percent in 1977 to 6.6 percent in 2014. In contrast, the share of public-sector workers who are union members fluctuated within a very narrow range and ended the period at a slightly higher level, 35.7 percent, than at the beginning. While the share of the workforce employed in the public sector fell from 18.7 percent to 15.2 percent over the period, the share of union members who are public-sector employees rose sharply, from 31.4 percent to 54.4 percent.

There is no question that the decline of union membership has had an impact on the growth of income inequality, although there is disagreement about how much. The union wage premium—that is, the increment to wages and benefits accruing solely from union membership with other relevant factors taken into account—has diminished since the 1980s. Still, union membership clearly boosts compensation—especially for private-sector employees, for men, for blue-collar workers, and for workers with no post-secondary education.[63] In fact, one study estimates that union decline explains between a fifth and a third of the growth in wage inequality among men.[64]

At the same time that the weakening of union economic power has affected the size of workers' paychecks and the conditions under which they work, union decline has diminished their political capacity to support policies that protect the economic interests of ordinary workers and to oppose policies that benefit the privileged. An indicator of the political weakness of organized labor is the finding in a recent study that, when asked to name their principal antagonists on the issues on which they were currently working, not one of the corporate lobbyists mentioned a union.[65] Thus, union decline has operated through both the workplace and politics to augment income inequality.

What explains the steep decline in the share of American workers who are union members? Several factors account for this trend.[66] One is structural changes in the American economy, in particular the decrease in manufacturing employment. Another is diminished support for unionization among workers. Unions themselves made miscalculations. Evidence suggests that the leadership of the American Federation of Labor and Congress of Industrial Organizations (AFL-CIO), especially George Meany, did not devote sufficient attention or resources to organizing. Furthermore, employers have been increasingly aggressive. Aided by consultants who specialize in "union prevention," businesses have become substantially more hostile to union-organizing drives in both tone and tactics.

Finally, the weakening of labor has undoubtedly had a political component.[67] A significant blow to organized labor unions was the passage in 1947 of the employer-friendly Taft-Hartley Act, which proscribed a number of labor practices and permitted states to pass "right-to-work" laws outlawing the union shop. Although attempts have been made to alter or repeal it, Taft-Hartley remains in place today. In fact, organized labor has not succeeded in realizing any of its major legislative goals in decades. During both the Carter and Obama administrations, Congresses controlled by Democrats handed legislative defeats to organized labor.[68]

Political developments in the early years of the Reagan administration are critical. In a turning point in labor history, during the summer of 1981, Reagan dismissed striking air traffic controllers and replaced them with nonunion employees, after which employers have felt free to replace striking workers. In addition, Reagan was able to name appointees to the National Labor Relations Board (NLRB) who were unfriendly to labor. The result was policy changes that have facilitated management's capacity to act aggressively against unions.[69] The NLRB was able to weaken worker protections under the National Labor Relations Act by overturning worker-friendly precedents, many of them long standing, through a series of decisions in carefully selected cases. At the same time, whether by accident or design, the number of decisions in cases of unfair labor practices dwindled, and the backlog of unresolved cases expanded to the largest number in history.[70] More recently, at the state level, bolstered by friendly state legislatures, Republican governors in some states have dealt with revenue shortfalls by cutting the medical benefits and pensions of unionized public employees and, more fundamentally, targeting their collective bargaining rights.

Conclusion

Economic deserts are unequally distributed. Moreover, they are more unequally distributed in the New Gilded Age than at any time in several generations and are more unequal in the United States than in most developed democracies. Those at the top have garnered most of the income gains, while incomes in the middle and lower ranges have stagnated, and the number of desperately poor has risen.

What we have seen undermines several clichés about economic life in America. For one, it is often argued that a rising economic tide lifts all boats. However, growing prosperity and productivity in recent decades have lifted the yachts but left the dinghies still grounded. Moreover, with the stagnation in middle- and lower-class income and earnings, no longer does American affluence imply that low-income workers are better off in absolute terms than they are elsewhere. Finally, in spite of rhetoric about America as the land of opportunity, well-educated, affluent parents are ordinarily able to pass their high status along to their children, and rates of upward mobility in the United States are actually lower than in most affluent democracies. The possibilities for those of modest origins to become successful have surely not increased in this era of increasing economic inequality. Indeed, they may have diminished.

It is difficult to sort out the causes of economic inequality, but there is agreement that technological change, international trade, and domestic outsourcing are significant factors. Although the role of politics is more controversial, an environment of government policy shapes the way the markets function, and government policies influence the distribution of income. In addition, government inaction has exacerbated income inequality. Public officials have had policy instruments at their disposal—for example, raising the minimum wage regularly or establishing prudent standards for mortgage loans—that might have decelerated the rate of growth of economic inequality.

Thus, the sum total of government action and inaction has been insufficient to keep up with growing income inequality in the United States and has had less impact on the increase than in other affluent democracies.

Another factor that has added to economic inequality is the decline of unions and the resulting reduction in the economic and political power of workers. Even though private-sector union membership is a fraction of what it once was, unionized workers still command better wages and benefits than otherwise similar non-union workers. The weakness of unions also has implications for the inequalities of political voice. Labor union membership has a mobilizing effect for individuals: compared to their non-union counterparts, union members are more likely to vote or to engage in other political activities. Furthermore, among organized interests, unions are the most important advocates for the economic needs and concerns of ordinary workers.

11

Has It Always Been This Way?

Inequality of political voice violates the democratic ideal of equal consideration of the needs and preferences of all citizens, but inequality that continues over time poses an even greater challenge to that democratic ideal. Persistently loud political voice from politically significant categories of citizens coupled with persistent quiescence of others is a deeper transgression. Policymakers inclined to listen to the messages they receive would be especially likely to pay attention to the voices they hear over and over. They would have particular incentives to heed the communications from those whose support they might solicit in the future. In this chapter, we show that SES inequalities in political voice have been a notable feature of American politics at least since we have had the tools to measure them systematically and that they have become, in complicated ways, more pronounced in recent years.

Understanding changes to the class bias in political voice requires detecting changes in both the SES stratification of individual components of political voice and the relative weight of those components among the forms of citizen input to politics. For any particular form of political expression, we need to keep in mind who is taking part on what issues and how much they are doing. More big political donations versus small ones or more demonstrations about climate change versus gun rights might exacerbate the upward SES bias in political voice.

Similarly, changes in the mix of activities that make up political voice have potential consequences for the SES structuring of political voice. For example, because contactors are, on average, higher in SES than protesters, a spike in the number of contacts directed to public officials relative to attendance at protests would produce an increase in the stratification of political voice. In particular, an increase in political contributions relative to other forms of political activity would boost the tilt of political voice toward the affluent. Because the number of hours an activist can devote to politics is finite, but the number of dollars is not, it is easier to multiply the volume of participatory input based on money. The result is an increase in the SES bias of political voice.

The Changing Stratification of Political Voice: What Should We Expect?

How should we expect the social class stratification of political voice to have changed over the past several decades? Not only is figuring out the bottom line complicated, but also the relevant social and political trends do not all point in the same direction.[1] Most obvious are two trends, discussed in Chapter 10, that would be expected to enhance the participatory advantage of those at the top in terms of SES. The first is the decline of the labor movement. The unionized work force is now not only smaller but also more white collar and better educated, thus diluting the capacity of unions to compensate for SES disadvantage when it comes to political activity. Second, most of the fruits of economic expansion since 1980 have accrued to a narrow slice at the top of the income ladder. The spectacular gains in income realized by the most affluent puts them in a position to increase their advantage with regard to forms of political activity dependent on financial resources—in particular, making contributions to political campaigns and causes.

In contrast, several theories with long pedigrees in the social sciences suggest that growing economic inequality would be met with political reaction rather than greater participatory inequality. Anthony Downs predicts that, in a democracy where citizens are all enfranchised and have equal votes, the many have nots would gang up on the haves and bring about redistributive policies, a process that would be more likely to occur as the distance between the average and median incomes diverged—as it has in recent decades.[2] In addition, a simplified version of Marxism suggests that widening gaps in income would generate anger, and even revolt, among those at the bottom of the ladder. Analogously, interest-group pluralists—who inhabit a different part of the political spectrum from Marx—would predict that, in reaction to growing income inequality, those left behind economically would organize themselves into new and numerically powerful interest groups to oppose their increasing relative disadvantage. Of course, history provides far fewer examples of such results than have been predicted by the theories. Contrary to the expectation of increasing agitation for redistributive relief, there is even some evidence that increasing economic inequality actually has a depressing, rather than a mobilizing, impact on political discussion and participation.[3]

Because education is such an important driver of political participation, we might also expect the aggregate increase in average educational attainment to be accompanied by a narrowing of the class-based gap in participation. Those further down on the socioeconomic scale are, in absolute terms, better educated than they once were, which might boost their political activity.

Although never as strong as their European counterparts, American political parties play an important role in mobilizing ordinary citizens. They have recently undergone a revival. While especially notable at the elite level, this resurgence is associated with increased efforts to organize on the ground and to mobilize the base and with increased ideological coherence and higher levels of partisan voting among citizens. We might expect this process of renewal to lead both to reduction in the SES differences in participation and to growth in overall levels of political activity.

Such an increase in aggregate levels of political participation has not materialized, however. In fact, overall rates of political activity declined in the later years of the twentieth century.[4]

Recent changes to the rules of politics, discussed in Chapter 12, could have the effect of exacerbating political inequalities, however. The most obvious is the series of judicial decisions that have relaxed substantially the rules governing campaign finance. Not only have the sums contributed to politics exploded recently, but the share of political donations from the very wealthy has also soared, thus rendering the least democratic form of political voice even less democratic. In addition, with regard to the least unequal participatory act, voting, changes at the state level to the laws governing voter turnout—in particular, the enactment of voter ID laws—may result in electorates that are less representative in class, as well as in racial or ethnic, terms.

Participatory Inequality over Time

Unequal political voice is a persistent feature of American politics. The distribution of the kinds of individuals and organized interests represented

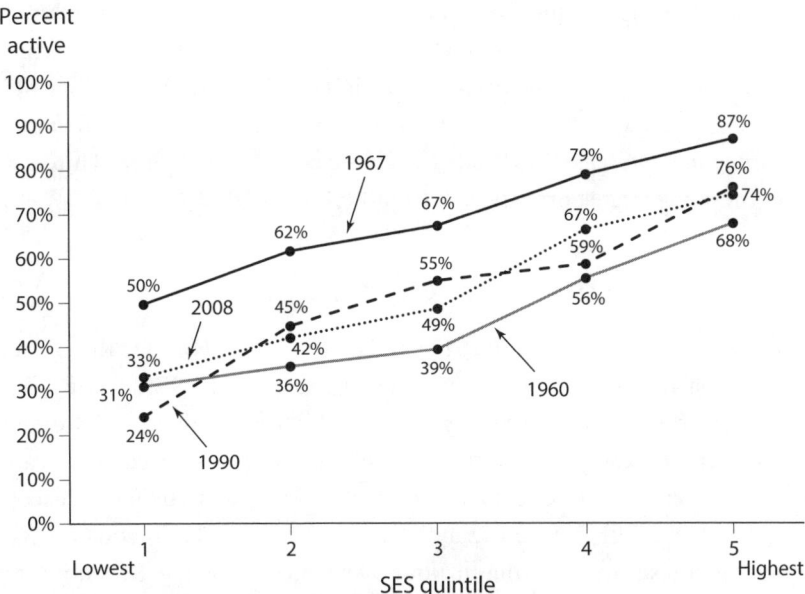

FIGURE 11.1. Continuing Stratification of Political Participation: Political Activity by SES Quintile, 1960, 1967, 1990, 2008

Sources: 1960—Civic Culture Study; 1967—Political Participation in America; 1990—Citizen Participation Study; 2008—Pew Internet and American Life Survey.
Note: The figure shows by SES quintiles the percentage engaging in at least one political act other than voting. The data for 1967, 1990, and 2008 are based on the same five measures of activity: working in a political campaign, contributing to a candidate or campaign, contacting a government official, belonging to a political organization, and working with others on a community issue. The data for 1960 are based on a somewhat different set of activities, although ones that closely parallel those used in the other studies.

in politics has been stable across several decades. Although public issues and citizen concerns may come and go, the affluent and well educated are consistently overrepresented. Figure 11.1, which presents data from surveys with similar questions about a variety of modes of participation beyond voting across half a century, shows that inequalities of political voice have been present in American politics for a long time.[5] In each of the surveys, dating back to 1960, the average amount of political activity rises steeply across five quintiles of socioeconomic status (SES). Presumably, the association between SES and political voice dates back much further than the half century for which we have data.

We can investigate this finding in several ways: comparing separate political acts with one another, comparing political activity with religious attendance, and comparing individual activity with the activity of organized interests. To consider questions about individual activity, we use the American National Election Studies (ANES) cumulative file (1952–2012), which asks in the same way over extended periods about both political participation and the two components of SES.[6] Then we use evidence from the *Washington Representatives* Study to explore changes in organized interests over the somewhat shorter period from 1981 to 2011.

INEQUALITY IN VOTING TURNOUT OVER TIME

We begin with voting. Figure 11.2 uses data from the ANES for the sixteen presidential elections between 1952 and 2012 to show the SES stratification in voting turnout.[7] Because voting turnout is high compared to engagement in other participatory acts, voting is—although structured by education and income—relatively more egalitarian than other kinds of participation except for protesting. Still, Figure 11.2 indicates a striking level of inequality. Notably, the lines tracing voting turnout over time for the five SES quintiles array themselves in order from top to bottom and never cross. Turnout in the highest-SES quintile has been rather consistent over the years, hovering around 90 percent. In the middle and the two lower quintiles, there has

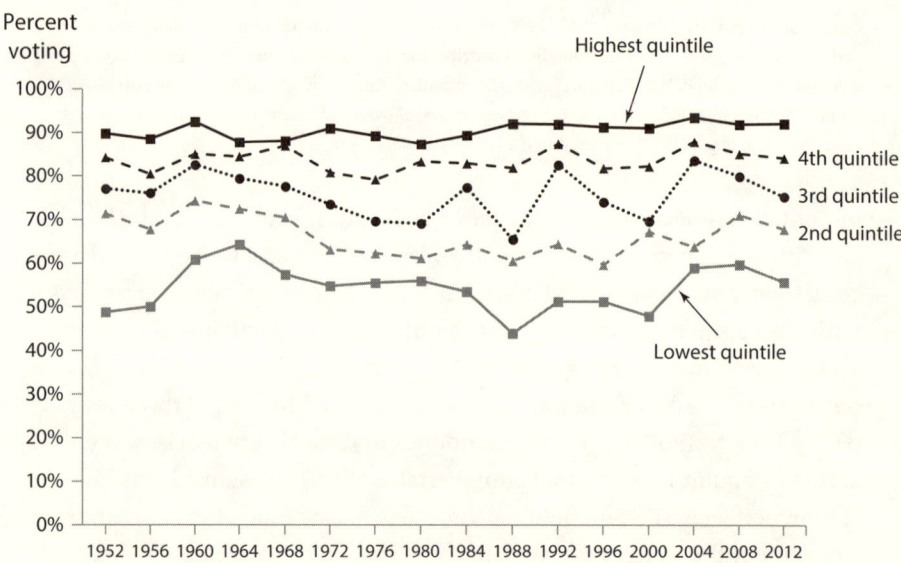

FIGURE 11.2. Voting Percentages over Time by SES Quintile, 1952–2012
Source: American National Elections Studies (1952–2012).

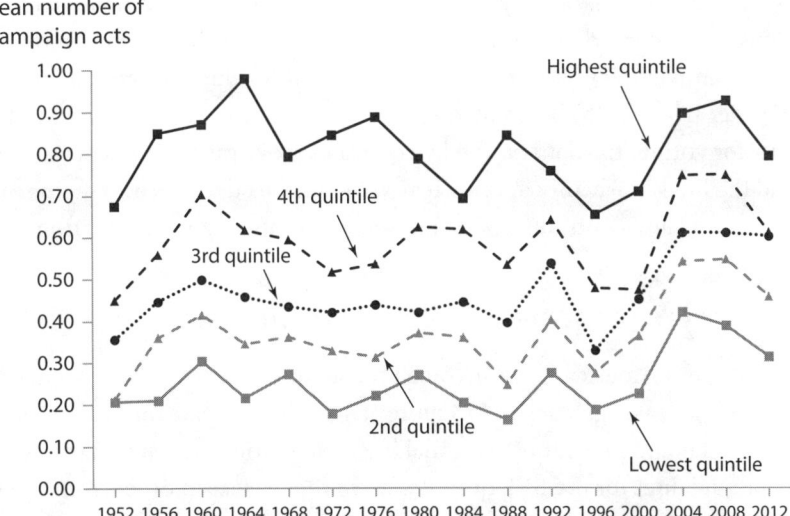

FIGURE 11.3. Persistence of Stratification of Campaign Activity: Mean Number of Campaign Acts over Time by SES Quintile, 1952–2012
Source: American National Election Studies (1952–2012).
Note: Campaign acts: working on a campaign, donating money to a campaign, going to campaign meetings, or trying to influence someone's vote.

been considerably more fluctuation; voting in the lowest quintile has varied between 40 percent and just over 60 percent. Consensus about persistent socioeconomic bias in voter turnout is not matched by agreement as to whether increasing economic inequality has affected inequality in voting. Perhaps surprisingly, in their analysis of turnout between 1972 and 2008, Jan Leighley and Jonathan Nagler say that what they "do *not* see is an increase in income bias in turnout that is anything like the increase in income inequality over this period."[8] However, their data predate most of the recent voter ID laws.

INEQUALITY IN OTHER ELECTORAL ACTIVITIES OVER TIME

When we move beyond voting to other, more demanding electoral activities that, at least in cross-sections, are characterized by a higher degree of stratification by social class, the patterns are roughly similar but differ in detail. Using ANES data for presidential elections over the same period, Figure 11.3 presents for each SES quintile the mean score on a scale of four campaign activities: working in a campaign, giving money to a campaign, going to a campaign meeting or rally, and trying to influence how someone votes.[9] Consistent with what we saw for voting in Figure 11.2, the lines showing mean campaign activity over time for the five SES quintiles array themselves in order from top to bottom and never cross. However, in contrast to the data for voting, the data for the five quintiles move more or less in tandem, and the lines are farther apart. Clearly, the past six decades have witnessed substantial and continuing SES differences in campaign participation.

THE SPECIAL CASE OF MAKING CAMPAIGN DONATIONS

Of the ways Americans get involved in electoral politics, giving money is clearly the least egalitarian. In Figure 11.4 we break apart the scale used in Figure 11.3 and present data on making contributions to campaigns. Once again, the lines for the SES quintiles array themselves in order from top to bottom and rarely cross. However, the distance between the rates for the highest quintile and the four lower quintiles is noteworthy. While the proportion of donors in the top quintile has varied over time and has sometimes reached nearly 30 percent, less than 5 percent in the lowest quintile typically contribute to political campaigns. Giving campaign money has long been highly stratified.

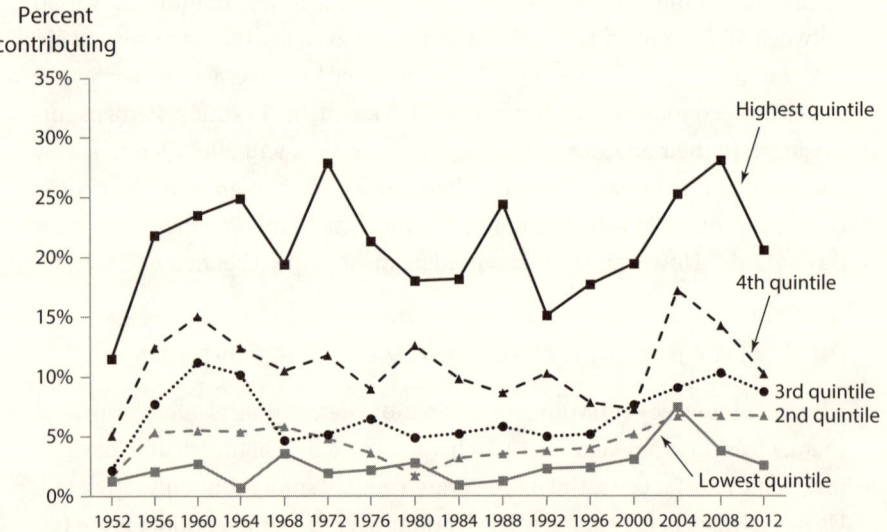

FIGURE 11.4. Contributing to Campaigns over Time by SES Quintile, 1952–2012
Source: American National Elections Studies (1952–2012).

In addition, making campaign donations seems to have become more stratified in the New Gilded Age. Although the proportion in the highest quintile who make campaign contributions has fluctuated over the period, it climbed steadily between 1992 and 2008, with a dip in 2012. The mix of campaign activities for those with very high SES has shifted, and giving money occupies more space in the participatory bundle.

Even more significant than any increase in the proportion of upper-SES activists who make contributions is the spectacular growth in the amounts contributed, very likely the result of recent judicial decisions that make it easier for those with deep pockets to contribute very large sums. Those at the top SES ladder not only are more likely to donate but are also in a position to give much larger amounts when they contribute. Therefore, socio-economic stratification in campaign giving is much more pronounced when we weight contributors by the size of their donations.

It is noteworthy that the elections in 2012 and 2014—elections in which the effects of the series of court decisions were beginning to be felt—were respectively the most expensive on record for presidential and mid-term elections. The total cost of federal campaigns continued to rise in 2016. Although campaign spending for the presidential election actually decreased, the growth in spending on congressional elections more than compensated.[10] But absolute amounts of campaign spending might not have implications for unequal political voice were it not for the fact that an increasing—and astonishing—share of campaign contributions derives from a small number of very big donors. According to the Sunlight Foundation, during the 2012 federal election cycle, 28 percent of all disclosed political contributions were made by the top ten-thousandth—or 1 percent of 1 percent—of the public.[11] Every single winning candidate for the House and Senate in 2012 received some money from this small group of just 31,385 people—a group that would not even fill a football stadium. Moreover, the vast majority of these 2012 winners, 84 percent, received more money in contributions from this elite one ten-thousandth than they did from *all* of their small donors (that is, those who gave $200 or less) combined. What is even more striking is that about half of the contributions from the 1 percent of 1 percent derived from the upper tenth of this small group, or the top hundred-thousandth of the nation's givers. A further indication of the extent to which mega-donors are dominating this important sphere of political activity is the meteoric increase in the absolute sums donated by the top ten-thousandth: in constant 2012 dollars, it required roughly $3,650 to be in the 1 percent of 1 percent of givers in 1990; by 2012, that figure had risen to $13,054.

This pattern shows no sign of abating. In the 2014 cycle, the 100 biggest campaign donors contributed nearly as much, $323 million, as the $356 million from the 4.75 million people who donated in amounts no larger than $200.[12] Well before the first presidential primary had taken place in 2016, $176 million had been collected in seed money—nearly half of it from only 158 families.[13] In fact, the sums donated by the ultra-rich have become so astronomical that, in what the *Washington Post* described as "the lament of the rich who are not quite rich enough for 2016," mere millionaires are feeling left behind by the attention being paid to billionaires:

> "A couple [of] presidential elections ago, somebody who had raised, say, $100,000 for a candidate was viewed as a fairly valuable asset," said Washington lobbyist Kenneth Kies. "Today, that looks like peanuts." . . . There is a palpable angst among mid-level fundraisers and donors that their rank has been permanently downgraded. One longtime bundler recently fielded a call from a dispirited executive on his yacht, who complained, "We just don't count anymore." . . . [According to] Bobbie Kilberg, a top Republican fundraiser in Northern Virginia who with her husband raised more than $4 million for Mitt Romney, "When you look at super-PAC money and the large donations that we're seeing, the regular bundlers feel a little disenfranchised."[14]

These patterns would be even more pronounced if we could include the so-called "dark money" in the totals. Dark money is outside spending, particularly through such groups as 501(c)(4) "social welfare" organizations that are not required to disclose their donors. Even more than ordinary campaign spending, dark money is dominated by very large donors. Dark money spending soared from $5.9 million in 2004 to $311.3 million in 2012.[15]

A COMPARISON WITH RELIGIOUS ATTENDANCE

Are all forms of voluntary activity highly stratified by social class? Consider the most common form of nonpolitical participation in American society, religious attendance. Religious institutions figure importantly in civil society in America and intersect with politics in many ways. They take stands on public issues. Those who attend religious services are exposed to political cues and to requests for political action. As we discussed in Chapter 3, those who have a deeper involvement in a religious institution—by, for example, taking part in educational, charitable, or social activities—develop civic skills

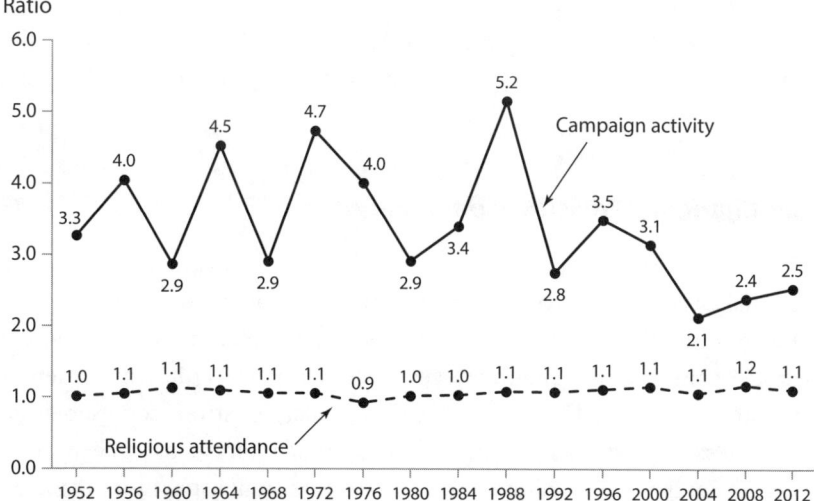

FIGURE 11.5. Ratio of Highest to Lowest SES Quintile over time for Campaign Activity and for Religious Attendance, 1952–2012
Source: American National Elections Studies (1952–2012).

that can be transferred to politics. Religious involvement is also closely related to individual political beliefs and issue positions: most notably, those who attend church regularly are more likely to take conservative positions on social and moral matters.

Figure 11.5 presents data from the ANES about two forms of activity: involvement in campaigns (as measured by the scale of four campaign activities used in Figure 11.3) and attendance at religious services.[16] The points on the top line represent, for each presidential election year, the ratio of the average level of campaign participation for the top SES quintile to the average level for the bottom quintile. Despite fluctuations, campaign activity is highly structured by social class.[17] Although the ratios are widely scattered, Figure 11.5 suggests that inequality in campaign activity may actually have decreased over time, especially in the past ten, or perhaps twenty, years.

The bottom line in Figure 11.5 presents corresponding figures for religious attendance.[18] There is a remarkable contrast between the stratification for campaign activity and that for religious attendance. While the ratios of top to bottom quintile for campaign activity range between 2.1 and 5.2, the ratios for religious attendance hover at about 1.1. A very slight class gap for religious attendance may have appeared since the mid-1980s.[19] However, the primary message of Figure 11.5 is that, in contrast to political activity, there seems to be virtually no SES stratification for religious attendance. The structuring of voluntary involvement by social class is far from preordained or inevitable.

The Changing Pressure Community

We can ask the same questions about political organizations—extending our analysis over time to consider the evolution of the Washington pressure community and assessing changes in the number and distribution of active organizations over a thirty-year span. Of special concern is whether the patterns described in Chapter 8—in particular, the strong representation of business interests in contrast to the economic interests of less economically advantaged—are unique to 2011 or are persistent aspects of organized interest representation in Washington.

In an era in which the costs of transportation and communications have fallen in relative terms and electronic technologies make it easier to stay in touch with both those at an organization's headquarters and the folks at the grassroots, organizations can move in and out of politics relatively easily. However, there have been many more entries than exits over the thirty-year period for which we have data, with the result that the number of organizations that take part in Washington politics has grown substantially. The increase in the number and influence of citizen groups—a broad category that includes various kinds of membership associations, such as identity groups and public interest groups—has been well documented.[20] What has garnered less attention is the explosive growth in the number of state and local governments as well as established but previously apolitical non-membership organizations—for example, hospitals, universities, and museums—that are active in Washington.

THE EVER-EXPANDING PRESSURE SYSTEM

Compared to the 1981 *Washington Representatives* directory with 6,691 organizations, the 2011 directory lists more than twice the number of organizations, 14,365, for an overall growth rate of 115 percent. With population growth, which is accompanied by more businesses, institutions, and membership organizations with policy concerns and claims on the government, we might expect more organized interest organizations. However, the growth in the number of organizations active in Washington has been considerably faster than the increase in population. In fact, the rate of increase in pressure groups is essentially the same as the rate of increase in federal expenditures. What is more, the rate of spending on lobbying rose even more quickly. Because we have data about lobbying spending only since 1998, we cannot track the whole period. However, between 1998 and 2011, lobbying spending rose sharply—increasing, in inflation-adjusted 2011 dollars, from $2.0 billion to $3.24 billion.[21] Clearly, organized advocacy is a growth industry.

From one point of view, the increase in the number of organizations active in Washington is unexpected because it seems to contradict a widely documented trend in American society, the decline in affiliations with membership associations.[22] However, we have seen that only a small minority of organizations active in Washington pressure politics are associations with individuals as members. Voluntary associations of individuals—the "interest groups" that absorb so much attention from students of pressure politics—are a small and diminishing share of the organizations involved in national politics. In 1981, such organizations constituted 14.9 percent of the organizations active in Washington; by 2011, that share had fallen to 11.3 percent.

Besides, the process by which increasing numbers of organizations have come to be involved in Washington politics has a self-reinforcing quality. One small category of organization that has grown steadily over the twenty-five-year period is firms of professionals, especially law firms. Many of these firms specialize in government relations, and they work hard to generate new clients. Similarly, in-house government relations professionals in organizations with offices in Washington provide intelligence to their employers about the relevance of unfolding political developments. In so doing, they find reasons for the organization to continue to have a presence in Washington—thus simultaneously justifying their existence while they protect the organizations that employ them. When new organizations are brought into politics through this process, their potential political antagonists have an incentive to become active as well.

A RECENT LEVELING OFF?

The rate of growth in number of organizations has varied substantially over the period since 1981, but it seems to have leveled off recently.[23] Figures from the Center for Responsive Politics indicate that, after steady yearly increases beginning in 1998 (the first year for which data are available), the number of lobbyists peaked in 2006 and, in inflation-adjusted terms, aggregate amounts spent on lobbying reached their high point in 2010 before declining slightly thereafter.[24]

Various explanations for the drop-off have been suggested.[25] With the recovery of the economy since the 2008 recession, blaming it on economic conditions is not convincing. One more plausible theory is that the end of earmarks has reduced the incentive for smaller organizations to lobby. Another is that, with the relaxation of campaign finance regulation, increasing sums are being devoted to campaign giving rather than to lobbying.[26] Still another is that, with partisan gridlock the operative principle in Washington, policy change is less likely and, therefore, organizations have less need to get involved in Washington politics. However, with issues like health care and tax reform—ordinarily magnets for lobbying—on the policy agenda, 2017 saw an uptick in lobbying activity.[27]

It is possible that the apparent diminution in the rate of increase is deceptive. A report from the Center for Responsive Politics found that nearly half of the lobbyists who filed reports in 2012 but not in 2013 were continuing to work for their original employers under job titles suggesting that they were still in the business of seeking political influence.[28] There is evidence that—in response to tightened regulations under the 2007 Honest Leadership and Open Government Act and to the requirement that registered lobbyists needed a special waiver to get a job in the Obama administration—"unlobbyists" are billing themselves as policy analysts or consultants rather than as lobbyists. They are calibrating their lobbying to stay just under the threshold for registration, emphasizing activities like grassroots lobbying (for which reporting is not necessary) or simply flouting the rules because enforcement is rare.[29] Rather than a decrease in lobbying activity, the result is an increase in the amount of activity that goes unreported.

DISPARATE GROWTH RATES ACROSS CATEGORIES OF ORGANIZATIONS

Table 11.1 shows that the expansion of the pressure system was quite uneven across various categories of organizations. The data in the first column of numbers show above-average growth rates among several kinds of citizen organizations: identity groups, public interest groups, and organizations that provide social welfare services or that advocate on behalf of the poor. However, other striking changes seem to have gone unnoticed by Washington watchers. One is the extraordinary growth both of organizations in the health and educational sectors and of state and local governments. Another

TABLE 11.1. Growth in the Pressure System, 1981–2011

	Relative Increase	Absolute Increase (number)
Corporations	71%	2,182
Trade and other business associations	41%	426
Occupational associations	41%	224
Unions	0%	0
Education	698%	712
Health	1,114%	680
Social welfare or poor	408%	133
Identity groups[a]	186%	337
Public interest	153%	386
State and local governments	421%	1,428
Foreign	52%	307
Other	294%	846
Don't know	14%	12
Total	115%	7,673

Source: Washington Representatives Study (2011).
[a]Includes organizations representing racial, ethnic, religious, or LGBT groups, the elderly, or women.

is the failure of the kinds of organizations that have traditionally dominated in pressure politics—trade associations, unions, and occupational associations—to keep pace with the overall rate of increase in the number of organizations in Washington politics. Especially striking is the fact that unions are the only one of the aggregated categories in Table 11.1 not to register an increase over the period. In addition, the increase in the number of trade and other business associations and the number of occupational associations did not keep up with the overall rate of growth of the Washington pressure community.

The second column of numbers in Table 11.1, which shows the changes in the absolute number of organizations listed, tells a somewhat different story. A high rate of increase may not imply many new organizations and vice versa. For example, a fairly high rate of increase for organizations providing social services and advocacy for the economically needy masks a quite small absolute increase. In contrast, for subnational governments and organizations in the health and education sectors, high rates of increase produced large absolute numbers of newly active organizations. In a different pattern, although the relative rate of increase for organizations representing business lagged, their absolute increase was the most substantial.[30] There were 2,182 more corporations and 426 more trade and other business associations in the 2011 directory than in 1981. Taken together, these changes mean that, in absolute terms, the increases in the kinds of organizations traditionally well represented in pressure politics—corporations, trade and other business associations, occupational associations of professionals and managers, and the like—dwarf the increases in the kinds of organizations that we have seen to be less well represented: public interest groups and organizations representing the less advantaged.

THE (MOSTLY) UNCHANGING DISTRIBUTION OF ORGANIZATIONS

Table 11.2 presents the distribution of organizations in the pressure system from 1981 to 2011. On balance, the overall pattern shows a great deal of continuity. Organizations representing broad publics and the disadvantaged continue to constitute only a small share of organized interest representation in Washington. Although the economic organizations that have traditionally dominated in the pressure system—corporations, trade and other business associations, occupational associations, and labor unions—command a somewhat smaller share of the pressure system than they did in 1981, they continue to represent a majority of organizations active in national politics.

As we discussed in Chapter 8, several categories of organizations represent the interests of the for-profit sector. Going beyond the data in Table 11.2, we include the following among the organizations that represent business: corporations, both domestic and foreign; trade and other business associations, again both domestic and foreign, which have corporations as members; occupational associations of business executives and professionals; and business-related think tanks and research organizations. These organizations representing business constituted 69.2 percent of all organizations listed in 1981 but only 51.2 percent in 2011—a substantial drop. Part of this decline almost certainly reflects a change in the rules for inclusion made by the editor of the *Washington Representatives* directory.[31] Even with the change in procedure, however, there were 2,721 more business-related organizations active in Washington politics in 2011 than in 1981—a substantial increase. In fact, combining all the unions, public interest groups, identity groups, and organizations representing the economically needy listed in 2011 yields a total that is just over half the number of *additional* organizations representing the private sector.

The diminution of the share of the pressure system occupied by traditional business and occupational organizations has not been accompanied by a corresponding enlargement in the share of the kinds of organizations

TABLE 11.2. The Changing Distribution of Organized Interests in Washington Politics

	Share of DC Organizations					Change in Share
	1981	1991	2001	2006	2011	1981–2011
Corporations	45.9%	33.8%	34.9%	36.1%	36.6%	-9.3%
Trade and other business associations	15.5	14.8	13.2	10.6	10.2	-5.3%
Occupational associations	8.2	8.7	6.9	5.2	5.4	-2.8%
Unions	1.6	1.5	1.0	0.8	0.7	-0.9%
Education	1.5	3.0	4.2	5.4	5.7	+4.2%
Health	0.9	2.4	3.5	4.4	5.2	+4.3%
Public interest	3.8	4.8	4.6	4.1	4.4	+0.6%
Identity groups[a]	2.7	3.5	3.8	3.8	3.6	+0.9%
Social welfare or poor	0.5	0.7	0.8	0.9	1.2	+0.7%
State and local governments	5.1	6.9	10.4	11.8	12.3	+7.2%
Foreign	8.7	10.2	7.7	6.5	6.2	-2.5%
Other	4.3	7.0	7.7	8.6	7.9	+3.6%
Don't know	1.3	2.7	1.4	1.7	0.7	-0.6%
Total	100.0%	100.0%	100.1%	99.9%	100.1%	
N	6,691	7,924	11,651	13,824	14,365	

Source: Washington Representatives Study (2011).
[a] Includes organizations representing racial, ethnic, religious, or LGBT groups, the elderly, or women.

that are traditionally underrepresented in pressure politics: organizations representing broad publics and the disadvantaged. Instead there has been explosive growth of subnational governments, especially local governments, and memberless organizations, especially in the health and education sectors. Taken together, the share accounted for by subnational governments and the health and educational sectors tripled over the three-decade period. The share of organizations representing public interests increased very slightly, from 3.8 to 4.4 percent. The small share of organized interests representing people in terms of their shared identities—racial, religious, ethnic, age, gender, and sexual orientation—was also slightly higher in 2011 than it had been in 1981.

Several kinds of organizations represent the economic interests of the less affluent: social welfare and poor people's organizations, occupational associations of nonprofessionals, and labor unions. Throughout the period under discussion, this group of organizations accounted for only a tiny fraction of the pressure system. However, between 1981 and 2011 that share decreased from 2.9 percent to 2.5 percent. Decomposing that figure into its constituents, the minute share of organizations representing the poor and social welfare increased slightly. In contrast, the share of organizations representing the occupational interests of the vast majority of American workers diminished. Moreover, when it comes to union strength, what is even more important than the number of unions is the decline in the number of members and the share of the workforce they enroll.

THE DECLINE OF LABOR UNIONS

Alone among all the aggregate categories of organized interests, labor unions did not register an absolute increase in the number of organizations, an outcome that results from the absolute decrease in the number of unions that organize blue-collar workers in the private sector. A corollary to this development is that between 1998 and 2012, union spending on lobbying rose 24 percent, while corporate lobbying spending increased 68 percent.[32] These findings dovetail with evidence about the steady decline in the proportion of private-sector employees who are unionized and the increasing share of union members with college degrees, especially among women. The result, as Theda Skocpol demonstrates, is a growing gap between the proportion of college-educated Americans who are members of a professional society and the proportion of non-college-educated Americans who are union members.[33]

The erosion of union membership in the working class also has consequences for the changing accent of political voice through individual-level political participation. Surveys conducted over a three-decade period allow us to track the proportion of all political activity undertaken by individuals that arises from union members. Because the surveys include somewhat different measures and somewhat different political acts, we should not make too much of any particular number.[34] However, the pattern of steady decrease is unmistakable. In 1967, 25 percent of all political acts were performed by union members. By 1990, this figure had decreased to 18 percent. It had fallen to 13 percent in 2000 and then to 11 percent in 2006. This decline is especially noteworthy in light of the gains over the period in the share of the unionized workforce that is college educated. What is also striking is the erosion in the share of political activity that arises from union members who are lower on the ladder of SES. In 1967, 4.6 percent of all political acts originated with union members in one of the two lower-SES quintiles. In

2006, the corresponding figure was 2.5 percent. In short, what we observe for individual activity accords with our findings about the pressure system.

Conclusion

This chapter has considered how social-class structuring of political voice through individual and organized interest activity has changed in an era of increasing economic inequality. We might suppose that, as income becomes more concentrated at the top, political voice would also become more unequal along social class lines. However, such factors as increasing levels of educational attainment and the growing strength of the political parties might have a mitigating impact.

The story is the same for individual participation and organized interest involvement. In both domains, political voice remains highly stratified by social class, and that stratification has been a feature of political activity for as long as we have been tracking it. Participatory inequality is not only pronounced but also enduring, evident in our data as far back as they go. However, in both domains the growing dominance of forms of political voice that depend on spending implies that, in the New Gilded Age, the sum total of citizen input to politics tilts even more heavily in the direction of the well-heeled.

For individuals, participatory inequality is evident in our data as far back as they go, which is the early 1950s. For the political act with the least social class structuring, voting, those in the top quintile are on average roughly twice as likely to go to the polls as those in the bottom quintile. For the political act that is most inegalitarian, making campaign contributions, those in the top quintile are approximately eight times more likely to make a donation than those in the bottom quintile.

The highly egalitarian pattern for religious attendance suggests that political participation may be unique. Not all forms of civic involvement share the socioeconomic stratification characteristic of political participation. On the contrary, religious attendance is characterized by only minimal class stratification.

As for the trajectory over time, SES bias in participation has varied over the years. Additive scales measuring the number of electoral and nonelectoral acts in which an individual has engaged show that, on average, it has not increased, but it has not diminished much either. The ups and downs of participatory inequality do not seem to be related to other obvious factors—in particular, to growing economic inequality. The possible exception is that a competitive presidential election may have a mobilizing effect, resulting in some amelioration of participatory inequality with respect to electoral activity. In short, our major conclusion is the extent of the participatory advantage enjoyed by the well-educated and affluent rather than any changes in the level of socioeconomic inequality in political activity.

Comparing the trajectories for different political acts shows evidence of increasingly unequal political voice related to increasingly unequal incomes. For attending campaign meetings and doing campaign work, involvement is actually less sharply structured by SES than in the past. In contrast, the propensity to make campaign contributions rises sharply at the very top of the SES ladder. As a consequence, contributions weigh more heavily in the bundle of campaign activities of the very affluent and well educated. Moreover, data measuring whether individuals made campaign donations do not account for how much they gave. As we saw in Chapter 3, the best predictor of the size of campaign contributions is a respondent's income. We also know that growing economic inequality has produced a super-stratum of donors able to afford very large donations. As aggregate campaign contributions have soared in recent years, a small set of mega-donors are responsible for an increasing share of giving. Thus, when it comes to the most expandable and most unequal form of individual political participation, making campaign contributions, inequality has grown over time in a way that is related to the rise in economic inequality.

When we focus on the activity of organizations rather than of individuals, we find parallel results. Although political scientists often emphasize the barriers to forming new membership groups and taking them into politics, the pressure community has expanded substantially. We found a striking increase in the number of organizations active in Washington politics: more than twice as many organizations were listed in the *Washington Representatives* directory in 2011 as in 1981. The overall distribution of kinds of organizations shows a great deal of continuity. Throughout the period, the representation of business was robust, and public interest groups and organizations representing the less advantaged were only a tiny share of the organizations active in Washington politics. In sum, a thirty-year march to Washington by organized interests entails expansion but not transformation.

Interestingly, although they continue to be dominant in the pressure system, in relative terms the rate of increase in some kinds of organizations that have traditionally formed the backbone of pressure politics—trade and other business associations, occupational associations, and unions—has not kept pace with the rate of increase in other kinds of organizations. However, the growth rates for the kinds of organizations that have traditionally been less well represented—public interest groups and organizations representing the less advantaged—have not been especially noteworthy. Instead, the marked expansion in the number of politically active organizations derives disproportionately from the education and health fields (categories dominated by organizations without members rather than by voluntary associations) and from state, and especially local, governments.

We should not overlook that, even small increases in some kinds of groups, such as citizen groups, have empowered those outside the traditional pressure group system and have exerted appreciable influence on policy.[35] By and large, however, the proliferation of organizational advocates reinforces the tendencies we have been emphasizing. While the growth rates for the various kinds of organizations representing business were not remarkable, the absolute changes were substantial, and business advocates remain a dominant force in the system.

During this period, the number of unions did not grow, a function of the decline in the number of blue-collar, private-sector unions. The declining proportion of the private-sector workforce enrolled in unions and the relative increase in the educational attainment of union members enfeebles the voice of people on lower rungs of the socioeconomic ladder. At the same time, in absolute terms, the increases in organizations representing business dwarf the increases in organizations advocating on behalf of either public goods or the disadvantaged. Indeed, nearly twice as many organizations representing the private sector were added over the period as there were unions, public interest groups, identity groups, and organizations representing the economically needy listed in 2011.

As we were working on this project, a friend asked, "Are you describing a new and disturbing trend or an old and disturbing process?" In response, we could only say, "Yes." Our consideration of the complicated and sometimes contradictory trends over three decades makes it clear that we are dealing with an expanded version of an old and disturbing process. Because pressure politics relies so heavily on the services of paid professionals, it facilitates the conversion of market resources into political advocacy. Throughout the period we have considered, pressure politics has been hospitable to the representation of the interests of the advantaged, especially business. As the chorus has unambiguously become larger, the voices of the advantaged have become louder.

At one point scholars were concerned that political participation by individuals was diminishing.[36] That slide seems to have tapered off, but it is clear that—unlike what we have seen for organized interests—the time-based activity of individuals has hardly increased. The simultaneous explosion in campaign giving and the growth in activity in pressure politics thus shift the relative weight of forms of political input in favor of those parts of the chorus that sing with an especially pronounced upper-class accent. Even though the distribution of organizations has not changed appreciably, when combined with the greater weight of campaign giving in the political activity of individuals, the alteration in the balance of individual and organizational voices has exacerbated inequalities of political voice.

12

Can We Do Anything about It?

Having painted a bleak picture of the skew in political voice toward the affluent and well educated, the obvious question is whether we can do anything about it. With political, educational, and social change, can we overcome some of the inequalities in political voice?

Our conclusions are not especially upbeat. Many proposed reforms would not have much impact on inequalities of political voice. Voting by mail, for example, seems to have the effect of raising the level of activity without decreasing inequalities of political voice.[1] In fact, because most people are not especially active in politics, the channels that transmit messages from citizens to public officials run at far below full capacity. Thus, simultaneous increases in the amount of activity and the extent to which it is unrepresentative are possible. Procedural reforms that are potentially more efficacious face political or constitutional obstacles.

That said, political change never occurs unless policy ideas are proposed and evaluated—ready when the political environment is more favorable. American history has witnessed periodic episodes of enthusiasm for political reform. Our era is not congenial to equalizing reform. The current poisonous partisan environment is hostile to equalizing efforts. Current constitutional interpretation rules out many kinds of reform. Neither of these is necessarily permanent. When a window opens in the future, reformers should be prepared with sound proposals for moderating political inequality.

Our focus is on changes that would make individual and organizational participation more representative of the American public in politically relevant ways—not only in terms of such demographic characteristics as social class, race, gender, or age but also in terms of preferences and needs for government policy. Ensuring equality of political voice does not prescribe any particular model of democracy along the continuum from elite autonomy to populist control in policymaking. However, it does require that expressions of political voice—through which citizens inform public officials about their circumstances and opinions and persuade them to listen—represent the public.

The Uphill Road to Reform

Democracy involves balancing multiple, often competing, values, not all of which can be maximized simultaneously. For example, we ask a great deal of elections: among them, to be free of corruption, to be competitive, to involve a large and representative share of the eligible voters, to increase the voters' faith in the political process, and to allow maximum opportunities for individuals to express—and to persuade others to heed—their views. When it comes to political voice, some of the most complicated procedural issues involve the trade-off between two of these goals, free speech and equality.

Moreover, the strong gravitational pull exerted by the political status quo in America is well known. As every textbook points out, our political system was constructed from the outset to diminish the possibilities for hasty change. Institutional arrangements present an impediment to policy change. Moreover, existing policies usually create stakeholders with an interest in maintaining those policies. Underlying the insight that "Policy makes politics" is that achieving policy change is difficult. Moreover, in the American federal system, many political arrangements with implications for inequalities of political voice—ranging from the laws mandating the disenfranchisement of felons to the regulation of corporate giving in state elections—are governed by state, not national, law. Bringing about nationwide reform involves changing up to fifty sets of laws—and perhaps myriad local ones—which is much more challenging than altering a single federal statute. Of course, constitutional amendments can bring about change on a national basis. Historically, constitutional amendments reduced inequalities of political voice by enfranchising former slaves in 1870 and women in 1920, outlawing the poll tax in 1964, and enfranchising young adults in 1971. However, the failure of many constitutional amendments—including, most recently, the attempt to establish equality under the law irrespective of gender through the Equal Rights Amendment—demonstrates the high hurdles imposed by requirements for congressional supermajorities and passage in three-fourths of the states.

Essential to the American political tradition are distrust of government, hostility to coercion, and a liberal celebration of the individual apart from inherited status. As a result, the political arrangements commonly used by other democracies to overcome political inequalities—for instance, registration of voters by the government, mandatory voter turnout, or reservation of seats in the legislature for underrepresented groups such as women—are less likely to be considered in the American context. Although public opinion surveys show that Americans are concerned about the role of money in politics, that concern coexists with the individualistic and anti-government strands of the liberal American tradition. The result is a political system that facilitates the conversion of market resources into political voice. Dovetailing with the American predilection for small government is the current climate of fiscal restraint, which takes off the table any expensive reform, such as schemes for public funding of election campaigns.

Anatole France noted famously: "The law, in its majestic equality, forbids the rich as well as the poor to sleep under bridges, to beg in the streets, and to steal bread." This observation points to the way that, even when fairly applied, the rules of politics have differential consequences across groups. When political arrangements are debated, contestants frequently choose to emphasize the abstract democratic norm that coincides with their political self-interest. For example, those who seek to prevent voter fraud by requiring presentation of photo ID at the polls argue that the integrity of voting process demands stiff safeguards even if they deter some legitimate voters. Concerned about equal representation, opponents of voter ID laws argue that they place a greater burden on voters of limited education or English language skills. Beneath this debate about democratic norms are partisan interests. It is hardly surprising that Democrats are less likely than Republicans to consider voter fraud a serious problem and are less enthusiastic about voter ID laws as a possible remedy. In fact, state legislators rarely cross party lines when votes are taken on voter ID bills. The controversies over many of the ostensibly procedural measures discussed later in this chapter are similarly imbued with partisan conflict.

Political Reform: Results or Consequences?

When it comes to political reform, it is a truism that "you want results and you get consequences." Political innovations frequently do not work out as expected. Assessments of the consequences of procedural reforms often contain the caveat that they have their intended impact "if correctly designed," thus attesting to the central role played by the details of program design in determining their effectiveness. It is often possible to find loopholes that can be exploited to subvert the best intentions for political change—a circumstance that seems to be the rule, not the exception, when it comes to campaign finance law. For example, the impact of limitations on the sums that individuals can donate to campaigns is weakened when smaller checks are "bundled" together.[2]

Furthermore, it is one thing to legislate and another to implement. For example, on the principle that low-income and disabled voters would be less likely to have cars or driver's licenses, the 1993 National Voter Registration Act (NVRA) contained provisions directing states to provide for voter registration not only at motor vehicle bureaus but also at public assistance agencies. According to a report issued by Project Vote and Dēmos, two nongovernmental organizations concerned with voter participation, compliance with the mandate for voter registration at public assistance agencies declined precipitously in the decade after the NVRA was passed and first implemented.[3]

In addition, procedural changes often bequeath unintended consequences. For example, the purpose of eliminating 60 percent of precincts in Los Angeles County in 2003 was to save money. An ancillary result was to reduce turnout by several percentage points when polling places had been moved to new and more distant locations.[4]

Not only do reforms sometimes produce unexpected results, but a procedural reform in the name of one democratic value may jeopardize others. For instance, opponents of same-day voter registration, a procedural reform that increases turnout, argue that it increases voter fraud. Surely, the integrity of the electoral process, which requires restricting ballot access to eligible voters, is also an important democratic principle.

The final reason that we are dubious about what can be achieved by procedural reform is that political inequalities are deeply rooted in social, educational, and economic inequalities. We have demonstrated the power and durability of the class skew in individual and collective political participation. Addressing inequalities of income and education is not a matter of a mere institutional quick fix but requires a political and social revolution involving a level of patience and a commitment of resources not characteristic of American policy. It is difficult to overestimate what would be required to cut through the web of interconnected political, social, economic, and educational circumstances in domains ranging from taxes to education to income support to medical care that sustain inequality among citizens. Nevertheless, certain eras in American history—of which the New Deal and Great Society are obvious examples—are characterized by bursts of policy activity with long-term consequences.

Voting: A More Representative Electorate?

As we saw in Chapter 4, turnout in the United States is anything but universal, and the American electorate overrepresents the well educated and affluent and, therefore, non-Hispanic whites. Although it seems logical that lowering the barriers to voting should produce higher turnout, procedural changes that make it more convenient to go to the polls have often been disappointing.[5] Perhaps surprisingly, higher turnout does not necessarily produce a more representative electorate. Even when new voters show up at the polls, they often replicate the kind of voters already casting ballots rather than those whose participation would render turnout more representative of the eligible electorate.

The franchise has never been universal. Even today, minors, some of the mentally incapable, and, in most states, convicted felons are disenfranchised. In the past citizens could not vote because of distinctions based, most notably, on property, race, and sex. The process of incorporating historically disenfranchised groups into the electorate has been a protracted and difficult one: Jacksonian-era reforms removed property qualifications; the Fifteenth (1870) and Nineteenth (1920) Amendments eliminated race- and sex-based qualifications, respectively; and various measures during the 1960s outlawed poll taxes, literacy tests, and other discriminatory policies and practices.

In contrast to the enfranchisement of women, which seems to have been settled once the Nineteenth Amendment was finally adopted in 1920, guaranteeing voting rights for African Americans has long been, and continues to be, contested territory.[6] The Fifteenth Amendment to the contrary, until the passage of the Voting Rights Act of 1965, the disenfranchisement of African Americans was an essential piece of Jim Crow in the South. Over its half-century existence, the Voting Rights Act (VRA) changed the South, and the explicit disenfranchisement of African Americans has been consigned to memory. That said, the VRA met with substantial opposition and efforts to dilute the power of black votes through discriminatory procedures and practices. The most recent chapter in a fraught history is the 5–4 decision in *Shelby* v. *Holder* (2013). Arguing that current conditions no longer require

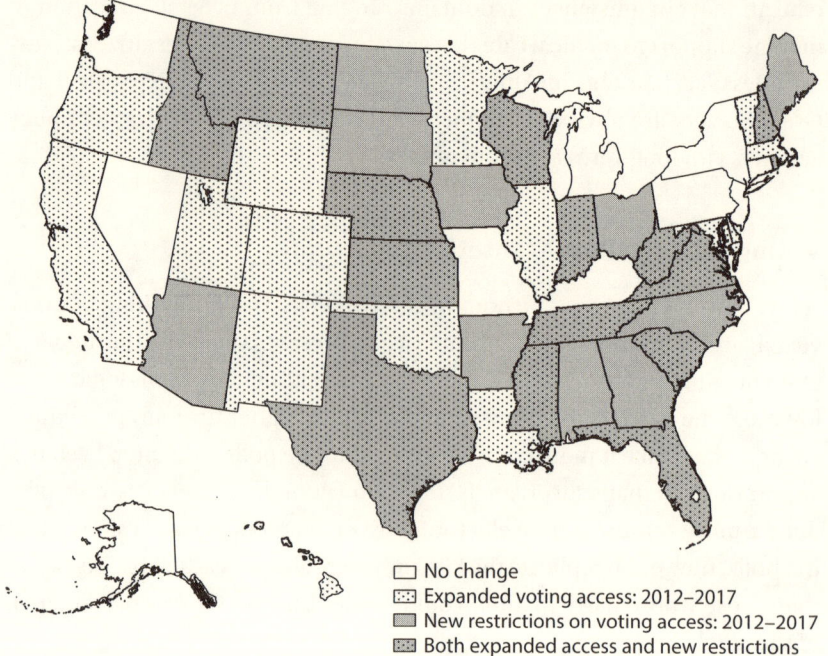

MAP 12.1. Recent Procedural Changes to the Regulations Governing Voting
Source: Map constructed using information on the Web site of the Brennan Center for Justice, https://www.brennancenter.org/analysis/voting-laws-roundup-2017; https://www.brennancenter.org/analysis/voting-laws-roundup-2016; https://www.brennancenter.org/analysis/voting-laws-roundup-2015; https://www.brennancenter.org/analysis/voting-laws-roundup-2014; https://www.brennancenter.org/analysis/election-2013-voting-laws-roundup; http://www.brennancenter.org/analysis/election-2012-voting-laws-roundup.
Note: States frequently alter their regulations governing voting. This map shows the situation as of August 2017.

such scrutiny, the Supreme Court held unconstitutional the requirement that jurisdictions with a history of voting discrimination must submit proposed changes in voting procedures for federal "preclearance." At this point, preclearance is no longer required, and Congress has declined to update the VRA so as to restore preclearance in a way that complies with *Shelby*.[7] Although it is too soon to know what the consequences will be at the polls, early soundings suggest that formerly covered jurisdictions have seized on the opportunity to make it more difficult for African Americans to vote.[8]

The recent skirmishes over the VRA illustrate Alex Keyssar's contention that the enfranchisement of adults in the United States entailed not only the unidirectional advance celebrated in high school civics but also periodic retreats. Our own era has witnessed a great deal of procedural fiddling with the rules that govern voting. Many states have imposed new requirements that raise barriers to voting—most notably, voter ID laws. What has attracted less attention is that even more states have facilitated turnout by, for example, providing for early voting or no-excuse absentee balloting.[9] Map 12.1 illustrates this combination of advance and retreat in recent years.

Delving into the political controversies over changing voting rules confirms the truism that, although conflict over political reform usually engages principled democratic rhetoric, what is usually at stake is political self-interest. Over the last generation, the voting wars have become increasingly partisan.

FACILITATING REGISTRATION

The first step to casting a ballot is voter registration. In most democracies, governmental authorities find eligible voters and register them. In contrast, in the United States, registration is voluntary and takes place at the initiative of citizens themselves. Like so much having to do with voting, there is wide variety among states. Map 12.2 shows the mix of arrangements: the largest group of states permit either election-day or online registration, but not both. Several states permit neither. North Dakota, in contrast, does not require voters to register. States also vary in the extent to which responsibility for managing registration is further devolved to local communities and the extent to which registration records contain errors.[10]

Assessments of various reforms suggest that it is easier to increase registration than to raise turnout. Hardest of all is increasing the representativeness of the electorate in terms of education, income, and race or ethnicity. The 1993 National Voter Registration Act (NVRA) most notably, mandated voter registration at motor vehicle registration bureaus and other government agencies as well as mail-in registration. Although the NVRA achieved its goal of raising registration rates, enhanced registration rates did not translate into higher turnout, much less a more representative electorate. Election-day registration seems unambiguously to raise turnout, but results are less conclusive when it comes to democratizing the composition of the electorate.[11]

Registration poses a barrier not only to the socioeconomically disadvantaged but also to new voters. Among the reforms aimed at facilitating registration for first-time voters are permitting high school students to pre-register at their schools when they turn sixteen; making registration a requirement for high school graduation; and permitting new citizens to register at their

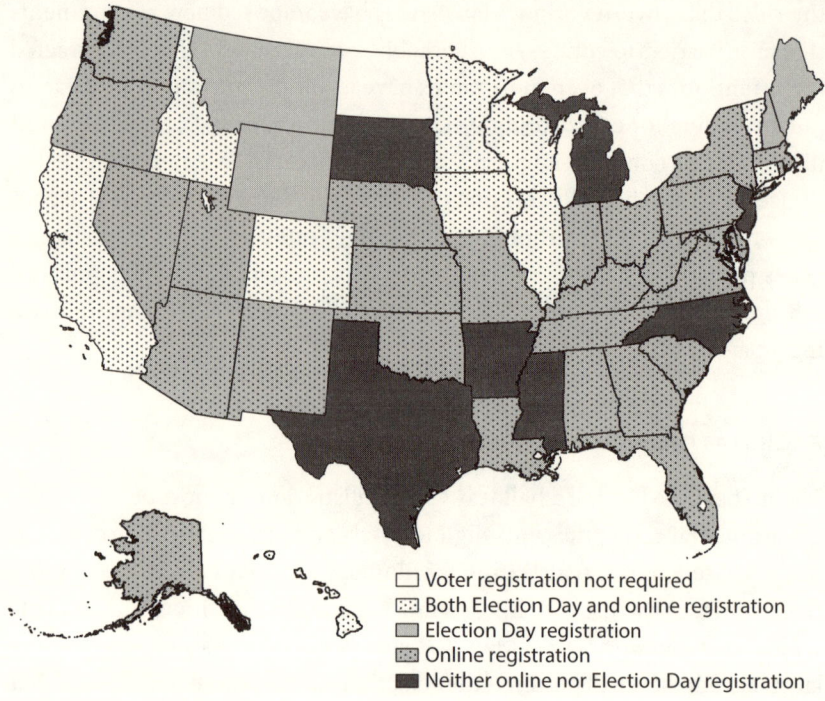

MAP 12.2. Voter Registration Arrangements
Source: Map constructed using information on the Web site of the National Conference of State Legislatures, http://www.ncsl.org/research/elections-and-campaigns/same-day-registration.aspx; http://www.ncsl.org/research/elections-and-campaigns/electronic-or-online-voter-registration.aspx.
Note: States frequently alter their regulations governing voter registration. This map shows the situation as of August 2017. In some cases, regulations on the books may not yet have been implemented.

naturalization ceremony.[12] Several states have pre-registration programs in place. One study found that those who pre-register in school vote at slightly higher rates than those who register after their eighteenth birthday and that the effect is somewhat stronger for African Americans and Latinos. Since evidence suggests that voting becomes habitual, there is good reason to make efforts to encourage new voters to turn out.[13] While not a silver bullet, under the right circumstances, pre-registration could modestly reduce the underrepresentation of the young and minorities among voters.[14]

MAKING VOTING MORE CONVENIENT

In more than two dozen other nations—among them, such democracies as Australia and Belgium—citizens are required to go to the polls at election time and may be fined if they do not.[15] Although evidence indicates that countries that have introduced compulsory voting have seen reductions in inequalities in turnout among social groups, mandating turnout as a means of equalizing citizen political voice would probably be a tough sell in a nation uneasy with public mandates.[16]

While compulsory voting does not fit comfortably with the individualistic American suspicion of coercion, states find that making voting less burdensome raises no such problems:

- *Early voting*, in which voters are permitted to vote in person on specified dates (usually including weekends) before Election Day at such sites as town hall, a public library, or community center;
- *No-excuse absentee balloting*, which may be temporary or permanent, in which voters receive and return an absentee ballot by mail; and
- *All-mail voting*, in which there is no in-person voting, and all ballots are received and returned through the mail.

Map 12.3 shows that a majority of states have adopted some version of these arrangements, but the details are crucial. With regard to early in-person voting, the consequences depend on the length of the early voting period and the number and location of voting sites. Many states permit early in-person voting on weekends, which provides a partial test of the proposition that conducting elections on weekends, as in so many of the democracies of Europe (rather than on Tuesdays) would raise turnout. Although absentee balloting is a mechanism with a long history, California pioneered no-excuse absentee voting in 1978, and since then, versions of these arrangements have been adopted in a majority of states. By 2008 more than a third of voters (34 percent) cast some kind of early ballot.[17] Early in-person voting has shown particular growth in popularity and, by 2008, the number of early in-person voters was roughly equivalent to the number of mail voters.

Ballots cast early or by mail suffer liabilities that offset the convenience to the elderly, disabled, the overly busy, and the away-from-home.[18] Such ballots are more likely to be compromised, cast in error, or contested, and are less likely to be counted. Because ballots cast early or by mail must be kept in a government office—in a number of states for as long as a month and a half—these voting arrangements pose security risks. Ballots could be lost or damaged either through accident or unwitting error or through the deliberate efforts of someone with a stake in the outcome. Furthermore, whether absentee ballots or part of a statewide program of elections by mail, ballots that arrive and are returned by mail present additional opportunities

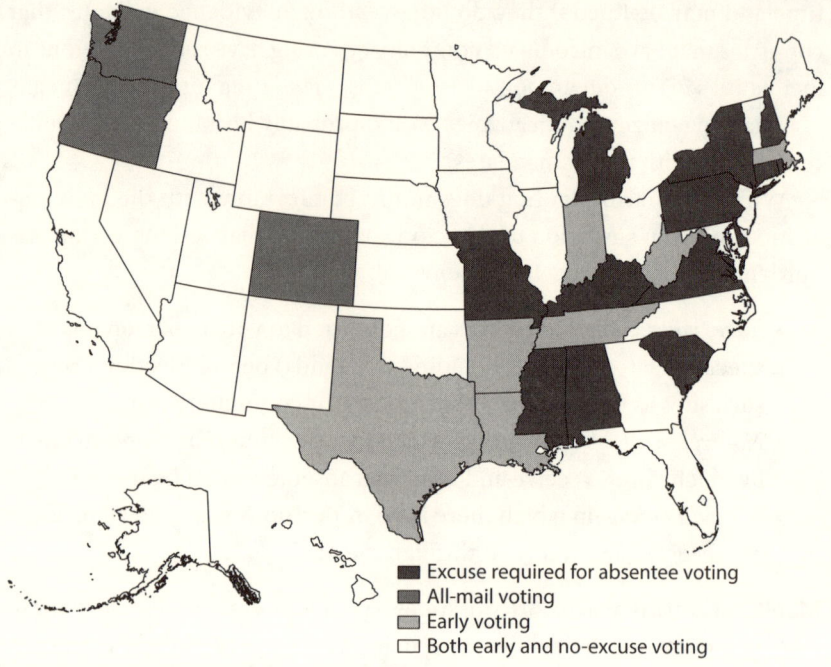

- Excuse required for absentee voting
- All-mail voting
- Early voting
- Both early and no-excuse voting

MAP 12.3. Early and No-Excuse Absentee Voting
Source: Map constructed using information on the Web site of the National Conference of State Legislatures, http://www.ncsl.org/research/elections-and-campaigns/absentee-and-early-voting.aspx.
Note: States frequently alter their regulations regarding absentee voting. This map shows the situation as of August 2017. Included among the states permitting early voting are some states that permit what is sometimes called "in-person absentee" voting even though they do not have early voting in the traditional sense. During a specified period before an election, voters may apply in person for an absentee ballot (without an excuse) at an election official's office and cast that ballot immediately after applying. Massachusetts has early voting in general elections in even-numbered years only. Six states (Arizona, California, Hawaii, Montana, New Jersey, and Utah) permit any voter to join a permanent absentee voting list and receive an absentee ballot automatically in future elections.

for things to go awry by chance or by design. Envelopes can get lost in the mail. When ballots are completed at home or, especially, a nursing home, privacy—and even the voter's intent—may be compromised by someone who offers to "help."[19] Even when signatures are compared, there is still the possibility that someone else actually filled it out. In short, the downside of voter convenience is the multiplication of the possibilities for invalidation, error, or fraud.

Reforms that make it easier to vote may have simply made it more convenient for those already inclined to vote to cast their ballots. Although there is some disagreement among scholars, these reforms have not raised turnout appreciably in national elections, and there is no evidence that any of these arrangements renders the electorate more representative of eligible voters.[20] In fact, because early in-person voting is especially attractive to older and better-educated voters, it may actually exacerbate existing biases in turnout.

MAKING VOTING MORE DIFFICULT: VOTER ID

Some procedural changes could actually reduce the representativeness of the electorate. Since 2000, a majority of states have raised barriers to voting by enacting or strengthening the requirements for voters to show identification at the polls in order to cast a ballot.

The politics of voter ID laws are complicated. On one hand, voter ID laws are generally popular with the public, attracting support across parties.[21] On the other, the issue has become extremely partisan with Republicans supporting voter ID laws and Democrats opposing them.[22] Furthermore, in an era in which the Democratic Party is more attractive to Latinos and, especially, African Americans, there is evidence that beneath the partisan politics of the adoption of voter ID laws is an unspoken politics of race.[23] The states that since 2010 have augmented their requirements for presenting ID to vote include nine of the twelve states with the fastest-growing Latino populations and seven of the eleven with the highest African-American turnout in 2008.[24] A former Republican staffer in the Wisconsin state senate reported that some of the legislators who attended a party caucus "'were literally giddy' over the [presumably negative] effect of the state's voter ID law on minorities and college students."[25]

As with other kinds of balloting regulations, states vary tremendously with regard to the details of voter ID provisions. Map 12.4 shows how the states line up with respect to two critical distinctions. One is the form of identification that is required: just a printed document specifying a name and address—for example, a recent bank statement or utility bill—as opposed to a photo ID. If the latter, it matters which particular forms of photo ID are acceptable. For example, Tennessee accepts a Tennessee handgun carry permit but not a student ID from a public Tennessee educational institution. The list of valid forms may be restrictive or expansive and may be more congenial to some kinds of voters than to others.

The second distinction is whether the voter ID law is strict. Although the details vary, in non-strict states, voters lacking the required ID are permitted

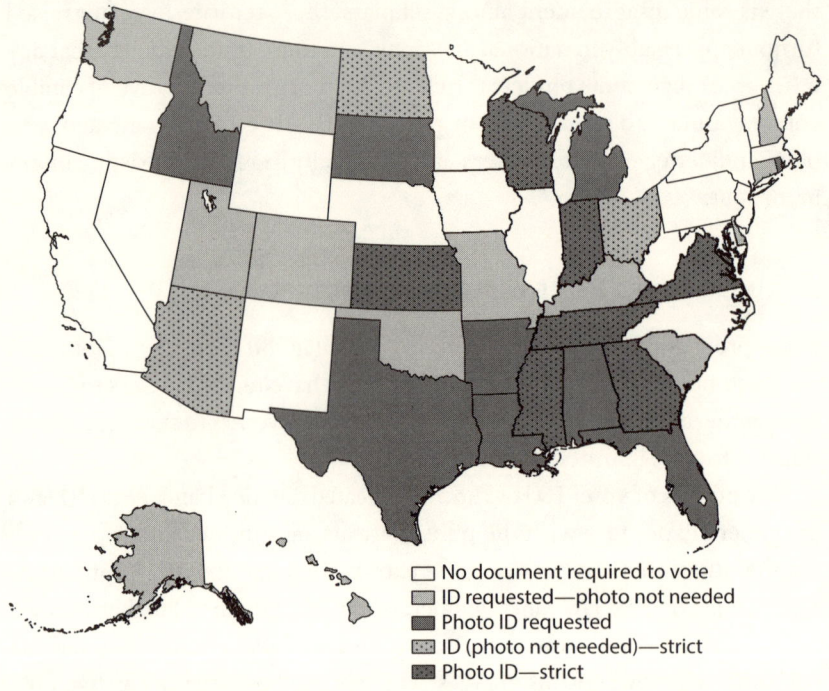

MAP 12.4. Voter Identification Requirements
Source: Map constructed using information on the Web site of the National Conference of State Legislatures, http://www.ncsl.org/research/elections-and-campaigns/voter-id.aspx.
Note: In the last decade, many states have changed their regulations regarding the presentation of identification when voting. This map shows the situation as of August 2017. In strict voter ID states, voters who cannot produce acceptable identification may vote on a provisional ballot. For a provisional ballot to be counted, additional steps must be taken within a specified period after Election Day.

to vote without taking further action—for example, by signing an affidavit or by having poll workers vouch for them. In strict voter ID states, voters are required to show one of the acceptable forms of identification. Those who are unable to do so cast a provisional ballot. For that ballot to be counted, the voter must, within a few days, return to an elections office with a valid form of identification. Although there is limited evidence about whether the requirement for a return visit to an election office constitutes a high hurdle, in Harris County, the county that contains Houston, only 27 of the 389 provisional voters across three elections in 2014 and 2015 eventually produced a valid ID.[26]

Proponents of voter ID requirements argue that they protect the integrity of the electoral process by restricting ballot access to eligible voters.

Soon after the 2016 election, Donald Trump claimed that he had been deprived of a popular vote victory by "serious voter fraud" in which "millions of people . . . voted illegally."[27] His ongoing comments, many on Twitter, focus on several forms of electoral corruption. The first is that many people are registered in two states and could, therefore, vote twice in a single federal election. Many people are registered in two states, which is not illegal, most often because they have moved and have not been removed from the voter rolls. However, little evidence suports the idea that they are actually casting more than one ballot in a single election. Trump has de-emphasized this potential source of voter fraud since it emerged that several people in his inner circle—including his daughter, Tiffany, and his son-in-law, Jared Kushner—are registered in two states.[28]

Although the problem of such double voting is not amenable to remedy through strict voter ID laws, careful upkeep of voter lists to purge voters who have moved, died, or are otherwise inactive is sound election administration and is mandated by the NVRA and, especially, the 2002 Help America Vote Act (HAVA). Unfortunately, maintaining the voter rolls is difficult, and zealous purging often removes eligible voters, especially if the standard for what constitutes an inactive voter is strict. People with very common names often have the same birthday, which can result in the ejection of eligible voters when voter rolls are purged. Persons of color are disproportionately likely to be removed as the result of such false positives. Vanita Gupta, a head of the civil rights division at the Justice Department in the Obama administration, cites Census data demonstrating that "minorities are overrepresented in 85 of the 100 most common last names."[29]

There is also little evidence for other forms of voter fraud cited by Trump. One is voter impersonation at the polls.[30] After all, an individual seeking to commit voter fraud must identify someone on the voter rolls who is unlikely to vote, perhaps a recently deceased voter, and then impersonate that person (and, if required, sign a poll book or provide such relevant information as an address) at a polling place staffed by locals who might actually know the voter whose identity is being assumed—a process that involves committing a felony in public. While this variant of voter fraud is potentially addressed by strict voter ID laws, it is no wonder that Indiana, which has a strict voter ID law that was blessed by the Supreme Court in a 2007 case, had never had a single prosecution for that form of voter fraud. An extensive initiative to uncover and document voter fraud in Texas found only thirteen indictments for voter fraud, none of which would have been prevented by a requirement to show photo ID at the polls.[31]

It has been argued that voter ID requirements are needed to protect against a form of fraud for which there is somewhat more evidence: registration fraud.[32] In the late years of the George W. Bush administration, considerable controversy surrounded the voter registration drives conducted in low-income and minority communities by ACORN, a now-defunct organizing and advocacy organization on the left. It seems that some of ACORN's canvassers had delivered registration forms containing false names like "Mickey Mouse." Registering fictitious people constitutes *registration fraud*. However, since Mickey Mouse never showed up at the polls, no voter fraud was committed. Even if he had, voter ID laws would not be necessary to safeguard against voter fraud. As a newly registered voter who had not registered in person, Mickey would have been required, under a provision of HAVA, to present verifying identification to cast his ballot if the registration form submitted by ACORN had not included that information or if election authorities had not been able to verify the information presented on the registration form.[33]

President Trump has repeatedly alleged that millions of unauthorized aliens cast ballots in 2016, a claim that has been discredited.[34] Trump is correct that ineligible immigrants do sometimes vote—the result of error as well as malfeasance—but his numbers are wide of the mark. For example, a review conducted in Ohio after the 2012 and 2014 elections, in which more than 8 million ballots were cast, found that 436 unauthorized immigrants were registered to vote, of which 44 voted.[35]

We have already mentioned that absentee ballots, as well as early in-person and mail ballots, present opportunities for election fraud.[36] For example, in hearings on North Carolina's quite stringent voter ID bill, a Democratic state senator observed that the state board of elections had found twenty-four times more instances of absentee ballot fraud than cases of voter impersonation.[37] Under the circumstances, it is ironic that less than a third of the states with voter ID laws, including a number with strict photo ID laws, require voter ID for absentee ballots.[38] Since absentee voters tend to have high levels of income and education, the net result of this configuration is to give even greater advantage to upper-SES voters.

Many of the voter ID laws are of recent vintage, some of them in effect only since 2016. Therefore, it is too early to render a verdict on their impact on the representativeness of the electorate. Unambiguous evidence indicates that people with low incomes and people who move frequently, groups that are disproportionately young and African American or Latino, are less likely to have a driver's license that is valid for voting purposes—that is, an unexpired license showing the voter's current name and address.[39] There is also some evidence that, in states without strict requirements for photo ID, African Americans and especially Latinos are more likely to be asked to show identification.[40] Studies conducted before the most recent round of new voter ID regulations do not come to a firm conclusion as to whether voter ID laws depress turnout and whether they operate in such a way as to produce an electorate that is less representative of eligible voters.[41] After all, the kinds of people who lack valid ID are also less likely to be engaged with politics and, hence, would be less likely to go to the polls even if no photo ID were required. However, a more recent study—which not only includes the states that have recently raised their requirements for presenting ID to vote but considers verified turnout rather than reported turnout—finds that, in fact, strict voter ID requirements have little impact on non-Hispanic white voters but depress turnout for Latinos, Americans of mixed race, and in primaries, African Americans.[42] Similarly, a survey conducted after the 2016 election in two Wisconsin counties showed considerable confusion among voters about Wisconsin's voter ID law and concluded that the law depressed turnout among registered voters, an effect that was especially pronounced among African Americans.[43]

A number of the most recent voter ID laws have been challenged in court. Although some have failed to pass muster with federal judges, the results are mixed, and the process is ongoing.[44] At the same time, President Trump appointed a Presidential Advisory Commission on Election Integrity. Controversial from the start, Trump abruptly shut down the Commission in January 2018[45] but he remains concerned about what he considers massive illegal voting in the 2016 presidential election. The story of voter fraud and attempts to address it continues to play out.

MAKING IT IMPOSSIBLE TO VOTE: FELON DISENFRANCHISEMENT

While there is residual uncertainty about whether voter ID laws obstruct turnout, state laws disenfranchising felons unambiguously keep many people from the polls.[46] As shown in Map 12.5, with the exception of Maine and Vermont, all states have some provision for the disenfranchisement of felons, and twelve states deny access to the ballot to some or all ex-felons who

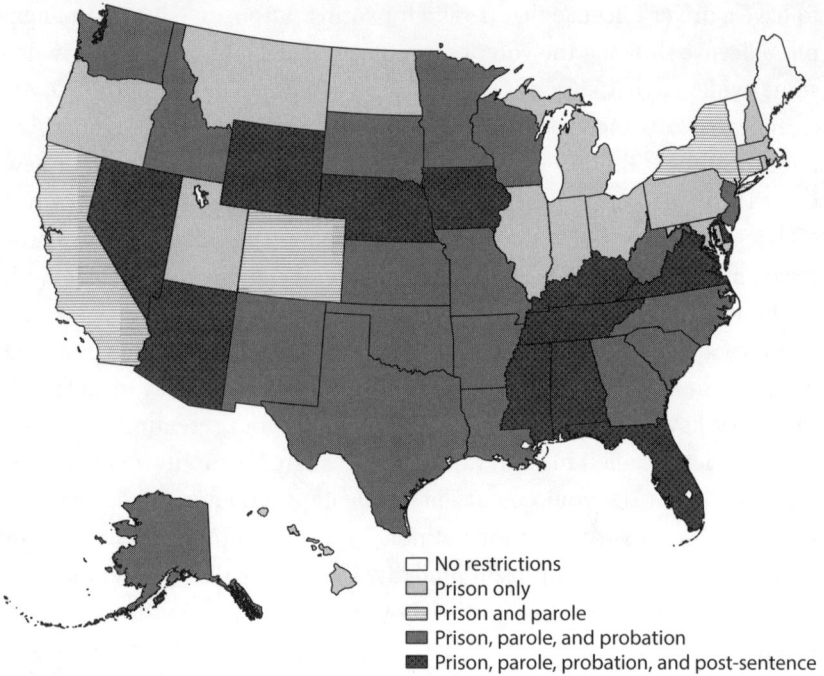

MAP 12.5. Felon Disenfranchisement
Source: Map constructed from the Web site of the The Sentencing Project, http://www.sentencingproject.org/publications/6-million-lost-voters-state-level-estimates-felony-disenfranchisement-2016/.
Note: States sometimes change their regulations regarding disenfranchisement of felons. This map shows the situation as of August 2017.

have completed their sentences and no longer have contact with the criminal justice system. With felon disenfranchisement laws that are far more punitive than in other developed democracies and incarceration rates that are six-to-ten times higher, the United States is unique—both in barring from the polls large numbers of felons who are not in prison and in the share of the electorate that is affected. In 2016 more than 6 million people (roughly 2.5 percent of the voting-age population) were denied access to the ballot. States with high proportions of African Americans are especially likely to have stringent laws, and there is good reason to believe that racial considerations played a significant role in their enactment. The rate of disenfranchisement for African Americans, 7.4 percent, is more than four times that for the rest of the voting-age population. In four states (Florida, Tennessee, Kentucky, and Virginia), more than one-fifth of African Americans of voting age are barred from voting, with even higher rates for young African-American males. Because felons have, on average, other characteristics associated with low turnout, felon disenfranchisement may not actually affect the outcomes of elections.[47] However, it unequivocally dampens turnout and renders the electorate less representative.

MOBILIZING VOTER PARTICIPATION

The Civic Voluntarism Model, discussed in Chapter 3, demonstrates that political activity often takes place because somebody asked. Since making voting easier is not a cure-all for bringing underrepresented groups into the electorate, voter mobilization through Get Out the Vote (GOTV) drives is a possible alternative. Field experiments—that is, randomized experiments that assess the impact of GOTV interventions in the context of actual elections—have brought systematic evidence to what has traditionally been the realm of anecdote, and we now know much more about what actually works when it comes to mobilizing voters. The key is personal contact:

> The more personal the interaction between campaign and potential voter, the more it raises a person's chances of voting. Door-to-door canvassing by enthusiastic volunteers is the gold standard mobilization tactic; chatty unhurried phone calls seem to work well, too. Automatically dialed, prerecorded GOTV phone calls, by contrast, are utterly impersonal and, evidently, wholly ineffective at getting people to vote.[48]

Appropriately conducted voter mobilization drives can raise turnout.

Do GOTV drives also make the electorate more representative? Canvassing in a low-income neighborhood with lots of low-propensity voters discovers many people to register, but relatively few of them end up voting—which means that campaigns often do not bother attempting to mobilize the least well-off. A swanky neighborhood populated by high-propensity voters yields fewer new registrants, but a higher proportion of them make it to the polls. In short, the efficacy of GOTV drives in reducing inequality depends on where they are conducted and what kind of voters are contacted.[49]

Recognizing their potential, those with a political stake in suppressing turnout have sought to pass legislation making it more difficult to conduct GOTV drives. A recent law in Florida imposed especially onerous conditions on those who sought to register others. With infractions potentially leading to a thousand-dollar fine and a felony conviction, even the normally nonpartisan and avowedly good government League of Women Voters has given up conducting voter registration drives there.[50]

Money-Based Participation: Campaign Finance

The possibilities for unequal political voice are especially pronounced when it comes to participation based on money, and a big bank account is virtually the sole prerequisite for making campaign contributions. Viewed cross-nationally, the American system of campaign finance is notable in the extent to which it relies on contributions from individuals and organized interests and does not depend on public funding to conduct its elections.[51] Many forms of campaign finance regulation bear directly on diminishing inequalities of political voice.[52] Among them are restrictions on campaign giving from such sources as labor unions, corporations, and government; restrictions on the size of contributions from individuals and political action committees; and schemes for the public funding of elections.

In addition to federal laws regulating campaign finance for federal elections are state and local laws. All states require some kind of disclosure of contributions; forty-four states impose some type of campaign contribution limits; and nineteen have some kind of public funding of electoral campaigns or political parties.[53] These public funding arrangements vary along several dimensions. Among them are the offices to which they apply: in Arizona and Connecticut, public financing is available to candidates in any statewide race as well as to candidates for legislative office. In contrast, in West Virginia, only candidates for state supreme court justice can qualify. State regulations also vary with regard to how many donations of what size must be raised before a candidate qualifies for public financing. Most states with public financing schemes provide qualifying candidates with matching funds up to a certain limit. However, four states (Arizona, Connecticut, Maine, and New Mexico) have "clean elections" programs, in which candidates who collect small contributions from a specified number of individuals qualify for a sum equal to the expenditure limit set for the election. Beyond the states, some large cities provide either full or partial public funding for citywide elections. Seattle has initiated an innovative program in which registered voters each receive four vouchers worth $25 each that can be donated to the candidates of their choice.[54] The consequences of Seattle's program bear watching.

Comparing the states with regard to campaign finance arrangements, Patrick Flavin finds that, in states with stricter campaign finance laws, a smaller proportion of campaign finance contributions derive from business interests and a higher proportion of the annual state budget is devoted to public welfare spending in general and to cash assistance programs in particular.[55]

Campaign finance regulation entails complex trade-offs among democratic values. Both public funding and caps on individual contributions can reduce inequalities in political voice, but contribution limits constrain the ability of those with the financial wherewithal to engage in what has now been defined as political speech. Limits on what candidates can raise or spend also impose constraints, but supporters argue that they render challengers more competitive.[56]

No fancy statistical studies are needed to ascertain that ceilings on contributions prevent those who are so inclined from devoting their resources to campaign donations. Such restrictions are unambiguously a constriction of individual liberty and are, therefore, to be taken seriously by anyone concerned about democracy. Whether such constraints constitute an infringement of free speech, however, is a more complicated and more highly contested matter. The Supreme Court first declared spending money to be a form of speech in *Buckley* v. *Valeo* (1976). Reviewing the 1974 amendments to the Federal Election Campaign Act, the Court stated in the majority opinion:

> A restriction on the amount of money a person or group can spend on political communication during a campaign necessarily reduces the quantity of expression by restricting the number of issues discussed, the depth of their exploration, and the size of the audience reached. This is because virtually every means of communicating ideas in today's mass society requires the expenditure of money. The distribution of the humblest handbill or leaflet entails printing, paper, and circulation costs. Speeches and rallies generally necessitate hiring a hall and publicizing the event. The electorate's increasing dependence on television, radio, and other mass media for news and information has made these expensive modes of communication indispensable instruments of effective political speech.[57]

Based on the principle that spending money is a form of constitutionally protected expression, the Court ruled that it would not permit certain kinds of restrictions—most importantly, on independent spending that is not coordinated with a candidate—but allowed many others. For three decades the Court hewed to this course, emphasizing the relevance of the First Amendment to campaign finance laws while permitting various forms of regulation. In *McConnell* v. *FEC* (2003), a divided court upheld most of the provisions of the Bipartisan Campaign Reform Act (BCRA).

After personnel changes, the Supreme Court subsequently issued a series of post-*McConnell* decisions, listed and summarized in Box 12.1, striking down several campaign finance provisions and affording greater First Amendment protection to political contributions as a form of speech.[58] Each of the Supreme Court decisions involved a 5–4 split—with stable coalitions of five conservative justices opposing four liberal ones.

The most significant and controversial decision was handed down in early 2010, when the Court struck down limits on corporate independent expenditures for political campaigns in its decision in *Citizens United* v. *FEC*. The case concerned a documentary produced in 2008 by a nonprofit corporation, Citizens United, and the television advertisements for this documentary, both of which were highly critical of then-presidential candidate Hillary Clinton. The FEC argued that such negative advertising was an unlawful independent expenditure under BCRA. Reversing a lower court's decision, the Supreme Court held that the BCRA provisions limiting corporate independent expenditures constituted an "outright ban on speech" and had a "substantial, nationwide chilling effect" on free speech.[59] In a reference that made unusually clear that campaign finance regulation involves trade-offs

---

BOX 12.1 Federal Court Decisions: Campaign Finance

Buckley v. *Valeo* (1976)

In a complex decision, the U.S. Supreme Court struck down on First Amendment grounds several provisions in the 1974 Amendments to the Federal Election Campaign Act, including limits on independent expenditures (that is, expenditures by outside groups or individuals not coordinated with candidates and political parties); limits on expenditures by candidates on their own campaigns; and limits on overall spending by campaigns. The opinion upheld limitations on the size of individual contributions to campaigns and mandatory disclosure and reporting provisions.

Federal Election Commission v. *Beaumont* (2003)

In a case involving a nonprofit pro-life advocacy group, the U.S. Supreme Court upheld (7–2) as consistent with the First Amendment a

BOX 12.1 (*continued*)

provision of the 1971 Federal Election Campaign Act (FECA) banning direct corporate donations to federal election campaigns.

McConnell v. *Federal Election Commission* (2003)

A divided U.S. Supreme Court upheld (5–4) major provisions of the Bipartisan Campaign Reform Act of 2002 (BCRA), including the ban on unrestricted ("soft money") donations made directly to political parties for such purposes as voter registration and mobilization and general party measures; and restrictions on the use of corporate or union treasury funds to finance electioneering communications before an election.

Wisconsin Right to Life v. *Federal Election Commission* (2007)

In another case involving a nonprofit pro-life advocacy group and First Amendment claims, a divided U.S. Supreme Court ruled (5–4) unconstitutional the limitations in BCRA on the use of corporate funds for certain political issue ads in the 60-day period prior to an election.

Davis v. *Federal Election Commission* (2008)

In another divided opinion, U.S. Supreme Court ruled (5–4) unconstitutional on First Amendment grounds BCRA's so-called Millionaire's Amendment, holding that equalizing electoral opportunities for candidates of different personal wealth was not permissible. The Millionaire's Amendment provided that contribution limits might be raised for candidates facing self-financed opponents whose contributions to their own campaigns exceeded a specified threshold ($350,000 for a House candidate).

Citizens United v. *Federal Election Commission* (2010)

In a case involving Citizens United's film *Hillary: The Movie*, which questioned Hillary Clinton's fitness to be president, a divided U.S. Supreme Court (5–4) disallowed on First Amendment grounds provisions of BCRA prohibiting corporations or unions from spending

BOX 12.1 (*continued*)

money to support or denounce individual candidates in elections. An expansive interpretation of corporate rights to free political speech and the status of political spending as a form of protected speech under the First Amendment, the opinion overruled decisions in two previous cases.

SpeechNow.org v. *Federal Election Commission* (2010)

Drawing on the ruling in *Citizens United*, the U.S. Court of Appeals for the District of Columbia extended the First Amendment protection given to electoral contributions. The unanimous decision held that, because the nonprofit entity SpeechNow sought to make independent expenditures only, it could accept contributions from individuals above the threshold of $5,000.

Arizona Free Enterprise Club's Freedom Club PAC v. *Bennett* (2011)

Citing the decision in *Davis*, a divided U.S. Supreme Court (5–4) invalidated as an unconstitutional burden on free speech a provision in the Arizona Citizens Clean Elections Act that triggered additional matching funds to candidates who accept matching funds from the state and are opposed by high-spending adversaries and independent groups.

McCutcheon v. *Federal Election Commission* (2014)

Once again narrowly divided, the U.S. Supreme Court (5–4) declared unconstitutional the overall cap ($117,000 in the 2011–2012 election cycle) on individual contributions in BCRA. The Court's plurality opinion argued that such aggregate limits "intrude without justification on a citizen's ability to exercise 'the most fundamental First Amendment activities.'"

Sources: Information about these cases is taken from the case summaries on the Web site of the Federal Election Commission (http://www.fec.gov/law/litigation) and the case briefs prepared by Oyez at ITT Chicago-Kent College of Law (https://www.oyez.org/cases).

among democratic values with consequences for equal political voice, Justice Roberts cited "*Buckley*'s explicit repudiation of any government interest in 'equalizing the relative ability of individuals and groups to influence the outcome of elections.'"[60]

At the time that *Citizens United* was decided, there was considerable discussion about the way that the case extended the rights of corporations as persons under the Fourteenth Amendment and recognized and enhanced their free speech rights under the First Amendment. Pundits predicted a flood of corporate contributions to campaigns. However, *Citizens United* was followed up by the appellate court decision in *SpeechNow* and the Supreme Court decision in *McCutcheon*, both of which freed up limitations on individual giving. What has happened since has not fully conformed to expectations. The predicted deluge of corporate money at the national level has not materialized—at least overtly. However, some evidence suggests that corporations are making donations that are harder to trace.[61]

Instead, in a trend that reflects the spiraling costs of campaigning and the soaring incomes of those at the top, the system has been swamped with cash from extremely wealthy individuals. "Super PACs," political action committees that operate independently of candidates and can accept unlimited contributions, have become important vehicles for campaign money.[62] Although they operate independently, FEC rulings no longer require a wall of separation between Super PACs and candidates. Thus, campaigns hungry for cash can raise much larger amounts from individuals with the resources to make large contributions. By contributing to Super PACs, affluent donors can get around the current contribution limit ($2,700) for individuals, a sum far beyond the capacity of all but the best-off donors. The national finance chairman of the presidential campaign of an unsuccessful Republican aspirant defended Super PACs by asking, "You know how hard it is to raise this money at $2,700 apiece?"[63] As we saw in Chapter 4, not only have the sums skyrocketed, but the giving has also become more and more concentrated—increasingly large shares of the total arise from a minuscule fraction of the public. At this point, it seems that the campaign finance environment is changing dramatically in ways that, if anything, render the playing field even less level.

Although the courts have not gone as far as some expected in extending the same principles in recent decisions to state and local laws, they continue to apply the First Amendment to giving money as a form of speech. While limitations on campaign giving can be justified in terms of avoiding corruption or the appearance of corruption, furthering political equality has been deemed constitutionally unacceptable. In fact, during the oral argument in the *Arizona Free Enterprise Club* case, Justice Roberts remarked, "this act was passed to, quote, 'level the playing field' when it comes to running for office. Why isn't that clear evidence that it's unconstitutional?"[64]

Public opinion disapproves of the current campaign finance regime, but the issue is not a high priority for ordinary citizens, and there is little taste for a political reform that would strain government budgets. Congress has not acted to introduce statutory or constitutional changes to blunt the effects of recent court decisions and is unlikely to do so in the near future. The experiments at the state and local levels offer possible models for change, and the political configuration on the Supreme Court and in Congress will not last forever. But current political and constitutional realities imply that, with respect to the form of political voice for which inequalities are most pronounced, meaningful reform is unlikely in the near future.

Equalizing Time-Based Activity

Reducing inequalities of political voice through time-based activity does not require procedural change to lower barriers but rather a strategy for developing and nurturing individual civic capacity. Participation is easier for those with skills and resources and such psychological orientations as political interest, knowledge, and efficacy that lead them to want and to be able to take part. Participation is also easier when there are strong mobilizing institutions, parties, and organized interests to communicate information about political issues, encourage and guide political involvement, and offer services to facilitate activity.

Addressing individual differences in civic skills and capacity would require a major public commitment—demanding both resources and patience and having no guarantee of positive outcome—for which Americans have shown little taste. Extending early education to all, improving the schools in our cities, making work more rewarding, and housing more affordable are, to us, worthy goals in themselves quite apart from their impact on political inequalities. But such social change is difficult and requires political will that is not obvious as we write. And, of course, the weak political constituency for raising the educational and economic well-being of those who have least is intimately and organically related to the very condition we seek to address: absence of political voice.

Another approach to developing the civic capacity of individuals focuses on political and civic institutions, for example, improving civic instruction in the schools.⁶⁵ Traditional civics classes are widespread but not especially effective, even at imparting knowledge.⁶⁶ However, advocates for programs focusing on civic education and service-based learning believe such programs can give a participatory boost to young people who might otherwise be inactive.⁶⁷

Extensive research indicates that, under certain conditions, civic education and service learning programs reduce political inequality by endowing young people whose parents are not well educated and affluent with the skills, knowledge, and other resources they need to engage with politics. Unfortunately, those who need these programs the most are least likely to enjoy the conditions that make them successful. Just as they are differentially endowed with so many participatory resources, those with well-educated and affluent parents are positioned to benefit differentially from well-designed programs of civic education. The result could parallel what we have seen for other reforms: to raise the overall level of civic commitment and political activity for the already advantaged rather than to reduce SES inequalities of political voice in the younger generation. In short, neither civic education nor service learning provides a silver bullet for the problem of political inequality.

Another approach is to foster the civic skills of adults. For example, Right Question Institute seeks "to make democracy work better by teaching a strategy that allows anyone, no matter their educational, income or literacy level, to learn to ask better questions and participate more effectively in decisions that affect them," so that they "can think for themselves and can effectively advocate for themselves, their families and their communities."⁶⁸ Although the Right Question Institute indicates that its methods produce promising results, these kinds of efforts have been tried only under limited circumstances.

Political innovations at the local level also promote political activity. For example, Chicago neighborhood councils with local control over policing and public schools seem to have engaged and benefited inner-city African American residents, although they seem not to have had the same positive effects for Spanish-speaking immigrants.⁶⁹ Another study finds that city-supported neighborhood associations "increase confidence in government and sense of community" and reports no evidence that the increased participation introduces racial or economic biases into the system.⁷⁰ Still, even this kind of intensive, local, city-supported participation did not seem to bring about fundamental change in the class bias of who participates.⁷¹

Yet another possibility derives from the fact that the design of government benefit programs can affect whether beneficiaries take part politically.[72] Universal policies rather than means-tested ones promote greater participation in politics, as do bureaucratic agencies that treat citizen-clients with respect and prompt service rather than with delays, negative assumptions, and invasions of privacy.[73]

TIME-BASED ACTS BY ORGANIZED INTERESTS

Equalizing political voice presents challenges analogous to those for campaign finance when it comes to activity by organized interests. As we saw in Chapters 8 and 9, because organized interest activity is undertaken by well-paid professionals, cash-strapped organizations are disadvantaged in ways that cannot be fully fixed by procedural tinkering. Still, just as campaign finance laws can disclose who is making donations and place some limitations on their contributions, state regulation of organized interests involved in politics can shed light on, and even limit, their efforts. Such regulations can include requirements for lobbying disclosure, restrictions on gifts to public officials, and rules governing when lobbyists can meet with public officials. Although it is difficult to prove causality, evidence shows that in states with stricter lobbying regulations, there is greater congruence between citizen attitudes and public policy.[74]

Advocates of broad public interests, whether liberal or conservative, are constrained in a somewhat different way—by their legal status as nonprofit groups. Contributions to these groups (as well as such nonprofits as museums, universities, and social service agencies) are tax deductible under section 501(c)3 of the federal tax code. While corporations are not limited in how much they lobby and may deduct any expenses associated with political advocacy from their taxable income, nonprofits are restricted in how much they are permitted to lobby.[75] These regulations do not erect an impermeable barrier between nonprofit executives and government officials, especially those in the executive branch. Instead a complex and contradictory dance takes place in which those in nonprofits cultivate relationships with policymakers. Lest their tax status be jeopardized, however, nonprofits feel constrained from using the full arsenal of tactics of advocacy that other organizations mobilize. This chilling effect potentially exacerbates inequalities of political voice among organizations representing different kinds of interests.

One promising—but probably politically controversial—proposal at the federal level would extend the principle of disclosure to lobbying through a "Congressional Lobbying Procedure Act" analogous to the 1946 Administrative Procedure Act.[76] Among its provisions would be a requirement for the electronic posting of both a report of any lobbying activity (including a brief summary of who was involved and what was discussed) and electronic copies of anything left behind (for example, research reports or draft legislation).

Conclusion

This discussion of the possibilities for equalizing political voice has been sobering. We have seen that anything that would make much difference in ameliorating inequalities of political voice is currently either politically infeasible or constitutionally proscribed; and anything that is currently both politically possible and constitutionally acceptable would not make much difference.

We have many reasons for caution. Beyond the inertial effect of the policy status quo in a system that places roadblocks in the path of policy change, the political obstacles to procedural reform are formidable—especially when the reform in question is expensive, requires action on the part of each of the states, threatens significant interests with stakes in current policies, or involves trade-offs with other cherished democratic values. Moreover, accomplishing the desired outcome is often difficult. Implementation may be lackadaisical. Determined stakeholders may find ways to exploit loopholes that subvert the original purpose. Even when implementation is vigorous and no one seeks to use details to undermine the achievement of the intended purposes, the results may not be as originally predicted. In short, procedural reforms often disappoint.

Nevertheless, some reforms do have an impact, and we do not want to stop experimenting. The challenge is to find innovations that not only raise participation but also produce a more representative set of activists.

With regard to electoral turnout, it seems reasonable to continue to ease registration requirements. Possible mechanisms include linking various state-level electronic databases so that a change of residence noted by the agencies that collect taxes or register motor vehicles automatically updates a voter's registration; introducing election day registration where it is not currently in place; and implementing more consistently the provisions of the National Voter Registration Act that mandate voter registration at public assistance agencies. Similarly, states should be able to improve the administration of elections so that the voting experience—the length of the lines, the skill and training of the election workers, the quality and accuracy of the balloting devices—is more positive and does not depend on the budget constraints of different municipalities. We urge reducing the constraints on voting by convicted felons, especially in states that prolong disenfranchisement beyond the period of supervision by the criminal justice system.

Equalizing political voice through time-based activity for those disadvantaged by low levels of education and income is challenging in a very different way. Bringing up the bottom of the educational and income hierarchies requires massive changes that are politically unlikely in the current environment. A more limited objective, however, would involve ongoing experimentation with service learning in the schools and civic education for youth and adults to find workable and effective programs.

In several respects, the tide seems to be running in an inegalitarian direction. We need to monitor the impact of both recent voter ID laws and the changes to the Voting Rights Act in the aftermath of the decision in *Shelby* to ascertain whether, as predicted, a less representative electorate materializes in the relevant jurisdictions. With respect to campaign finance, the current constitutional environment is especially hostile. Even in the context of virtually unfettered private giving, a robust form of public financing of elections would probably have equalizing consequences. Currently, however, it is very unlikely on political grounds. Still, we urge continued experimentation as well as close scrutiny of the results of the voucher program in Seattle and the various public funding schemes in the states that have enacted them. Advocates of a more representative system of electoral funding might explore ways to loosen the links between the Super PACs, which engage in independent spending only, and the candidates with which they are unofficially affiliated and to make more transparent the "dark money" donated to nonprofits.

Overall, for each of the reforms we have discussed, there is a trade-off between political feasibility and consequences for inequalities of political voice: the changes that would have the greatest impact are the least likely to happen. Still, a group of incremental changes, each one relatively contained, might cumulatively reduce inequalities of political voice. After all, American history, which has been punctuated by periodic bursts of procedural reform, has probably not witnessed its last.

13

Unequal Voice in an Unequal Age

During the debate in the House of Representatives over the Bill of Rights in 1789, the politically astute Elbridge Gerry of Massachusetts—who twenty-three years later would lend his name to the politically motivated carving of electoral districts eponymously known as gerrymandering—asserted that citizen voice must help legislators become informed about the public's opinions:

> We cannot, I apprehend, be too well informed of the true state, condition, and sentiment of our constituents. . . . I hope we shall never shut our ears against that information which is to be derived from the petitions and instructions of our constituents. . . .
>
> I hope we shall never presume to think that all the wisdom of this country is concentrated within the walls of this House. Men, unambitious of distinctions from their fellow-citizens, remain within their own domestic walk, unheard of and unseen, possessing all the advantages from a watchful observance of public men and public measures, whose voice, if we would descend to listen to it, would give us knowledge superior to what could be acquired amidst the cares and bustles of public life; let us then adopt the amendment and encourage the diffident to enrich our stock of knowledge with the treasure of their remarks and observations.[1]

Gerry's effort to include a nonbinding right for citizens "to instruct their Representatives" in the First Amendment failed. James Madison argued that, if the intent was, as Gerry advocated, to make the instructions nonbinding, the protections of free speech and press in the proposed First Amendment rendered the clause unnecessary. If the clause were to be interpreted "to say that the people have a right to instruct their representatives in such a sense as that the delegates are obliged to conform to those instructions," great mischief might ensue.[2] Although Gerry did not succeed, there seems to have been no quarrel then—or now—with his understanding that democratic governance required the people's right to make their wishes known and all representatives' responsibility to be "well informed of the true state, condition, and sentiment of our constituents." This book has shown how far we are from achieving that result.

John F. Kennedy's experiences campaigning in the West Virginia Democratic primary in 1960 provide a vivid example of the potential power of exposure to the "unheard of and unseen." His encounter with Appalachian poverty altered his perspective and inspired policy action when he took office. "Just imagine kids who never drink milk," he said to an assistant.[3]

In an age of inequality, such retail politics has a diminished role, and learning about the "true state, condition, and sentiment" of the people has become more complicated. With the increased importance of money-based forms of political voice in the mix of messages about what citizens want and need, public officials hear disproportionately about the experiences and preferences of the affluent and well-educated rather than the less advantaged. In a 2013 address to a conference at Yale, Connecticut Democratic Senator Chris Murphy described sitting in a cubicle at a call center at the headquarters of the Democratic National Committee and dialing for dollars. Acting as a rational prospector by "not calling anybody who doesn't have the chance of giving me at least $1,000," a sum far in excess of what the vast majority of donors could afford, Murphy described the rarified nature of the issues discussed in those calls: "I talked a lot more about carried interest [a tax provision giving favorable treatment to the earnings of partners at private equity firms and hedge funds] in that call room than I did at the supermarket." He continued to elaborate:

> In Connecticut, right, you spend a lot of time on the phone with people who work in the financial markets . . . and so you're hearing a lot about, you know, problems that, you know, bankers have and not a lot of problems that people who work at the mill in Thomaston Connecticut have . . . I go out of my way to try to be proactive in the way that I interact with

my constituents, in part, because I know that when I've been raising money, I'm not hearing from a representative sample.[4]

Murphy's perception that he—and all other public officials—are not hearing from a representative sample is at the heart of our argument. Our subject has been the inequality of political voice in America: how the public's preferences and concerns are conveyed to governing officials, where they come from, and how they are expressed by individuals and organizations. Some preferences and concerns receive louder and more sustained expression than others. Some people and some organizations have megaphones, and others speak in a whisper. A single theme has appeared and reappeared with remarkable consistency: the power and durability of the links between inequalities of political voice and socioeconomic status (SES).

Many of the matters we have considered are newsworthy. As citizens we are, like everyone else, fascinated by what attracts the public spotlight and, where relevant, we have inserted examples into the text. However, we have also looked beyond widely reported cases to develop a broader picture of the disparities of political representation. In bringing systematic evidence to matters that are sometimes fodder for exposés, we found that what grabs attention is not necessarily typical. In a series of boxes throughout this chapter, we highlight examples of the sometimes unexpected findings that emerge from systematic analysis.

Unequal Political Voice: Individuals

Our findings reinforce previous research, including our own, that demonstrates the strong association between individual SES and political activity. The Civic Voluntarism Model, discussed in Chapter 3, clarifies the relationship between SES and political activity by mapping the pathways through which SES has its impact. Although we ordinarily combine educational attainment and family income into a single measure of SES, education is at the root of most forms of individual participation. Those who are well educated are more likely to be politically interested, informed, and efficacious and to have the kinds of jobs that yield high incomes. Furthermore, they are likely to have the kinds of involvement at work and in religious institutions and nonpolitical organizations that permit the development of civic skills and lead to requests for political activity. In sum, educational attainment is associated with nearly every other factor that fosters political activity among individuals.

> **BOX 13.1 You might think . . .**
>
> that social movements overcome participatory inequalities by mobilizing into politics those who are less affluent and well educated.
>
> *In fact*, some social movements—for example, the labor movement at the end of the nineteenth century and Black Lives Matter much more recently—do bring less-advantaged publics into politics. But the United States has a long tradition of mobilizations of middle-class adherents, including the abolition, temperance, environmental, and Tea Party movements.

When it comes to making political contributions, however, what matters is not education—or any of the multiple participatory factors that are related to education. The only factor with a substantial impact on the size of political contributions is family income. At a time when running for office requires stratospheric sums and those with deep pockets are permitted to make virtually unlimited donations, a large share of political money derives from a small number of affluent people whose experiences and needs are quite different from those of ordinary citizens.

The political world does not have to operate this way. No iron law states that all voluntary involvements must be structured by educational and economic advantage. The connection between SES and activity we find for political participation does not exist for attendance at religious services, which is fairly similar across all socioeconomic levels.

> **BOX 13.2 You might think . . .**
>
> that recruitment of political activists democratizes political voice by bringing into politics a more representative set of participants.
>
> *In fact*, those who seek to get others to act in politics act as rational prospectors, looking for people who will say yes when asked and participate effectively when they get involved. By targeting recruits who possess attributes that are associated with participation, rational prospectors bring into politics participants who are higher in SES than those who become active on their own initiative.

Can such SES differences be overcome by social movements like the civil rights movement? Not ordinarily. Processes of political recruitment—mobilizing people for everyday political activity not just for episodic social movements—typically exacerbate SES differences when "rational prospectors" seek to mobilize those who are more likely to participate.

DO ACTIVISTS REPRESENT NONACTIVISTS?

Political inequality would not be a problem if activists had the same views as those who do not take part. Unfortunately, the noisy and the silent differ in many ways. We have looked beyond voting and public opinion surveys to consider both more demanding forms of political participation that are richer in information and measures of politically relevant characteristics beyond the opinions registered in response to questions preselected by survey researchers. We have found that those who speak least loudly through individual participation are distinctive in many ways that are germane to politics. For example, they are less likely to report both being in very good health and, before the Affordable Care Act kicked in, having health insurance. They are more likely to need government assistance as measured by their poverty-level incomes, to cut back spending on such basics as food, to delay health care, or to rely on means-tested government benefits. In addition, when those of limited education and income do take part in politics, their political activity is animated by a distinctive bundle of issue concerns, one that emphasizes basic human needs. Furthermore, they are more likely than their more affluent and highly educated counterparts to deliver messages urging greater government efforts to alleviate economic need. Thus, just as Senator Murphy indicated, the underrepresentation of the less well-off has political consequences.

SOCIAL CLASS AND GROUP DIFFERENCES IN POLITICAL VOICE

Political input through citizen voice is unrepresentative not only with respect to social class, but also with respect to gender and race or ethnicity. Once socioeconomic disparities between men and women and among African Americans, Latinos, and non-Hispanic whites are taken into account, group differences in political activity diminish, often to the point of statistical insignificance. However, the story does not end there. For one thing, disparities among groups in SES are not mere accident but instead result from social and sometimes political processes that create and reinforce group differences in income and education. That is, class differences among groups based on gender or on race or ethnicity have everything to do with those other social statuses. Furthermore, these group-based inequalities of political voice are still politically important even if they are explained by differences in social class, because public officials hear less from some groups than others—with potential consequences for equal political responsiveness to the needs of those groups.

UNEQUAL POLITICAL VOICE ON THE INTERNET

New technologies constantly disrupt the conduct of politics—offering new opportunities for political learning and discussion, the creation of links among like-minded individuals, and the attempt to influence political outcomes. Digital technologies make it easier to recruit activists and transform the ways citizens take part politically. In additon, traditional forms of activity take on new electronic forms—such as sending e-mails rather than "snail mail" to public officials or making political contributions without resort to check, envelope, or stamp. Because the political capacities of digital technologies are a work in progress, we must interpret with caution any conclusions drawn from the 2008 and 2012 surveys conducted in cooperation with the Pew Internet and American Life Project. However, results so far suggest the continuation of patterns of unequal voice.

Data from the Pew surveys show the increase of both Internet access and social media use between 2008 and 2012, with the result that the digital divide—the class-based gap between those with and without digital connections—has narrowed but not closed. Nonetheless, the optimistic prediction by early techies that the Internet would reduce the social-class structuring of political participation has not been borne out. For those forms of political participation with an online counterpart to traditional offline activity, the Internet has not leveled the political playing field. Just as it does offline, the strong association between social class and political participation obtains for political participation on the Internet. As might be expected, these class-based disparities translate into gaps in online political participation among non-Hispanic whites, African Americans, and Latinos, gaps that do not disappear when Internet access is taken into account. Evidence from 2008, when the young dominated the brave new world of social networking, suggested that political uses of social networking might reduce SES bias. However, the familiar pattern of structuring by SES was, once again,

> BOX 13.3 You might think...
>
> that Internet-based political activity would be free of the educational and income stratification that characterizes offline participation.
>
> *In fact*, contrary to expectations in the early days of the Internet, the SES bias of participatory acts carried out online—for example, signing a petition, contacting a senator, or making a campaign contribution to a candidate for governor—replicates the pattern for their offline counterparts.

visible in data from 2012, even as political participation anchored in social networking had increased substantially over the four-year period.

The Internet does function as an equalizer across age groups. On one hand, youthful deficits in most forms of political activity do not appear for political participation on the Web. On the other hand, this boost derives more from the fact that younger cohorts are much more likely than their elders to be Internet users and not from any greater propensity among Internet users to use the Internet for political purposes. Whether successive cohorts among the young will continue to act as pioneers in the rapidly evolving domain of the Web or whether the rapid diffusion of Internet literacy and connectivity will close the generation gap in Internet use is an open question.

Unequal Voice through Organized Interests

Interest organizations serve as a major vehicle for the expression of citizen voice. Our findings about the interests represented by organizations reinforce what we learned about individual political voice. Although the range of organized interests active in Washington politics is astonishingly broad, it does not even approximate equal voice. No advanced musical training is needed to hear that the unheavenly chorus of organized interests sings with the same upper-class accent as do politically active individuals.

Judging the representativeness of the organized interest system is complicated. In contrast to the circumstance for individual-level participation, where the baseline for measuring equal voice is the population, there is no natural baseline of organizations from which to measure over- and underrepresentation. Nothing like a random sample of individuals, active and inactive, can be used to compare the voice of the active organizations.

In addition, while individuals can be presumed to speak for themselves and to have equal weight as citizens, no such assumptions are possible about representation by organizations. Because organizations have vastly different numbers of members, no organizational equivalent exists of the democratic principle of one person, one vote. Besides, since the members of an association invariably differ in their preferences and concerns, it is often difficult to determine for whom an organization speaks. Further complicating matters is the fact that only a small minority of organized interests in Washington politics are voluntary associations of individuals. Instead, they are either memberless organizations (such as corporations, think tanks, or hospitals) or associations of such memberless organizations. When a memberless organization (such as an art museum) is politically active, it is not clear whose interests are being served—those of its management, board, staff, artists, donors, or visitors.

In spite of representational complexities, when we placed the thousands of organizations active in Washington into a set of 96 categories, the result did not even approximate equality of political voice. Both the free rider problem and the resource constraint problem have profound effects on whose voices are heard through the medium of collective representation. The interests of the advantaged, especially business, are well represented. In

---

BOX 13.4 You might think . . .

that most organizations active in Washington resemble the National Rifle Association, AARP, and the Teamsters Union in having lots and lots of members.

In fact, most membership organizations active in national politics—professional associations like the American Academy of Adoption Attorneys, with fewer than 500 members, and trade associations like Alliance of Automobile Manufacturers, with only 12—have relatively few members. Even more importantly, a majority of organizations in Washington—most commonly corporations but also hospitals and universities—are "memberless," with no members in the ordinary sense.

> **BOX 13.5 You might think . . .**
>
> that every possible interest has an organization to advocate on its behalf in Washington.
>
> *In fact,* many interests with a seeming stake in public policy are not represented by organizations. Examples include those caring for aging relatives at home, workers required to sign non-compete clauses, SNAP recipients, holders of sub-prime mortgages, parents seeking high-quality child care, and any unskilled worker who is not in a union.

contrast, two kinds of interests receive much less extensive representation: broad public interests and the economically disadvantaged.

Compared to the number of people who presumably have an interest in such broad public interests as wildlife protection, clean government, low-cost energy, highway safety, or access to firearms, the number of organizations advocating for public goods is relatively small, accounting for less than 5 percent of the organizations listed in the 2011 *Washington Representatives* directory. In any political controversy, a public interest on one side may be opposed by a different public interest on the other. The existence of such competing public goods means that, although, when taken together, public interest organizations lean in a somewhat liberal direction, public goods favored by conservatives are also represented.

ORGANIZED INTEREST REPRESENTATION: ADVANTAGED AND DISADVANTAGED

Just as they are in individual political participation, the economically disadvantaged are underrepresented in pressure politics. Organizations that advocate on behalf of the poor are relatively scarce; organizations of the poor themselves are extremely rare; and organizations of those who benefit from means-tested government programs acting on their own behalf are, quite simply, nonexistent. Less frequently noted is the dearth of organizations advocating for the economic interests of those with ordinary jobs and middle-class incomes. With respect to the non-occupational economic interests of these lower- and middle-class groups, there are few, if any, organizations representing people who live in rental housing, who receive the

Earned Income Tax Credit, whose jobs have been outsourced, or whose pensions are not vested.

With respect to occupational interests, although they have a long history in advocating for the economic interests of ordinary people and mobilizing them to take part in politics, labor unions are small in number and declining in membership. The few associations that enroll nonprofessional and nonmanagerial workers tend to represent those in occupations that demand relatively high levels of skill and that confer relatively high levels of pay and status. Thus, unless they are unionized, which is increasingly uncommon for private-sector workers, those who work in low-skill jobs have no occupational associations at all to represent their interests. In contrast, professionals and managers have many occupational associations to represent them.

What is more, business is quite well represented among organizations in Washington politics. American corporations comprise by far the single largest category of organized interest; adding in other kinds of business interests—for example, trade associations and foreign corporations—just over half (52 percent) of the all organized interests in Washington are associated with business.

In an exception to the overall pattern of interest representation in Washington, the very small number of organizations that represent people on the basis of some noneconomic identity (for example, race or ethnicity, nationality, gender, age, sexual orientation, or gender identity) represent the less advantaged: African Americans and Latinos rather than non-Hispanic whites, women rather than men, gay rather than straight, children and the elderly rather than middle-aged, and so forth. Still, the mainstream organizations that advocate on the basis of a wide variety of interests other than shared identity—usually joint economic interests—hardly neglect the concerns and preferences of middle-aged white men, in particular, those among them who are well educated and affluent.

ORGANIZED INTEREST ACTIVITY

As with individual participation, organizations can vary the volume of input for any form of political action, with the result that political voice is not necessarily proportional to the number of active organizations. The distribution of lobbying expenditures is skewed especially sharply in the direction of well-heeled organizations. Because an organization testifies at a congressional hearing at the behest of congressional policymakers, the distribution of congressional testimonies is much less concentrated in the direction of the haves. The specialized nature of the issues that dominate the docket of the Supreme Court implies that certain kinds of organizations—in particular, state and local governments as well as identity groups and public interest groups—figure as important in the filing of amicus briefs with the Court.

Overall, however, the activity of Washington organizations mirrors the upper-class distribution of political organizations. Organizations representing the advantaged, especially business, weigh heavily when compared to organizations representing the disadvantaged—whether defined in terms of identity or economic wherewithal—and broad public interests.

There is no form of organized interest input for which activity on behalf of the poor registers more than a trace—whether by organizations advocating for the poor or by organizations that provide social services. Such organizations account for 2 percent of the congressional testimonies and amicus briefs and less than 1 percent of the lobbying expenditures.

Few organizations other than unions represent the economic interests of nonprofessional, non-managerial workers, and none at all represent the interests of unskilled workers. As a result, unions are responsible for just about all organized interest activity on behalf of workers other than professionals and managers. As individual organizations, unions are, on average, the most active kind of organization. However, because there are so few of them, they account for only 1 percent of the lobbying expenditures, 1 percent of the amicus briefs, and 3 percent of the congressional testimonies.

We cannot specify some theoretical share of activity that should represent public goods. Still, the portion of activity deriving from public interest groups is surely quite low. Organizations representing such diffuse public interests account for 11 percent of the congressional testimonies, 13 percent of the amicus briefs, and, presumably reflecting the regulations affecting 501(c)3 organizations, a mere 2 percent of lobbying expenditures. It is worth noting that for no form of organized interest involvement does activity by public interest organizations—which include many more organizations advocating on behalf of public goods like low taxes and national security that appeal to conservatives than is generally realized—outweigh activity by organizations representing business.

Organizations representing business, taken together, are the modal kind of organization for each kind of activity, except for filing amicus briefs, where they are in second place to state and local governments. Most striking is the fact that business organizations are responsible for more than three-fourths (77 percent) of lobbying expenditures.

Dollar Politics and Unequal Political Voice

Throughout the book we have pointed to the special challenge posed by forms of political voice that rely on money: how to reconcile inequalities of market resources with the desire to establish a level playing field for democracy. While all democracies face the dilemma of how much to regulate the free use of unequal resources in pursuit of political objectives, the United States allows more freedom than any other industrialized country in the legal use of market resources to influence political outcomes—especially and increasingly when it comes to campaign finance.

THE DUAL FUNCTIONS OF MONEY

Of the various resources that individuals and organizations bring to political activity—among them time, political skills, allies, capable staffers, and an appealing message—money is unusual in that it is simultaneously both a resource for political participation and a source of political contestation. Inequalities in income and wealth are much more likely to follow the boundaries of politically relevant categories—not only social class but also race or ethnicity and gender. Conflicts between the articulate and inarticulate or between the busy and the leisured do not usually occur in American politics. Political issues that pit economic interests against one another are common.

In addition, among political resources, financial resources are particularly unevenly distributed. Comparing the best and worst off with respect to money and spare time, the most affluent person is relatively much better off than the most leisured one. Political resources differ in the extent to which they can be substituted for one another, but money is perhaps the most fungible—a characteristic that is especially important to political organizations that hire in-house staff or outside firms to assist in political advocacy.

Because money is both a resource and a source of political contestation, political money, unlike other political resources, is regulated in terms of both the ways it can be used and under certain circumstances, the amounts that can be spent. In spite of such restrictions, when the medium of participatory input is cash, the volume of political activity can be multiplied in a way not possible for other political acts. Even the most assiduous demonstrator can attend only so many protests, but the amounts legally given by heavy-hitter donors can be very, very substantial. In addition, because family income predicts not just the likelihood that an individual will make a political contribution but also the size of the contribution, major contributions originate from an extremely thin slice of affluent donors. A very high proportion of campaign contributions come from the richest respondents whose wealth has skyrocketed in the New Gilded Age.

As the costs of running for office zoom upward, not only do candidates devote more and more time to raising money at the expense of focusing on making policy or meeting with constituents, but they also spend increasing amounts of time in the company of wealthy donors, hearing about what is on their minds.[5] As he was leaving the House after 16 years, Steve Israel of New York described having "attended glamorous Washington galas, the ones where thousands of eyes make no eye contact, where pupils constantly rove in search of someone more powerful." In the spirit of Senator Chris Murphy's comments quoted earlier, Israel enumerated that he had "spent roughly 4,200 hours in call time, attended more than 1,600 fund-raisers just for my own campaign and raised nearly $20 million in increments of $1,000, $2,500 and $5,000 per election cycle."[6]

Furthermore, the high costs of campaigning may be linked to the recent increase in the magnitude of the economic gulf that separates ordinary members of the public from members of the House and Senate, more than half of whom were millionaires in 2012.[7] The sharp climb in the cost of running a campaign means that public office may become relatively more attractive to those who have substantial assets that they can invest on their own behalf and to those who have wealthy friends willing to back their candidacies.[8] The bottom line is that congressional aspirants are less and less likely to be experiencing themselves—or to interact frequently with others who are experiencing—the buffeting of ordinary economic life, with potential consequences for their views about what government should or should not be doing.[9]

An important part of the escalation in campaign costs is the series of federal court decisions—most notably, *Citizens United* v. *FEC*, which gave corporations greater freedom to engage in unlimited independent spending during campaigns. These court decisions have pushed the balance of campaign finance further in the direction of interests with deep pockets. Law professor Paul A. Freund's response to *Buckley* v. *Valeo* (1976), the decision that first interpreted campaign donations as a form of speech, seems germane in the aftermath of *Citizens United:* "They say that money talks. I thought that was the problem, not the solution."[10]

POLITICAL VOICE FOR HIRE

Individual political participation and organized interest activity both tilt in the direction of the advantaged because they rely on the mobilization of the resources of time, money, and skills for expressions of political voice. Our inquiry has, however, uncovered important distinctions. With the significant exception of making political contributions, individual political participation is anchored in education, and the individuals who take part act for themselves. While wealthy activists may dip deeply into their large bank accounts to fund favored candidates and causes, they do not ordinarily multiply their other activities by hiring mercenaries to attend demonstrations in their stead or by contracting with a political Cyrano to compose especially articulate letters to public officials.

In contrast, the critical resource for politically active organizations is money. At least at the state and national levels, a substantial share of an organization's political budget is devoted to the purchase of the time and the specific expertise of professional advocates. An organization with a large budget hires the expertise it needs—lobbyists, researchers, tax attorneys, public relations experts, and so on. Hiring high-priced talent helps organizations ensure their political effectiveness and multiplies the volume of their political input. In short, in Washington pressure politics, money buys time and skills.

Spending on lobbying grew rapidly in recent years, rising from $1.45 billion in 1998 to a peak of $3.52 billion in 2010 and then leveling off. In 2016, lobbying spending was $3.15 billion before ticking up notably during 2017.[11] In constant dollar terms, this increase outpaced any of such usual metrics of social change such as population. In addition, between 1981 and 2011, the number of firms of professionals listed in the *Washington Representatives* directory, most of them law and public relations firms that engage in organized interest advocacy for hire, multiplied by a factor of nearly twelve.

Data assembled as the result of the reporting requirements imposed by the Lobbying Disclosure Act of 1995 show unambiguously that the heavenly chorus is especially unrepresentative for lobbying activity. Of the lobbying expenditures in 2010 and 2011, 1 percent came from labor unions, 2 percent from groups organized around some noneconomic identity such as race or religion, 2 percent from organizations representing broad public interests, and less than 1 percent from organizations that provide social services or advocate on behalf of the poor. In contrast, 77 percent came from organizations representing business interests. The lobbying section of the heavenly chorus contains many voices, and it unambiguously sings with an upper-crust accent.

The Same Melody or a New Tune?
Persistent Inequality and a Changing Mix

Inequalities of political voice have been durable over time for both individuals and organized interests. In Chapter 11 we discussed trends with possible consequences for inequalities of political voice. The obvious assumption is that soaring economic inequality, coupled with the attrition of union membership and power, would exacerbate political inequality. However, we noted that several political theories that otherwise have little in common—Downsian, Marxist, and pluralist—converge in predicting the opposite result: that the disadvantaged would organize to protect their interests. In addition, rising levels of educational attainment in the public, the increasing institutional strength of the political parties, and the greater efforts by parties to mobilize voters would also have a contrary equalizing impact on unequal voice. Hence, we brought no clear expectations to the matter of how inequalities of political voice have changed in the New Gilded Age.

Data about individuals from four different cross-sectional surveys over a fifty-year period as well as six decades of time-series data from the American National Election Studies (ANES) about election-related participation reveal that political participation has been structured by socioeconomic differences since we have had surveys to measure citizen political involvement. Although all activities are stratified, voting is the most nearly equal, campaign contributions the least, and other political acts fall in between.

BOX 13.6 You might think . . .

that, because educational attainment and political participation are strongly associated, one consequence of the increasing educational level of the public would be a corresponding increase in aggregate levels of political activity.

In fact, despite the substantial aggregate increase of educational attainment among American adults since World War II, most forms of political participation have not increased demonstrably. Contributions to campaigns, however, have skyrocketed.

> **BOX 13.7 You might think...**
>
> that pronounced SES-based inequalities characterize all voluntary activity, not just political participation.
>
> *In fact*, SES stratification is most evident for political participation. The bias toward the well-educated and affluent is much less pronounced for nonpolitical secular activity and is barely perceptible for religious attendance.

In each case, the lines tracing political participation over time for the five SES quintiles arrange themselves neatly from the highest to the lowest and rarely cross. In addition, the finding that attendance of religious services, unlike political participation, is not stratified by class holds over the long run.

Perhaps surprisingly in an era of increasing levels of income inequality, the association between class and participation does not seem to have become more pronounced in recent decades. Indeed, with the possible exception that competitive presidential elections may ameliorate participatory inequalities, the peaks and valleys of participatory inequality do not seem to track trends in economic inequality or other obvious factors. As a matter of fact, the trajectories over time of relative inequality for different political acts do not move in sync. In short, what is most striking is not the inexplicable irregularities in the extent of participatory inequality across the decades but rather the remarkable persistence of that inequality—espe-

> **BOX 13.8 You might think...**
>
> that the New Gilded Age ushered in a new era of plutocracy with greatly enhanced inequalities of political voice.
>
> *In fact*, the story is complicated. For at least a half century, nearly all forms of political voice have tilted in the direction of the well-educated and affluent. However, the increased importance of modes of political advocacy that depend on money—both lobbying and campaign contributions—implies an even louder voice for the affluent in recent years.

cially when viewed in contrast to the absence of stratification in religious service attendance.

THE PERSISTENCE OF ORGANIZATIONAL VOICE

Data over a thirty-year period about the kinds of organizations active in Washington tell a story about the persistence of organizational voice that is parallel to what we saw for individuals. The overall distribution of interests represented shows a great deal of continuity as the number of organizations in the pressure system increased substantially between 1981 and 2011.

Although the traditional titans of pressure politics—corporations, trade and other business associations, occupational associations of professionals and managers, and the like—remain dominant, their share has diminished. However, this reconfiguration has not meant an upsurge in the share of the kinds of organizations that are traditionally underrepresented in pressure politics: organizations representing broad publics and the disadvantaged. Instead, the share of organizations in the pressure system accounted for by subnational governments and the health and educational sectors, taken together, more than tripled between 1981 and 2011, at which point these sectors accounted for nearly a quarter of the organizations active in Washington. Besides, even though the growth rates for the categories of organizations representing business were relatively low over the period, in absolute terms, the number of additional business-related organizations was nearly twice the total obtained when all the unions, public interest groups, identity groups, and organizations representing the economically needy listed in 2011 were added together.

BOX 13.9 You might think . . .

that there has been an explosion in the number of organizations advocating for such underrepresented groups as broad publics and the disadvantaged.

In fact, there has been no upsurge in the number of organizations representing broad publics and the disadvantaged in Washington politics. Instead the number of state and, especially, local governments and memberless organizations—such as universities and hospitals—has exploded.

> **BOX 13.10 You might think . . .**
>
> that powerful unions provide a counterweight to corporate political and economic power.
>
> *In fact*, both the share of workers who are unionized and the absolute number of union members have diminished in recent decades. These massive losses have taken place entirely among private-sector union members, who have traditionally been less well educated and less white-collar than their public-sector counterparts, with the result that a union member is now more likely to be a professional than a factory worker.

The only category that did not register growth in absolute numbers over the quarter-century period was unions. The overall number of unions was flat, and the number of unions representing blue-collar workers actually declined. Considering union membership rather than the number of unions, the unionized share of the workforce and, even, the absolute number of union members declined markedly, which means that fewer workforce members are exposed to the politicizing aspects of labor union membership, in particular, the cultivation of civic skills and exposure to requests for political action. The erosion of union membership was confined almost entirely to private-sector union members, who have traditionally been lower in SES than their public-sector counterparts, with the result that union members have, on average, moved up the socioeconomic ladder in recent decades. The result for individual-level participation is quite striking: in 2006, the share of individual participatory acts attributable to union members was much lower than what it had been in 1967, even though, on average, union members gained in SES over the period.

In sum, the organized interest chorus has grown, and the particular singers have changed, but the mix of voices is quite similar.

POLITICAL INEQUALITY: BOTH PERSISTENT AND GROWING

At least since there have been relevant data, regardless of whether we focus on individuals or on political organizations, the unheavenly chorus has been singing with an upper-class accent. Several developments are now working together to exacerbate inequality of political voice. One of them is the decline of unions, especially blue-collar unions of private-sector workers.

In addition, the mix of individual and organizational activities that constitute the cacophony of inputs into politics has shifted, and modes of political expression that depend on financial resources occupy greater space in the bundle. Campaign costs have shot up, and the federal courts have loosened restrictions on the sums contributed by individuals and corporations. Political contributions assume greater relative importance among activists, especially those at the very top of the of the social-class ladder, whose capacity to donate has grown substantially in recent decades. At the same time, organized interest activity—a form of political input for which market resources figure as especially important—has increased substantially. Taken together, these tendencies further tilt the playing field of democracy toward the well-off.

Hence, we discern two trends. On one hand, what is remarkable about political voice in American democracy is how unequal it has been for so long. On the other, when we take into account changes in the mixture of political inputs, those inequalities seem to be becoming more pronounced. As we finish this book, events in Washington throw these themes into relief. In December, 2017, Congress passed and President Trump signed a major overhaul of federal taxes that seems to confirm our analysis of unequal political voice. The details of the bill reveal both an overall bias in the direction of the affluent and the impact of lobbying by well-organized, but often narrow, interests. The bill lowers taxes on large estates by increasing the estate tax exemption. While reduction in the corporate income tax rate from 35 percent to 21 percent is permanent, many of the provisions that benefit middle-income taxpayers expire after five years.[12] Among those receiving favorable tax treatment are craft brewers, owners of golf courses, and real estate developers.[13] The tax bill had surprisingly lukewarm public support.[14] Why were Republicans in Congress so impatient to pass a bill that is not especially popular with the taxpaying public? Representative Chris Collins (R-NY) has an answer that resonates with the conclusions of our inquiry. He told reporters, "My donors are basically saying 'get it done or don't ever call me again.'"[15]

A New Burst of Reform?

Chapter 12 assessed the possibilities for change that might reduce these inequalities of political voice. We argued that anything that would make much difference in ameliorating inequalities of political voice is currently either politically infeasible or constitutionally proscribed; and anything that is currently both politically possible and constitutionally acceptable would not make much difference.

We cited several barriers standing in the way of effective policy change to promote greater equality of political voice. Some of those factors pertain to attempts at political reform in any democracy; some are enduring aspects of politics in America. Others are specific to the contemporary scene. For one thing, reforms often entail trade-offs between democratic values. Such voting reforms as extended early voting and no-excuse absentee balloting might have the effect of raising turnout while undermining the integrity of the vote count, because ballots that spend a couple of weeks in city hall might, by accident or design, get damaged or lost.

Besides, reforms do not always work out as intended. For example, the National Voter Registration Act (NVRA), commonly known as "Motor Voter," did not produce the expected boost in turnout. Those who registered to vote in state motor vehicle bureaus did not always show up at the polls. And one feature of the NVRA, the provision for voter registration in the kind of government offices that are visited by the poor—for instance, public assistance offices—has been implemented incompletely. Although numerous states have introduced reforms like same-day registration and early voting that make it easier to cast a ballot, even the procedural changes that actually enhance turnout do not necessarily result in a more representative electorate.

Aspects of American politics also serve as obstacles to equalizing change. It is well known that the policy status quo exerts a strong gravitational pull. Multiple constitutional, legal, and institutional features of American gov-

---

BOX 13.11 You might think . . .

that reforms making it easier to vote would raise turnout and, in turn, make the electorate more representative of the adult population.

In fact, democratizing the electorate is not easy. Many reforms designed to raise turnout fail to do so. Even reforms that boost turnout do not necessarily make the electorate more representative. Instead, the additional voters drawn to the polls replicate the characteristics of the core electorate.

ernment imply that it is much harder to realize policy change than to block it. In addition, consistent with both the individualistic tradition of distrust of solving collective problems through governmental intervention and the robust guarantees of freedom of expression in the First Amendment, American democracy is more hospitable than many of its counterparts around the world to the conversion of market resources into political voice. Activities that are a public responsibility in democracies around the world—for example, registering voters or funding parties and campaigns—are left to the private initiative of individuals and political organizations in the United States. Similarly, turnout is mandatory in many democracies, a form of governmental coercion that would be offensive to American traditions. On a much broader scale, Americans have traditionally been averse to governmental efforts that elsewhere address the educational and income inequalities that nourish unequal political voice. In addition, the unusual strength of First Amendment takes off the table many restrictions that might partially equalize political voice by placing a ceiling on expression.

What is more, contemporary developments, such as political polarization, further exacerbate unequal political voice by generating battles over the procedural rules of politics and elections. It is common political wisdom that the rules of politics are rarely neutral in their political effects, and therefore, that principled conflicts over political procedure often mask conflicts over political interest. Bitter partisan struggles now rage over such procedural matters as the rules governing voter ID requirements, voter registration drives, and campaign finance. Because persons of color, especially African Americans, are disproportionately Democratic in their voting habits, these partisan controversies have become enmeshed in racial politics as well. As of this writing, Trump has disbanded his commission on voter fraud with results that are as yet undetermined but are unlikely to be friendly to the cause of equal political voice. Under the present circumstances, democratizing policy reforms are politically unlikely.

Recent federal court decisions also suggest hostility toward political reform. A series of decisions defining political contributions as a form of constitutionally protected speech under the First Amendment has gutted federal campaign finance law. Not only have the aggregate amounts donated to campaigns skyrocketed, but also the amounts contributed by very rich donors have shot up as well. Thus, the mode of political expression characterized by the greatest inequality of all has become much more unequal.

In addition, the Supreme Court decision voiding the "preclearance" provision of the Voting Rights Act (VRA) seems to make it easier for the politically motivated to erect barriers to the ballot box. This decision is, in fact, amenable to legislative relief, but it is difficult to imagine at present the emergence of the kind of bipartisan support that operated until recently to renew the VRA several times in the past. In short, more immediate circumstances interact with long-term regularities in American politics to reduce the probabilities for equalizing reform.

The original Gilded Age gave way to the Progressive Era—part of a pattern in American history in which periods of reform follow eras of unbridled free enterprise.[16] It seems that we were due for such a period during the 1990s.[17] Instead, the go-go Reagan Era morphed into the New Gilded Age. Still, that missed opportunity for political change does not necessarily foreclose the possibilities for reform in the future.

Although Americans are supportive of voter ID laws, which surely do not function to make turnout more representative, public opinion data from a variety of sources show a perhaps surprising public recognition of inequality and a receptiveness toward ameliorating it. More than three-quarters (76 percent) of the respondents to the 2012 American National Election Study (ANES) said that the income gap between rich and poor is either much or somewhat larger than it was twenty years ago. Only 6 percent said that the difference is somewhat or much smaller. Not only do Americans agree that income inequality has grown, but they are not especially happy about it. Nearly two-thirds of Americans (66 percent, including 57 percent of Republicans and 76 percent of Democrats) reported in a 2015 Gallup Poll that they are not satisfied with the way income and wealth are distributed in United States. When asked in a May 2014 CBS survey whether they think that all Americans have an equal chance to influence the election process or that wealthy Americans have more of a chance to influence the election process than other Americans, three-quarters (including 63 percent of Republicans and 78 percent of Democrats) replied that wealthy Americans have more influence. And 61 percent of the respondents to the 2012 ANES (including 60 percent of Republicans and 64 percent of Democrats) agreed that the government should be able to place limits on how much money corporations and unions can give to a political candidate.

Thus, strong evidence shows that Americans in both parties recognize, at least in broad outline, the kinds of economic and political inequalities that are so fundamental to twenty-first century America and are willing to support corrective action. Although the issues of economic and political inequality may not be situated at the top of the list of political priorities for most members of the public, these survey results suggest that public push-back would be unlikely to be an impediment to reform efforts should the political opportunity arise. Although the current political and constitutional environment does not seem conducive to efforts to ameliorate economic and political inequality, at some point the window may once again open, as it has periodically in the past. If that happens, fewer will have megaphones and more will speak clearly rather than in whispers. Then we shall move closer to delivering on the promise of American democracy.

NOTES

Preface

1. See https://en.wikipedia.org/wiki/List_of_largest_houses_in_the_United_States (accessed on June 22, 2016). Our enumeration includes houses on the list that are under construction or have been demolished.

2. Sidney Verba, Kay Lehman Schlozman, and Henry E. Brady, *Voice and Equality: Civic Voluntarism and American Politics* (Cambridge, MA: Harvard University Press, 1995).

3. Kay Lehman Schlozman, Sidney Verba, and Henry E. Brady, *The Unheavenly Chorus: Unequal Political Voice and the Broken Promise of American Democracy* (Princeton, NJ: Princeton University Press, 2012).

Chapter 1: Introduction

1. With the exception of the first one, these examples were culled from the media around the country in a one-month period: Suzanne Gamboa, "Clinton Camp Laboring to Stop Sanders from Siphoning Latino Support," NBC News, February 12, 2016, at http://www.nbcnews.com/news/latino/clinton-camp-laboring-stop-sanders-siphoning-latino-support-n517351 (unless otherwise noted, accessed March 7, 2016); Darren Samuelsohn, "Why Bernie Sanders Is Obsessed with 17-Year Olds," *Politico Magazine*, January 31, 2016, at http://www.politico.com/magazine/story/2016/01/iowa-2016-bernie-sanders-youth-vote-213577; Bill Allison, "Singer, Griffin Give Combined $5 Million to Super-PAC Backing Rubio," *Bloomberg*, January 31, 2016, at http://www.bloomberg.com/politics/articles/2016-01-31/singer-griffin-give-combined-5-million-to-super-pac-backing-rubio; Shaun Towne, "Truckers Blare Opposition to Tolls outside RI Statehouse," WPRI, February 10, 2016, http://wpri.com/2016/02/10/truckers-blare-opposition-to-tolls-outside-ri-statehouse/; "Governor Bevin Signs Historic Pro-Life Legislation During Right to Life Rally," at http://kentucky.gov/Pages/Activity-stream.aspx?n=KentuckyGovernor&prId=32 (accessed on August 5, 2016); John Lauritsen, "Chicken Farm Expansion Ruffles Neighbors' Feathers," CBS Minnesota, February 10, 2016, at http://minnesota.cbslocal.com/2016/02/10/chicken-farm-expansion-ruffles-neighbors-feathers/; Jillian Jorgenson, "Mitchell-Lama Residents Back Bill de Blasio's Affordable Housing Plan," *Observer*, February 8, 2016, at http://observer.com/2016/02/mitchell-lama-residents-back-bill-de-blasios-affordable-housing-plan/; Jillian Raftery, "Seattle Neighbors Want More Input in Effort to Solve Homeless Crisis," MYNorthwest.com, February 8, 2016, at http://mynorthwest.com/11/2907964/Seattle-neighbors-want-more-input-in-effort-to-solve-homeless-crisis; Lisa Rathke, "Maple Syrup Producers Question Foods Labeled Maple," *U.S. News and World Report*, February 16, 2016, at http://www.usnews.com/news/business/articles/2016-02-16/maple-syrup-producers-question-foods-labeled-maple (accessed August 5,

2016); Robert Pear, "Lobbying for Drug Makers and Fending Off Anger over Prices," *New York Times,* February 27, 2016.

2. Robert A. Dahl, *Polyarchy: Participation and Opposition* (New Haven, CT: Yale University Press, 1971), p. 1.

3. Robert A. Dahl, *On Political Equality* (New Haven, CT: Yale University Press, 2006), p. 4.

4. Sidney Verba, Kay Lehman Schlozman, and Henry E. Brady, *Voice and Equality: Civic Voluntarism in American Politics* (Cambridge, MA: Harvard University Press, 1995), p. 38.

5. Charles E. Lindblom and Edward J. Woodhouse, *The Policy Making Process*, 3rd ed. (Englewood Cliffs, NJ: Prentice Hall, 1993), p. 111.

6. On these distinctions among participatory acts, see Sidney Verba and Norman H. Nie, *Participation in America* (New York: Harper and Row, 1972), chap. 3; and Verba, Schlozman, and Brady, *Voice and Equality*, pp. 44–46.

7. Figures taken from the Web sites of the two organizations: http://www.aarp.org/about-aarp/ and http://www.mohscollege.org/about-the-acms (accessed June 16, 2016).

8. Figure taken from the Web site of Center for Responsive Politics https://www.opensecrets.org/lobby/top.php?showYear=2015&indexType=s (accessed June 16, 2016).

9. Illegal aliens have been deported when their illegal status was discovered through their political speech. In *Reno v. American-Arab Anti-Discrimination Committee*, 525 U.S. 471 (1999), the Supreme Court affirmed their right to speak out but did not overturn their deportation, arguing that they were deported for their illegal residential status, not for their speech.

10. *Minor v. Happersett* (1875).

11. See Jeff Manza and Christopher Uggen, *Locked Out: Felon Disenfranchisement and American Democracy* (New York: Oxford University Press, 2006) and Amy Lerman and Vesla Weaver, *Arresting Citizenship: The Democratic Consequences of American Crime Control* (Chicago: University of Chicago Press, 2014).

12. We have dealt with participatory stratification based on race and gender in other writings. On race, ethnicity, and political activity, see Sidney Verba, Kay Lehman Schlozman, Henry Brady, and Norman H. Nie, "Race, Ethnicity, and Political Resources: Participation in the United States," *British Journal of Political Science* 23 (1993): 453–497; and Sidney Verba, Kay Lehman Schlozman, Henry Brady, and Norman H. Nie, "Race, Ethnicity and Participation," in *Classifying by Race*, ed. Paul E. Peterson (Princeton, NJ: Princeton University Press, 1995). On gender, see Nancy Burns, Kay Lehman Schlozman, and Sidney Verba, *The Private Roots of Public Action* (Cambridge, MA: Harvard University Press, 2001); as well as Kay Lehman Schlozman, Nancy Burns, and Sidney Verba, "Gender and the Pathways to Participation: The Role of Resources," *Journal of Politics* 56 (1994): 963–990; Kay Lehman Schlozman, Nancy Burns, Sidney Verba, and Jesse Donahue, "Gender and Citizen Participation: Is There a Different Voice?" *American Journal of Political Science* 39 (1995): 267–293; Sidney Verba, Nancy Burns, and Kay Lehman Schlozman, "Knowing and Caring about Politics: Gender and Political Engagement," *Journal of Politics* 59 (1997): 1051–1072; Nancy Burns, Kay Lehman Schlozman, and Sidney Verba, "The Public Consequences of Private Inequality: Family Life and Citizen Participation," *American Political Science Review* 91 (1997): 373–389; and Kay Lehman Schlozman, Nancy Burns, and Sidney Verba, "What Happened at Work Today? A Multi-Stage Model of Gender, Employment, and Political Participation," *Journal of Politics* 61 (1999): 29–54.

13. We recognize that there is no agreement as to the appropriate terms for the three racial/ethnic groups on which we focus in our analysis. We e-mailed six noted Latina/o scholars to ask their advice and received five answers with four sets of suggestions as to the preferred terms. We thank them for their prompt and thoughtful replies. We then did a word count for the major journals in political science and found that, by far, the most common set of terms was that suggested by two of our five correspondents: Latino, African American (or, sometimes, black), and non-Hispanic white.

14. For a more extensive discussion, see Kay Lehman Schlozman, Sidney Verba, and Henry E. Brady, *The Unheavenly Chorus: Unequal Political Voice and the Broken Promise of American Democracy* (Princeton, NJ: Princeton University Press, 2012), chap. 4.

15. James Madison, "The Federalist No. 63," in *The Federalist: Alexander Hamilton, John Jay, and James Madison,* ed. Robert Scigliano (New York: Modern Library, 2000), pp. 403–404.

16. Alexander Hamilton, "The Federalist No. 71," in *Federalist*, ed. Scigliano, p. 458.

17. A particularly important early work is Samuel Stouffer, *Communism, Conformity, and Civil Liberties* (New York: Doubleday, 1955). A recent extension of this tradition is Christopher H. Achen and Larry M. Bartels, *Democracy for Realists* (Princeton, NJ: Princeton University Press, 2016).

18. Joseph Schumpeter, *Capitalism, Socialism, and Democracy* (New York: Harper & Brothers, 1942).

19. Madison, "Federalist No. 10," in *Federalist*, ed. Scigliano, p. 54. On Madisonian democracy, see Robert A. Dahl, *A Preface to Democratic Theory: Expanded Edition* (Chicago: University of Chicago Press, 2006), chap. 1.

20. See the discussion of Madison in Robert A. Dahl, *How Democratic Is the American Constitution?* (New Haven, CT: Yale University Press, 2002), 33–37.

21. We designed and conducted the Citizen Participation Study, which forms the basis for the analysis in Verba, Schlozman, and Brady, *Voice and Equality*, in conjunction with the late Norman H. Nie. These data can be accessed as follows: Sidney Verba, Kay Lehman Schlozman, Henry E. Brady, and Norman Nie, "American Citizen Participation Study, 1990," ICPSR06635-v1 (Ann Arbor, MI: Inter-university Consortium for Political and Social Research [distributor], 1995), at https://doi.org/10.3886/ICPSR06635.v1.

22. The American National Election Studies (ANES). "ANES 2012 Time Series Study," ICPSR35157-v1 (Ann Arbor, MI: Inter-university Consortium for Political and Social Research [distributor], 2016-05-17), at https://doi.org/10.3886/ICPSR35157.v1.

23. We were fortunate to have been able to work with Lee Rainie and Scott Keeter of the Pew Internet and American Life Project in the design of these two surveys: The Pew Internet and American Life Project, August Tracking Survey 2008. Survey by Princeton Survey Research Associates International, August 12–31, 2008; The Pew Internet and American Life Project, Civic Engagement Survey 2012. Survey by Princeton Survey Research Associates International, July 16–August 7, 2012, at http://www.pewinternet.org/dataset/august-2012-civic-engagement/.

24. *Washington Representatives* (Washington, DC: Columbia Books).

25. The data can be accessed at Kay Schlozman, Traci Burch, Philip Edward Jones, Hye Young You, Sidney Verba, and Henry E. Brady, "Washington Representatives Study (Organized Interests in Washington Politics)—1981, 1991, 2001, 2006, 2011," ICPSR35309-v1 (Ann Arbor, MI: Inter-university Consortium for Political and Social Research [distributor], 2014-09-15), at https://doi.org/10.3886/ICPSR35309.v1.

Chapter 2: What Do We Mean by Political Voice?

1. On these distinctions among participatory acts, see Sidney Verba and Norman H. Nie, *Participation in America* (New York: Harper and Row, 1972), chap. 3; and Sidney Verba, Kay Lehman Schlozman, and Henry E. Brady, *Voice and Equality* (Cambridge, MA: Harvard University Press, 1995), pp. 44–46.

2. On the many ways in which the vote is unique as a participatory act, see Verba, Schlozman, and Brady, *Voice and Equality*, pp. 120–121, 358–361.

3. For discussion of the limitations of conventional definitions of participation and references, see Pippa Norris, *Democratic Phoenix: Reinventing Political Activism* (Cambridge: Cambridge

University Press, 2002), pp. xii, 190 ff.; Dietlind Stolle and Marc Hooghe, "Review Article: Inaccurate, Exceptional, One-Sided or Irrelevant? The Debate about the Alleged Decline of Social Capital and Civic Engagement in Western Societies," *British Journal of Political Science* 35 (2004): 154; Cliff Zukin, Scott Keeter, Molly Andolina, Krista Jenkins, and Michael X. Delli Carpini, *A New Engagement? Political Participation, Civic Life, and the Changing American Citizen* (Oxford: Oxford University Press, 2006), pp. 5–10; and Lawrence R. Jacobs, Fay Lomax Cook, and Michael X. Delli Carpini, *Talking Together: Public Deliberation and Political Participation in America* (Chicago: University of Chicago Press, 2009), p. 153. For a contrasting perspective, see Ben Berger, "Political Theory, Political Science, and the End of Civic Engagement," *Perspectives on Politics* 7 (2009): 335–350.

4. For examples and discussion of creative participation, see Michele Micheletti and Andrew McFarland, eds., *Creative Participation: Responsibility-Taking in the Political World* (Boulder, CO: Paradigm, 2010); and Andrew S. McFarland, *Boycotts and Dixie Chicks: Creative Participation at Home and Abroad* (Boulder, CO: Paradigm, 2011).

5. See Jacobs, Cook, and Delli Carpini, *Talking Together*, pp. 23–24, 35–36.

6. Although an extensive literature—much of it theoretical and philosophical—is devoted to deliberative democracy, investigations of how ordinary citizens engage in discussions about politics are less common. For a systematic survey-based study of political discussions, see Jacobs, Cook, and Delli Carpini, *Talking Together*.

7. Jacobs, Cook, and Delli Carpini, *Talking Together*, p. 37.

8. See the discussion and references in Kay Lehman Schlozman, Sidney Verba, and Henry E. Brady, *The Unheavenly Chorus: Unequal Political Voice and the Broken Promise of American Democracy* (Princeton, NJ: Princeton University Press, 2012), pp. 135–137.

9. On the theme of changing levels of turnout and participation, see, among others, Ruy A. Teixeira, *The Disappearing American Voter* (Washington, DC: Brookings Institution, 1992); Steven J. Rosenstone and John Mark Hansen, *Mobilization, Participation, and Democracy in America* (New York: MacMillan, 1993); Robert D. Putnam, *Bowling Alone: The Collapse and Revival of American Community* (New York: Simon and Schuster, 2000); Martin P. Wattenberg, *Where Have All the Voters Gone?* (Cambridge, MA: Harvard University Press, 2002); and Stephen Macedo, Yvette Alex-Assensoh, Jeffrey M. Berry, Michael Brintnall, David E. Campbell, Luis Ricardo Fraga, and Archon Fung, *Democracy at Risk: How Political Choices Undermine Citizen Participation and What We Can Do about It* (Washington, DC: Brookings Institution, 2005).

10. Turnout figure is for the Voter Eligible Population, as reported on the Web site of the United States Elections Project, http://www.electproject.org/2012g (accessed on April 11, 2016).

11. These figures are taken from Web sites of the organizations mentioned: http://www.aarp.org/about-aarp/?intcmp=FTR-LINKS-WWA-ABOUT; https://home.nra.org/about-the-nra/; http://www.ufcw.org/; https://www.nahb.org/en/about-nahb.aspx; http://www.ncga.com/about-ncga/mission-vision; http://www.abfnet.org/?page=37; http://www.api.org/about; and http://www.aia-aerospace.org/membership/our_members/ (accessed June 29, 2016).

12. Robert Michels, *Political Parties: A Sociological Study of the Oligarchical Tendencies of Modern Democracy*, trans. Eden Paul and Cedar Paul (New York: Dover, 1959).

13. The importance of political representation by organizations that are not voluntary associations of individuals was first discussed by Robert H. Salisbury in "Interest Representation: The Dominance of Institutions," *American Political Science Review* 78 (1984): 64–76.

On the implications for democratic representation of political advocacy by memberless organizations, see Kay Lehman Schlozman, Philip Edward Jones, Hye Young You, Traci Burch, Sidney Verba, and Henry E. Brady, "Organizations and the Democratic Representation of Interests: What Does It Mean When Those Organizations Have No Members?" *Perspectives on Politics*

13: (2015) 1017–1029. See also David Lowery, Virginia Gray, Jennifer Anderson, and Adam J. Newmark, "Collective Action and the Mobilization of Institutions," *Journal of Politics* 66 (2004): 684–705.

14. R. Edward Freeman, *Strategic Management: A Stakeholder Approach* (Boston: Pitman, 1984), p. 46.

15. See Nick Anderson, "For-Profit Schools Lobby to Avoid Proposed Federal Aid Rule," *Washington Post*, October 22, 2010; and David Halperin, "The Perfect Lobby: How One Industry Captured Washington, DC," *The Nation*, April 3, 2014.

16. U.S. Government Accountability Office, "For-Profit Colleges: Undercover Testing Finds Colleges Encouraged Fraud and Engaged in Deceptive and Questionable Marketing Practices," 2010, at http://www.gao.gov/products/GAO-10-948T, accessed April 1, 2015.

17. For a more detailed discussion of this issue, see the arguments and citations in Schlozman, Verba, and Brady, *Unheavenly Chorus,* chaps. 5 and 10.

18. *Citizen's Guide to Influencing Elected Officials* (Washington, DC: TheCapitolNet, 2010), p. 34.

19. Christopher Rowland, "A Funds Family at Risk, Fidelity Went to War," *Boston Sunday Globe*, October 19, 2014.

20. Katharine Seelye, "White Families Seek Gentler War on Heroin," *New York Times*, October 31, 2015.

21. Emmarie Huetteman, "In Rare Congressional Consensus, Opioid Crisis Bill Passes," *New York Times*, July 14, 2016.

22. Julie Hirschfeld Davis, "Pro-Israel Group Went 'All In' but Suffered a Stinging Defeat," *New York Times*, September 11, 2015; and Eric Lipton, "Intense Lobbying Failed to Assure Deal by Comcast," *New York Times*, April 25, 2015.

23. The literature on this subject is substantial, and reviewing it is well beyond our current task. A classic and still highly relevant analysis of the difficulty of connecting the public and elected officials is Christopher H. Achen, "Measuring Representation," *American Journal of Political Science* 22 (1978): 475–510. See also John Zaller, *The Nature and Origins of Mass Opinion* (Cambridge: Cambridge University Press, 1992); and Lawrence R. Jacobs and Robert Y. Shapiro, *Politicians Don't Pander: Political Manipulation and the Loss of Democratic Responsiveness* (Chicago: University of Chicago Press, 2000).

24. See Warren E. Miller and Donald E. Stokes, "Constituency Influence in Congress," *American Political Science Review* 57 (1963): 45–56. For additional discussion and citations, see Schlozman, Verba, and Brady, *Unheavenly Chorus*, p. 141.

25. See Sidney Verba and Norman H. Nie, *Participation in America: Political Democracy and Social Equality* (New York: Harper and Row, 1972), pp. 301–308 and chaps. 17 and 18; Kim Quaile Hill and Jan E. Leighley, "The Policy Consequences of Class Bias in State Electorates," *American Journal of Political Science* 36 (1992): 351–365; Kim Quaile Hill, Jan E. Leighley, and Angela Hinton-Andersson, "Lower-Class Mobilization and Policy Linkage in the U.S. States," *American Journal of Political Science* 39 (1995): 75–86; Jessica Trounstine and Zoltan Hajnal, "Where Turnout Matters: The Consequences of Uneven Turnout in City Politics," *Journal of Politics* 67 (2005): 515–535; and Daniel E. Bergan, "Does Grassroots Lobbying Work? A Field Experiment Measuring the Effects of an E-Mail Lobbying Campaign on Legislative Behavior," *American Politics Research* 37 (2009): 327–352.

26. Andrea Louise Campbell, *How Policies Make Citizens: Senior Political Activism and the American Welfare State* (Princeton, NJ: Princeton University Press, 2003).

27. Larry M. Bartels, *Unequal Democracy: The Political Economy of the New Gilded Age* (New York and Princeton, NJ: Russell Sage Foundation and Princeton University Press, 2008), pp. 275–282.

In Yosef Bhatti and Robert S. Erikson, "How Poorly Are the Poor Represented in the U.S. Senate?" in *Who Gets Represented?*, ed. Peter K. Enns and Christopher Wlezien (New York: Russell Sage Foundation, 2011), chap. 8, Bhatti and Erikson raise methodological concerns about Bartels's approach but conclude (p. 241): "Our reinvestigation is not directly contradictory to Bartels's findings."

28. Bartels, *Unequal Democracy*, p. 282. Emphasis in the original.

29. Martin Gilens, *Affluence and Influence: Economic Inequality and Political Power in America* (Princeton, NJ: Princeton University Press, 2012), chaps. 3–4.

30. See, for example, James N. Druckman and Lawrence R. Jacobs, in "Segmented Representation: The Reagan White House and Disproportionate Responsiveness," and Elizabeth Rigby and Gerald C. Wright, "Whose Statehouse Democracy? Policy Responsiveness to Poor versus Rich Constituents in Poor versus Rich States," in *Who Gets Represented?* ed. Enns and Wlezien, chaps. 6 and 7; Thomas J. Hayes, "Responsiveness in an Era of Inequality: The Case of the U.S. Senate," *Political Research Quarterly* 66 (2012): 585–589; Patrick Flavin, "Income Inequality and Policy Representation in the American States," *American Politics Research* 40 (2012): 29–59; Elizabeth Rigby and Gerald C. Wright, "Political Parties and Representation of the Poor in the American States," *American Journal of Political Science* 57 (2013): 552–565; and Larry M. Bartels, "Political Inequality and American Democracy," *Extensions*, Winter 2016, pp. 4–9.

31. See John D. Griffin and Brian Newman, *Minority Report: Evaluating Political Equality in America* (Chicago: University of Chicago Press, 2008), pp. 195–196, and passim; John D. Griffin and Brian Newman, "Voting Power, Policy Representation, and Disparities in Voting's Rewards," *Journal of Politics* 75 (2013): 52–64; Daniel M. Butler and David E. Broockman, "Do Politicians Racially Discriminate against Constituents? A Field Experiment on State Legislators," *American Journal of Political Science* 55 (2011): 463–477.

32. Martin Gilens and Benjamin I. Page, "Testing Theories of American Politics: Elites, Interest Groups, and Average Citizens," *Perspectives on Politics* 12 (2014): 564–581.

33. James A. Stimson, "The Issues in Representation," in *Who Gets Represented?* ed. Enns and Wlezien, p. 347.

34. T. H. White, *The Once and Future King* (New York: Berkley Books, 1939), p. 557.

35. On the value of case studies and their relation to causal quantitative analysis, see the discussion and citations in Schlozman, Verba, and Brady, *Unheavenly Chorus*, pp. 288–291.

36. See Beth Leech, "Lobbying and Influence," in *The Oxford Handbook of American Political Parties and Interest Groups*, ed. L. Sandy Maisel and Jeffrey M. Berry (Oxford: Oxford University Press, 2010), pp. 540–541.

37. Frank Baumgartner, Jeffrey Berry, Marie Hojnacki, David C. Kimball, and Beth Leech, *Lobbying and Policy Change: Who Wins, Who Loses, and Why* (Chicago: University of Chicago Press, 2009). For a discussion of their findings, see Schlozman, Verba, and Brady, *Unheavenly Chorus*, pp. 296–304. Others have found a way to sample political controversies more directly. See Gilens, *Affluence and Influence*; and Paul Burstein, *American Public Opinion, Advocacy, and Policy in Congress: What the Public Wants and What It Gets* (New York: Cambridge University Press, 2014).

38. John W. Kingdon, *Agendas, Alternatives, and Public Policy* (Boston: Little Brown, 1984), p. 52. See also Roger W. Cobb and Marc Howard Ross, *Cultural Strategies of Agenda Denial: Avoidance, Attack, and Redefinition* (Lawrence: University of Kansas Press, 1997), p. 208.

39. Baumgartner et al., *Lobbying and Policy Change*, p. 255.

40. Michael Isikoff, "A Ban Gets Shot Down," *Newsweek*, April 6, 2009, p. 6.

41. On the significance of service provision in the lobbying process and the importance of the information function of lobbying, see the discussion and citations in Schlozman, Verba, and Brady, *Unheavenly Chorus*, pp. 299–301.

42. Rogan Kersh, "Corporate Lobbyists as Political Actors," in *Interest Group Politics*, ed. Allan J. Cigler and Burdett A. Loomis, 6th ed. (Washington, DC: CQ Press, 2002), p. 227.

43. See Leech, "Lobbying and Influence," pp. 541–544; and Lynda W. Powell, *The Influence of Campaign Contributions in State Legislatures* (Ann Arbor: University of Michigan Press, 2012), pp. 16–19.

44. Timothy A. Byrnes, *Catholic Bishops in American Politics* (Princeton, NJ: Princeton University Press, 1991), pp. 6–8.

45. Leech, "Lobbying and Influence," p. 537.

46. Leech, "Lobbying and Influence," p. 540.

47. For a wide-ranging narrative account of the persistent role of business in shaping policy on the economy for thirty years beginning in the 1970s—that is, through periods of Democratic and Republican control in Washington—see Jacob S. Hacker and Paul Pierson, *Winner-Take-All Politics: How Washington Made the Rich Richer—And Turned Its Back on the Middle Class* (New York: Simon and Schuster, 2010).

48. Baumgartner et al., *Lobbying and Policy Change*, chap. 10.

49. Baumgartner et al., *Lobbying and Policy Change*, p. 212.

50. For a helpful review essay, see Richard A. Smith, "Interest Group Influence in the U. S. Congress," *Legislative Studies Quarterly* 20 (1995): 89–139. For additional discussion and citations, see Schlozman, Verba, and Brady, *Unheavenly Chorus*, pp. 305–308.

51. Stephen Ansolabehere, John M. de Figueiredo, and James M. Snyder Jr., "Why Is There So Little Money in U.S. Politics?" *Journal of Economic Perspectives* 17 (2003): 116. However, some systematic empirical analyses find positive results for the effects of contributions. See Thomas Stratmann, "Some Talk: Money in Politics; A (Partial) Review of the Literature," *Public Choice* 124 (2005): 135–156.

52. See, for example, Powell, *Influence of Campaign Contributions*, pp. 180–183.

53. Michael Malbin, "Rethinking the Campaign Finance Agenda," *The Forum* 6, no. 1 (2008): 2, at http://www.bepress.com/forum/vol6/iss1/art3 (accessed June 23, 2010).

54. Smith, "Interest Group Influence," p. 93. On the difficulty of distinguishing access from influence, especially when access is unequal, see Kay Lehman Schlozman and John T. Tierney, *Organized Interests and American Democracy* (New York: Harper and Row, 1986), pp. 164–165; and Frank J. Sorauf, "Political Action Committees," in *Campaign Finance Reform: A Sourcebook*, ed. Anthony Corrado, Thomas E. Mann, Daniel R. Ortiz, Trevor Potter, and Frank J. Sorauf (Washington, DC: Brookings Institution Press, 1997), pp. 121, 127.

55. John R. Wright, "Lobbying and Committee Voting in the U.S. House of Representatives," *American Political Science Review* 84 (1990): 418.

56. Robert D. McFadden, "Charles Keating, Key Figure in the 1980s Savings and Loan Crisis, Dies at 90," *New York Times*, April 2, 2014.

57. See donor perspectives in *Inside the Campaign Finance Battle: Court Testimony on the New Reforms*, ed. Anthony Corrado, Thomas E. Mann, and Trevor Potter (Washington, DC: Brookings Institution Press, 2003), pp. 297–316.

58. Robert Rozen, "Large Contributions Provide Unequal Access," in *Inside the Campaign Finance Battle*, ed. Corrado, Mann, and Potter, p. 297.

59. Powell, *Influence of Campaign Contributions*, p. 21.

60. Joshua L. Kalla and David Broockman, "Campaign Contributions Facilitate Access to Congressional Officials: A Randomized Field Experiment," *American Journal of Political Science* 60 (2016): 545–558.

61. John P. Heinz, Edward O. Laumann, Robert L. Nelson, and Robert H. Salisbury, *The Hollow Core: Private Interests in National Policy Making* (Cambridge, MA: Harvard University Press, 1993), p. 409.

62. Anthony J. Nownes, *Total Lobbying* (Cambridge: Cambridge University Press, 2006), p. 32.

Chapter 3: The Roots of Citizen Participation

1. This chapter condenses and modifies the complex argument made in Sidney Verba, Kay Lehman Schlozman, and Henry E. Brady, *Voice and Equality: Civic Voluntarism in American Politics* (Cambridge, MA: Harvard University Press, 1995). We are grateful to Harvard University Press for permission to draw heavily on the arguments and data in various chapters of *Voice and Equality* (in particular, chaps. 1, 5, 9–15).

We encourage interested readers to consult the original, which contains a much more nuanced presentation, supported by extensive multivariate analysis and embellished by detailed variable definitions, copious explanatory notes, and citations. We invite those with concerns about such matters as ambiguities of causal direction to see our discussions of methodological issues. We recognize the losses incurred by presenting such an abbreviated version of our argument and so few citations to others' work.

2. By encompassing resources, engagement, and recruitment, the CVM accommodates a rich array of explanatory factors. It is not, however, exhaustive. Our analysis does not include all aspects of the political system that have been found to be significant for political participation, for example, the correspondence between public officials and constituency in terms of race or ethnicity, and the role of legal institutions and requirements (such as registration and voting laws).

3. For a set of essays that bring new perspectives and more recent data to the CVM, see *Resources, Engagement, and Recruitment: New Advances in the Study of Civic Voluntarism*, ed. Casey Klofstad (Philadelphia: Temple University Press, 2016). Klofstad's essay includes an excellent overview of the CVM.

4. Because it is the only survey that contains all the variables in the CVM, throughout this chapter, we use data from the 1990 Citizen Participation Study. Whenever possible, we tested our findings using data taken from several more recent surveys. In no case did we find anything contradictory to what is reported here.

The 1990 survey measures money and time directly: money as family income; free time as the residual time available to an individual after accounting for the hours spent doing necessary household tasks of all sorts, including child care; working for pay, which includes commuting and work taken home (for those in the work force); studying or going to school (for those taking courses toward a degree); and sleeping.

5. The findings in the remainder of this paragraph are drawn from Nancy Burns, Kay Lehman Schlozman, and Sidney Verba, *The Private Roots of Public Action: Gender, Equality, and Political Participation* (Cambridge, MA: Harvard University Press, 2001), pp. 184–185, 249.

6. For discussion and citations, see Sara Chatfield and John Henderson, "Untangling the Education Effect: Moving Educational Interventions into the Experimental Frontier," in *Resources, Engagement, and Recruitment*, ed. Klofstad, chap. 13.

7. The ability to communicate effectively, as measured in the 1990 survey by respondents' linguistic facility and their proficiency in English, is, obviously, critical for most forms of political action. See Verba, Schlozman, and Brady, *Voice and Equality*, pp. 305–308, 356–364, 433.

8. Information in this paragraph is taken from U.S. Census Bureau, *Statistical Abstract of the United States: 2012*, 131st ed. (Washington, DC: U.S. Government Printing Office, 2012), tables 229–231, pp. 151–152.

9. The discussion in this paragraph is drawn from Burns, Schlozman, and Verba, *Private Roots*, pp. 281–290.

10. This assumption, of course, figures importantly in the literature on participatory democracy: that participation leads to political involvement and interest. Classic statements are in Rousseau and John Stuart Mill. See also Carole Pateman, *Participation and Democratic Theory*

(Cambridge: Cambridge University Press, 1970); and Benjamin R. Barber, *Strong Democracy: Participatory Politics for a New Age* (Berkeley and Los Angeles: University of California Press, 1984).

For discussion of the methodologically complex matter of the causal status of psychological orientations to politics, elaboration of variable definitions, and bibliographical references, see Verba, Schlozman, and Brady, *Voice and Equality*, pp. 343–348, Appendix B.7, Appendix D.

11. For data about income, see Verba, Schlozman, and Brady, *Voice and Equality*, p. 349.

12. For full data supporting these conclusions, see Burns, Schlozman, and Verba, *Private Roots*, p. 293. On the extent to which disparities in psychological engagement with politics contribute to the relatively modest gender gap in participation and the way that those disparities are anchored in the understanding that politics is a man's game, see chaps. 4, 11.

13. The Citizen Participation Study contained two sets of items about requests for activity. For discussion, see Verba, Schlozman, and Brady, *Voice and Equality*, Appendix B.8.

14. See Henry E. Brady, Kay Lehman Schlozman, and Sidney Verba, "Political Mobility and Political Reproduction from Generation to Generation," *Annals of the American Academy of Political and Social Science* 657 (2015): 149–173. For discussion of causal direction and the validity of survey items that require adult respondents to recall childhood experiences, see Verba, Schlozman, and Brady, *Voice and Equality*, chap. 15; and Burns, Schlozman, and Verba, *Private Roots*, chap. 5.

15. For extensive citations of the literature on political socialization, see Kay Lehman Schlozman, Sidney Verba, and Henry E. Brady, *The Unheavenly Chorus: Unequal Political Voice and the Broken Promise of American Democracy* (Princeton, NJ: Princeton University Press, 2012), p. 179. For literature reviews, see Paul Allen Beck, "The Role of Agents in Political Socialization," in *Handbook of Political Socialization*, ed. Stanley Allen Renshon (New York: Free Press, 1979), pp. 115–141; Virginia Sapiro, "Not Your Parents' Political Socialization: Introduction for a New Generation," *Annual Review of Political Science* 7 (2004): 1–23; and M. Kent Jennings, "Political Socialization," in *The Oxford Handbook of Political Behavior,* ed. Russell J. Dalton and Hans-Dieter Klingemann (Oxford: Oxford University Press, 2009), pp. 29–44.

16. For arguments consistent with this perspective, see M. Kent Jennings and Richard G. Niemi, *The Political Character of Adolescence* (Princeton, NJ: Princeton University Press, 1974), p. 22; and Stanley Allen Renshon, in "The Role of Personality Development in Political Socialization," in *New Directions in Political Socialization*, ed. David C. Schwartz and Sandra Kenyon Schwartz (New York: Free Press, 1975), p. 48.

17. The questionnaire items covered whether respondents had taken any courses that required students to pay attention to current events; students in the respondent's high school were concerned about current events and politics; students in the respondent's high school were encouraged to debate and make up their own minds about current events; students in the respondent's high school were allowed to complain if they thought something was unfair; the respondent was concerned about current events and politics; the respondent was active in school sports; the respondent was active in school government; and the respondent was active in other school clubs or activities.

18. Not surprisingly, respondents' retrospective reports on whether they cared about current events in high school are strongly related to adult activity. This measure may be tainted by backward projection of current views and is thus not entirely trustworthy. In addition, having taken a course that includes discussion of current events—an experience shared by 79 percent the of high school graduates in the sample that may reflect either respondent choice or a school requirement—is related, though somewhat less strongly, to future activity.

19. For extensive data analysis and discussion of our methods and findings, see Sidney Verba, Nancy Burns, and Kay Lehman Schlozman, "Unequal at the Starting Line: Creating Participatory

Inequalities across Generations and among Groups," *American Sociologist* 34 (2003): 45–69; and Sidney Verba, Kay Lehman Schlozman, and Nancy Burns, "Family Ties," in *The Social Logic of Politics: Personal Networks as Contexts for Political Behavior*, ed. Alan S. Zuckerman (Philadelphia: Temple University Press, 2005), chap. 5.

20. These regularities, which emerge from the Citizen Participation Study conducted in 1990, are confirmed by data for 2010 from the U.S. Census Bureau, *Statistical Abstract of the United States: 2012*, tables 588 and 593, pp. 378, 381. It should be noted that, although their labor force participation rates are roughly similar, African Americans and Latinos have higher rates of unemployment than do non-Hispanic whites.

21. For a detailed examination of the skill-building opportunities provided by different religious groups, including various different Protestant denominations, see David E. Campbell, "Doing the Lord's Work: How Religious Congregations Build Civic Skills" in *Resources, Engagement, and Recruitment*, ed. Klofstad, chap. 4.

22. Multivariate analysis confirms that, with other factors taken into account, Catholics exercise fewer civic skills in church than do Protestants. See Verba, Schlozman, and Brady, *Voice and Equality*, p. 324–325.

23. What follows is a brief summary of a complex data analysis. For variable definitions, complete results, and discussions of statistical issues and problems of causal direction, see Verba, Schlozman, and Brady, *Voice and Equality*, pp. 350–364, 388–390, 440–445, 538–546.

24. The index of overall participation is an additive scale that includes measures of the following activities: voting; working in a campaign; making a campaign contribution; contacting a public official; attending a protest, march, or demonstration; serving in a voluntary capacity on a local governmental board or attending meetings of such a board; working informally with others in the community to deal with some community issue or problem; and being affiliated with an organization that takes stands in politics.

25. For an interesting analysis of participation in different generations among Latino and Asian-American immigrants, see S. Karthick Ramakrishnan and Sono Shah, "Latinos, Asian Americans, and the Voluntarism/Voting Gap," in *Resources, Engagement, and Recruitment*, ed. Klofstad, chap. 3.

26. Data from the 2012 American National Election Study suggest that, more than two decades after the Citizen Participation Study, abortion continues to mobilize activity. Even after SES and political interest are taken into account, those who are pro-choice and those who are pro-life are significantly more active than those who take positions on abortion in the middle of the scale.

Chapter 4: Who Exercises Political Voice?

1. "Erin Burnett Outraged at All-Male Senate Health Care Panel," Alexander King, CNN, Saturday May 6, 2017 (5:07 PM ET), at http://www.cnn.com/2017/05/06/us/erin-burnett-women-health-care-cnntv/.

2. Quoted in "Republicans Defend Having No Women in Health Care Group," Dana Bash, Lauren Fox, and Ted Burnett, CNN, Friday May 5, 2017 (5:29 PM ET), at http://www.cnn.com/2017/05/05/politics/senate-republican-health-care-men/.

3. For discussion of socioeconomic stratification and references to works providing evidence for its role in enhancing participation, see Sidney Verba, Kay Lehman Schlozman, and Henry E. Brady, in *Voice and Equality: Civic Voluntarism in American Politics* (Cambridge, MA: Harvard University Press, 1995), chaps. 7, 9–12. For a dissent from the consensus on the impact of education on political participation, see Cindy D. Kam and Carl L. Palmer, "Reconsidering the

Effects of Education on Political Participation," *Journal of Politics* 70 (2008): 612–631; and Adam J. Rerinsky and Gabriel S. Lenz, "Education and Political Participation: Exploring the Causal Link," *Political Behavior* 33 (2011): 357–373. For an alternative perspective, see John Henderson and Sara Chatfield, "Who Matches? Propensity Scores and Bias in the Causal Effects of Education on Participation," *Journal of Politics* 73 (2011): 646–658.

4. The SES measure, which is used throughout this work, is constructed to give equal weight to family income and the respondent's educational attainment. For detailed information about how we constructed the measure of SES and why we chose to include *family* income and the *respondent's* educational attainment, see Kay Lehman Schlozman, Sidney Verba, and Henry E. Brady, *The Unheavenly Chorus: Unequal Political Voice and the Broken Promise of American Democracy* (Princeton, NJ: Princeton University Press, 2012), p. 123.

5. The 2012 ANES measured informal community activity by asking about "attending a meeting about an issue facing the community or schools."

Surveys taken at different times vary in whether they show an association between SES and protest. Data about protest activity from the 1990 Citizen Participation Study show an overall pattern of stratification similar to that for the 2012 ANES. However, data from the 2008 Pew Internet and American Life Survey do not show an upward tilt. The explanation may be the small number of protesters in any survey. Or the explanation may lie in the changing nature of the issues animating demonstrations. For example, it is likely that environmental protesters are, on average, higher in SES than pro-life demonstrators.

6. The SES groups were constructed using the same technique described earlier but dividing the respondents into percentiles rather than quintiles.

7. We used the 1990 Citizen Participation Study, which allows us to differentiate local from national activity in a way that has not been replicated. Not only did that survey ask separately about voting in presidential and local elections, but it also allows us to distinguish local from national activity with respect to six acts: working in a campaign; contributing to a campaign; contacting a public official (elected and nonelected); taking part in a protest, march, or demonstration; and being affiliated with an organization that takes stands in politics.

8. Because the data in Figures 4.1 and 4.4 are drawn from different surveys conducted several years apart, the numbers for contacting and making a campaign donation are not identical in the two figures, but the pattern is the same.

9. The data about discussing politics were generated by combining two items from the August Tracking 2008 survey sponsored by the Pew Internet and American Life Project. Respondents were asked how often they discussed politics and public affairs with others, first "on the Internet by e-mail or instant message, or on a social networking site, or in an online chat," and second, "in person, by phone, or in a letter." The data on boycotting are taken from the 2005 Citizenship, Involvement, Democracy (CID) Survey. Respondents were presented with a list of actions they might have taken, preceded by this question: "Over the past 5 years have you done any of the following [actions] to express your opinion about an issue or your support for a cause: Boycotting a product . . . ?"

Compared to the probability of engaging in the other three acts, that of engaging in political discussion rises more steeply, from the lowest through the middle SES quintile, and then levels off slightly for the upper two quintiles. For the other three acts, the slope is shallower at the bottom and steeper at the top.

The CID survey can be accessed at Marc M. Howard, James L. Gibson, and Dietlind Stolle, "United States Citizenship, Involvement, Democracy (CID) Survey, 2006," ICPSR04607-v2 (Ann Arbor, MI: Inter-university Consortium for Political and Social Research [distributor], 2016-10-11), at https://doi.org/10.3886/ICPSR04607.v2. (Note that, although the date attached to the archive is 2006, the survey was actually conducted in 2005.)

10. Jan Teorell, Paul Sum, and Mette Tobiasen, in "Participation and Political Equality: An Assessment of Large-Scale Democracy," in *Citizenship and Involvement in European Democracies*, ed. Jan W. van Deth, José Ramón Montero, and Anders Westholm (London: Routledge, 2007), pp. 392–398, find a relationship between education and political consumerism for European democracies.

11. By focusing separately on race or ethnicity on one hand and gender on the other, we do not mean to overlook the matter of gender differences in racial or ethnic groups (or of racial and ethnic differences within gender groups), issues sometimes called "intersectionality." For an extended treatment of intersectionality with regard to political participation, see Nancy Burns, Kay Lehman Schlozman, and Sidney Verba, *The Private Roots of Public Action* (Cambridge, MA: Harvard University Press, 2001), chap. 11.

One important intersectional matter involves the extent to which high rates of incarceration of young males of color in recent decades imply that survey data on political participation may overestimate the rates of activity of Latino and, especially, African American males in their twenties and thirties because the incarcerated are not included in surveys.

12. In fact, the 2012 survey sponsored by the Pew Internet and American Life Project showed no gender gap at all. On a scale of eight participatory acts, men scored an average of 2.04 and women an average of 2.05. On the disparity between men and women in participation, see Nancy Burns, Kay Lehman Schlozman, Ashley Jardina, Shauna Shames, and Sidney Verba "What Happened to the Gender Gap in Participation?" in *100 Years of the Nineteenth Amendment*, ed., Lee Ann Banaszak and Holly McCammon (Oxford and New York: Oxford University Press), in press.

13. Information taken from Peter Olsen-Phillips, Russ Choma, Sarah Bryner, and Doug Weber, "The Political One Percent of the One Percent: Megadonors Fuel Rising Cost of Elections in 2014," April 30, 2015 at http://sunlightfoundation.com/blog/2015/04/30/the-political-one-percent-of-the-one-percent-megadonors-fuel-rising-cost-of-elections-in-2014/ (accessed on January 25, 2016). Seventy-six percent of the 1 percent of the 1 percent were men. The gender of 2 percent could not be determined.

Chapter 5: The Noisy and the Silent

1. Franklin Roosevelt, "The Forgotten Man," April 1932, at http://newdeal.feri.org/speeches/1932c.htm (accessed on December 29, 2016).

2. Raymond E. Wolfinger and Steven J. Rosenstone, *Who Votes?* (New Haven, CT: Yale University Press, 1980), chap. 6.

3. See Stephen Earl Bennett and David Resnick, "The Implications of Non-voting for Democracy in the United States," *American Journal of Political Science* 34 (1990): 771–802. Sidney Verba, Kay Lehman Schlozman, and Henry E. Brady, in *Voice and Equality: Civic Voluntarism in American Politics* (Cambridge, MA: Harvard University Press, 1995), pp. 204–205, also confirmed the Wolfinger and Rosenstone analysis. In "The Political Implications of Higher Turnout," *British Journal of Political Science* 31 (2001): 179–192, Benjamin Highton and Raymond E. Wolfinger repeated the analysis and confirmed the earlier finding. They also looked at the demographic characteristics of nonvoters and found (p. 191) "that no single characteristic is shared by a majority of those who did not vote in 1992 or 1996; the 'party of non-voters' is rather diverse." However, they do not compare the distributions of voters and nonvoters with respect to demographic characteristics. While the "party of non-voters" is surely diverse, it is not representative of the electorate as a whole.

4. Jan E. Leighley and Jonathan Nagler, *Who Votes Now?: Demographics, Issues, Inequality, and Turnout in the United States* (Princeton, NJ: Princeton University Press, 2014), chap. 6.

5. Leighley and Nagler, *Who Votes Now?*, p. 171. (Emphasis in the original.)

6. The discussion in this section draws on Verba, Schlozman, and Brady, *Voice and Equality*, chap. 7.

7. See Marc Morje Howard, James L. Gibson, and Dietlind Stolle, "The U.S. Citizenship, Involvement, Democracy Survey" (Washington, DC: Center for Democracy and Civil Society, Georgetown University, 2005). The CID survey can be accessed at Marc M. Howard, James L. Gibson, and Dietlind Stolle, "United States Citizenship, Involvement, Democracy (CID) Survey, 2006," ICPSR04607-v2 (Ann Arbor, MI: Inter-university Consortium for Political and Social Research [distributor], 2016-10-11, 2006), at https://doi.org/10.3886/ICPSR04607.v2. (Note that although the date attached to the archive is 2006, the survey was actually conducted in 2005.)

8. The three-item scale measuring attitudes on social issues includes one question about abortion and two about gay rights.

Details about question-wording and scale construction for both the 2005 and the 1990 data and the logic behind the decision to use the mean rather than the median position can be found in Kay Lehman Schlozman, Sidney Verba, and Henry E. Brady, *The Unheavenly Chorus: Unequal Political Voice and the Broken Promise of American Democracy* (Princeton, NJ: Princeton University Press, 2012), pp. 243–247. The survey items were somewhat different in 1990.

9. These results are confirmed by analyses of data from the ANES.

10. Alan Abramowitz, *The Disappearing Center: Engaged Citizens, Polarization, and American Democracy* (New Haven, CT: Yale University Press, 2010), chap. 3.

11. The participation scales included seven information-rich activities (march, board member, Internet petition, in-person petition, political organization, contacting official, and contacting government office).

12. The additive scale of economic attitudes includes eight items: government guarantee jobs; government services or reduce spending; aid to blacks; guarantee equal opportunity; unequal chances are a problem; gone too far in pushing equal rights; better off if we worried less about equality; and not a big problem if some have more chance in life.

13. Respondents were shown a list of eight different political movements. They were considered "active" in a particular movement if either they said that they "actively participate" or they had "in the past 12 months . . . attended a meeting, protest, rally or any other event associated" with it.

14. It is not surprising that those with the most pro-choice views were less likely to be active in support if the women's rights movement than were those with the most pro-life views to be active in support of the pro-life movement. Although reproductive rights are a central concern among women's rights advocates, the link between attitudes on abortion and the pro-life movement is much more direct.

15. When we considered the SES of the groups along the continuum from extremely liberal to extremely conservative, we noted a symmetrical M-shaped pattern in which the liberal or conservative groups that were, on average, highest in SES were not those at the ends, those who called themselves "extremely liberal" (1) or "extremely conservative" (7), but those who placed themselves in the next categories, that is, those who called themselves "liberal" (2) or "conservative" (6). The groups at the two extremes and the moderates were roughly equivalent in average SES and were significantly lower in SES than any other group.

16. On this point, see Mark C. Alexander, "*Citizens United* and Equality Forgotten," in *Money, Politics, and the Constitution*, ed. Monica Youn (New York: Century Foundation, 2011), pp. 161–163.

17. What was then called food stamps was renamed the Supplemental Nutritional Assistance Program (SNAP) in the 2008 farm bill. AFDC was replaced by Temporary Assistance to Needy Families (TANF) in the Personal Responsibility and Work Opportunity Reconciliation Act of 1996.

18. The data in Table 5.3 are taken from Verba, Schlozman, and Brady, *Voice and Equality*, Figure 7.12, p. 218.

19. To the best of our knowledge, no national survey subsequent to the 1990 Citizen Participation Study has asked activists open-ended questions about the issues and concerns behind their participation. The discussion in this section is drawn from Verba, Schlozman, and Brady, *Voice and Equality*, pp. 84–91, 93–96, 220–225, 247–251, 260–263. See these sections for the treatment of various technical issues in the coding and analysis of these data.

20. We defined socioeconomic advantage and disadvantage so as to produce groups of roughly equal size, each representing about one-sixth of the sample. The advantaged are those with at least some college education and a family income over $50,000 ($91,300 in 2015 dollars), and the disadvantaged are those with no education beyond high school and a family income below $20,000 ($36,500 in 2015 dollars).

21. The issue-based political act is the unit of analysis, and the figures represent the proportion of all issue-based activities for which the respondent mentioned, among other things, a particular set of policy concerns.

22. To ensure that what was on people's minds was actually communicated to public officials, we focus solely on those information-rich activities in which an explicit message can be sent: contacting a public official, attending a protest, doing campaign work or making contributions accompanied by a communication to the candidate, taking part in informal activity to solve a community problem, or doing voluntary service on a local governing board (such as the school board or zoning board). Thus, we omit voting, attending meetings of a local board on a regular basis, and campaigning for or contributing to a candidate when the activity is not accompanied by an explicit message.

23. A detailed exposition of the evidence that underlies the discussion in this section can be found in Verba, Schlozman, and Brady, *Voice and Equality*, pp. 220–225.

Chapter 6: Do Digital Technologies Make a Difference?

1. Johnathan Silver, "Petition Seeks Ban on Sex Offender Pen Pals," Texas Tribune, April 20, 2016, at https://www.texastribune.org/2016/04/20/petition-ban-prisoner-access-pen-pals-on line/; Sheila Burke and Erik Schelzig, "Transgender Bathroom Bill Fails in Tennessee Legislature," April 18, 2016, at http://bigstory.ap.org/article/b2551210164b45ffa7a8369ba7975290/tennessee-transgender-bathroom-bill-dead-session; Shasta Kearns Moore, "Sabin Protests Class Sizes on YouTube," *Portland Tribune*, September 17, 2015, at http://portlandtribune.com/pt/9-news/273457-148352-sabin-protests-class-sizes-on-youtube; Mark Pazniokas, "Malloy Hears from Homeowners with Crumbling Basements," *Connecticut Mirror*, March 30, 2016, at http://ctmirror.org/2016/03/30/malloy-hears-from-homeowners-with-crumbing-foundations/ (all accessed April 24, 2016).

2. This chapter draws from and extends the analysis in Kay Lehman Schlozman, Sidney Verba, and Henry E. Brady, *The Unheavenly Chorus: Unequal Political Voice and the Broken Promise of American Democracy* (Princeton, NJ: Princeton University Press, 2012), chap. 16, which contains extensive bibliographical discussion and citations not repeated here.

3. Michael Margolis and Gerson Moreno-Riaño, *The Prospect of Internet Democracy* (Burlington, VT: Ashgate, 2009), p. 17; see also pp. 22, 150. A thoughtful assessment of the implications for democracy of controversies that go viral can be found in Archon Fung and Jennifer Shkabatur, "Viral Engagement: Fast, Cheap, and Broad, but Good for Democracy? in *From Voice to Influence: Understanding Citizenship in a Digital Age*, ed. Danielle Allen and Jennifer S. Light (Chicago: University of Chicago Press, 2015), chap. 7.

4. We are very grateful to Lee Rainie and Scott Keeter for having responded to our initial suggestion about the importance of collecting systematic national data comparing online and offline participation, for allowing us to be partners in the design of the questionnaires, and for making those data available to us.

5. On this point, see David Karpf, "The Internet and Political Campaigns," *The Forum* 11 (2013): 421–422.

6. References to sources on which the discussion in this section is based can be found in Schlozman, Verba, and Brady, *Unheavenly Chorus,* pp. 487–488.

7. For alternative ways of thinking about the impact of the Internet on political activity, see, among others, Pippa Norris, *Digital Divide: Civic Engagement, Information Poverty, and the Internet Worldwide* (Cambridge: Cambridge University Press, 2001), pp. 229–231, as well as the essays in *From Voice to Influence,* ed. Allen and Light, especially Joseph Kahne, Ellen Middaugh, and Danielle Allen, "Youth New Media, and the Rise of Participatory Politics," chap. 2.

8. For contrasting perspectives, see the sources cited in Schlozman, Verba, and Brady, *Unheavenly Chorus,* p. 488; Jody C. Baumgartner and Jonathan S. Morris, "MyFaceTube Politics: Social Networking Web Sites and Political Engagement of Young Adults," *Social Science Computer Review* 28 (2010): 24–44; Bruce Bimber and Lauren Copeland, "Digital Media and Political Participation over Time in the U.S." *Journal of Information Technology and Politics* 10 (2013): 125–137; Rosa Borge and Ana Cardenal, "Surfing the Net: A Pathway to Participation for the Politically Uninterested?" *Policy & Internet* 3, no. 1 (2011): Article 3; Shelley Boulianne, "Does Internet Use Affect Engagement? A Meta-Analysis of Research," *Political Communication* 26 (2009): 193–211; Meredith Conroy, Jessica T. Feezell, and Mario Guerrero, "Facebook and Political Engagement: A Study of Online Political Group Membership and Offline Political Engagement," *Computers in Human Behavior* 28 (2012): 1535–1546; and R. J. Maratea, *The Politics of the Internet* (Lanham, MD: Lexington Books, 2014), chaps. 5, 8.

9. Norris, *Digital Divide,* pp. 230–231.

10. Quoted in Bruce Bimber, *Information and American Democracy* (Cambridge: Cambridge University Press, 2003), p. 151.

11. Figure cited in Bimber, *Information and American Democracy,* p. 159; on the history and remarkable politics of the E-Rate program, see pp. 150–161.

12. Figure cited in Karen Mossberger, Caroline J. Tolbert, and Mary Stansbury, *Virtual Inequality: Beyond the Digital Divide* (Washington, DC: Georgetown University Press, 2003), p. 129.

13. Karen Mossberger, Caroline Tolbert, and Ramona McNeal, *Digital Citizenship: The Internet, Society, and Participation* (Cambridge, MA: MIT Press, 2008), p. 1, define "digital citizens" as those who use the Internet on a daily basis. These authors demonstrate the impact on various outcomes, including political participation, of digital citizenship. We choose a much lower threshold, because we are interested in filtering out those who, through lack of access, interest, or capacity, do not use the Internet at all.

14. As usual, we use a scale based on education and family income and divide respondents into rough quintiles.

15. On age-related disparities in political activity, see the discussion and references in Schlozman, Verba, and Brady, *Unheavenly Chorus,* chap. 8.

16. An additional aspect of uneven Internet access and use has received somewhat less attention. Although some convergence has occurred, those who live in rural areas continue to be disadvantaged with regard to online access. See data from the Pew Internet and American Life Project in John B. Horrigan and Maeve Duggan, "Home Broadband 2015," at http://www.pewinternet.org/2015/12/21/home-broadband-2015/ (accessed April 18, 2016).

17. For a demonstration in 2010 of the potential of online voter mobilization that used Facebook users, see Robert M. Bond, Christopher J. Fariss, Jason J. Jones, Adam D. I. Kramer, Cameron

Marlow, Jaime F. Settle, and James H. Fowler, "A 61-Million-Person Experiment in Social Influence and Political Mobilization," *Nature* 489 (2012): 295–298.

18. The findings presented in this section are confirmed by the results of parallel analysis (not shown) of similar, but not identical, items contained in the 2012 American National Election Study.

19. The offline activity scale includes the following: contacted a national, state, or local government official in person, by phone call or by letter, about an issue that is important to you; signed a paper petition; sent a "letter to the editor" by regular mail to a newspaper or magazine; contributed money to a political candidate or party or any other organization or cause in person, by phone call, or through the mail. The online activity scale includes the following: contacted a national, state, or local government official online, by e-mail or by text message, about an issue that is important to you; signed a petition online; sent a "letter to the editor" to a newspaper or magazine online by e-mail or text message; contributed money online to a political candidate or party or any other organization or cause. The two scales are associated with a .50 Pearson correlation.

20. To the extent possible, we confirmed these findings using the limited data about online participation in the 2012 American National Election Study.

21. In the interests of brevity, we do not present results, which are parallel, for five-item scales using data from the 2008 Pew survey. See Schlozman, Verba, and Brady, *Unheavenly Chorus*, pp. 495–498.

22. Reflecting changes in the forms of social media over the four-year period, the questions in the 2008 and 2012 surveys sponsored by the Pew Internet and American Life Project are somewhat different:

Do you ever:
>2008: Use a social networking site like MySpace, Facebook, or LinkedIn.com?
>Use Twitter or another "micro-blogging" service to share updates about yourself or to see updates about others?
>2012: Use a social networking site like Facebook, LinkedIn or Google Plus?
>Use Twitter?

23. See, for example, Cliff Zukin, Scott Keeter, Molly Andolina, Krista Jenkins, and Michael X. Delli Carpini, *A New Engagement? Political Participation, Civic Life, and the Changing American Citizen* (Oxford: Oxford University Press, 2006), chap. 4.

24. Once again, consistent with the continuing evolution of the Internet, the 2008 and 2012 surveys sponsored by the Pew Internet and American Life Project differ somewhat in the items measuring political engagement on social media:

>2008: Thinking about what you have done on social networking sites like Facebook and MySpace, have you . . .
>Started or joined a political group, or group supporting a cause or a social networking site?
>Signed up as a "friend" of any candidates on a social networking site?
>Posted political news for friends or others to read on a social networking site?
>2012: Now thinking about how you use Twitter, or social networking sites such as Facebook and Google Plus . . .
>Do you currently belong to a group on a social networking site that is involved in political or social issues, or that is working to advance a cause?
>Do you currently follow any elected officials, candidates for office or other political figures on a social networking site or on Twitter?
>Do you ever use social networking sites or Twitter to post links to political stories or articles for others to read?

25. The relatively high level of political engagement on social media in the lowest SES level shown in the data for 2008 is perhaps a puzzle. It turns out that, among those who are politically engaged on social media, a high proportion of the low-SES are twentysomethings. Measuring SES among younger respondents is tricky, especially if they are still in school. When answering questions about income, they may consider their family income to be that derived from their own earnings or, especially if they are still living at home, that of their birth family. Particularly among those still in school, their own current incomes may not be especially predictive of their future earning power. Their SES is under construction: if they graduate, the educational component of their eventual SES will, by definition, rise. Their measured incomes are artificially depressed by their student status, but their incomes will be likely to rise more sharply than those of members of their cohort who leave school earlier. Forty-two percent of the respondents under thirty in the 2008 Pew survey reported still being in school either full or part time. For further discussion, see Schlozman, Verba, and Brady, *Unheavenly Chorus,* pp. 511–515.

26. We confirmed these assertions by conducting simple ordinary least squares regressions, in which online political participation was predicted by race or ethnicity, Internet use, and SES. Even with the latter two taken into account, there was a negative coefficient for being Latino or African American as opposed to non-Hispanic white.

27. These assertions were also confirmed with simple regressions.

Chapter 7: Social Movements and Ordinary Recruitment

1. For additional data analysis, detailed technical information, and extensive citations, see Henry E. Brady, Kay Lehman Schlozman, and Sidney Verba, "Prospecting for Participants," *American Political Science Review* 93 (1999): 153–168; and Kay Lehman Schlozman, Sidney Verba, and Henry E. Brady, *The Unheavenly Chorus: Unequal Political Voice and the Broken Promise of American Democracy* (Princeton, NJ: Princeton University Press, 2012), chap. 15.

2. For representative examples of the various views in the vast literature on social movements, see, among others, Hadley Cantril, *The Psychology of Social Movements* (Huntington, NY: R. E. Krieger, 1941); Anthony Oberschall, *Social Conflict and Social Movements* (Englewood Cliffs, NJ: Prentice-Hall, 1973); Doug McAdam, *Political Process and the Development of Black Insurgency 1930–1970* (Chicago: University of Chicago Press, 1982); William Gamson, *The Strategy of Social Protest,* 2nd ed. (Belmont, CA: Wadsworth, 1990); Aldon Morris and Carol McClurg Mueller, eds. *Frontiers of Social Movement Theory* (New Haven, CT: Yale University Press, 1992); Anthony Oberschall, *Social Movements: Ideologies, Interests, and Identities* (New Brunswick, NJ: Transaction, 1993); Doug McAdam, Sidney Tarrow, and Charles Tilly, *Dynamics of Contention* (New York: Cambridge University Press, 2001); Gerald Davis, Doug McAdam, Mayer N. Zald, and W. Richard Scott, eds., *Social Movements and Organization Theory* (New York: Cambridge University Press, 2005); Charles Tilly and Sidney Tarrow, *Contentious Politics* (Boulder, CO: Paradigm, 2007); David S. Meyer, *The Politics of Protest: Social Movements in America* (New York: Oxford University Press, 2007); and Sidney G. Tarrow, *Power in Movement: Social Movements and Contentious Politics,* 3rd ed. (New York: Cambridge University Press, 2011).

3. Tarrow, *Power in Movement,* pp. 7–8, emphasis in the original.

4. Gamson, *Strategy of Protest,* p. 16.

5. Doug McAdam, John D. McCarthy, and Mayer N. Zald, "Social Movements" in *Handbook of Sociology,* ed. Neil J. Smelser (Newbury Park, CA: Sage, 1988), pp. 707–711; McAdam, Tarrow, and Tilly, *Dynamics of Contention,* pp. 38–48.

6. See McAdam, *Political Process and Black Insurgency,* esp. pp. 128–132.

7. See, for example, the argument and citations in Jennifer Earl, Jayson Hunt, R. Kelly Garrett, and Aysenur Dal, "New Technologies and Social Movements," in *The Oxford Handbook of Social Movements*, ed. Donatella Della Porta and Mario Diani (Oxford: Oxford University Press, 2015), chap. 22.

8. Elizabeth Day, "#BlackLivesMatter: The Birth of a New Civil Rights Movement," *The Guardian,* July 19, 2015.

9. Charles M. Payne, *I've Got the Light of Freedom* (Berkeley: University of California Press, 1995), p. 133.

10. McAdam, McCarthy, and Zald, "Social Movements," p. 702. In *Affirmative Advocacy: Race, Class and Gender in Interest Group Politics* (Chicago: University of Chicago Press, 2007), Dara Z. Strolovich makes this point about political organizations that represent disadvantaged groups.

11. See John D. McCarthy and Mayer N. Zald, "Resource Mobilization and Social Movements: A Partial Theory," *American Journal of Sociology* 82 (1977): 1212–1241.

12. See, for example, Jo Freeman, *The Politics of Women's Liberation* (New York: David McKay, 1975); Yen Le Espiritu, *Asian American Panethnicity: Bridging Institutions and Identities* (Philadelphia: Temple University Press, 1992); and Belinda Robnett, *How Long? How Long? African-American Women in the Struggle for Civil Rights* (New York: Oxford University Press, 1997).

13. Of course, eschewing leadership and division of labor imposes costs when it comes to efficiency and effectiveness in accomplishing movement objectives.

14. Tarrow, *Power in Movement*, pp. 96–98.

15. See, for example, Daniel Schlozman, *When Movements Anchor Parties* (Princeton, NJ: Princeton University Press, 2015), chap. 2. There is disagreement about whether the natural evolution of social movements into more sustainable forms undermines their capacity to activate and represent the disadvantaged. For contrasting views, see Frances Fox Piven and Richard A. Cloward, *Poor People's Movements: Why They Succeed, How They Fail* (New York: Pantheon, 1977); and the essays in "Symposium: Poor People's Movements," *Perspectives on Politics* 1 (2003): 707–735.

16. Because it is the only survey that includes the array of relevant variables needed, we are forced to use data from the Citizen Participation Study of 1990 in this analysis.

17. Thus, what we know about the characteristics of recruiters is derived from reports of targets. To the extent that we are making inferences about the intentions of recruiters, we are doing so on the basis of revealed preferences.

18. Because a small proportion of respondents were active both spontaneously and in response to a request, the sum of these two numbers may exceed the numbers active in Figure 7.1.A.

19. Income predicts who is asked to donate, not who will agree to do so. Hence, the pattern in these data reflects processes of selection by recruiters, not decisions by their targets to say yes.

20. Information in this paragraph is taken from Alexander Hertel-Fernandez, "How Employers Recruit Their Workers into Politics—And Why Political Scientists Should Care," *Perspectives on Politics* 14 (2016): 410–421. See also Andrew Ross Sorkin, "In Politics, Workers Follow Boss's Lead," *New York Times*, September 6, 2016.

21. See the analyses and references in, among others, Janelle Wong, *Democracy's Promise: Immigrants and American Civic Institutions* (Ann Arbor: University of Michigan Press, 2006), esp. chaps. 3, 9; S. Karthick Ramakrishnan and Irene Bloemraad, "Introduction: Civic and Political Inequalities," in *Civic Hopes and Political Realities,* ed. S. Karthick Ramakrishnan and Irene Bloemraad (New York: Russell Sage Foundation, 2008), chap. 1; and Kristi Andersen, *New Immigrant Communities: Finding a Place in Local Politics* (Boulder, CO: Lynne Rienner, 2010), esp. chaps. 1, 2, 5.

The received wisdom of the effectiveness of the historical urban party machines in bringing immigrants into politics has come in for some revision. See, for example, Steven Erie, *Rainbow's End: Irish Americans and the Dilemmas of Urban Machine Politics, 1840–1985* (Berkeley: University of California Press, 1988); and Gerald Gamm, *The Making of New Deal Democrats* (Chicago: University of Chicago Press, 1989).

Chapter 8: Who Sings in the Heavenly Chorus?

1. This chapter draws from the intellectual framework contained in Kay L. Schlozman and John T. Tierney, *Organized Interests and American Democracy* (New York: Harper and Row, 1986), chap. 4; and Kay Lehman Schlozman, Sidney Verba, and Henry E. Brady, *The Unheavenly Chorus: Unequal Political Voice and the Broken Promise of American Democracy* (Princeton, NJ: Princeton University Press, 2012), chaps. 10–14. For further discussion and additional bibliography, see chaps. 10, 11.

2. James C. Scott, "Handling Historical Comparisons Cross-Nationally," in *Political Corruption: Concepts and Contexts*, 3rd ed., ed. Arnold J. Heidenheimer and Michael Johnston (New Brunswick, NJ: Transaction, 2002), p. 135, emphasis in the original. In a similar vein, Mark E. Warren asserts that "corruption of democracy is a violation of the norm of equal inclusion of all affected by a collectivity," in "What Does Corruption Mean in a Democracy?" *American Journal of Political Science* 48 (2004): 334. For a discussion of concern about corruption as rooted in concern about inequality and an alternative perspective, see Zephyr Teachout, *Corruption in America: From Benjamin Franklin's Snuff Box to Citizens United* (Cambridge, MA: Harvard University Press, 2014), chap. 16.

3. Transparency International constructs scores on the basis of ratings in surveys of businesspeople and country analysts. In the past five years, the United States has been ranked between 16 and 19 every year (behind most of the countries of northern Europe as well as Canada, New Zealand, Australia, and Singapore) and ranked eighteenth out of 176 countries in 2016. See https://www.transparency.org/research/cpi/overview (accessed June 18, 2017).

4. For a helpful discussion that includes a variety of perspectives on the question of equal political voice when representation is by organizations, see David Lowery, Frank R. Baumgartner, Joost Berkhout, Jeffrey M. Berry, Darren Halpin, Marie Hojnacki, Heike Klüver, Beate Kohler-Koch, Jeremy Richardson, and Kay Lehman Schlozman, "Images of an Unbiased Interest System," *Journal of European Public Policy* 22 (2015): 1212–1231.

5. For more detailed discussion and references to the extensive literature, see Schlozman, Verba, and Brady, *Unheavenly Chorus*, pp. 275–281.

An alternative perspective from that presented here, that of population ecology theory, draws from insights in the biological sciences and shifts the focus from the micro-level processes that lead to the formation of individual organizations to a macro-level consideration of organized interest communities. See Virginia Gray and David Lowery, in *The Population Ecology of Interest Representation* (Ann Arbor: University of Michigan Press, 1996). While their work is more theory driven and less descriptive than ours and they have different intellectual concerns, to the extent that our analyses intersect, our findings are similar.

6. E. E. Schattschneider, *Semi-Sovereign People* (New York: Holt, Rinehart and Winston, 1960); Mancur Olson Jr., *The Logic of Collective Action: Public Goods and the Theory of Groups* (Cambridge, MA: Harvard University Press, 1965).

7. Schattschneider, *Semi-Sovereign People*, p. 35.

8. James Q. Wilson, *Political Organizations* (New York: Basic Books, 1973), especially chaps. 2, 3.

9. See, for example, Robert H. Salisbury, "An Exchange Theory of Interest Groups," *Midwest Journal of Political Science* 13 (1969): 1–32; and Norman Frolich, Joe A. Oppenheimer, and Oran R. Young, *Political Leadership and Collective Goods* (Princeton, NJ: Princeton University Press, 1971).

10. Jack L. Walker, *Interest Groups in America: Patrons, Professions, and Social Movements* (Ann Arbor: University of Michigan Press, 1991), especially chap. 5.

11. Anthony J. Nownes, "Patronage and Citizen Groups: A Reevaluation," *Political Behavior* 17 (1995): 203–221.

12. On the subject of social movement organizations, see, for example, John D. McCarthy and Mayer N. Zald, "Resource Mobilization and Social Movements: A Partial Theory," *American Journal of Sociology* 82 (1977): 1212–1241; and Mayer N. Zald and John D. McCarthy, *Social Movements in an Organizational Society* (New Brunswick, NJ: Transaction, 1987); David Meyer, *The Politics of Protest: Social Movements in America* (Oxford: Oxford University Press 2007), pp. 36–37.

13. Robert H. Salisbury, in "Interest Representation: The Dominance of Institutions," *American Political Science Review* 78 (1984): 64–76, first pointed to the significance of what he called "institutions" in interest representation. See also David Lowery, Virginia Gray, Jennifer Anderson, and Adam J. Newmark, "Collective Action and the Mobilization of Institutions," *Journal of Politics* 66 (2004): 684–705.

Kay Lehman Schlozman, Philip Edward Jones, Hye Young You, Traci Burch, Sidney Verba, and Henry E. Brady explore the meaning for democratic representation when memberless organizations dominate among organizations active in politics in "Organizations and the Democratic Representation of Interests: What Does It Mean When Those Organizations Have No Members?" *Perspectives on Politics* 13: (2015): 1017–1029.

14. The Washington Representatives Study contains data for 1981, 1991, 2001, 2006, and 2011 and includes profiles of more than 40,000 organizations that are or have been active in national politics. Of these organizations, more than 33,000 were listed in one of the *Washington Representatives* directories. The others were retrieved from government archives as having been active in other ways, such as making PAC contributions or filing amicus briefs. Most of the data presented in Chapters 8, 9, and 11 draw on the information provided on organizations listed in the directories. For detailed information about the directory and the data base constructed from it, see Schlozman, Verba, and Brady, *The Unheavenly Chorus*, Appendix C.

The directory, *Washington Representatives* (Washington, DC: Columbia Books), is published annually. Note that it includes neither organizations that drop in on Washington politics on an occasional basis without maintaining an ongoing presence nor organizations whose participation is confined to writing checks to campaigns, testifying before federal regulatory agencies, or filing *amicus* briefs. In addition, the directory does not list organizations active only in state or local politics, an omission with possible consequences for our concern with the socioeconomic inequalities of political voice. It is possible that the disadvantaged achieve greater voice—for example, through neighborhood groups—in local politics than in national politics.

15. For details on the coding of organizational membership status, see Schlozman et al., "Organizations and Democratic Representation."

16. See Steven Greenhouse, "The Mystery of the Vanishing Pay Raise," *New York Times*, October 31, 2015.

17. Throughout this chapter, we use the names of real organizations that appear somewhere in the Washington Representative database. However, the names listed in any directory may have changed since then. In addition, organizations do sometimes go out of business. As a result, some of the organizations chosen for illustrative purposes may no longer exist.

18. To accommodate organizations that, in the nature of their organizational mission, membership, or structure, really do belong in more than one category, our coding rules permitted us

to place an organization into as many as three categories. For discussion, see Schlozman, Verba, and Brady, *Unheavenly Chorus*, pp. 340–344.

19. For extensive bibliographical citations and a cogent critique of the possibility of drawing inferences from counts of organizations, see David Lowery and Virginia Gray, "Bias in the Heavenly Chorus: Interests in Society and before Government," *Journal of Theoretical Politics* 16 (2004): 5–29. Many of their criticisms had been noted in earlier works—including Schlozman and Tierney, *Organized Interests and American Democracy*, chap. 4.

20. We looked more closely at the detailed categories to ensure that they were not obscuring compensatory tendencies. We found, on the contrary, that the distribution of organizations into categories actually may have underestimated the extent of bias in the pressure system. When appropriate data were available, we found that within any particular category of organizations, large and affluent organizations are much more likely than smaller ones to be represented in Washington politics. In addition, survey data show that members and supporters of organizations that take stands in politics are stratified by social class. Furthermore, even among those affiliated with such organizations, the affluent and well educated are more likely to be activists and to feel represented by the organization. For evidence and discussion, see Schlozman, Verba, and Brady, *The Unheavenly Chorus*, chap. 13.

21. This figure includes corporations (both domestic and foreign), trade and other business associations (again, both domestic and foreign), farm organizations, occupational associations, labor unions, and institutions and organizations in the health and educational sectors. (In Table 8.3, foreign corporations and foreign trade and other business organizations are in the category of foreign organizations. Farm organizations are grouped with "other organizations.")

22. Using data coded from approximately 19,000 1996 lobbying reports, Frank R. Baumgartner and Beth L. Leech, in "Interest Niches and Policy Bandwagons: Patterns of Interest Group Involvement in National Politics," *Journal of Politics* 63 (2001): 1191–1213, find (as shown in their tables 1–2) a distribution of lobbying organizations not very different from that described here.

23. The umbrella category "corporations" includes partnerships and sole proprietorships; U.S. subsidiaries of foreign corporations; and for-profit firms of professionals, such as law and consulting firms as well as corporations.

24. There is widespread agreement on this point, even among scholars who disagree in their assessments of the aggregate weight of business interests in politics. A helpful review article is David M. Hart, "'Business' Is Not an Interest Group: On the Study of Companies in American National Politics," *Annual Review of Political Science* 7 (2004): 47–69.

25. Baumgartner and Leech, in "Interest Niches and Policy Bandwagons," p. 1204, find that on many issues only one or two interests are involved and that "business advantage, while great overall, is even more striking in the cases where the fewest interest groups are active." Using a very different kind of data, Gilens and Page show how rare it is for business interests to oppose one another in a policy controversy. Martin Gilens and Benjamin I. Page, "Testing Theories of American Politics: Elites, Interest Groups, and Average Citizens," *Perspectives on Politics* 12 (2014): 575.

26. See, for example, Mark A. Smith, *American Business and Political Power: Public Opinion Elections and Democracy* (Chicago: University of Chicago Press, 2000). For a contrary account of the activity and success of business in influencing policy, see Jacob S. Hacker and Paul Pierson, *Winner-Take-All Politics: How Washington Made the Rich Richer and Turned Its Back on the Middle Class* (New York: Simon and Schuster, 2009).

27. Following the categorization used by the Census, we include fishing and forestry along with farming.

28. On the role of unions as "vigorous champion on pocketbook issues" for middle- and working-class Americans, see Hacker and Pierson, *Winner-Take-All Politics*, p. 143.

29. Frank R. Baumgartner, Jeffrey M. Berry, Marie Hojnacki, David C. Kimball, and Beth L. Leech, *Lobbying and Policy Change: Who Wins, Who Loses, and Why* (Chicago: University of Chicago Press, 2009), pp. 10–11.

30. Figures are taken from the Web site of the Bureau of Labor Statistics, http://www.bls.gov/news.release/union2.nr0.htm (accessed September 19, 2015).

31. In categorizing occupational associations as professional associations, we followed the U.S. Census definition of professional occupations, which includes certain occupations (for example, professional athlete) that do not fully conform to this criterion.

32. The remainder of the paragraph is based on a comparison of the data about other occupational associations in our database with U.S. Census data found at www.census.gov/compendia/statab/labor_force_employment_earnings/ (accessed September 26, 2006).

33. For details of coding decisions, see Schlozman, Verba, and Brady, *The Unheavenly Chorus*, pp. 328–331. We have mentioned the puzzle of inferring representation for memberless organizations that have no individual members. In the right-hand column in Figure 8.1, we make the perhaps unwarranted assumptions that corporations and trade associations represent the interests of managers and executives and that all organizations in the educational and health sectors represent the interests of the professionals that staff such institutions.

34. The pattern of results changes somewhat if we consider only membership associations of individuals (and omit such memberless organizations as corporations, universities, and hospitals and associations of memberless organizations). Under these circumstances, professionals are very substantially overrepresented and managers are somewhat overrepresented. However, blue-collar and service workers, along with those out of the workforce, continue to be very substantially underrepresented.

35. Many such organizations not only engage in advocacy but also provide direct services. Our coders were instructed to consider the overall balance in organizational activities in placing an organization into one of the two categories.

36. Jeffrey M. Berry with David Arons, *A Voice for Nonprofits* (Washington, DC: Brookings Institution, 2003), p. 65.

37. We are aware that the term *identity groups* is a contested one and use it to denote organizations in which the organizing principle is some noneconomic demographic characteristic.

38. See Richard Witmer and Frederick J. Boehmke, "American Indian Incorporation in the Post–Indian Gaming Regulatory Act Era," *Social Science Journal* 44 (2007): 127–145. Especially as interpreted by the Supreme Court, the Indian Gaming Regulatory Act has increased the political involvement of tribal governments with state governments. See the essays in *The New Politics of Indian Gaming*, ed. Kenneth N. Hansen and Tracy A. Skopek (Reno: University of Nevada Press, 2011).

39. This point is made by Andrew S. McFarland in *Public Interest Lobbies: Decision Making on Energy* (Washington, DC: American Enterprise Institute, 1976), chap. 2.

40. The correlation coefficient is .04. Gilens and Page, "Testing Theories of American Politics," 570–571.

41. Matt Grossman, *The Not-So-Special Interests* (Stanford, CA: Stanford University Press, 2012), pp. 54–55, finds that "the mean socio-economic status of a constituency is significantly correlated with the number of organizations and staff."

Chapter 9: Representing Interests through Organizational Activity

1. "America Can Save $1 Trillion and Get Better Health Care" CNN Opinion, June 27, 2017, at http://www.cnn.com/2017/06/27/opinions/fixing-americas-health-care-sachs/index.html.

2. Using 2001 as the base year, we recorded data from the 2001 Washington Representatives directory, organizations' Web sites, congressional sources, the Federal Election Commission (FEC), Supreme Court records, opensecrets.org, and politicalmoneyline.com about the resources and political activities of organizations active in national politics. We then added data for spending on lobbying to include 2006 and 2011. Unfortunately, we were unable to find an analogous source that would allow us to aggregate data about organizational activity in the executive branch.

3. Thomas Holyoke, in "Choosing Battlegrounds: Interest Group Lobbying across Multiple Venues," *Political Research Quarterly* 56 (2003): 325–336, considers the multiple factors at play in an organization's decision about whether to get involved and its decision about how intensely to get involved.

4. For a concise summary of the various tactics of influence at the disposal of organized interest representatives and the policy venues in which they can be marshaled, see Anthony J. Nownes, *Total Lobbying* (Cambridge: Cambridge University Press, 2006), pp. 16–26.

5. See the arguments made and the literature cited in, for example, Beth L. Leech and Frank R. Baumgartner, "Lobbying Friends and Foes in Washington," in *Interest Group Politics*, ed. Allan J. Cigler and Burdett A. Loomis, 5th ed. (Washington, DC: CQ Press, 1998), chap 10; Marie Hojnacki and David C. Kimball, "The Who and How of Organizations' Lobbying Strategies in Committee," *Journal of Politics* 61 (1999): 999–1024; and Richard L. Hall and Alan V. Deardorff, "Lobbying as Legislative Subsidy," *American Political Science Review* 100 (2006): 69–84.

6. See, for example, Hojnacki and Kimball, "Organizations' Lobbying Strategies," and Stephen Ansolabehere, James M. Snyder Jr., and Micky Tripathi, "Are PAC Contributions and Lobbying Linked? New Evidence from the 1995 Lobby Disclosure Act," *Business and Politics* 4 (2002): 131–155. For an alternative perspective, see Nolan McCarty and Lawrence S. Rothenberg, "Commitment and the Campaign Contribution Contract," *American Journal of Political Science* 40 (1996): 872–904.

7. See Sanford C. Gordon and Catherine Hafer, "Flexing Muscle: Corporate Political Expenditures as Signals to the Bureaucracy," *American Political Science Review* 99 (2005): 245–261.

8. For discussions of factors predisposing an organization to choose in-house or outside representation, see Kay Lehman Schlozman, Sidney Verba, and Henry E. Brady, *The Unheavenly Chorus: Unequal Political Voice and the Broken Promise of American Democracy* (Princeton, NJ: Princeton University Press, 2012), pp. 397–399; and Lee Drutman, *The Business of America Is Lobbying* (Oxford and New York: Oxford University Press, 2015), pp. 134–137.

9. On grassroots lobbying, see Thomas L. Gais and Jack L. Walker Jr., "Pathways to Influence in American Politics," in *Mobilizing Interest Groups in America*, ed. Jack L. Walker Jr. (Ann Arbor: University of Michigan Press, 1991), chap. 6; and Ken Kollman, *Outside Lobbying* (Princeton, NJ: Princeton University Press, 1998).

10. Hojnacki and Kimball, "Organizations' Lobbying Strategies," p. 1000.

11. Sharon Beder, "Public Relations' Role in Manufacturing Artificial Grass Roots Coalitions," *Public Relations Quarterly* 13 (1998): 20–23; and Thomas P. Lyon and John W. Maxwell, "Astroturf: Interest Group Lobbying and Corporate Strategy," *Journal of Economics and Management Strategy* 13 (2004): 561–597.

12. Linda L. Fowler and Ronald G. Shaiko, "The Grass Roots Connection: Environmental Activists and Senate Roll Calls," *American Journal of Political Science* 31 (1987): 485.

13. Hojnacki and Kimball, "Organizations' Lobbying Strategies," p. 1004.

14. Gais and Walker, "Pathways to Influence," p. 258.

15. R. Kenneth Godwin, *One Billion Dollars of Influence: The Direct Marketing of Politics* (Chatham, NJ: Chatham House, 1988).

16. William P. Browne, "Organized Interests, Grassroots Confidants, and Congress," in *Interest Group Politics*, ed. Allan J. Cigler and Burdett A. Loomis, 4th ed. (Washington, DC: CQ Press, 1995), pp. 284–285.

17. Detailed discussion of the propensity of organizations in different categories to engage in various forms of advocacy and extensive citations can be found in Schlozman, Verba, and Brady, *Unheavenly Chorus*, chap. 14.

18. We used information from the Center for Responsive Politics, which discusses its sources and coding methods at https://www.opensecrets.org/lobby/methodology.php. If opensecrets.org did not have any information about the lobbying spending of an organization, we also consulted the data contained at politicalmoneyline.org (now CQMoneyLine).

19. On the LDA of 1995, see Ronald G. Shaiko, "Making the Connection: Organized Interests, Political Representation, and the Changing Rules of the Game in Washington Politics," in *The Interest Group Connection: Electioneering, Lobbying, and Policymaking in Washington*, ed. Paul S. Herrnson, Ronald G. Shaiko, and Clyde Wilcox, 2nd ed. (Washington: Congressional Quarterly Press, 2005), pp. 17–19; and Jonathan D. Salant, "Highlights of the Lobby Bill," *CQ Weekly Online*, December 2, 1995, p. 3632. For additional details, see "Provisions: Bill Targets Lobbying Law Loopholes," *CQ Weekly Online*, November 11, 1995, pp. 3477–3478. Recent changes are summarized in a memo from the Clerk of the U.S. House of Representatives, "Lobbying Disclosure Act Guidance," http://lobbyingdisclosure.house.gov/amended_lda_guide.html (accessed on September 22, 2015).

20. In 2006, political scientist James Thurber estimated that about 100,000 people were involved in government influence, a figure much greater than the number of registered lobbyists at the time. Quoted in Lisa Caruso, "What's in a Number?" *National Journal*, March 26, 2006.

For discussion of the multiple reasons that we were able to find data about lobbying expenditures for only 62 percent of the organizations listed in the 2011 directory, see Schlozman, Verba, and Brady, *Unheavenly Chorus*, pp. 408–409.

Note that unless they establish a parallel, non-tax-deductible 501(c)4 arm, organizations that fall into the 501(c)3 designation under the tax code—that is, nonprofits for which contributions are tax deductible—are legally enjoined from undertaking significant lobbying, though not from engaging in many other kinds of political activity. For discussion of how an arcane tax provision, "H election," can permit nonprofits to ignore lobbying limits, see Jeffrey M. Berry with David F. Arons, *A Voice for Nonprofits* (Washington, DC: Brookings Institution, 2003), pp. 54–65.

21. This finding is similar to that contained in Frank R. Baumgartner and Beth L. Leech, in "Interest Niches and Policy Bandwagons: Patterns of Interest Group Involvement in National Politics," *Journal of Politics* 63 (2001): table 3.

22. On testifying as a form of advocacy by organized interests, see Kevin M. Leyden, "Interest Group Resources and Testimony at Congressional Hearings," *Legislative Studies Quarterly* 20 (1995): 431–439; and John R. Wright, *Interest Groups and Congress* (Boston: Allyn and Bacon, 1996), pp. 40–43.

23. See Leyden, "Interest Group Resources and Testimony," p. 433. With respect to executive branch lobbying, Scott R. Furlong, in "Exploring Interest Group Participation in Executive Policymaking," in *The Interest Group Connection*, ed. Herrnson, Shaiko, and Wilcox, p. 284, makes the point that, even with the *Federal Register* now available online, keeping tabs on executive branch activity is likely to be time-consuming and expensive.

24. For three forms of activity we were able to locate and code the activity of all organizations that took part—including organizations not listed in the 2001 *Washington Representatives* directory. The directory lists only 32.2 percent of the organizations that testified in Congress, 29.5 percent of those that filed an amicus brief, and 47.7 percent of those that made a PAC donation during the specified periods. For reasons other than error, the directory is not a complete

listing for these forms of activity. According to Valerie Sheridan of Columbia Books, organizations move in and out of Washington politics, and the directory for any given year is a snapshot as of a particular date. Therefore, because our measures for testifying, filing briefs, or making PAC donations each cover at least two years, it is likely that some of the active organizations were listed on the Web site of the directory or in a directory for another year but not in the 2001 directory. In addition, the directory does not list any organization that testifies but does not have a Washington presence or a PAC that is run out of an office in Washington.

25. An especially clear account of organized interest activity in the courts can be found in Lee Epstein, "Courts and Interest Groups," in *The American Courts: A Critical Assessment*, ed. John B. Gates and Charles A. Johnson (Washington, DC: CQ Press, 1992), chap. 13.

26. See, for example, Epstein, "Courts and Interest Groups;" and Joseph D. Kearney and Thomas W. Merrill, "The Influence of Amicus Curiae Briefs on the Supreme Court," *University of Pennsylvania Law Review* 148 (2000): 751–754.

27. On this point, see Lucius J. Barker, "Third Parties in Litigation: A Systemic View of the Judicial Function," *Journal of Politics* 29 (1967): 53 ff.

28. See Bruce J. Ennis, "Effective Amicus Briefs," *Catholic University Law Review* 33 (1984): 606; Gregory A. Caldeira and John R. Wright, "Organized Interests and Agenda Setting in the U.S. Supreme Court," *American Political Science Review* 82 (1988): 1111; Donald Songer and Reginald S. Sheehan, "Interest Group Success in the Courts: Amicus Participation in the Supreme Court," *Political Research Quarterly* 46 (1993): 351–352; Kevin T. McGuire and Barbara Palmer, "Issue Fluidity on the Supreme Court," *American Political Science Review* 89 (1995): 696; James F. Spriggs II and Paul J. Wahlbeck, "Amicus Curiae and the Role of Information at the Supreme Court," *Political Research Quarterly* 50 (1997): 371–373; Luther T. Mumford, "When Does the Curiae Need an Amicus?" *Journal of Appellate Practice and Process* 1 (1999): 281–282; and Paul M. Collins Jr., "Friends of the Court: Examining the Influence of Amicus Curiae Participation in U.S. Supreme Court Litigation," *Law and Society Review* 38 (2004): 813.

29. For two different estimates of the cost of drafting an amicus curiae brief, see Caldeira and Wright, "Organized Interests and Agenda Setting," p. 1112; and Gregory A. Caldeira and John R. Wright, "Amici Curiae before the Supreme Court: Who Participates, When, and How Much?" *Journal of Politics* 52 (1990): 800. On the strategic calculations made by those who file amicus briefs, see Lisa A. Solowiej and Paul M. Collins Jr., "Counteractive Lobbying in the U.S. Supreme Court," *American Politics Research* 37 (2009): 670–699.

30. On this point, see Lee Epstein and C. K. Rowland, "Debunking the Myth of Interest Group Invincibility in the Courts," *American Political Science Review* 85 (1991): 206; and Thomas G. Hansford, "Information Provision, Organizational Constraints, and the Decision to Submit an Amicus Curiae Brief in a U.S. Supreme Court Case," *Political Research Quarterly* 57 (2004): 219–230.

31. In a mail survey of lawyers who represented petitioners before the Supreme Court at the agenda stage, Kevin T. McGuire, "Amicus Curiae and Strategies for Gaining Access to the Supreme Court," *Political Research Quarterly* 47 (1994): 825, found that 23 percent of them solicited amicus briefs on their clients' behalf.

32. See Kevin T. McGuire and Gregory A. Caldeira, "Lawyers, Organized Interests, and the Law of Obscenity: Agenda Setting in the Supreme Court," *American Political Science Review* 87 (1993): 723–724, and Collins, "Friends of the Court."

33. For detailed results and discussion of how these data were assembled, see Schlozman, Verba, and Brady, *Unheavenly Chorus*, pp. 416–420.

34. Because many briefs were signed by more than one organization, we refer to signings as the unit of analysis rather than to briefs.

35. See Adam Liptak, "Justices Offer Receptive Ear to Business Interests," *New York Times*, December 19, 2010.

36. On the multiple ways that organizations get involved in campaigns, see Paul S. Herrnson, "Interest Groups and Campaigns: The Electoral Connection," in *The Interest Group Connection*, ed. Herrnson, Shaiko, and Wilcox, chap. 2.

37. Federal Election Committee data taken from Harold W. Stanley and Richard G. Niemi, *Vital Statistics on American Politics 2009–2010* (Washington, DC: CQ Press, 2010), pp. 91 and 93; and Harold W. Stanley and Richard G. Niemi, *Vital Statistics on American Politics 2013–2014* (Washington, DC: CQ Press, 2013), pp. 94–95.

38. https://www.opensecrets.org/pacs/toppacs.php (accessed August 2, 2017).

39. https://www.opensecrets.org/overview/topindivs.php (accessed August 2, 2017).

40. Jonathan Weisman, "G.O.P. Reveals Donors and the Price of Access," *New York Times*, September 24, 2014; and Chisun Lee and Lawrence Norden, "The Secret Power behind Local Elections," *New York Times*, June 26, 2016.

Chapter 10: Growing Economic Inequality and Its (Partially) Political Roots

1. Paul Krugman, "Now That's Rich," *New York Times*, May 9, 2014.

2. Josh Bivens, "Walton Family Net Worth is a Case Study Why Growing Wealth Concentration Isn't Just an Academic Worry," Economic Policy Institute Working Economics Blog, posted October 3, 2014, at http://www.epi.org/blog/walton-family-net-worth-case-study-growing/ (accessed December 18, 2015).

3. The minimum wage for 1978 is found at U.S. Department of Labor, Wage and Hour Division, "History of Federal Minimum Wage Rates under the Fair Labor Standards Act, 1938–2009," at http://www.dol.gov/whd/minwage/chart.htm; cost of living adjustment is taken from U. S. Department of Labor, Bureau of Labor Statistics, "CPI Inflation Calculator," at http://www.bls.gov/data/inflation_calculator.htm; the rate of growth of CEO pay (including the value of stock options exercised in a given year plus salary, bonuses, restricted stock grants, and long-term incentive payouts) for chief executives of the top 350 U.S. firms is taken from Lawrence Mishel and Alyssa Davis, "CEO Pay Has Grown 90 Times Faster Than Typical Worker Pay since 1978," Economic Policy Institute, July 1, 2015, at http://www.epi.org/publication/ceo-pay-has-grown-90-times-faster-than-typical-worker-pay-since-1978/ (all accessed December 26, 2015).

4. Data are for the thirty-four members of the Organisation for Economic Co-operation and Development (OECD). The poverty rate is the proportion of the population whose incomes are below half the median for the population as a whole. *OECD Factbook 2014: Economic, Environmental and Social Statistics* (Paris: OECD Publishing, 2014), pp. 66–67, at http://dx.doi.org/10.1787/factbook-2014-en (accessed December 18, 2015).

5. Catherine Rampell, "Freebies for the Rich," *New York Times Magazine*, September 29, 2013.

6. See, for example, Mark D. Brewer, *Split: Class and Cultural Divides in American Politics* (Washington, DC: CQ Press, 2007); Larry M. Bartels, *Unequal Democracy* (Princeton, NJ: Princeton University Press, 2008); and Jeffrey M. Stonecash, "Class in American Politics," in *New Directions in American Politics*, ed. Jeffrey M. Stonecash (New York: Routledge, 2010), chap. 7.

7. For extensive additional bibliography and discussion of technical matters, see Kay Lehman Schlozman, Sidney Verba, and Henry E. Brady, *The Unheavenly Chorus: Unequal Political Voice and the Broken Promise of American Democracy* (Princeton, NJ: Princeton University Press, 2012), chap. 3. See also Thomas Piketty and Emmanuel Saez, "Income Inequality in the United States, 1913–1998," *Quarterly Journal of Economics* 118 (2003): 1–39; Gary Burtless and Christopher Jencks, "American Inequality and Its Consequences," in *Agenda for the Nation*, ed. Henry J. Aaron, James M Lindsay, and Pietro S. Nivola (Washington, DC: Brookings Institution,

2003), chap. 3; Lawrence Mishel, Josh Bivens, Elise Gould, and Heidi Shierholz, *The State of Working America*, 12th ed. (Ithaca, NY: Cornell University Press, 2012); Thomas Piketty, *Capital in the Twenty-First Century*, trans. Arthur Goldhammer (Cambridge, MA: The Belnap Press of Harvard University Press, 2014), esp. part III; Anthony Atkinson, *Inequality: What Can Be Done?* (Cambridge, MA: Harvard University Press, 2015), chap. 1.

8. There is controversy among economists about the long-used official definition of poverty. An alternative measure, which takes account of in-kind government benefits, shows lower rates of poverty among children and higher rates among adults, especially the elderly. See Benjamin Bridges and Robert V. Gesumaria, "The Supplemental Poverty Measure (SPM) and Children: How and Why the SPM and Official Poverty Estimates Differ," *Social Security Bulletin* 75 (2015): 55–81; and Kathleen Short, "The Supplemental Poverty Measure: 2014," Report Number: P60-254, *Current Population Reports*, September 2015, at https://www.census.gov/library/publications/2015/demo/p60-254.html (accessed on July 31, 2016).

9. Joseph E. Stiglitz, *The Price of Inequality* (New York: W. W. Norton, 2013), p. 20. On desperate poverty, see Kathryn J. Edin and H. Luke Shaefer, *$2.00 a Day: Living on Almost Nothing in America* (Boston: Houghton Mifflin Harcourt, 2015).

10. Mishel, Bivens, Gould, and Shierholz, *State of Working America*, p. 196.

11. Mishel and Davis, "CEO Pay Has Grown." The figure is for chief executives of the top 350 U.S. firms and includes the value of stock options exercised in a given year plus salary, bonuses, restricted stock grants, and long-term incentive payouts.

12. Gretchen Morgenson, "Comparing Paychecks with CEOs," *New York Times*, April 12, 2015.

13. See Lucian Bebchuk and Jesse Fried, *Pay without Performance: The Unfulfilled Promise of Executive Compensation* (Cambridge, MA: Harvard University Press, 2004).

14. Cited in Robert B. Reich, *Beyond Outrage* (New York: Random House, Vintage Books, 2012), p. 11.

15. Stiglitz, *Price of Inequality*, p. 257.

16. On the erosion of the private welfare state, see Michael B. Katz, *The Price of Citizenship: Redefining the American Welfare State* (New York: Henry Holt, 2001), chaps. 6–8; and Jacob S. Hacker, *The Great Risk Shift: The Assault on American Jobs, Families, Health Care, and Retirement and How You Can Fight Back* (Oxford: Oxford University Press, 2006).

17. Figure taken from Employment Benefit Research Institute, *EBRI Databook on Employee Benefits*, table 5.1a, at https://www.ebri.org/pdf/publications/books/databook/DB.Chapter%2005.pdf (accessed on March 8, 2016).

18. Emmanuel Saez and Gabriel Zucman, "Wealth Inequality in the United States since 1913: Evidence from Capitalized Income Data," *Quarterly Journal of Economics* 131 (2016): 520, 523.

19. Discussion in this paragraph is taken from Mishel, Bivens, Gould, and Shierholz, *State of Working America*, pp. 376, 385–395.

20. This section draws on arguments and data in Burtless and Jencks, "American Inequality"; Timothy M. Smeeding, "Public Policy, Economic Inequality, and Poverty: The United States in Comparative Perspective," *Social Science Quarterly* 86 (2005), 955–983; Picketty, *Capital*, especially chaps. 8–9; and Atkinson, *Inequality*, chap. 2.

Making cross-national comparisons with regard to these issues poses technical dilemmas. See these sources as well the discussions and citations in Schlozman, Verba, and Brady, *The Unheavenly Chorus*, pp. 76–79.

21. Atkinson, *Inequality*, p. 26.

22. Picketty, *Capital*, p. 265.

23. Smeeding, "Public Policy, Inequality, and Poverty," pp. 971–973. See also Alan Krueger, "The Rise and Consequences of Inequality," presentation made to the Center for American Progress, January 12, 2012, Figure 10, at https://www.americanprogress.org/events/2012/01/12/17181

/the-rise-and-consequences-of-inequality/ (accessed December 30, 2015); and Janet C. Gornick and Branko Milanovic, "Income Inequality in the United States in Cross-National Perspective: Redistribution Revisited," LIS Center Research Brief, May 4, 2015, at https://www.gc.cuny.edu/CUNY_GC/media/CUNY-Graduate-Center/PDF/Centers/LIS/LIS-Center-Research-Brief-1-2015.pdf (accessed January 14, 2017).

24. David Leonhardt and Kevin Quealy, "U.S. Middle Class Is No Longer World's Richest," *New York Times*, April 23, 2014.

25. Richard B. Freeman, *When Earnings Diverge: Causes, Consequences, and Cures for the New Inequality in the United States* (Washington, DC: National Policy Association, 1997), p. 19.

26. Lawrence Mishel, Jared Bernstein, and Heidi Shierholz, *The State of Working America, 2008/2009* (Ithaca, NY: Cornell University Press and ILR Press, 2009), p. 382, fig. 8E.

27. Mishel, Bivens, Gould, and Shierholz, *State of Working America*, p. 143, fig. 3A.

28. In a vast literature, see, for example, P. M. Blau and O. D. Duncan, *The American Occupational Structure* (New York: Wiley, 1967); Robert M. Hauser and David L. Featherman, *The Process of Stratification* (New York: Academic Press,1977); Michael Hout, "More Universalism, Less Structural Mobility," *American Journal of Sociology* 93 (1988): 1358–1400; Harry B. G. Ganzeboom, Donald J. Treiman, and Wout C. Ultee, "Comparative Intergenerational Stratification Research," *Annual Review of Sociology* 17 (1991): 284; Burtless and Jencks, "American Inequality"; the essays in Samuel Bowles, Herbert Gintis, and Melissa Osborne Groves, eds., *Unequal Chances: Family Background and Economic Success* (Princeton, NJ: Princeton University Press, 2005); and the essays in Julia B. Isaacs, Isabel V. Sawhill, and Ron Haskins, eds., *Getting Ahead or Losing Ground: Economic Mobility in America* (Washington, DC: Brookings Institution and Economic Mobility Project, 2008).

29. On the class gaps in child well-being, see Robert D. Putnam, *Our Kids: The American Dream in Crisis* (New York: Simon and Schuster, 2015). With respect to the educational system, see the essays and references in *Whither Opportunity? Rising Inequality, Schools, and Children's Life Chances*, Greg J. Duncan and Richard J. Murnane, eds. (New York: Russell Sage, 2011), in particular, Duncan and Murnane, "Introduction," chap. 1; Sean F. Reardon, "The Widening Academic Achievement Gap between the Rich and the Poor: New Evidence and Possible Explanations," chap. 5; and Martha J. Bailey and Susan M. Dynarski, "Inequality in Postsecondary Education," chap. 6.

30. An exception to the pattern of growing gaps between rich and poor children is diminution in the disparity in health between rich and poor for children and young adults. See Margot Sanger-Katz, "Bucking a Health Trend, Fewer Kids Are Dying," *New York Times*, June 19, 2016.

31. Miles Corak, "Income Equality, Equality of Opportunity, and Intergenerational Mobility," *Journal of Economic Perspectives* 27 (2013): 79–102, fig. 1. See also Krueger, "Rise and Consequences of Inequality."

32. Discussion of such factors is in Uri Dadush, Kemal Dervis, Sarah Puritz Milsom, and Bennett Stancil, *Inequality in America: Facts, Trends, and International Perspectives* (Washington, DC: Brookings Institution Press, 2012), chap. 4. See also Atkinson, *Inequality*, chap. 3.

33. Atkinson, *Inequality*, p. 147.

34. Testimony before the Massachusetts legislature, cited without additional bibliographic information in Paul Kens, *Lochner v. New York: Economic Regulation on Trial* (Lawrence: University Press of Kansas, 1998), p. 19. On the extent to which executive pay reflects forces other than the operations of markets, see Bebchuk and Fried, "Pay without Performance," parts I and II.

35. Christopher Jencks, "Why Do So Many Jobs Pay So Badly?" in *Inequality Matters*, ed. James Lardner and David A. Smith (New York: New Press, 2005), p. 134.

36. For evidence and citations supporting the contention that government benefits reduce poverty, see James P. Ziliak, "Income, Program Participation, and Financial Vulnerability: Research and Data Needs," *Journal of Economic and Social Measurement* 40 (2015): 34–36.

37. Edin and Shaefer, *$2.00 a Day*, p. 7.

38. Marianne Bitler and Hilary Hoynes, "The More Things Change, the More They Stay the Same? The Safety Net and Poverty in the Great Recession," *Journal of Labor Economics* 34 (2016): S403–S444.

39. Congressional Budget Office, "The Distribution of Household Income and Federal Taxes, 2011," November 12, 2014, pp. 25–27, at https://www.cbo.gov/publication/49440 (accessed on January 2, 2016). A parallel CBO analysis undertaken three years earlier found the opposite: a decrease in the redistributive impact of government benefits between 1979 and 2007. See Congressional Budget Office, "Trends in the Distribution of Household Income between 1979 and 2007," October 25, 2011, xii, at https://www.cbo.gov/publication/42729 (accessed on January 2, 2016).

40. Dottie Rosenbaum and Brynne Keith-Jennings, "SNAP Costs and Caseloads Declining," Center on Budget and Policy Priorities, March 8, 2016, at http://www.cbpp.org/research/food-assistance/snap-costs-and-caseloads-declining (accessed on August 16, 2016).

41. Material in the paragraph is taken from David Cay Johnston, "The Great Tax Shift," in *Inequality Matters*, ed. Lardner and Smith, pp. 168–173.

42. Institute on Taxation & Economic Policy, "Who Pays?: A Distributional Analysis of the Tax Systems in All Fifty States," 5th ed., January 2015, at http://www.itep.org/whopays/full_report.php (accessed on January 2, 2016).

43. Congressional Budget Office, "Distribution of Household Income," fig. 15. See also Andrew Fieldhouse, "Rising Income Inequality and the Role of Shifting Market-Income Distribution, Tax Burdens, and Tax Rates," Economic Policy Institute, June 14, 2013, at http://www.epi.org/publication/rising-income-inequality-role-shifting-market/ (accessed on January 2, 2016).

44. Information in this paragraph is taken from Stiglitz, *Price of Inequality*, pp. 89–92; and Ronald P. Formisano, *Plutocracy in America (Baltimore: Johns Hopkins University Press, 2015)*, pp. 77–80.

45. For information about the estate tax, see Darien B. Jacobson, Brian G. Raub, and Barry W. Johnson, "The Estate Tax: Ninety Years and Counting," Internal Revenue Service, Compendium of Federal Transfer Tax and Personal Wealth Studies, volume 2, chap. 1, at https://www.irs.gov/pub/irs-soi/11pwcompench1aestate.pdf; IRS, "Estate Tax," https://www.irs.gov/pub/irs-soi/ninetyestate.pdf; and Chye-Ching Huang and Brandon DeBot, "Ten Facts You Should Know about the Federal Estate Tax," Center on Budget and Policy Priorities, March 23, 2015, at http://www.cbpp.org/sites/default/files/atoms/files/1-8-15tax.pdf (all accessed on January 2, 2016).

46. Atkinson, *Inequality*, pp. 181–182. See also Piketty, *Capital*, pp. 499, 508.

47. Among others, this argument is made by Picketty, *Capital*, pp. 508–512, who finds no evidence that the explosion in compensation has been accompanied by enhanced productivity by high earners.

48. Joseph E. Stiglitz, "Rewriting the Rules of the American Economy," Roosevelt Institute, 2015, at http://rooseveltinstitute.org/rewriting-rules-report/ (accessed on January 14, 2017).

49. Dean Baker and Jared Bernstein, *Getting Back to Full Employment* (Washington, DC: Center for Economic and Policy Research, 2013); and Lawrence Mishel, John Schmitt, and Heidi Shierholz, "Wage Inequality: A Story of Policy Choices," *New Labor Forum* 23 (2014): 26–31.

50. Council of Economic Advisers Brief, "Labor Market Monopsony: Trends, Consequences, and Policy Responses," October, 2016, at https://www.whitehouse.gov/sites/default/files/page/files/20161025_monopsony_labor_mrkt_cea.pdf (accessed January 15, 2017).

51. Craig K. Elwell, "Inflation and the Real Minimum Wage: A Fact Sheet" (Washington, DC: Congressional Research Service, 2014), table 1, at https://www.fas.org/sgp/crs/misc/R42973.pdf (accessed on March 8, 2016).

52. Atkinson, *Inequality*, p. 149.

53. Lawrence Mishel and Ross Eisenbrey, "How to Raise Wages: Policies That Work and Policies That Don't," Washington, DC: Economic Policy Institute Briefing Paper 391, March 16, 2015, p. 10.

54. Daniel Weissner, "Trump Administration Moves Closer to Undoing Overtime Pay Rule," *Reuters*, July 25, 2017, at https://www.reuters.com/article/us-usa-labor-overtime-idUSKBN1A A2DZ (accessed on August 2, 2017).

55. These and other practices are discussed in Stiglitz, "Rewriting the Rules"; and Council of Economic Advisers Issue Brief, "Labor Market Monopsony: Trends, Consequences, and Policy Responses," October 2016, at https://obamawhitehouse.archives.gov/sites/default/files/page/files/20161025_monopsony_labor_mrkt_cea.pdf. The specific examples of lower-wage workers who are required to sign non-competes are taken from p. 8 of "Labor Market Monopsony."

56. Rachel Abrams, "Trapped in Fast Food's Slow Lane," *New York Times*, September 28, 2017.

57. Stiglitz, "Rewriting the Rules," p. 47.

58. For conflicting views on the causes of the 2008 financial crisis, see the Financial Crisis Inquiry Commission, *The Financial Crisis Inquiry Report* (Washington, DC: U.S. Government Printing Office, 2011) including the two dissenting reports at https://www.gpo.gov/fdsys/pkg/GPO-FCIC/pdf/GPO-FCIC.pdf (accessed January 14, 2016). Material in the remainder of this section is taken from Elizabeth Warren and Amelia Warren Tyagi, *The Two-Income Trap* (New York: Basic Books, 2003), pp. 126–129, 152–156; Stiglitz, *Price of Inequality*, pp. 46, 93, 112–115, 239–245, 252, 310; Reich, *Beyond Outrage*, 6, 57–58.

59. One provision in the 2005 bankruptcy act made it extremely difficult to discharge private student loans—in contrast to, for example, consumer debt—through bankruptcy. See Ron Lieber, "Student Debt and a Push for Fairness," *New York Times*, June 5, 2010.

60. Robert B. Reich, "Rolling Back Inequality," *American Prospect*, Spring 2015, pp. 28–29.

61. Data taken from the Union Membership and Coverage Database, constructed by Barry Hirsch and David Macpherson, at http://www.unionstats.com/ (accessed December 31, 2015).

62. Robert J. Flanagan, "Has Management Strangled U.S. Unions?" *Journal of Labor Research* 26 (2005): 35, table 1. See Mishel, Bernstein, and Shierholz, *State of Working America, 2008/2009*, p. 375. Of the thirteen countries for which they present data, union coverage is lowest in the United States.

63. See Lawrence Mishel, "Unions, Inequality, and Faltering Middle-Class Wages," Economic Policy Institute, August 29, 2012, at http://www.epi.org/publication/ib342-unions-inequality-faltering-middle-class/ (accessed on January 4, 2016); and Jake Rosenfeld, *What Unions No Longer Do* (Cambridge, MA: Harvard University Press, 2014), chaps. 2, 3.

64. Bruce Western and Jake Rosenfeld, "Unions, Norms, and the Rise in U.S. Wage Inequality," *American Sociological Review* 76 (2011): 532.

65. Lee Drutman, *The Business of America Is Lobbying* (Oxford and New York: Oxford University Press, 2015), pp. 78–79.

66. For a more extensive discussion and additional bibliographical sources, see Schlozman, Verba, and Brady, *Unheavenly Chorus*, pp. 87–94; as well as Richard B. Freeman, *America Works: The Exceptional U.S. Market* (New York: Russell Sage Foundation, 2007), chap. 5. See also Michael Goldfield, *The Decline of Organized Labor in the United States* (Chicago: University of Chicago Press, 1987); Richard B. Freeman and Lawrence Katz, "Rising Wage Inequality: The United States vs. Other Advanced Countries," in *Working under Different Rules*, ed. Richard B. Freeman (New York: Russell Sage Foundation, 1994); Jacob S. Hacker and Paul Pierson, *Winner-Take-All Politics: How Washington Made the Rich Richer and Turned Its Back on the Middle Class* (New York: Simon and Schuster, 2010), pp. 56–61; and Rosenfeld, *What Unions No Longer Do*, chap. 1.

67. On these factors, see Nelson Lichtenstein, *State of the Union* (Princeton, NJ: Princeton University Press, 2002), chaps. 3–4.

68. See Hacker and Pierson, *Winner-Take-All Politics*, pp. 127–132, 278–279.

69. On the NLRB under Reagan, see Paul Alan Levy, "The Unidimensional Perspective of the Reagan Labor Board," *Rutgers Law Journal* 16 (1985): 269–390; Terry Moe, "Interests, Institutions, and Positive Theory: The Politics of the NLRB," *Studies in American Political Development* 2 (1987): 266–271; and James A. Gross, *Broken Promise: The Subversion of U.S. Labor Relations Policy, 1947–1994* (Philadelphia: Temple University Press, 1995), chap. 13.

70. Gross, *Broken Promise*, p. 253.

Chapter 11: Has It Always Been This Way?

1. Figuring out how increasing inequality in income should affect participatory inequality in not a simple matter. See Henry E. Brady, "An Analytical Perspective on Participatory Inequality and Income Inequality," in *Social Inequality*, ed. Kathryn M. Neckerman (New York: Russell Sage Foundation, 2004), chap. 17.

2. See Anthony Downs, *An Economic Theory of Democracy* (New York: Harper and Row, 1957), chap. 10; and Allan H. Meltzer and F. Scott Richard, "A Rational Theory of the Size of Government," *Journal of Political Economy* 89 (1981): 914–927.

3. Frederick Solt, "Economic Inequality and Democratic Political Engagement," *American Journal of Political Science* 52 (2008): 48–60. On the complex steps between the onset of social or economic change and actual political mobilization, see, for example, Sidney Tarrow, *Power in Movement: Social Movements and Contentious Politics*, 2nd ed. (New York: Cambridge University Press, 1998); and Doug McAdam, Sidney Tarrow, and Charles Tilly, *Dynamics of Contention* (New York: Cambridge University Press, 2001).

4. Major works documenting the erosion of turnout and political participation in the latter years of the past century include Ruy A. Teixeira, *The Disappearing American Voter* (Washington, DC: Brookings Institution, 1992); Steven J. Rosenstone and John Mark Hansen, *Mobilization, Participation, and Democracy in America* (New York: Macmillan, 1993); Robert D. Putnam, *Bowling Alone: The Collapse and Revival of American Community* (New York: Simon and Schuster, 2000); Martin P. Wattenberg, *Where Have All the Voters Gone?* (Cambridge, MA: Harvard University Press, 2002); and Stephen Macedo, Yvette Alex-Assensoh, Jeffrey M. Berry, Michael Brintnall, David E. Campbell, Luis Ricardo Fraga, and Archon Fung, et al., *Democracy at Risk: How Political Choices Undermine Citizen Participation and What We Can Do about It* (Washington, DC: Brookings Institution, 2005).

The absence of an increase in participation suggests that *relative* rather than *absolute* levels of education are consequential for political participation. For an argument that it is relative education that matters, see Norman H. Nie, Jane Junn, and Kenneth Stehlik-Barry, *Education and Democratic Citizenship in America* (Chicago: University of Chicago Press, 1996).

5. The data are drawn from the following studies: 1959—Gabriel Almond and Sidney Verba, *The Civic Culture* (Princeton, NJ: Princeton University Press, 1963); 1967—Sidney Verba and Norman H. Nie, *Participation in America* (New York: Harper and Row, 1972); 1990—Sidney Verba, Kay Lehman Schlozman, and Henry E. Brady, *Voice and Equality: Civic Voluntarism in American Politics* (Cambridge, MA: Harvard University Press, 1995); 2008—August Tracking 2008 Survey of the Pew Internet and American Life Project. The data for 1967, 1990, and 2008 are based on the same five measures of activity: working in a political campaign, contributing to a candidate or campaign, contacting a government official, belonging to a political organization, and working with others on a community issue. The data from 1960 are based on a somewhat different set of activities: acting to influence a local policy, acting to influence a national policy, taking part in a campaign, belonging to a party organization, and belonging to a nonpolitical organization that takes political stands.

Because our purpose is to illustrate continuity of stratification, what counts is the similarity in the upward slope of the lines.

6. The ANES data begin in 1948, but the participation items beyond voting are available only from 1952 onward.

7. Because voting turnout in nonpresidential years is inevitably lower than in presidential elections, we restrict our analysis to the sixteen presidential elections between 1952 and 2012.

There is a very large literature treating the fact that surveys tend to overestimate turnout. See, for example, Brian D. Silver, Barbara A. Anderson, and Paul R. Abramson, "Who Overreports Voting?" *American Political Science Review* 80 (1986): 613–624; Verba, Schlozman, and Brady, *Voice and Equality*, pp. 613–619; Henry E. Brady, "Conceptualizing and Measuring Political Participation," in *Measures of Political Attitudes*, ed. John P. Robinson, Philip R. Shaver, and Lawrence S. Wrightsman (San Diego, CA: Academic Press, 1999), vol. 2, chap. 13; and Michael P. McDonald, "On the Over-report Bias of the National Election Study Turnout Rate," *Political Analysis* 11 (2003): 180–186. On the problems with survey samples, see, for example, Barry C. Burden, "Voter Turnout and the National Election Studies," *Political Analysis* 8 (2000): 389–398.

An important insight in this literature is the definition of the Voting-Eligible Population (VEP) as an alternative to the Voting-Age Population (VAP). See Michael P. McDonald and Samuel L. Popkin, "The Myth of the Vanishing Voter," *American Political Science Review* 95 (2001): 963–974. Although the ANES turnout measure that we use is about 16 percentage points higher than the VEP, it is correlated at .878 with the VEP and .747 with the VAP. The ANES turnout measure thus captures the movement in the VEP, but it overestimates the level of turnout.

8. Jan E. Leighley and Jonathan Nagler, *Who Votes Now?: Demographics, Issues, Inequality, and Turnout in the United States* (Princeton, NJ: Princeton University Press, 2014), p. 28. Emphasis in the original.

9. A fifth campaign-related item, displaying a candidate button or sign, was added in 1956. However, to use the longest possible time series, we do not use this item in our scale. Including this item has no effect on the results.

10. See https://www.opensecrets.org/overview/cost.php?display=T&infl=Y (accessed on July 17, 2017).

11. This figure as well as all information in the remainder of this paragraph is taken from the Web site of the Sunlight Foundation, http://sunlightfoundation.com/blog/2013/06/24/1pct_of_the_1pct/ (accessed June 23, 2015).

In 2014, the 1 percent of the 1 percent were responsible for a slightly higher proportion of total disclosed giving, 29 percent. See Peter Olsen-Phillips, Russ Choma, Sarah Bryner and Doug Weber, "The Political One Percent of the One Percent in 2014: Mega Donors Fuel Rising Cost of Elections," Center for Responsive Politics, April 30, 2015, https://www.opensecrets.org/news/2015/04/the-political-one-percent-of-the-one-percent-in-2014-mega-donors-fuel-rising-cost-of-elections/ (accessed on June 25, 2015).

12. Kenneth P. Vogel, "Big Money Breaks Out," *Politico*, December 29, 2014, at http://www.politico.com/story/2014/12/top-political-donors-113833 (accessed on July 5, 2016).

13. Nicholas Confessore, Sarah Cohen, and Karen Yourish, "From Only 158 Families, Half the Cash for '16 Race," *New York Times*, October 11, 2015.

14. Matea Gold and Tom Hamburger, "For 2016 Campaign: Out with the Rich, in with the Really Rich," *Washington Post*, March 26, 2015.

15. Center for Responsive Politics, https://www.opensecrets.org/outsidespending/disclosure.php (accessed July 17, 2017).

16. In making this comparison, we recognize that these are very different kinds of acts that are measured differently. Religious attendance is measured in terms of how frequently the re-

spondent attends religious services. Political activity is measured by an additive scale consisting of dichotomies measuring whether the respondent has been active at all.

17. We replicated this analysis for Republicans and Democrats separately and found no obvious differences—except for consistently higher average SES of Republicans.

18. The question about religious attendance was asked using somewhat different versions over the period. From 1952 through 1968, respondents were asked about the regularity of their attendance at services, and "3" corresponds to "Often." From 1972 through 2008, the options were more specific, and "3" corresponds to "Once or twice a month."

19. We obtain exactly the same result for 1973–2008 when we use data from the General Social Survey. In their massive study of religious behavior in the United States, Putnam and Campbell also note the more recent emergence of an educational gap in religious attendance. See Robert D. Putnam and David E. Campbell, *American Grace: How Religion Divides and Unites Us* (New York: Simon and Schuster, 2010), pp. 252–253.

20. See, in particular, Jeffrey M. Berry, *The New Liberalism* (Washington, DC: Brookings Institution, 1999).

21. See Center for Responsive Politics, at https://www.opensecrets.org/lobby/ (accessed June 25, 2015).

22. Using somewhat different arguments and kinds of evidence, both Robert Putnam and Theda Skocpol demonstrate an erosion in participation in voluntary associations. See Robert D. Putnam, *Bowling Alone: The Collapse and Revival of American Community* (New York: Simon and Schuster, 2000), especially chap. 3; and Theda Skocpol, *Diminished Democracy: From Membership to Management in Civic Life* (Norman: University of Oklahoma Press, 2003), especially chaps. 3–6.

23. Some of the variability may stem from procedural changes in the way that the *Washington Representatives* directory is assembled. On these procedural changes, see Kay Lehman Schlozman, Sidney Verba, and Henry E. Brady, *The Unheavenly Chorus: Unequal Political Voice and the Broken Promise of American Democracy* (Princeton, NJ: Princeton University Press, 2012), p. 350; and Kay Lehman Schlozman, Philip Edward Jones, Hye Young You, Traci Burch, Sidney Verba, and Henry E. Brady, "Louder Chorus—Same Accent: The Representation of Interests in Pressure Politics, 1981–2011," in *The Organization Ecology of Interest Communities: Assessments and Agendas* ed. David Lowery, Darren R. Halpin, and Virginia Gray (London: Palgrave Macmillan, 2015), chap. 9.

24. See, Center for Responsive Politics, at http://www.opensecrets.org/lobby/ (accessed July 18, 2017); and Will Tucker, "For Lobbying, Gravity's Pull Continues, Floor Not Found Yet," January 26, 2016, at http://www.opensecrets.org/news/ (accessed on February 1, 2016). Lobbying spending peaked at $3.52 billion in 2010 and varied between $3.15 and $3.33 billion between 2011 and 2016. The number of registered lobbyists crested at 14,818 in 2007 and has diminished since then. In 2016 it stood at 11,166.

25. Lee Drutman, *The Business of America Is Lobbying* (Oxford and New York: Oxford University Press, 2015), pp. 223–225.

26. Kate Ackley, "Billionaire Donors Bypass K Street," *CQ Weekly,* July 6, 2015.

27. https://www.opensecrets.org/lobby (accessed February 8, 2018).

28. See Dan Auble, "Waning Influence? Part 1: Tracking the 'Unlobbyist,'" Washington, DC: Center for Responsive Politics, March 18, 2014. See also Dan Auble, "Lobbyists 2012: Out of the Game or Under the Radar?" Washington, DC: Center for Responsive Politics, March 20, 2013; and Kate Ackley, "Street Talk: The Curious Cases of Vanishing Lobbyists," *Roll Call,* April 1, 2013.

29. For discussion and copious examples of how former members of Congress are able to walk through the revolving door without having to register as lobbyists, see Isaac Arnsdorf, "The Lobbying Reform that Enriched Congress," *Politico,* July 3, 2016, at http://www.politico

.com/story/2016/06/the-lobbying-reform-that-enriched-congress-224849 (accessed on July 14, 2016).

30. The absolute number of corporations listed actually fell from 1981 to 1991 before rebounding substantially from 1991 to 2011. In fact, from 1991 to 2001 and from 2001 to 2011, the increase in the number of corporations outpaced the increase in the overall number of organizations. Our suspicion is that the decline reflects the fact that the *Washington Representatives* directory included the dockets of the regulatory agencies as a source of information in its 1981 enumeration but not in its 1991 enumeration. For elaboration, see Schlozman, Verba, and Brady, *Unheavenly Chorus*, pp. 352–354.

31. In fact, the share of business organizations dropped much less substantially between 1991 and 2011. While the number of corporations listed declined between 1981 and 1991, in no other category was there a decrease over this period in the absolute number of organizations. Across all categories other than corporations, the number of organizations increased by 56 percent from 1981 to 1991.

32. Drutman, *Business of America*, p. 14.

33. See Skocpol, *Diminished Democracy*, pp. 212–219.

34. The data are drawn from the following studies: 1967, "Participation in America Survey"; 1990, "Citizen Participation Study"; 2000, "Social Capital Community Benchmark Survey," Saguaro Seminar, Kennedy School of Government, Harvard University; and 2006, "Social Capital Community Survey," Saguaro Seminar, Kennedy School of Government, Harvard University. These surveys are available at the major political science data repositories, including the Interuniversity Consortium for Political and Social Research. While the specific acts differ somewhat from survey to survey, each of these surveys contains a set of questions about such political acts as voting, contacting officials, or taking part in campaigns.

35. Berry, *New Liberalism*.

36. See, in particular, Steven J. Rosenstone and John Mark Hansen, *Mobilization, Participation, and Democracy in America* (New York: Macmillan, 1993); and Putnam, *Bowling Alone*.

Chapter 12: Can We Do Anything About It?

1. See Adam J. Berinsky, Nancy Burns, and Michael W. Traugott, "Who Votes by Mail? A Dynamic Model of the Individual-Level Consequences of Voting-by-Mail Systems," *Public Opinion Quarterly* 65 (2001): 178–197; and Adam J. Berinsky "The Perverse Consequences of Electoral Reform in the United States," *American Politics Research* 33 (2005): 471–491.

2. Fred Wertheimer and Susan Weiss Manes, "Campaign Finance Reform: A Key to Restoring the Health of Our Democracy," *Columbia Law Review* 94 (1994): 1126–1159. They note (pp. 1140–1141) that, although checks in a bundle originate from many sources, the "bundler" who gathers checks and delivers them to a candidate or campaign gets the credit.

3. Douglas R. Hess and Scott Novakowski, *Unequal Access: Neglecting the National Voter Registration Act*, February 2008, p. 5, at http://www.demos.org/sites/default/files/publications/UnequalAccessReport-web%282%29.pdf (accessed April 2, 2016). After careful consideration, the report (p. 6) discredits explanations other than uneven implementation for the decline in the number of registrations at public assistance agencies.

4. Henry E. Brady and John McNulty, "Turning Out to Vote: The Costs of Finding and Getting to the Polling Place," *American Political Science Review* 105 (2011): pp. 115–134.

5. For analysis of a number of procedural changes designed to raise turnout and their relationship to the Civic Voluntarism Model, see Barry C. Burden and Logan Vidal, "How Resources, Engagement, and Recruitment Are Shaped by Election Rules," in *Resources, Engagement, and*

Recruitment: New Advances in the Study of Civic Voluntarism, ed. Casey Klofstad (Philadelphia: Temple University Press, 2016), chap. 5.

6. For the history of voting rights for African Americans in the South, see, for example, Alexander Keyssar, *The Right to Vote: The Contested History of Democracy in the United States*, rev. ed. (New York: Basic Books, 2009), especially chaps. 4, 8, 9; and Ari Berman, *Give Us the Ballot: The Modern Struggle for Voting Rights in America* (New York: Farrar, Straus, and Giroux, 2015).

7. For a history of the Voting Rights Act through the Obama Administration, see Jesse H. Rhodes, *The Ballot Blocked* (Stanford, CA: Stanford University Press, 2017).

8. Michael Wines, "Is Target of New Voting Laws Fraud or Blacks?" *New York Times*, August 1, 2016.

9. See Jan E. Leighley and Jonathan Nagler, "Absentee Ballot Regimes: Easing Costs or Adding a Step," in *Election Administration in the United States*, ed. R. Michael Alvarez and Bernard Grofman (New York: Cambridge University Press, 2014), p. 144.

10. For discussion of errors in registration records, as well as other matters mentioned in this paragraph, see R. Michael Alvarez and Thad E. Hall, "Resolving Voter Registration Problems: Making Registration Easier, Less Costly, and More Accurate," in *Election Administration*, ed. Alvarez and Grofman, chap. 10.

11. For discussion and summary of the literature, see Thad E. Hall, "US Voter Registration Reform," *Electoral Studies* 32 (2013): 589–596; and Jan E. Leighley and Jonathan Nagler, *Who Votes Now? Demographics, Issues, Inequality, and Turnout in the United States* (Princeton, NJ: Princeton University Press, 2014), chap. 4. For somewhat divergent results, see Matthew R. Knee and Donald P. Green, "The Effects of Registration Laws on Voter Turnout: An Updated Assessment," in *Facing the Challenge of Democracy: Explorations in the Analysis of Public Opinion and Political Participation*, ed. Paul M. Sniderman and Benjamin Highton (Princeton, NJ: Princeton University Press, 2011), pp. 312–328; and Elizabeth Rigby and Melanie J. Springer, "Does Electoral Reform Increase (or Decrease) Political Equality?" *Political Research Quarterly* 64 (2011): 420–434.

12. See Tova Andrea Wang, *Politics of Voter Suppression* (Ithaca, NY: Cornell University Press, 2012), pp. 102, 112, 134.

13. See John H. Aldrich, Jacob M. Montgomery, and Wendy Wood, "Turnout as Habit" *Political Behavior* 33 (2011): 535–563; and citations in Kay Lehman Schlozman, Sidney Verba, and Henry E. Brady, *The Unheavenly Chorus: Unequal Political Voice and the Broken Promise of American Democracy* (Princeton, NJ: Princeton University Press, 2012), p. 173.

14. Michael P. McDonald and Matthew Thornburg, "Registering the Youth through Voter Preregistration," *N.Y.U. Journal of Legislation and Public Policy* 13 (2010): 551–572.

15. See "What Is Compulsory Voting?" available on the Web site of the International Institute for Democracy and Electoral Assistance, http://www.idea.int/vt/compulsory_voting.cfm (accessed February 23, 2016).

16. Political scientists are divided about compulsory voting. See, among others, Arend Lijphart, "Unequal Participation: Democracy's Unresolved Dilemma," *American Political Science Review* 91 (1997): 1–14; Aina Gallego, "Understanding Unequal Turnout: Education and Voting in Comparative Perspective," *Electoral Studies* 29 (2010): 239–247; Mark N. Franklin, "Electoral Engineering and Cross-National Turnout Differences: What Role for Compulsory Voting?" *British Journal of Political Science* 29 (1999): 205–216; and Benjamin Highton and Raymond E. Wolfinger, "The Political Implications of Higher Turnout," *British Journal of Political Science* 31 (2001): 179–192.

17. Associated Press data cited in Paul Gronke, "Early Voting after *Bush v. Gore*," in *Election Administration*, ed. Alvarez and Grofman, p. 122.

18. See Adam Liptak, "Error and Fraud at Issue as Absentee Voting Rises," *New York Times*, October 7, 2012; and Wang, *Politics of Voter Suppression*, pp. 140–141.

19. Richard K. Scher, *The Politics of Disenfranchisement: Why Is It So Hard to Vote in America?* (Amonk, NY: M. E. Sharpe, 2011), chap.3.

20. For the effects on turnout in national elections, see the discussion and references in Leighley and Nagler, "Absentee Ballot Regimes," p. 151; Wang, *Politics of Voter Suppression*, p. 139; and Leighley and Nagler, *Who Votes Now?*, pp. 109–118. For the effects on voter representativeness, see the discussion and references in David Hill, *American Voter Turnout* (Boulder, CO: Westview Press, 2006), pp. 138–139; Gronke, "Early Voting," pp. 134, 138; and Rigby and Springer, "Does Electoral Reform Increase."

21. Charles Stewart III, "What Hath HAVA Wrought? Consequences, Intended or Not, of the Post-*Bush* v. *Gore* Reforms" in *Election Administration*, ed. Alvarez and Grofman, p. 96.

22. Seth C. McKee, "Politics Is Local: State Legislator Voting on Restrictive Voter Identification Legislation," *Research and Politics* (2015): 1–7.

23. Keith G. Bentele and Erin E. O'Brien, "Jim Crow 2.0: Why States Consider and Adopt Restrictive Voter Access Policies," *Perspectives on Politics* 11 (2013): 1088–1116; and McKee, "Politics Is Local."

24. Renée Loth, "Prepare for Voter Whiplash," *Boston Globe*, May 9, 2016.

25. Michael Wines and Manny Fernandez, "Stricter Rules over Voter IDs Reshape Races," *New York Times*, May 2, 2016.

26. Wines and Fernandez, "Stricter Rules over Voter IDs."

27. Michael D. Shear and Maggie Haberman, "Trump Promotes a Baseless Claim on Illegal Voting," *New York Times*, November 28, 2016.

28. Erin McCann, "Who Is Registered to Vote in Two States? Some in Trump's Inner Circle," *New York Times*, January 27, 2017.

29. Vanita Gupta, "The Voter Purges Are Coming," *New York Times*, July 19, 2017.

30. Lorraine Minnite, *The Myth of Voter Fraud* (Ithaca, NY: Cornell University Press, 2010), especially chaps. 1, 3, 4 and Appendix 1; Stewart, "What Hath HAVA Wrought?" pp. 93–94, 96–97; Wang, *Politics of Voter Suppression*, pp. 76, 80; and Berman, *Give Us the Ballot*, pp. 254–257, 296–297, 308.

31. Chandler Davidson, "Historical Context of Voter Photo-ID Laws," *PS: Political Science and Politics* 42 (2009): 94–95.

32. On registration fraud, see Stewart, "What Hath HAVA Wrought?" pp. 96–97; Berman, *Give Us the Ballot*, pp. 296–297.

33. The information in this paragraph is drawn from Berman, *Give Us the Ballot*, pp. 296–297. For an extended case study that documents the targeting of ACORN in several states by groups allied with the Republican Party and demonstrates the flimsiness of much of the evidence against ACORN, see Minnite, *Myth of Voter Fraud,* pp. 94–99. We are grateful to Myrna Vasquez of the Brennan Center for clarifying in an e-mail the requirements for showing ID for first-time voters registered by a third-party registration drive.

34. Michael D. Shear and Emmarie Huetteman, "Meeting with Top Lawmakers, Trump Repeats an Election Lie," *New York Times*, January 24, 2017.

35. Michael D. Shear and Peter Baker, "Pledge to Find Election Fraud Few Say Exists," *New York Times*, January 26, 2017.

36. On the many kinds of voting fraud other than the kind deterred by voter ID laws, see Scher, *Politics of Disenfranchisement*, pp. 143–146.

37. Cited in Berman, *Give Us the Ballot*, p. 297.

38. Berman, *Give Us the Ballot*, p. 258–259, 297; and the Web site of Vote.org, https://www.vote.org/voter-id-laws/ (accessed August 16, 2016).

39. On the issues discussed in this paragraph, see the findings and citations in Charles Stewart III, "Voter ID: Who Has Them? Who Shows Them?" *Oklahoma Law Review* 66 (2013–2014): 21–52.

40. Lonna Rae Atkeson, Lisa Ann Bryant, Thad E. Hall, Kyle L. Saunders, and R. Michael Alvarez, "A New Barrier to Participation: Heterogeneous Application of Voter Identification Policies," *Electoral Studies* 29 (2010): 66–73; Rachael V. Cobb, D. James Greiner, and Kevin Quinn, "Can Voter ID Laws Be Administered in a Race-Neutral Manner? Evidence from the City of Boston in 2008," *Quarterly Journal of Political Science* 7 (2012); 1–33; and Stewart, "Voter ID: Who Has Them?" p. 48.

41. See M. V. Hood III and Charles S. Bullock III, "Much Ado about Nothing? An Empirical Assessment of the Georgia Voter Identification Statute," *State Politics and Policy Quarterly* 12 (2012): 394–414; Rene R. Rocha and Tetsuya Matsubayashi, "The Politics of Race and Voter ID Laws in the States: The Return of Jim Crow?" *Political Research Quarterly* 67 (2014): 666–679; and Stewart, "Voter ID: Who Has Them?" pp. 28–30, 48–50.

42. Zoltan Hajnal, Nazita Lajevardi, Lindsay Nielson, "Voter Identification Laws and the Suppression of Minority Votes," *Journal of Politics* 79 (2017): 363–379.

43. Kenneth R. Mayer and Scott McDonell, "Voter ID Study Shows Turnout Effects in 2016 Wisconsin Presidential Election," September 25, 2017, at https://elections.wisc.edu/news/voter-id-study/Voter-ID-Study-Release.pdf (accessed on November 24, 2017).

44. Michael Wines and Alan Blinder, "Voter ID Laws Take a Beating in U.S. Courts," *New York Times*, July 30, 2016.

45. Michael Tackett and Michael Wines, "Trump Disbands Commission on Voter Fraud," *New York Times*, January 3, 2018.

46. Discussion and data in this paragraph are taken from Jeff Manza and Christopher Uggen, *Locked Out: Felon Disenfranchisement and American Democracy* (New York: Oxford University Press, 2006); and Christopher Uggen, Ryan Larson, and Sarah Shannon, *6 Million Lost Voters: State-Level Estimates of Felony Disenfranchisement, 2016* (Washington, DC: The Sentencing Project, 2016), p. 3, at http://www.sentencingproject.org/publications/6-million-lost-voters-state-level-estimates-felony-disenfranchisement-2016/ (accessed on August 3, 2017).

47. On the issue of whether felon disenfranchisement laws actually alter election outcomes, see the discussion and citations in Khalilah L. Brown-Dean, "Felon Disenfranchisement after *Bush* v. *Gore*: Changes and Trends," in *Election Administration*, ed. Alvarez and Grofman, p. 207.

48. Donald P. Green and Alan S. Gerber, *Get Out the Vote: How to Increase Voter Turnout*, 3rd ed. (Washington, DC: Brookings Institution Press, 2015), p. 9.

49. For contrasting conclusions about the consequences of GOTV efforts for the representativeness of the electorate, see Ryan D. Enos, Anthony Fowler, and Lynn Vavreck, "Increasing Inequality: The Effect of GOTV Mobilization on the Composition of the Electorate, *Journal of Politics* 76 (2014): 273–288; Green and Gerber, *Get Out the Vote,* 136–138; and David W. Nickerson, "Do Voter Registration Drives Increase Participation? For Whom and When?" *Journal of Politics* 77 (2015):88–101.

50. Berman, *Give Us the Ballot*, pp. 261–262.

51. On political finance arrangements around the world, see Pippa Norris and Andrea Abel Van Es, eds., *Checkbook Elections?: Political Finance in Comparative Perspective* (New York: Oxford University Press, 2016); Robert G. Boatright, ed., *The Deregulatory Moment?* (Ann Arbor: University of Michigan Press, 2015); Elin Falguera, Samuel Jones, and Magnus Ohlman, eds., *Funding of Political Parties and Election Campaigns: A Handbook on Political Finance* (Stockholm: International Institute for Democracy and Electoral Assistance, 2014), especially chaps. 7–8; and Susan E. Scarrow, "Political Finance in Comparative Perspective," *Annual Review of Political Science* 10 (2007): 193–210.

52. For extensive references to the literature on campaign finance reform and its effects, see Schlozman, Verba, and Brady, *Unheavenly Chorus*, pp. 546–552; Kenneth R. Mayer, "Public Election Funding: An Assessment of What We Would Like to Know," *The Forum* 11 (2013): 365–384; and Michael J. Malbin, *Citizen Funding for Elections: What Do We Know? What Are the Effects? What Are the Options?* (Washington, DC: Campaign Finance Institute, 2015), at http://www.cfinst.org/pdf/books-reports/CFI_CitizenFundingforElections.pdf (accessed on March 1, 2016).

53. These figures and other information in this paragraph are taken from the Web site of the National Conference of State Legislators, http://www.ncsl.org/research/elections-and-campaigns/public-financing-of-campaigns-overview.aspx (accessed on March 1, 2016).

54. Russell Berman, "Seattle's Experiment with Campaign Funding," *The Atlantic*, November 10, 2015, at https://www.theatlantic.com/politics/archive/2015/11/seattle-experiments-with-campaign-funding/415026/ (accessed March 5, 2016).

55. Patrick Flavin, "Campaign Finance Laws, Policy Outcomes, and Political Equality in the American States," *Political Research Quarterly* 68 (2015): 77–88. In a further elaboration ("State Campaign Finance Laws and the Equality of Political Representation, *Election Law Journal* 13 [2014]: 362–374), he finds that it is stringent disclosure requirements that are associated with equality of political representation.

56. Political scientists have found mixed results with regard to the impact of such limits on incumbency retention. See Mayer, "Public Election Funding," pp. 370–374.

57. *Buckley* v. *Valeo* (1976), p. 9. On the *Buckley* decision, see Frank J. Sorauf, *Money in American Elections* (Glenview, IL: Scott Foresman, 1988), pp. 235–246.

58. Notably, neither BCRA's "Millionaire's Amendment," which was disallowed in *Davis* v. *FEC* (2008), nor the Arizona provision that was struck down in *Arizona Free Enterprise Club* v. *Bennett* (2011) restricts political expenditures. In fact, both provisions facilitated them.

59. *Citizens United* v. *Federal Election Commission* (2010), opinion of the Court, written by Justice Kennedy. For an interpretation of the extent to which *Citizens United* was a departure from previous legal interpretations and transformed the Founders interpretation of what constituted corruption, see Zephyr Teachout, *Corruption in America: From Benjamin Franklin's Snuff Box to Citizens United* (Cambridge, MA: Harvard University Press, 2014), esp. chap. 13.

60. Concurring opinion (p. 8), written by Justice Roberts. Justice Kennedy included a similar comment (p. 34) in his majority opinion. For contrasting views on the consequences of *Citizens United* for equality, see Samuel Issacharoff, "On Political Corruption," and Mark Alexander, "*Citizens United* and Equality Forgotten," in *Money, Politics, and the Constitution: Beyond Citizens United*, ed. Monica Youn (New York: Century Foundation Press, 2011), chaps. 8, 10.

61. Jonathan Weisman, "G.O.P. Error Reveals Donors and the Price of Access," *New York Times*, September 25, 2014.

62. On Super PACs, see Richard Hasen, *Plutocrats United: Campaign Money, the Supreme Court, and the Distortion of American Elections* (New Haven, CT: Yale University Press, 2016), pp. 33–34.

63. Nicholas Confessore, "Walker's Exit Shows limits of 'Super PACs,' Even Those Flush with Cash," *New York Times*, September 23, 2015.

64. Quoted in Hasen, *Plutocrats United*, p. 86. Hasen argues that a constitutionally permissible regime of campaign finance regulation can incorporate concern for equality.

65. For discussion and references, see Schlozman, Verba, and Brady, *Unheavenly Chorus*, pp. 567–571.

66. On the prevalence of civics courses, see Richard G. Niemi and Julia Smith, "Enrollments in High School Government Classes: Are We Short-Changing Both Citizenship and Political Science Training?" *PS: Political Science and Politics* 34 (2001): 281–287. On the performance of

students in such courses, see Robert L. Dudley and Alan R. Gitelson, "Civic Education, Civic Engagement, and Youth Civic Development," *PS: Political Science and Politics* 36 (2003): 263–267.

67. For a review of a variety of approaches to civic learning, see Peter Levine, *The Future of Democracy: Developing the Next Generation of American Citizens* (Medford, MA: Tufts University Press, 2007), chap. 7.

68. Right Question Institute Web site, http://www.rightquestion.org/ (accessed on March 5, 2016).

69. See Archon Fung and Erik Olin Wright, *Deepening Democracy: Institutional Innovations in Empowered Community Governance* (New York: Verso, 2003); and Wesley G. Skogan, *Police and Community in Chicago: A Tale of Three Cities* (New York: Oxford University Press, 2006).

70. Jeffrey M. Berry, Kent E. Portney, and Ken Thompson, *The Rebirth of Urban Democracy* (Washington DC: Brookings Institution, 2003), p. 14.

71. Berry, Portney, and Thompson, *Rebirth of Urban Democracy*, pp. 284–285. See also Kaifeng Yang and Kathe Callahan, "Citizen Involvement Efforts and Bureaucratic Responsiveness: Participatory Values, Stakeholder Pressures, and Administrative Practicality," *Public Administration Review* 67 (2007): 249–264.

72. See, for example, Joe Soss, *Unwanted Claims: The Politics of Participation in the U.S. Welfare System* (Ann Arbor: University of Michigan Press, 2000); Andrea Campbell, *How Policies Make Citizens: Senior Political Activism and the American Welfare State* (Princeton, NJ: Princeton University Press, 2003); Suzanne Mettler, *Soldiers to Citizens: The G.I. Bill and the Making of the Greatest Generation* (Ithaca, NY: Cornell University Press, 2005); and Joe Soss, Jacob S. Hacker, and Suzanne Mettler, eds., *Remaking America: Democracy and Public Policy in an Age of Inequality* (New York: Russell Sage Foundation, 2007).

73. Campbell, in *How Policies Make Citizens*, uses Social Security as an example of the former in each case, and welfare as an example of the latter.

74. Patrick Flavin, "Lobbying Regulations and Political Equality in the American States," *American Politics Research* 43 (2015): 304–326.

75. The argument in this paragraph is taken from Jeffrey M. Berry with David F. Arons, *A Voice for Nonprofits* (Washington, DC: Brookings Institution, 2003). Berry probes the relationship between nonprofits and government and the impact of 501(c)3 tax status.

76. Lee Drutman, *The Business of America Is Lobbying* (Oxford and New York: Oxford University Press, 2015), pp. 230–232.

Chapter 13: Unequal Voice in an Unequal Age

1. Elbridge Gerry, quoted in Robert A. Goldwin, *From Parchment to Power: How James Madison Used the Bill of Rights to Save the Constitution* (Washington, DC: American Enterprise Institute Press, 1997), pp. 116–117. The account of the fate of the amendment and Madison's rejoinder is taken from pp. 114–118.

2. James Madison, quoted in Goldwin, *From Parchment to Power*, p. 117.

3. Quoted in Theodore H. White, *The Making of the President 1960* (New York: Atheneum, 1961), p. 126. A number of Kennedy biographies and histories of his administration emphasize the impact of what he saw in West Virginia. See, for example, Arthur M. Schlesinger, Jr., *A Thousand Days: John F. Kennedy in the White House* (Boston: Houghton Mifflin, 1965), pp. 1007–1008.

4. Chris Murphy, "Opening Remarks by Sen. Chris Murphy for the ISPS Conference on Money and Politics," New Haven, CT, Yale University, Institute for Social and Political Studies, May 5, 2013, at http://www.youtube.com/watch?v=kLfVpET_r5A&list=PLqHnHG5X2PXAo8rhYsOVedp0V8Kiwnylh&index=3 (accessed July 12, 2016).

5. See Mark Alexander, "*Citizens United* and Equality Forgotten," in *Money, Politics, and the Constitution: Beyond Citizens United,* ed. Monica Youn (New York: Century Foundation Press, 2011), pp. 160–163.

6. Steve Israel, "Confessions of a Congressman," *New York Times,* January 8, 2016.

7. Study conducted by the Center for Responsive Politics, reported by Russ Choma, "Millionaires' Club: For First Time, Most Lawmakers Are Worth $1 Million-Plus," January 9, 2014, at http://www.opensecrets.org/news/2014/01/millionaires-club-for-first-time-most-lawmakers-are-worth-1-million-plus/ (accessed July 13, 2016).

8. Eric Lichtblau, "Economic Slide Took a Detour at Capitol Hill," *New York Times,* December 27, 2011.

9. See Nicholas Carnes, *White-Collar Government: The Hidden Role of Class in Economic Policy Making* (Chicago: University of Chicago Pres, 2013), for a discussion of the distinctive attitudes and floor votes of the rare blue-collar or service workers who have served in recent years in Congress.

10. Paul A. Freund, quoted in Anthony Lewis, *Freedom for the Thought That We Hate: A Biography of the First Amendment* (New York: Basic Books, 2007), p. 178.

11. Figures taken from calculations by the Center for Responsive Politics, at https://www.opensecrets.org/lobby/ (accessed August 3, 2017).

12. Ron Lieber and Tara Siegel Bernard, "What's in the Tax Bill, and How It Will Affect You," *New York Times,* December 16, 2017, at https://www.nytimes.com/2017/12/16/your-money/taxplan-changes.html (accessed on February 15, 2018); Heather Long, "In Political Gamble, GOP Gives Permanent Tax Cuts to Corporations, but Not People," *Washington Post,* November 15, 2017, at https://www.washingtonpost.com/news/wonk/wp/2017/11/15/in-political-gamble-gop-gives-permanent-tax-cuts-to-corporations-but-not-people/?utm_term=.eef433e09d60 (accessed on November 19, 2017).

13. Jim Tankersley and Kenneth Vogel, "Hidden in Senate Bill: Tax Gifts for Select Few," *New York Times,* November 16, 2017; Dan Wilchins and Prashant Gopal, "One Tax Loophole Untouched So Far: The Trump Golf-Course Break," *Bloomberg,* November 9, 2017, at https://www.bloomberg.com/news/articles/2017-11-09/one-tax-loophole-untouched-so-far-the-trump-golf-course-break; Eric Levitz, "GOP Plan Retains Tax Break for Golf-Course Owners," *New York Magazine,* November 9, 2017, at http://nymag.com/daily/intelligencer/2017/11/gop-plan-retains-tax-break-for-owners-of-golf-courses.html (both accessed on November 19, 2017); Lynnley Browning and Benjamin Bain, "Trump, Real Estate Investors Get Late-Added Perk in Tax Bill," *Bloomberg,* December 17, 2017, at https://www.bloomberg.com/news/articles/2017-12-18/trump-real-estate-investors-get-last-minute-perk-in-tax-bill (accessed on February 15, 2018).

14. John Sides, "Here's the Incredibly Unpopular GOP Tax Reform Plan—In One Graph," *Washington Post,* November 18, 2017, at https://www.washingtonpost.com/news/monkey-cage/wp/2017/11/18/heres-the-incredibly-unpopular-gop-tax-reform-plan-in-one-graph/?utm_term=.d4d8a7fab402 (accessed on November 19, 2017).

15. Dylan Scott, "House Republican: My Donors Told Me to Pass the Tax Bill 'Or Don't Ever Call Me Again,'" *Vox,* November 7, 2017, at https://www.vox.com/policy-and-politics/2017/11/7/16618038/house-republicans-tax-bill-donors-chris-collins (accessed on November 19, 2017).

16. Arthur M. Schlesinger Jr., *The Cycles of American History* (Boston: Houghton Mifflin, 1986).

17. This point is made by Lee Drutman, *The Business of America Is Lobbying* (Oxford: Oxford University Press, 2015), pp. 222–223.

INDEX

AARP, 8, 32, 103, 163
abortion, 43; gender and abortion as issue, 109; and issue commitment, 64, 77–78, 98–100, 104, 105–7; party identification or ideology and, 95–96; race or ethnicity and abortion as issue, 106
Abramowitz, Alan, 97
accountability: political voice and, 2, 4–7; responsiveness of policymakers, 4–5, 35–38, 206, 257–58; voting and, 24–25
ACORN, 240
activism. *See* political activists
advantage, economic: American public as relatively "affluent," 193–95, 204; and attitude toward social welfare programs, 106; campaign contributions and, 13, 17, 76–77, 87–88, 214, 249, 266–67; civic skill development and, 57–58, 69–72; defined, 292n20; education and, 17, 79, 194; family and intergenerational, *ix*, 65–67, 79, 194–95, 204; income growth, 188–92, 197–98, 207; Internet and social media access of, 112–14; organizations and representation of, 150–51, 173–74, 181–82, 188; overrepresentation of the affluent, 5, 15, 38, 87–88, 208–9, 214, 226, 227, 249, 256, 258, 269–70; and participation, 65–67, 93; policy interests linked to, 38, 103, 106, 256–57; "rational prospecting" and, 143–44; recruitment and, 72, 136, 143–44, 256–57; tax policy advantages for, 197–98, 272; time-based political activity and, 52–53. *See also* socioeconomic status (SES)
affluence. *See* advantage, economic
Affordable Care Act, 84, 100–101, 191, 259
African Americans: civic skills and, 57–58, 67, 68–72; discriminatory disenfranchisement of, 10, 231–32, 237, 241–42; education and political participation by, 54–55, 67–68, 91; as identity group, 33, 163, 177; income inequality and, 12, 91–92, 192, 259–60; lobbying and advocacy for, 177; online activities and, 126–28, 131, 260; participation by, 91–92, 107–8, 110; party identification and, 60, 274; policy concerns, 107–8, 110; psychological engagement with politics, 60, 67; recruitment of, 63, 72–73; SES and group differences in political voice, 12, 75, 259–60; time as political resource, 53; as underrepresented, 12, 110, 290n11; use of term, 280n13; voting by, 234, 237, 240–42 (*see also* discriminatory disenfranchisement *under this heading*)
age: activism and, 85; Internet use and, 115–16, 120–23, 128, 260–61; lobbying organizations and, 103; online political activity and, 120–21, 260–61; participation in political activities and, 85, 112–13, 115, 120–21, 260–61; political voice and, 3, 38–39; SES and, 120–21; and stakeholder status in government programs, 85, 102–3, 110, 163; voter registration and, 233–34; voting and, 112–13, 163, 233–36, 234
agriculture as organized interest, 159
Aid to Families with Dependent Children (AFDC), 102, 104, 196–97
"American Dream," 193–95
American National Election Studies (ANES), *xi*, 18, 86–87, 94–95, 97–99, 142–43, 210, 269, 275
amicus briefs, 25, 27, 172–74, 178–80, 184
Ansolabehere, Stephen, 45
Arizona Free Enterprise Club's Freedom Club PAC v. Bennett, 248, 250
Asian Americans, 132–33
astroturf (artificial grassroots lobbying campaigns), 172
attitudes: about economic equality, *xi*, 95–96, 276; about political equality, 249, 276

319

Bartels, Larry, 38
basic human needs: organizations and advocacy for the disadvantaged, 162–63; as participatory issue, 11, 77–78, 104–10, 162, 259; race or ethnicity and issue of, 107–8, 110
Baumgartner, Frank, 40–41, 45
Berry, Jeffrey, 40–41, 45, 163
Bipartisan Campaign Reform Act, 46, 245, 247–48
Black Lives Matter, 103, 107, 131, 133, 258
blacks. *See* African Americans
bribes, 148–50
Buckley v. *Valeo*, 245–46, 248, 267
Burnett, Erin, 83–84
Bush, George W., 239–40
business interests: amicus briefs, 181; astroturf campaigns and, 172; CEO compensation, 191, 195; *Citizens United* v. *FEC* and right to political speech, 154; corporations as memberless organizations, 8, 34, 154, 262; "dark money" contributions and, 181–82, 253; as diverse or conflicting, 158; lobbying and, 42, 46, 173–77, 183, 219, 222, 252; as multi- or transnational, 28, 182; organizations and representation of, 38, 157–58, 163, 182–84, 225, 265; as overrepresented, 38, 46, 156–58, 161–62, 173, 181–84, 216, 219–21, 225, 263, 265, 268, 270, 275; PACs and, 180–81; policy actions favorable to, 35, 200–201; restrictions on campaign contributions from, 10, 180, 244, 245–48, 275; tax code and, 197–98, 272; testimony before Congress, 178; trade or other business associations, 220. *See also specific*

campaign contributions: access to policymakers and, 45–47; "buying access" and, 46; campaign finance laws, 244–50, 271–72; corruption and, 148–49; "dark money," 181–82, 214, 253; disclosure requirements for, 244; financial sector as source of, 256–57; inequality of political voice and, 12–13; innovative local systems for equitable, 244; limits on, 7, 10, 26; measuring influence of, 45–47; mega-donors, 213–14; as most unequal political activity, 144, 208, 212–13, 224, 269; and overrepresentation of the affluent, 208, 248, 266–67; PACs and volume of, 180; political engagement and, 76–77; as protected political speech, *xi*, 2, 9–10, 17, 244–49, 267, 274; public disapproval of current policy, 249; public funding alternatives, 244; recruitment of, 53, 136–37; regulation of, 45, 136, 180–81; SES and, 87–88, 136–37, 208, 212–14, 223–24, 248, 256–58, 266–67; spontaneous or self-initiated, 136–37; trends over time, 212–14. *See also* campaign finance laws
campaign costs, 165–67
campaign finance laws, 243–50, 271–72
campaign meetings or rallies, 24, 87, 211–12, 224
campaign work, 30, 51–52, 86–87, 95–97, 101, 224, 292n22
Campbell, Andrea, 37–38
case studies, 39–40, 44
causality, 43–44
Center for Responsive Politics, 217–18
characteristics, politically relevant, 5, 11–13, 30, 83–85, 266. *See also* specific
Citizen Participation Study, 18–19, 66, 95–96, 101–5, 134
citizenship rights, 9–10
Citizens United v. *Federal Election Commission*, 17, 154, 213, 246–48, 267
civic capacity. *See* civic skills
civic education, 74, 250, 253
civic involvement, 89
civic skills: adult acquisition of, 55–58, 250; of American public, 13–15; civic capacity and, 250–51; civic voluntarism model and, 3, 73, 79; defined, 51–52; education and, 11, 14, 54–58, 74, 80, 250–51, 253; equality of political voice and, 250; families and political socialization, 56–58, 65–66, 79; gender and, 56–58, 69–73; high school experience and, 54–55, 66–67, 73–74, 76, 232; nonpolitical organizations and development of, 55–56, 68–71; race or ethnicity and, 54–58, 67–69, 71–72; recruitment and, 140; religious institutions and, 55–56, 58, 68–69, 68–72, 79–80, 257; as resource for political participation, 51–52, 54–58, 73–74; service learning programs, 250; SES and, 11, 56–58, 68–69, 80, 257; skepticism regarding general public's, 14–15; time-based activities and, 76, 250–51; unions and development of, 272; workplace and development of, 11, 55–56, 68–73, 257
civic voluntarism model (CVM), 3; civic skill development and, 3, 73, 79; defined and described, 50–51, 73; Get Out the Vote (GOTV) and, 243; knowledge or interest and, 3; political efficacy, 3, 54,

INDEX 321

73; psychological engagement with politics and, 73; recruitment and, 73; resources and, 73; SES model compared with, 78–79
civil rights as participatory issue, 107–8
civil rights movement, 131–33
class bias. *See* socioeconomic status (SES)
Clinton, Bill, 41
Clinton, Hillary, 246–47
collective action model, 150–52
Collins, Chris, 273
communicating directly with policymakers, 292n22; limits on opportunity for, 7; lobbying and, 171; preference communication and, 4, 25, 27, 35, 85; socioeconomic barriers to, 102, 104–6, 110, 256
community participation. *See* local political participation
Congressional Lobbying Procedure Act, 253
congressional testimony. *See* testimony before Congress
conservatism: campaign contributions and, 96; polarization and, 95–100; public interest and, 166; social issues and, 94–95; social movements and, 131
conservative organizations, 165, 167, 177
Constitution, U.S., 9–10, 13, 213, 245–50, 255–56, 275
consumer groups, 165–66, 167
contact with policymakers. *See* communicating directly with policymakers
controversies, political, 40–41
corporations. *See* business interests; memberless organizations
corruption, 148–50
creative participation, 28–29, 83, 89
crime as participatory issue, 106–8

Dahl, Robert, 2–3
"dark money" contributions, 181–82, 214, 254
Davis v. Federal Election Commission, 246
de Figueiredo, John, 45
Democratic Party, 96, 141–43, 237; race or ethnicity and affiliation with, 237, 275
demographics: politically relevant characteristics and, 84; race or ethnicity and political voice, 3
disadvantage, economic: advocacy organizations for the poor, 157, 162–63, 168, 176–77, 180, 218–19, 220–21, 225, 251–52, 263, 268; barriers to organization and, 151–52; basic human needs as issue, 11, 77–78, 104–10, 162, 259; campaign contributions and, 77; civic skill development and, 65–67, 69–73, 250, 253; definition of term, 292n20; direct contact with policymakers and, 102, 104–6, 110, 256; education and, 92, 194–95; family and intergenerational poverty, 65–67, 194–95; family influence on political participation, 65–67; income trends and income inequality, 207; issue commitments and, 77–78; labor unions as representation, 207, 221–22 (*see also* low-skilled workers *under this heading*); low-skilled workers and, 159–60, 160–61, 168, 184, 222, 262; the needy as constituency, 162–63; occupational associations as representation, 150, 160 (*see also* labor unions *under this heading*); organizations as representation, 150–51, 157, 162–63, 168, 176–77, 180, 183, 218–22, 224–25, 251–52, 258, 261–64, 268; race or ethnic identity and, 91–92; social movements and mobilization, 131–33; stakeholders in government welfare programs, 77–78, 104–6, 110, 162–63, 259; underrepresentation and, 5, 28, 30, 77, 104–6, 110, 150–52, 157, 160–64, 167–68, 183, 220, 221–22, 225, 262–64, 268; upward mobility and, 194–95, 204; voting by, 233; wage gap and growth of economic inequality, 195–96. *See also* socioeconomic status (SES)
disclosure requirements: for campaign contributions, 244, 246; for lobbyists, 175, 252, 268
discussion, political, 28–29
Dodd-Frank Wall Street Reform and Consumer Protection Act, 201
Downs, Anthony, 207, 269

earmarks, 218
Earned Income Tax Credit, 162, 168, 197, 264
economic inequality: compensation for economic elite, 192; concentration of wealth and, 207; earnings and wages, 189–92; education and, 194; explanations for increasing, 195–203; family circumstances and, 194–95; government benefits and, 102, 174, 196; household income and, 188–92; household wealth and, 192; increasing income of the affluent, 207; increasing level of, 4, 86–87, 188–92; inequality of political voice and, 4, 26, 187–88, 206–11, 223; inherited wealth, 192; intergenerational transmission of, 194–95; market efficiency and, 195; measures of, 188–89;

economic inequality (*cont.*)
political response to, 207, 268–69; social advantages and, 194; social mobility and, 194–95, 204; taxation and, 192–93, 197–98, 272. *See also* advantage, economic; disadvantage, economic

education: access to resources linked to, 53 (*see also* income *under this heading*); African Americans and, 12, 67–68; capacity and, 30; civic skills and, 11, 14, 54–58, 74, 80, 250–51, 253; employment and, 53, 54, 70–71, 159–60; family or parental education as influence, 66–68, 79, 194; gender and, 54–55, 90, 92; income and, 17, 53–54, 190–91; Internet access in schools, 115; as issue commitment, 77, 104–10; Latinos and, 12, 54, 57, 67–68; as organized interests (*see* education organizations); participation and, 12, 17, 54–55, 66–68, 74, 78, 79–80, 208, 257–58, 267, 268; party identification and, 60; political voice and, *x*, 274; psychological engagement with politics and, 60–61; race or ethnicity and, 54–55, 67–68, 91; recruitment and level of, 62–63, 140; religious institutions and, 71–72; school experiences as influence on participation, 54, 66–67; SES Measure and, 289n4; time-based acts and, 53, 76, 254; transmission of social class linked to, 65–66, 78–80, 194; unequal opportunities for, 17–18, 65–66, 194, 231–32; voting and, 76, 229

education organizations: increase in, 169, 218, 221, 225, 270; as memberless, 8, 34, 153, 159, 262, 271; as representation, 156, 158, 173, 218–21, 225, 271

efficacy, political, 3, 54, 59–60

elections: campaign donations and election cycles, 91, 213–14; campaign work and, 27, 30, 51–52, 86–87, 95–97, 101, 224, 292n22; Downsian model and, 207; economic issues and, 95–97; social issues and, 95–97

electoral activity: campaign contributions (*see* campaign contributions); campaign meetings, 24, 87, 211–12, 224; campaign work, 27, 30, 51–52, 86–87, 95–97, 101, 224, 292n22; voting (*see* voting)

Electoral College, 31

employment: full employment as policy objective, 199; minimum wage, 199; overtime pay, 199. *See also* workplace or job

environmental issues, 165–66

equality in U.S.: as democratic value, 2–3, 9–10, 13–15, 48, 206, 228

equality of political voice, 3–4, 5, 29–30, 48–49, 228; equal consideration and, 6; pressure system and, 151, 154; proportional representation and, 5

Equal Rights Amendment, 228–29

expertise, political: of citizenry, 14–15; as limited resource, 26–27; paid political experts, 17, 148 (*see also* lobbying); pressure politics and hired, 225

extremity of opinion: disproportionate political voice and, 97–100

Facebook. *See* social media

families: family income and political participation, 56–57, 62–63, 140, 257–58; gender and family-related political concerns, 109–10; intergenerational transmission of economic advantage, *ix*, 65–67, 79, 194–95, 204; parental education as factor in political participation, 65–68; parents of school-aged children, 64, 77, 166–67; political participation and, 51, 56–57, 62–63, 65–66, 73–74, 140, 257–58; political socialization in, 56–58, 65–66, 79

Federal Election Campaign Act, 180–81, 245

Federal Election Commission v. *Beaumont*, 246–47

"Federalist No. 10" (Madison), 16

Federal Regulation of Lobbying Act, 175

felon disenfranchisement, 241–42

Fifteenth Amendment, 231

financial sector, 200–201

First Amendment, 9–10, 13, 255–56; as adequate guarantee of right to political speech, 255–56; campaign finance law and, 245–50, 273–74

Flavin, Patrick, 244

food stamps (Supplemental Nutrition Assistance Program or SNAP), 110, 197

Fourteenth Amendment, 9–10, 248

France, Anatole, 229

free riders, 151–52, 156, 164, 167, 169, 183, 262

Freund, Paul A., 267

gay rights, 5, 95–96, 143

gender: civic skills and, 56–58, 67–73, 71; disenfranchisement of voters based on, 231; education and, 54–55, 90, 92; and family-related political concerns, 109–10; identity groups and organizational representation, 163–64; inequality of political voice and, 12; Internet use and, 126–28;

of mega-donors, 91; participation and, 12, 89–91, 109–10, 126–28; policy concerns and, 109–10; and political engagement, 60, 67; political resources and, 53–54; and representation, 83; SES and, 12, 89–92
Gerry, Elbridge, 255–56
Gilens, Martin, 38
government relations firms, 217
grassroots lobbying, 32, 42, 171–72, 175, 218
Gupta, Vanita, 239

Hamilton, Alexander, 14
Hanna, Mark, 12–13
health care: as business, 169; individual health and exercise of political voice, 85, 100–101; policy and legislation, 83–84; SES and access to, 100–101, 191, 259
health organizations: increase in, 169, 216, 218–21, 225, 270; lobbying and, 158–59, 162–63, 173, 176, 218–19; as memberless, 8, 34, 153, 159–60, 262, 270; as representation, 156, 158, 173, 218–21, 225, 270
Heinz, John P., 47
Help America Vote Act (HAVA), 239–40
Hispanics. *See* Latinos
Hojnacki, Marie, 40–41, 45
Honest Leadership and Open Government Act, 218
hospitals. *See* memberless organizations

identity groups, 222; amicus briefs and, 184; as class-based groups, 164; lobbying and, 177, 182, 216, 220–21; organizations and representation for, 163–64, 177, 182–83, 184, 221; SES and group differences in political voice, 259–60; testimony before Congress and, 178, 184. *See also* specific
immigrants, 5, 30; illegal voting by, 240; recruitment into political activity, 141–42, 250–51
income: CEO compensation, 192–93; gains in income by the affluent, 192–93, 207; government benefits as, 30, 64, 77, 85, 101–3, 162–63, 192–93, 196, 251, 259, 305n8; labor unions and higher wages, 202; minimum wage, 16, 199; political contributions and, 13, 16–17, 52–53, 74, 76–77, 80, 136–37, 207–8, 212–14, 224; SES Measure and, 289n4; taxes on unearned, 197–98; time-based acts and, 253; wage gap and growth of economic inequality, 189–91, 195–96; wage suppression in U.S., 193
income inequality: American affluence as compensation for, 193; concentration of income and wealth, *ix*, 16, 188–89, 192–93, 207, 269, 275; decline in union membership linked to, 201–5; factors contributing to, 195–203; financial sector growth linked to, 200–201; labor market and, 198–201; participation disparities linked to, 52; public policy as influence on, 16, 196–201; reactionary politics and, 207–8; redistribution and, 188–89, 192–93, 196–98, 207–8; in U.S. compared with other nations, 192–95. *See also* advantage, economic; disadvantage, economic
individualism, American, 229, 236, 273
information, political: Americans and lack of, 14, 59; digital technologies and access to, 112–13, 117–18; education and, 60–61; as measure of political engagement, 59–60; participation and, 74; voting and, 74
interest groups. *See* organized interests
interest-groups pluralism, 207–8
Internet: access to, 3, 112–17, 120–21, 128, 260; age and use of, 115–16, 120–23, 128, 260–61; creative participation and, 28; the "digital divide," 114–17, 120–21, 123–25, 128, 260; digital participation in politics, 3, 28–29, 122–23; "discursive participation" and, 28–29; gender and use of, 126–28; measuring political uses of, 112–13; mobilization and, 28; online *vs.* offline political participation, 114, 117–21; Pew Internet and American Life Project, 18, 260; race or ethnicity and use of, 113, 126–28; recruitment via, 114, 117–20; and social-class structuring of political participation, 118, 120–21, 124, 223; socioeconomic status and use of, 114–20, 124–25, 128, 260–61; unequal political voice and, 260–61
issue commitments, 50–51, 64, 77–78
issue constituencies, 64, 77–78

Jencks, Christopher, 196

Keating, Charles, 46, 148
Keeter, Scott, 113
Kennedy, John F., 256
Keyssar, Alex, 232–33
Kies, Kenneth, 214
Kimball, David C., 40–41, 45
Kingdon, John, 41

labor unions, 153, 159–62; amicus brief filings by, 180; antiunion activity, 203; civic skill development and, 271; decline of, 201–5,

labor unions (*cont.*)
207, 219, 222–23, 225, 270–71; income inequality and decline of, 201–5; lobbying by, 174, 176–77, 222, 268; low-skill workers and, 159–60, 168, 184, 222; as membership organizations, 7, 32, 153, 156, 157; membership statistics, 159–60, 201–2, 222, 271; PACs and, 180–81; participation in political activity, 207, 222–23; policy changes and weakening of, 203–4; private *vs.* public sector, 159–60, 202, 225, 271; recruitment and, 201, 204–5, 222–23; as representation, 7, 32, 160, 181, 184, 201, 202, 204–5, 207, 221–22, 225; resources for political action and, 203; restrictions on political giving, 244, 247, 275; Taft-Hartley Act and weakening of, 203; testimony before Congress, 178; wage premium and, 202

Latinos: civic skills and, 57–58, 67, 68–72; as economically disadvantaged, 91–92; education and political participation by, 54–55, 67–68, 91; income inequality and, 192; lobbying and advocacy for, 177; online activity and, 126–28, 260; participation by, 91–92, 107–8, 110; policy concerns and, 107–8, 110; political engagement of, 60, 67; psychological engagement with politics, 60; recruitment of, 63, 72–73; SES and group differences in political voice, 12, 54–55, 67–69, 75, 259–60; time as political resource, 53; as underrepresented, 12, 110, 290n11; voting by, 234, 237, 240–41

Laumann, Edward O., 47
Leech, Beth, 40–41, 44, 45
legal actions. *See* amicus briefs; Supreme Court
Leighley, Jan, 95–96, 211
LGBT organizations, 143
LGBT rights as a participatory issue, 5, 95, 143
liberalism: ideology and voter ID laws, 237; lobbying expenditures and, 177; polarization and, 95–100; political participation and, 97–98; public interest and, 166
Lindblom, Charles E., 6
lobbying, 17; astroturf (artificial grassroots campaigns), 172; business interests as overrepresented, 38, 46, 156–58, 161–62, 173, 181–84, 216, 219–21, 225, 265, 268, 270; decline in activity, 217–18; direct contact with policymakers, 171; disclosure requirements, 175, 252–53, 268;

educational organizations and, 218–19; expenditures on, 171–77, 183, 267–68; experts or expertise and, 42, 175, 225; grassroots, 32, 42, 170, 171–72, 175, 218; health organizations and, 158–59, 162–63, 173, 176, 218–19; identity groups and, 177, 182, 216, 220–21; influence of, 44–45, 47–48, 171; labor unions and, 174, 176–77, 222, 268; occupational associations and, 225–26; public interest groups and, 164–67, 176–77, 216, 218–20; public interests groups, 220–21; registration requirements, 218; social welfare organizations and, 214; state or local governments and, 174, 176, 178; testimony before Congress, 177–78; trends over time, 217–18, 267–68

Lobbying Disclosure Act (LDA), 175, 268
local governments. *See* state or local governments
local political participation, 2, 4, 24–26, 74, 88–89, 250–51

Madison, James, 13–14, 16, 255–56
Malbin, Michael, 45
market outcomes: policy influences on, 198–201
Marxism, 207–8, 269
McConnell v. *Federal Election Commission*, 245, 246, 247
McCutcheon v. *Federal Election Commission*, 248, 249
Medicaid, 102, 104, 110
Medicare, 37–38, 84–85, 102, 104, 110, 163
memberless organizations, 8, 32, 34, 153–54, 262; grassroots lobbying and, 172; health and education sectors and, 8, 34, 153, 262, 271; increase of, 216, 225; political pressure and, 216; public interest groups, 166–67; questions of representation and, 34, 152–54, 158–59; stakeholders and, 8, 34, 154
membership organizations: benefits of participation through, 152; decline in, 217
Michels, Robert, 34
Miller, Warren, 37
"Millionaire's Amendment," 247
minimum wage, 199
Minor, Virginia, 10
"minorities rule," 15–16
money-based political activities: amicus briefs, costs of, 179; corruption and, 148–49; costs of political contests, 165–67; as essentially unlimited, 207; inequalities of market resources, 12–13, 266; inequalities

of political voice linked to, 13, 25–26, 31, 38, 44–47, 87–88, 101, 144, 183–84, 188–89, 256–57; lobbying expenditures, 171–77, 183, 267–68; money as resource, 51–54, 207; money as substitute for time, 148, 266; policy results and, 38, 44–45. *See also* campaign contributions; PACs
"Motor Voter" law. *See* National Voter Registration Act (NVRA)
Murphy, Chris, 256–57

Nagler, Jonathan, 95–96, 211
National Labor Relations Act, 203
National Voter Registration Act (NVRA), 230, 233, 239, 253, 274
Native Americans, 164, 177
Nelson, Robert L., 47
Nineteenth Amendment, 231
nonprofits, 501(c) organizations, 10, 163, 252–53, 302n20
Norris, Pippa, 114
Nownes, Anthony J., 47–48

Obama, Barack, *vi*, 36, 92, 113, 203, 218
occupational associations, 157, 159–62, 168, 173, 174, 176–77, 219–22, 300n31. *See also* labor unions; professional associations
Occupy movement, 98–100, 133, 143
Olson, Mancur, 150–52
organizations: barriers to creation of, 150–52, 168, 224; benefits of membership or participation through, 152; civic skill development and, 69–73; memberless, 262; requests for political activity in, 51, 62, 72–73, 75. *See also* organized interests
organized interests: amicus briefs and, 184; business or corporations and, 155–63, 182–83, 220–22, 270; campaign contributions and, 148; case studies and role of interest organizations, 39–40; categories of, 155–57, 220; corruption and, 148–50; differences between individual and collective political voice, 7–8, 33–34; expertise and, 148, 171; free riders and, 151–52, 156, 164, 167–69, 183, 262; government relations firms, 217; identity groups and representation via, 163–64, 182–83, 221; increase in, 155–57, 169, 216–25; inequality of political voice and, 3, 154–57, 160–62, 167–68, 181, 183–84, 188, 204–5; information as resource of, 27, 42, 148; local governments (*see* state or local governments); measuring political capacity of, 171–74; measuring political voice of, 8–9, 31–32, 41–43, 150; memberless, 8, 32, 34, 152–54, 158–59, 166–67, 172, 216, 225, 271; membership organizations, 7, 153, 217 (*see also* labor unions; professional associations); and mobilization for political action, 147–48; money as primary resource of, 148; nonprofits, 501(c), 10, 163, 252–53, 302n20; occupational organizations, 220–21; PACs and, 25, 148; policy influence of, 4, 39–40; political strategies and tactics of, 42, 169–72; public interest, 151, 164–67, 174, 177, 182–83, 184, 221, 262–63; race or ethnicity and representation via, 163–64; regulation of, 251; as representation, 8, 48, 152–53, 157, 161–63, 183, 221–22, 224–25, 261–64, 270–72; representation of advantaged and disadvantaged by, 150–51, 157, 173–74, 181–83, 188, 221–22; resource constraints and, 32–33, 156, 167, 169, 170, 183, 262; resource inequalities among, 171, 176–77, 183; role in democratic process, 149–50; services provided to policymakers, 42; social movements and, 133; social welfare advocacy and, 162–63, 177, 214, 218, 221–22; socioeconomic status and representation, 151, 160–61; state or local governments, 182–83, 221; tactics, 169–70; testimony before Congress, 177–78, 184; time-based activities and, 252; trade associations, 7; trends in distribution over time, 220. *See also* lobbying

PACs: corporations and businesses and, 181–82; dark money and, 181–82; influence of, 44–45; lobbying and, 180–81; Super PACs, 248, 253; unions and, 180–81; volume of campaign contributions and, 180
Page, Benjamin, 38
parents of school-aged children, 64, 77, 166–67
participation in political activities, 5; age and, 85, 112–13, 115, 120–21, 260–61; civic skills and, 55–58, 69–71, 250–51; creative, 28–29, 89; decline in, 29–30, 208, 225–26; democracy and, 5; demographic distinctions and, 84–85; digital (*see* Internet); education and, 12, 17, 54–57, 66–70, 74, 78, 79–80, 208, 257–58, 267, 268; extremity of opinion and, 95–100; factors linked to unequal, 10–11, 50–52, 73–77; families and inter-generational influence on, 56–57, 62–63, 65–68, 140, 257–58; First Amendment and guaranteed rights

participation in political activities (*cont.*) to, 9–10; gender and, 53–58, 60, 67, 71, 109–10, 126–28; group differences and, 67–68; influence on policy, 37–38; institutional affiliation and, 68–73, 75 (*see also* education; religious institutions); issue commitments and, 64, 77–78; local political innovation to encourage, 250–51; oppositional, 132; organizations as means of, 147, 152; parental education and, 67–68; personal stake in policy and, 64–65; policy concerns and activism, 103–4; predicting overall, 73–74; psychological engagement with politics, 58–61; race or ethnicity and, 53, 57–58, 60, 62–63, 67–73, 75, 89–92, 107–8, 126–28; "rational prospecting" and targeted recruitment, 138–39; recruitment as catalyst for, 50–51, 61–63, 138–39; resources and, 11, 50–58; SES and, 56–57, 62–63, 65–66, 85–88, 89, 120–21, 208–10, 223–24, 259–60; social class stratification of, 223–24; state or local governments and opportunities for, 88–89; time-based, 76, 225–26; time *vs.* money as input, 24–26, 52–54; trends over time, 208–16, 223–24. *See also* campaign contributions; civic voluntarism model (CVM); social movements; voting

parties, political: gridlock and, 218; as measure of political engagement, 60; measuring strength of, 60; polarization and, 95–100; recruitment by, 141–43; role in democracy, 141–43; voter ID laws and, 237

Payne, Charles M., 132

Pew Internet and American Life Project, 18, 260

Piketty, Thomas, 192

polarization, 95–100, 275

policymakers: communicating directly with, 4, 7, 25, 27, 35, 85, 102, 105–6, 110, 120, 171, 256, 292n22; democratic governing structure and access to, 169; influence of political voice on, 35–37, 206; and policy as remedy for income inequality, 200; public preferences and, 6, 35–38; responsiveness of, 4–5, 35–38, 206, 257–58; services provided by organizations to, 42

policy results: lobbying and, 42; measuring, 42–43; partisan gridlock and lack of, 218; political voice linked to, 35–37, 39–43, 49, 225; public opinion as influence on, 37–39; victory contrasted with influence, 43

political activists: higher SES of, 37, 110, 141, 213, 258; issue polarization among, 97–100, 109–10; policy commitments and, 64; policy concerns and, 103–4; representation of nonactivists, 259

political capacity of general public, 14–15, 50. *See also* civic skills

political efficacy, 59; civic voluntarism model and, 73, 79; recruitment and, 138–39

political engagement. *See* psychological engagement with politics

political inequality, 4, 8; activism and, 259; attitudes about, 275; civic skill and reduction in, 250–51; groups differences and, 67. *See also* voice, political

politically relevant characteristics, 5, 11–13, 30, 83–85, 266. *See also* specific

political mobilization. *See* recruitment; social movements

political reforms. *See* reforms, political

political voice. *See* voice, political

poor people. *See* disadvantage, economic

preferences: communicative value of political activities, 85; direct communication and expression of, 27; poverty and lack of opportunities to express, 110; voting as expression of, 4, 85

pressure politics. *See* lobbying; organized interests

professional associations, 7–9, 153, 157, 160, 177, 262, 300n31. *See also* occupational associations

protest, 2, 24, 25, 30, 95, 292n22; civic skills and, 26; creative participation and, 28; as expression of preference, 25; measurement of, 6–7; mobilization of outsiders, 130–31; participation in, 86; as personal investment of time, 25, 148, 266; recruitment requests, 62; social movements and, 129–30; socioeconomic status and, 289n5

psychological engagement with politics, 58–61; civic voluntarism model (CVM) and, 73; extremity of opinion and, 97–99; issue commitments and, 64; measurement of, 58–61; and participation, 58–61; political information and, 59–60. *See also* efficacy, political; information, political

public good or public interest, 251; amicus briefs and, 180, 184; as contested or disputed, 166–67, 262–63; lobbying expenditures and, 177; organizations and advocacy for, 151, 164–66, 177, 262–63 (*see also* public interest groups); as underrepre-

sented by organizations, 151, 164, 167, 174, 184, 262–63
public interest groups, 222, 224–25, 262–63; free rider problem and, 167; ideology of, 166–67; as memberless organizations, 166–67; policy issues and, 164–66

race or ethnicity: civic skills and, 54–58, 67–73; civil rights issues and, 107–8; digital divide and, 260; disenfranchisement of voters based on, 10, 231–32, 237, 241–42; education and, 92; identity groups and organizational representation, 163–64; inequality of political voice and, 12, 89–92, 107–8, 259–60; intersectionality and, 33; lobbying and identity groups, 177; mobilization and, 133; participation and, 53, 57–58, 60, 62–63, 67–73, 75, 89–92, 107–8, 126–28; policy concerns and, 107–8, 110; political disadvantages and, 12, 53; political resources and, 53; psychological engagement with politics and, 60; recruitment and, 72–73; SES and, 89–92, 259–60; voting and, 234. *See also* African Americans; Asian Americans; Latinos; Native Americans
Rainie, Lee, 113
rational prospecting, 74–75, 130, 138–41, 144, 256, 258. *See also* recruitment
Reagan, Ronald, 196, 199, 203
recruitment: adult institutions and requests for activity, 72–73; of campaign contributions, 53; as catalyst for participation, 50–51; civic voluntarism model (CVM) and, 73; coercion and, 141; economic disadvantage and participation requests, 132; education and, 62–63; everyday contacts and, 133–34; Get Out the Vote (GOTV), 243; grassroots, 130–31, 171–72; immigrants and, 141–42, 250–51; income and, 62; information and, 144; institutions and, 68–73; job or workplace as site of, 68–73; leverage and, 139, 144; locating potential targets for, 75, 138–39; measurement of, 61–62, 134, 144; of the disadvantaged, 132; organizations and, 68–73, 147–48; personal relationships and, 139–41, 144, 243; political efficacy and, 138–39; political parties and, 141–43; race or ethnicity and, 62, 72–73; religious institutions and requests for activity, 72–73; requests as measure of, 61–62, 134; SES and, 130, 134–37, 138, 143–44, 256–57; social media and, 117–19; social movements and, 129–31, 143–44; social networks and, 62; spontaneous, self-initiated mobilization, 134–36. *See also* rational prospecting
reforms, political, 4; barriers to, 272–73; campaign finance law, 230; consequences of, 229–30, 253; constitutional expansions of the franchise, 228–29; to encourage voter participation, 230; policy barriers to, 252; to promote equality of political voice, 227–28; unexpected consequences of, 229–31; to voting process, 17, 229–30, 233–34, 243, 253
religious attendance: compared to political participation rate, 209–10, 214–16, 223
religious institutions: civic skill development and, 69–73, 79–80; civil rights mobilization and, 131; denominational differences in political recruitment, 72; identity groups and organizational representation, 163–64; recruitment to political participation and, 68–73
representative democracy: equal political voice and, 14–15, 48; gerrymandering or electoral district boundaries, 31; role of Electoral College, 31; and skepticism about political capacity of citizens, 14
Republican Party, 95–96, 141–43, 237
requests for political activity. *See* rational prospecting; recruitment
resources, political: campaign contributions as (*see* campaign contributions); civic voluntarism model (CVM) and, 73; different types of, *x*, 3, 4–5, 25–26, 73, 132; time as (*see* time-based political activities); unequal distribution of, 52
Right Question Institute, 250
"right to work" laws, 203
Roosevelt, Franklin Delano, 94
Rosenstone, Steven, 94–95

Salisbury, Robert, 47
Sanders, Bernie, *xi*
scandals, 148–49
Schattschneider, E.E., 150–52, 156–57
Schumpeter, Joseph, 15
Scott, James C., 148–49
SES. *See* socioeconomic status (SES)
Shelby v. Holder, *xi*, 231–32, 253
silent political voices, 35, 47, 259
Skocpol, Theda, 222
Smith, Richard, 45

Smith-Connally Act, 180
Snyder, James, 45
social media, 28–29, 122–26, 128, 131, 143, 260; campaigning and, 143. *See also* Internet
social movements, 131–33, 258; as hierarchical and exclusionary organizations, 132–33; mobilization and, 3, 142–43; and representative political voice, 131–33; SES and participation in, 132–33, 142–44
Social Security, 33, 37–38, 84–85, 102, 104, 110, 163
social welfare organizations, 156, 162–63, 173, 176–77, 214, 218–19, 221–22
social welfare programs: beneficiaries as stakeholders in, 77, 109–10, 259; beneficiaries as underrepresented, 259; benefits as income, 30, 64, 77, 85, 101–3, 102, 162–63, 192–93, 196, 252, 259, 305n8; campaign contributions from stakeholders in, 102–3; income inequality and, 196–97; issue commitment and, 64, 77; organizations and representation of beneficiaries of, 162–63; political activity and stakeholders in, 102–3, 168, 252; welfare reforms and changes in, 196–97
socioeconomic status (SES), 3; affluence and social advantages, 52; attitude toward needs-based government programs and, 104–6; basic human needs as participatory issue, 77–78, 104–6, 110, 259; campaign contributions and, 256–58; civic skills and, 65–66, 257; defined, 5, 86, 289n4; digital political participation and, 120–21; economic circumstance and issue commitment, 104–5; education and, 190–91, 257; families as influence on political participation, 56–57, 62–63, 65–68, 140, 257–58; group differences in political voice linked to, 259–60; health and political activism, 100–101; income and education, 17, 53–54; increasing inequality in, 16–18; Internet use and, 114–20, 124–25, 128, 260–61; organizational representation and, 151, 160–61; the poor as underrepresented by organizations, 183; quintiles defined, 86; recruitment and, 72–73, 141; social movements and, 142–44; unequal participation and voice linked to, 11–12, 75, 109–10, 222–24, 257–58. *See also* advantage, economic; disadvantage, economic
speech, political: campaign contributions as protected, *xi*, 9–10, 245–49, 267, 275;

First Amendment guarantees, 9–10, 245–47, 275; free speech as democratic value, 9–10, 25, 29, 228, 245; of individuals *vs.* organizations, 10
SpeechNow.org v. *Federal Election Commission*, 248, 249
state or local governments, 179–80, 222; amicus briefs and, 179–80, 184; civic skill development and, 74; increase in numbers of organizations, 218; lobbying and, 174, 176, 178; as organized political interests, 74, 153, 156, 157, 173, 182–83, 216, 218–19, 221, 271; participation and, 88–89; pressure politics and, 271; taxation systems of, 197–98; testimony before Congress, 178; voting in local *vs.* presidential elections, 88
Stevens, John Paul, 154
Stiglitz, Joseph, 198
Stimson, James A., 38
Stokes, Donald, 37
subnational governments. *See* state or local governments
Sunlight Foundation, 213
Sun Oil decision, 180–81
Super PACs, 248
Supplemental Nutrition Assistance Program (SNAP), 110, 197
Supreme Court: *Arizona Free Enterprise Club's Freedom Club PAC* v. *Bennett*, 248, 250; *Buckley* v. *Valeo*, 245, 246, 248, 267; *Citizens United* v. *Federal Election Commission*, 17, 154, 213, 246–48, 267; *Davis* v. *Federal Election Commission*, 247; *Federal Election Commission* v. *Beaumont*, 246–47; *McConnell* v. *Federal Election Commission*, 245, 247; *McCutcheon* v. *Federal Election Commission*, 248, 249; and political contributions as protected speech, *xi*, 9–10, 17, 244–49, 267, 275; and rights of organizations to free speech, 10; *Shelby* v. *Holder*, *xi*, 231–32, 253; and voting rights, 10; *Wisconsin Right to Life* v. *Federal Election Commission*, 247
surveys: as accurate measure of preferences, 5, 30, 41; as snapshots in time, 30, 103–4

Taft-Hartley Act, 180, 203
taxes: business interests and tax code advantages, 197, 272; Earned Income Tax Credit (EITC), 197; income inequality and, 188–89, 197–98; local and state, 197–98; as political issue, 104–7, 109; rates in U.S *vs.* other nations, 198; as redistribution, 192–

93, 196, 197–98; on unearned income, 197–98
Tea Party (Taxed Enough Already), 98–100, 103, 131–33, 143
Telecommunications Act, 115
Temporary Assistance to Needy Families (TANF), 167, 196–97
testimony before Congress, 27; as expression of preference, 25; organizations and, 177–78, 184
Tillman Act, 10, 180
time-based political activities, 76; campaign meetings or rallies, 24, 87, 211–12, 224; campaign work, 27, 30, 51–52, 86–87, 95–97, 101, 224, 292n22; civic skills and, 250–51; employment as barrier to participation in, 53; SES and, 87–88, 224, 253; as substitute for money contributions, 266; and time as limited resource, 12–13, 25–26, 51–54, 207; trends over time, 211–12, 224. *See also* communicating directly with policymakers; protest
Tocqueville, Alexis de, 74, 147
trade and business associations, 153, 158, 166, 219–21, 220–21. *See also* business interests
Transparency International Corruption Perceptions Index, 149, 297n3
Trump, Donald, 200, 238–40; political insurgency and, *xi*; Presidential Advisory Commission on Election Integrity established by, 241
Twitter. *See* social media

The Unheavenly Chorus (Schlozman, Verba, Brady), *x–xi*
unions. *See* labor unions
U.S. Congress: congressional testimony, 18–19, 173, 184; influence of campaign contributions, 272; influence of political contributions, 45–47, 170, 175; responsiveness of, 37–38; services provided by organized interests to, 42; tax reforms, 197, 272
U.S. Constitution, 9–10, 13, 213, 245–50, 255–56, 274

voice, political: accountability of government and, 2, 4–7; age and, 3, 113–14; citizenship and opportunities for, 9–10; defined, 27–29; democracy and mechanisms for expression of, 2–3, 6, 24–25, 228; direct *vs.* indirect, 24–25, 27; forms of, 4, 23–27, 206–7; government responsiveness to inequalities in, *ix–x*, 16–18,
228–29, 272–75; majority and minority dynamics and, 15–16; measuring inequality of, 6–7, 31–33; money and efficacy of, 38; opportunities or channels for expression, 2–3; organizations as (*see* organizations); organized interests and (*see* organized interests); pressure system and inequality of, 150–52 (*see also* lobbying); reforms to ensure equality of (*see* reforms, political); role in representative democracy, 2, 3, 5, 6, 13–16, 29–30, 48, 228; SES and stratification of, 11, 206–7, 223 (*see also* advantage, economic); time and, 52–54; voting as, 4
Voice and Inequality (Verba, Schlozman, Brady), *x*
voter fraud, 229–30, 238–41, 274
voter ID laws, 17, 208, 229, 233, 237–41, 253, 275
voter registration: election day registration, 253; reforms to encourage participation, 17, 229–30, 233–34, 243, 253; voter fraud *vs.* registration fraud, 239–40
voting: absentee and early, 233, 235–36, 240; barriers to, 10, 17, 208, 231–32, 237–38, 241–42 (*see also* voter ID laws *under this heading*); as civil right, 231, 239; compulsory, 234–35, 274; CVM and, 243; discriminatory disenfranchisement of voters, 10, 231–32, 237, 241–42; as egalitarian, 210–11, 269; election day registration, 253; as expression of preference, 4, 24–25, 85; felon disenfranchisement, 241–42; fraud, 229–30, 236, 238–41, 274; gerrymandering voting districts, 255; Get Out the Vote (GOTV) and, 243; habituation and, 234; in local *vs.* presidential elections, 88; by mail, 227, 235–36; mandatory voting systems, 235, 253, 274; "preclearance" provisions, *xi*, 232, 274; provisional ballots, 238; race or ethnicity and turnout, 240–41; registration reforms to encourage participation, 17, 229–30, 233–34, 243, 253; restrictions on, 208 (*see also* discriminatory disenfranchisement *under this heading*); restrictions on access to, 208, 231–33; SES and, 76, 210, 211, 223; trends over time, 211–12; turnout, 17, 29, 76, 210–11, 231, 240–41; turnout as unrepresentative of electorate, 231, 235–37, 240–41, 243, 253; voter ID laws, 17, 208, 229, 233, 237–41, 253, 275; vote suppression, 243
Voting Rights Act, *xi*, 231–33, 253, 274–75

wages, 189–91; labor unions and higher, 202; minimum wage as policy issue, 16, 199; policy as influence on labor market, 198–201

Washington Representatives Study, 18–19, 153–57, 160–61, 164, 169, 171, 176, 216–17, 220, 224, 262

Wisconsin Right to Life v. *Federal Election Commission*, 246

Wolfinger, Raymond, 94–95

women: discriminatory disenfranchisement of, 10; intersectionality and, 33; issues and policy concerns of, 98–100, 109–10, 129, 143; as politically disadvantaged, 12, 53–54. *See also* gender

Woodhouse, Edward J., 6

working class: low-skilled workers, 159–61, 168, 184, 222; mobilization of, *xi*, 141; as underrepresented by organizations, 184; union membership and representation of, 222; voting by, *xi*

workplace or job: civic skill development and, 69–73; political coercion and, 141; recruitment to political activity and, 68–73, 141

Wright, John, 46

A NOTE ON THE TYPE

This book has been composed in Adobe Text and Gotham. Adobe Text, designed by Robert Slimbach for Adobe, bridges the gap between fifteenth- and sixteenth-century calligraphic and eighteenth-century Modern styles. Gotham, inspired by New York street signs, was designed by Tobias Frere-Jones for Hoefler & Co.